U N E S C O

SURVEY OF OCEANIC COLLECTIONS

IN

MUSEUMS IN THE UNITED KINGDOM AND THE IRISH REPUBLIC

prepared by

Peter Gathercole and Alison Clarke

(1979)

(CC-80/WS/58)

P R E F A C E

This inventory of specimens and related information from Oceania, to be found at present in museums in the United Kingdom and Ireland, was commissioned within the framework of the Unesco programme for the Promotion of Appreciation and Respect of Cultural Identity, and more specifically as an integral part of the project for the study of Oceanic cultures.

Recommendation 13 of the inaugural meeting of the Advisory Committee for the Study of Oceanic Cultures (Tonga, 1975) affirmed the need for information on Oceanic material culture in museums and private collections throughout the world.

In this connection, the work to be undertaken was to be divided into two stages :

1) a world-wide inventory in general terms of numbers of objects from each island group in the various collections in the nations of the world;

2) a systematic recording of the individual artefacts including their associated documentation and photography.

The ultimate aim of the project is to constitute and make available a photographic archive and associated documentation of the material culture of each island area.

On the basis of a preliminary report in which information acquired from 80 museums was summarised, the present inventory lists in greater detail the data previously collected, bringing the number of museums covered to a total of 173.

The inventory is divided into two parts :

- Part I describes how the information was acquired, discusses its reliability and aspects of its significance and explains the method of presentation of the data.

- Part II sets out the information in detail.

T A B L E   O F   C O N T E N T

PART I

1. ACQUISITION OF INFORMATION

At the outset, the aims of the survey were defined as the following :

(i) to determine the extent of Oceanic collections in museums in the United Kingdom and Ireland;

(ii) to pinpoint the major collections;

(iii) to recommend ways in which a fully detailed inventory of all collections might be obtained;

(iv) to suggest ways in which the information in this report, and any subsequently obtained, could be made more widely known, in order to stimulate further research.

The information presented in this report was obtained in two stages, on the basis of prior knowledge, visits, circularisation and correspondence.

Stage 1 - List of relevant museums

This list was compiled from :

a. data summarised in a preliminary report, most of which had been obtained by museum visits.

b. a pilot and non-detailed survey of all ethnographic collections in museums in the United Kingdom undertaken by the Museum Ethnographers' Group in 1978. This survey only listed gross holdings by continent for each museum.

c. a similar survey of holdings in military museums carried out by M.D. McLeod, Keeper of the Museum of Mankind, and incorporated in (

d. replies to an appeal letter in the Museums Bulletin. (The fact that few replies were received indicated that the coverage obtained from a - c was reasonably complete).

Stage 2 - Acquisition of data

e. Where not already available from the work undertaken in the preliminary report, details of holdings were obtained from the listed museums, discussed usually by correspondence, and arranged on the specially designed tabular sheets which provide the format of Part II of this report. The relevant sheets were then sent to each museum concerned for checking.

.../...

The checked sheets comprise the information included in Part II, which also contains information about the history, documentation and publication of each collection, or of individual items, in the museum concerned. An indication of the amount of work involved may be gauged from the fact that it included c. 300 items of correspondence.

2. RANGE AND RELIABILITY OF INFORMATION

We are reasonably confident that the number covered represents the great majority of public holdings of Oceanic material in the United Kingdom and Ireland (It is important to note that no private collections are included). The only serious exception of which we are aware is the collection in the Museum of Mankind, where despite our efforts, and those of Mrs. Dorota Starzecka, the Assistant Keeper concerned, it proved impossible to organise the recording of this large and important collection, reported to be not less than 27,000 objects, in a way consistent with the other entries. For the time being, only a general entry has been made for the Museum of Mankind in Part II.

Various methods were used to obtain information for the preliminary report. Some was by correspondence, but much resulted from personal visits by either Gathercole or colleagues from either this country or overseas who were visiting U.K. museums for purposes of research. These colleagues, whose names are listed on page (7), and others within the U.K., often supplied data about particular museum collections, and these sources are noted on the first page of the individual report forms. Also included here are data obtained from an initial survey undertaken by Mr. R. Hutchings, then of Liverpool Museum, in 1966 and 1969.

For the great majority of the museums included here for the first time, however, the information was obtained by letter, unchecked by any personal examination of the specimens. This naturally raises the question of the reliability of the information obtained. The most that we can say is that the information is as accurate as we can make it, given the constraints of this form of survey. Many collections are, unfortunately, poorly documented, identified and localised. Many of our museum correspondents are not, perforce, ethnographers, let alone Pacific specialists. The data obtained therefore reflect varying levels of surviving documentation and curatorial knowledge. Clearly every museum listed should have its objects inspected by a Pacific specialist. In the meantime, we have done all we can to assist museums by correspondence, and to make apparent any ambiguities or uncertainties in the lists.

.../...

The point to stress, however, is that this report is only the first step in making available a large body of information on the history of Oceania which must be improved and extended by Pacific scholars, not least from the Pacific region itself. If we had sought accuracy for each entry, this report would never have been completed. We hope that it will stimulate further research by Pacific scholars interested in material culture. If this happens, we shall have achieved one of our aims.

One of the aspects of accuracy to which we have given much attention is the presentation of the information in a way consistent for all museums. Many ambiguities can be expected to arise concerning both the classification and the localisation of objects. An object often had several uses, and one use may have been favoured above others by field collectors as providing a suitable descriptive term. Alternatively, a simple term might have become accepted into museum parlance despite evidence that other, more elaborate ones were actually more accurate. An example is the Australian "throwing stick", which we also found variously termed "spear thrower", "throwing club", "non-returning boomerang" or "game(stick)", and not necessarily in five different museums.

In drawing up the descriptive tables used in Part II, we were painfully aware of the need for uniformity and the absence of an agreed terminology. If all objects had been seen, then, theoretically at least, a wholly consistent terminology could have been employed. The most we could do in the circumstances was to use a judicious mixture of generally accepted terms, arranged into generic groups, drawing on the generic/specific system employed by Beatrice Blackwood in her valuable paper, "The Classification of Artefacts in the Pitt Rivers Museum, Oxford", Occasional Papers in Technology, 11 (Pitt Rivers Museum, Oxford, 1970).

In dealing with the problem of using suitable past/present names of islands, we have relied on the listings drawn up by the Pacific Manuscripts Bureau, Canberra, and, to a lesser degree, the culture groupings used by C.R.H. Taylor in his Pacific Bibliography (2nd ed. Oxford 1965) pp. 589-591. The result is naturally a compromise, comparable to that used by Dr. A.L. Kaeppler in her current survey of Oceanic objects in museums in the U.S.A. However, we looked to common usage and practical expediency in forming our tables, hoping that they will prove to be clear and functional.

As a footnote to the discussion on the entries for Oceania, it should be noted that, unlike these, the entries for Australia are rarely arranged by area. This is simply because Australian provenances have been recorded only rarely, apart from some collections in major museums.

.../...

3. COMMENTS ON THE SIGNIFICANCE OF DATA

Generally, the newly acquired information supports the statements concerning significance of the material reviewed in 1977 (see pp. 3-4). Most of the objects are sufficiently small and portable to have been carried without difficulty by sea half-way across the world. Examples of larger and rarer objects are the Maori House at Clandon Park, Surrey, items of house architecture from New Zealand, New Guinea and New Caledonia (e.g. Museum of Mankind, Oxford, Cambridge and Manchester), canoes (e.g. Museum of Mankind, Belfast, Cambridge, Liverpool, Norwich and Oxford), and large slit gongs from the New Hebrides (Cambridge). Certain types predominate, particularly in smaller museums : ornaments, weapons, clothing, and model canoes. The quantity of weapons indicates either a mass turnover to non-indigenous weapons after initial colonisation, or a brisk trade in "weapons" made for sale (notably clubs), or more probably, both. The Solomon Islands, Fiji and the Gilbert Islands are prime examples. It is evident that, in the case of most collections in smaller museums, or those in larger institutions devoted mainly to other specialisms, the Pacific material represents a final phase in the sociology of collecting, where objects have been "screened" by a series of exchanges, starting with an island exchange and passing perhaps from collector to dealer to another collector, and so on. The most important period of time involved is generally from the onset of effective and persistent island contact to 1939 (plus a tail-piece after 1945 to c. 1960), with a period of numerical intensity from 1880 to 1930. This period saw the major trading activities in Britain of such persons as the dealers W.O. Oldman and W.D. Webster ; the staff of Fenton's and Steven's Salerooms in London ; the private collectors Beasley, Fuller, Oldman and Wellcome, and the museum men Braunholtz, Edge-Partington, (British Museum), Von Hügel (Cambridge) and Balfour (Oxford). These men, along with others with less definitive interests, formed the nucleus of a market which was fed by objects provided from Oceania. These objects were obtained mainly from travellers, missionaries, colonial administrators and soldiers who came home on leave or retirement from the British South Pacific Empire. Prices were usually low, because Oceanic ethnography had not yet become, at least to any significant extent, an area of "primitive art".

This process of exchanges, which we have only briefly summarised here, affected the quality of the objects as ethnographic data. The more they passed through the exchange "screens", the less they retained any representative character of the cultures from which they came, and the smaller were the chances of them retaining associated documentation. They became stripped of their original social context and tended to exist *in vacuo* as collectors'

.../...

specimens. The results can be seen in all museums, but are particularly evident in the smaller ones whose ethnographic collections derive mainly from home, usually locally-based, collectors or dealers. This does not mean that the collections should be ignored. We believe that all objects can be sources of ethnohistorical research. But their usefulness depends on the general level of sophistication of material culture studies. As the latter improves, so the relevance of the smaller, undocumented collections will become clearer.

It is only to be expected that collections at the Museum of Mankind, the larger cities and the Universities are both larger and more immediately useful. They have been less "screened", have often been obtained directly from the field collectors, and are therefore broader in scope and better documented. This is particularly true of the Oxford and Cambridge collections, and is probably the case for the majority of the collection at the Museum of Mankind. Other examples are to be found, for example, at Belfast, Exeter, Edinburgh, Glasgow (both museums), Liverpool, Manchester, and at a number of military museums. At the same time, we emphasise that recent improvements in the level of research in Pacific ethnohistory in Britain is narrowing the "utility gap" between documented and undocumented collections. In the course of our survey we have learnt of research under way at Hastings, Leeds, Bristol and Saffron Walden. It is clear that our entries concerning documentation and the names of collectors will require considerable updating over the next few years, as the pace of research increases and the results of this survey become known. We have borne these points in mind in framing our recommendations.

P A R T II

4. GUIDE TO PART II

The lists are arranged in alphabetical order by the name of the city or town concerned. Where more than one museum per location is included, each is distinguished by a suitable abbreviation in parenthesis, e.g. London (Horniman); London (Museum of).

The information for each museum is set out factually and succinctly on three or more sides or pages. An explanation of the layout of Side I appears below. Sides II and III, with additional pages if required by the size of the collection, comprise lists of objects and of their provenances arranged

.../...

in tabular form. The provenances are listed vertically on Side II and repeated on Side III. The list of artefactual types spreads horizontally over Side II on to Side III. Explanatory notes on the choice of location names and of types are included at the end of this section.

5. SIDE I

On Side I the name, address and current telephone number of the museum, together with the designation of the person to contact, are on the top left. On the top right is the abbreviated name, below which is a summary indication of the source and date of the information. As mentioned above (pp. 3-4), our information was obtained in a variety of ways, including visits by specialists. These sources are shown by the following abbreviations :

1.	R. Hutchings	Part surveys done by Mr. Hutchings, then Keeper of Ethnology, Liverpool Museum, in 1966 and 1969. The latter survey was confined to New Guinea (especially Asmat) material.
2.	Visits and letters:	
	AC	Alison Clarke
	PG	Peter Gathercole
	ALK	Adrienne L. Kaeppler, Anthropologist, Bernice P. Bishop Museum, Honolulu.
	GSP	G. Stuart Park, Director, Auckland Institute and Museum, Auckland.
	SP	Steven Phelps, Research Student, Cambridge Univeristy.
	DRS	David R. Simmons, Ethnologist, Auckland Museum.
3.	MEG	Initial register of ethnographic collections compiled by the Museum Ethnographers' Group in 1978, including one of collections in military museums conducted by M. D. McLeod, Keeper, Museum of Mankind.

Other abbreviations are self-explanatory.

In the middle of Side I, is a section headed Notes. This includes numerous brief explanatory comments concerning items listed in the tables, for example, the quality and completeness of the data, information concerning disposals* etc. These notes often refer

.../...

* Information on disposals refers to whole collections, not solely Oceanic ones. When known, details on acquisition and transferal of these collections are added here.

to the artefactual category "Other", or to other categories where extra information is available, e.g. that some of the Fijian barkcloth at Aberdeen was made for presentation to King Edward VII. This section is meaningless without reference to Sheets II and III.

Below this section are two headed Dates of Collection/Acquisition and Donors/Collectors/Former Owners respectively. Following them is a section headed Documentation where we list :

- whether or not the collection is accessioned, sorted or catalogued
- supporting information, i.e. printed works, manuscripts, letters, photographs (negatives and prints), paintings, drawings, engravings, sound recordings, films
- the museum's publications) selected
- references in other works) selected

At the bottom of the page is a small section headed Comment. Comments are kept brief, being limited mainly to the significance of the collection and sometimes to work under way relating to it. Absence of comment usually means that the collection has not been seen, not that the information supplied provides insufficient ground for comment. Although we are very aware of the research opportunities which these collections provide, we feel that it would be pointless to expand on this matter until a more complete inventory has been established.

6. SIDES II AND III

A. Provenances

Usually arranged by island groups. Where necessary, additional locations are added at the end of the printed list.

Oceania, unprovenanced: if provenance is unknown or unspecified, objects are entered here.

Australia: subdivided only for Cambridge, Oxford (Pitt Rivers)

Admiralty: Ninigo listed separately

Banks: includes Torres Islands

New Guinea: subdivided only for Cambridge, Liverpool, Oxford (Pitt Rivers)

Solomon: subdivided only for Cambridge, Oxford (Pitt Rivers)

Austral: as in Taylor

Cook: as in Taylor

Society: Tahiti distinguished where possible

Gambier: Mangareva distinguished where possible

Outliers: defined conventionally (e.g. as in Bellwood, The Polynesians, 1978) and listed separately where possible.

.../...

B. Artefactual Types

These are listed under 74 categories and, where appropriate, sub-categories, e.g. clothing is not only a category in itself, but also has sub-categories of -skirt, -belt and -cloak. Numbers of listed objects are shown where possible. An X indicates an unknown number. Broken, incomplete, part or related objects, copies, models (except canoes) are entered under the appropriate category, e.g. box lid under box, wrist guard under bow, spear rest under spear, quiver under arrow, and so on.

The arbitrary nature of any classification system, uncertainties over some attributions, and the volume of objects dealt with, together mean that numerous objects do not fit into the defined categories. These objects are listed under the heading Other and are explained in the notes on Side I. Entries accompanied by an asterisk are also referred to here. Owing to the amount of information available for some museums, extra notes are included for these museums after their detailed sheets.

Entries under Other include :

Toys, e.g. amusements, puzzles and games for all ages (but excluding toy musical instruments or weapons, which are placed under their own related categories).

Large quantities of archaeological but loosely or poorly defined objects, such as stone cores and flakes.

Biological specimens, e.g. hair or crania, but not such items as ornamented skulls or preserved heads, which are included under ceremonial objects.

Fakes, objects made for export, metal and other post-contact objects.

Objects of uncertain provenance.

Odd, insignificant or indeterminate objects.

Some examples of the coverage of categories

Category		Examples
barkcloth	:	most objects made or partly made of barkcloth, including samples
clothing	:	shoes, hats, ceremonial costumes
belt	:	girdles, waistbands
cloak	:	capes, mantles
personal ornament	:	ceremonial ornaments, status ornaments, non-specified pendants

.../...

head ornament	:	hair ornaments, headbands, headdresses, some helmets, wigs
arm ornament	:	all specified as worn on arm or wrist
neck, breast ornament	:	gorgets, neck pendants, <u>tiki</u>(s)
toilet apparatus	:	surgical, depilatory, scarifying and tattooing tool mirrors and back scratchers
staff, stick	:	staves, batons, staves of office, message sticks, walking sticks, unspecified sticks
ceremonial object	:	those clearly connected with dance, mourning, burial, religious actions (excluding magical), e.g. clubs, spears, food bowls, <u>tambua</u>, ornamented skull or preserved heads of persons or animals
board	:	ceremonial shields, tablets
adze	:	some actually axes
bullroarer	:	<u>churinga</u>
carving	:	both figurative and non-figurative; architectural, ornamental; human heads
figure, image	:	anthropomorphic figures
magic, medicine	:	objects associated with performance (except surgica and charms, amulets)
charm	:	fetishes, amulets; protective, invoking objects
musical instrument	:	shell trumpets, jewsharps, musical bows, friction instruments
flute, pipe	:	whistles
rattle	:	jingles, bells
currency	:	shells, feathers, fishhooks; other non-ceremonial exchange objects
transport	:	aids to transport of goods e.g. straps, loops, potrings; tree-climbing devices, roller skates
headrest	:	"stools", pillows
basket	:	fishing baskets
dish, vessel	:	bowls, trays, platters, cups, gourds

.../...

utensil	:	generally any used in preparation and consumption of food; food scrapers, stirrers, spoons, ladles, cannibal forks, food knives
pottery	:	generally pottery vessels, sherds (but pot-making tools under tools)
smoking pipe	:	cigarette holders
fire, light	:	objects associated with fire making and with lighting, e.g. lamps, candles
tool	:	drills, knives (used as tools), polishing, cutting, gouging tools, digging sticks, hoes, spades, paint-brushes, mesh gauges
adze	:	hafted or non-hafted, including archaeological; includes hafts, axes, but excludes ceremonial (where known)
pounding	:	mortars, pestles, hammer stones
grinding	:	may include archaeological grindstones
needle, awl	:	may include netting needles
weaving	:	looms, warp boards, shuttles, spinning tools
barlcloth	:	beaters, design aids, pattern boards, printing blocks
navigation	:	steering paddles, fullsize canoes, bailers, other parts, sailing charts
paddle	:	including mini (toy?) paddles
ornament	:	for prow, stern (excluding charms)
model	:	dugouts, rafts, canoes, outriggers, other parts
hunting	:	bird arrows, trapping devices (excluding fishing), weapons specified for hunting, mantraps
fishing	:	lines, lures, traps, arrows (where specified), kites, rods, bait
fishhook	:	often attached to lines, lures
spear	:	spears with multiple points are classed as harpoons
net	:	may include some hunting nets in error

.../...

float, sinker	:	weights
weapon	:	non-specified weapons, swords, beheading knives, armour
club	:	all non-ceremonial and status (chief's) clubs; maces; throwing clubs
spear	:	spearheads, points
dagger	:	knives used as weapons (excluding Australia); cassowary bone daggers
bow	:	includes those used in games; wristguards
arrow	:	includes those used in games; arrowheads, quivers
raw material	:	generally illustrating manufacture e.g. dyes, pigments, foods, samples of shell, bone, stone, feathers, clay, ivory
cord	:	rope, string, plaited samples, sennit (sinnet), twined material
other	:	includes flywhisks, boomerangs, some preserved heads, suspension hooks, house/shrine models, toys of all forms

R E C O M M E N D A T I O N S

The intention behind the original survey was that the information obtained would enable Unesco to plan a fully detailed inventory of U.K. collections undertaken by a number of visiting experts. The result would be much more than a survey ; it would be a complete and accurate inventory embracing a full photographic coverage, i.e. a major research tool. This was a plausible ideal scheme, given the number of museums then thought to be involved.

Now that our survey has included so many more museums, this proposal acquires a new aspect. There is much more material, both artefactual and documentary, to deal with, and more places to visit. Although the number of artefacts involved has not increased by a massive amount (all the major collections, apart from the Museum of Mankind, were covered in the 1977 report), the figures included here are more accurate than previously reported, and many more smaller collections are included. We have not done a total "head count" because some of the numbers reported are approximate, but the following totals provide a guide. The collections at the Museum of Mankind, Cambridge, Oxford (Pitt Rivers), Horniman, Liverpool, Manchester and Brighton total about 130,000 objects. If one adds the other collections, allows for new data, and compensates for inaccuracies in recording, the total holdings in the U.K. to be inventoried probably amount to about 160,000 objects.

We doubt if it is realistic to propose handing this number solely by means of a comprehensive mobile specialist survey. It is bound to be expensive and slow to implement. The impetus created by the present survey may well be lost. Of equal importance is the fact that a programme which is implemented wholly externally ignores the vital contribution which could be made by U.K. museum curators themselves, and by visiting or resident scholars. For these reasons we strongly favour a more varied approach to the question of how to provide a detailed inventory, and suggest the following course of action :

1. Unesco should approach the museums having the major collections with the proposal that their sections of the inventory should be compiled on a co-operative basis. The detailed arrangements would vary, but the intention would be that the museums provide complete documentary and photographic data (where these exist) and, if possible, assistance in transcribing.

2. More scholars and students, especially from the Pacific countries, should be encouraged to visit museums in metropolitan countries, both to improve their knowledge and to raise standards of identification and documentation. Their work could be incorporated into the inventory. They should supply copies of notes, publications, photographs etc. to a central archive, the core of which would be the information and associated papers on which this report is based.

.../...

3. A mobile team of recorders should nonetheless be recruited to inventory those collections which cannot be dealt with by the above means. This work is likely to include some of the larger collections, but it is probable that numerous smaller ones will have to be covered, i.e. those at museums not yet visited and those lacking specialist curatorial knowledge.

4. It would be useful to set up a small organisation to co-ordinate and sustain these activities over the next few years. We consider that a secretariat should be established under the auspices of the British National Commission for Unesco, which should also maintain the central archive proposed above. We recognise that, in these days of economic constraint, it may be difficult to keep the inventory project in being, but it has a greater chance to succeed if it is closely tied to the growth of scholastic research already evident, and to the obvious concern of museums to improve their documentation.

5. Encouragement and specialist advice should be given to museums to improve the identification and care of objects when required.

6. The report should be kept open, and further information added as necessary.

7. Museums should be encouraged to notify Unesco, and the U.K. Secretariat, if set up, when new material is obtained or collections are moved, etc.

8. Serious consideration should be given to the question of recording objects now in private collections and those which come onto the open market, either through the antique trade or privately.

D E T A I L E D   L I S T S   O F   C O L L E C T I O N

(arranged by alphabetical order)

<u>List of Museums Entries by Location</u>

Abbotsford
Aberdeen
Aldershot
Arbroath
Arundel
Aylesbury
Ayr
Barnet
Barrow-in-Furness
Bath
Batley
Belfast
Belsay
Bideford
Birchington
Birmingham (M)
Birmingham (Uni)
Blackburn (M & AG)
Blackburn (SC)
Bolton
Bournemouth
Bradford
Brighton
Bristol
Burnley
Bury
Bury St Edmunds(M)
Bury St Edmunds (Reg)
Campbeltown
Camborne
Cambridge
Canterbury (City)
Canterbury (Reg)
Cardiff
Carmarthen
Chatham
Chelmsford
Cheltenham
Chertsey
Christchurch
Clandon
Clitheroe
Colchester
Coventry
Cuckfield
Darlington
Derby(M & AG)
Derby (Schools)
Devizes
Dewsbury (see Batley)
Doncaster
Dorchester
Dover
Dublin
Dumfries
Dundee
Durham (DLI)
Durham (Gulb)
East Cowes
Edinburgh (Music)
Edinburgh (RSM)
Elgin
Exeter (MM)
Exeter (RAMM)
Forres
Glasgow (H)
Galsgow (M & AG)
Godalming
Grays
Greenock
Guernsey
Halifax
Hartlepool
Hastings
Hatfield
Hertford
Horsham
Huddersfield (see Batley)
Hull
Ilfracombe
Ipswich
Jersey
Keswick
Kew
Kilmarnock
King's Lynn
Kingston
Kirkcaldy (JMS)
Kirkcaldy (M & AG)
Leeds
Leicester
Lewes
Lincoln (CCM)
Lincoln (MLL)
Liverpool (E)
Liverpool (Maritime)
London (Admiralty)
London (CI)
London (Courtauld)
London (Cuming)
London (Greenwich)
London (Hendon)
London (Horniman)
London (LSE)
London (Museum of)
London (Museum of Mankind)
London (NAM)
London (RGS)
London (Science-Engineering)
London (Science-Naviga)
London (UCL)
London (Wellcome)
Macclesfield
Maidenhead
Maidstone
Maldon
Manchester
Mansfield
Middlesbrough
Montrose
Newcastle (Brown)
Newcastle (Hancock)
Northampton (M & AG)
Northampton (Reg)
Norwich (NMS)
Norwich (UEA)
Nottingham
Nuneaton
Orpington
Oxford (Ash)
Oxford (PR)
Paisley
Perth
Peterborough
Peterhead
Plymouth
Pocklington
Portsmouth
Port Sunlight
Rochester
Rossendale
Rotherham
Rugby
Saffron Walden
St Albans
St Helens
St Neots
Salford
Salisbury
Scarborough
Sheffield (City)
Sheffield (Reg)
Southampton
Southport
South Shields
Stamford
Stirling
Stoke-on-Trent
Torquay
Truro
Tunbridge Wells
Wakefield (M)
Wakefield (SMRS)
Warrington
Warwick
Welshpool
Whitby
Winchester
Wisbech
Wolverhampton
Yarmouth
York (Castle)
York (YM)

Total : 173

Name	Home of Sir Walter Scott Abbotsford	ABBOTSFORD
Address	Abbotsford near Galashiels Scotland	Sources & Dates of Information R. Hutchings 1966 Visit ALK 1974 MEG 1978 Letter
Telephone	0896-2043	
Contact	Secretary	

Notes

Oceania: weapons
New Zealand: patu
Tonga: fishook

Dates of Collection/Acquisition	Donors/Collectors/Former Owners
	Leverian Bullock

Documentation

Reference: A. Kaeppler, 1974, "Cook Voyage Provenance of 'Artificial Curiousities' of Bullock's Museum", Man, 9:68-92.

Comment

Sir Walter Scott's house. Objects in his collection of weapons.

ABERDEEN

Name: Anthropological Museum

Address: Marischal College
University of Aberdeen
Aberdeen AB9 1AS

Telephone: 0224-40241

Contact: Curator

Sources & Dates of Information

R. Hutchings 1966
Visits GSP 1974, DLS 1978
MEG 1978
Letter 1979
catalogue 1912

Notes

Total Oceanic collection: c. 2500 items.

*Australia-- other: boomerangs 13, toy 1, misc. 2
*Fiji-- barkcloth: made for King Edward VII
other: hook (Tongan type)
*New Guinea-- belt: of barkcloth
navigation: steering paddle
*New Hebrides-- bags: of barkcloth
*Polynesia unprovenanced-- mats: "20" includes some baskets
*New Zealand-- other: head, head model

Dates of Collection/Acquisition

Donors/Collectors/Former Owners

Documentation

Museum publication: Illustrated Catalogue of the Anthropological Museum, Marischal College, University of Aberdeen, Reid, 1912. (copy in Haddon Library, Cambridge)

Comment

Important, valuable collection. This information derived from ~~1912~~ Catalogue which needs checking when circumstances permit. Full-time curator appointed effective 1 July 1979.

Anthropological Museum

ABERDEEN

Provenance ↓ / Artefact →	TOTAL	OTHER	barkcloth	CLOTHING	-skirt	-belt	-cloak	PERS. ORN.	-head	-ear,nose	-arm	-neck,breast	comb	fan	toilet app.	staff,sti	CERE. O	-mask	-board	-adze	-paddle	-bullroarer	carving	fig.,image	magic,med.	charm	MUSICAL INS.	-drum,gong	-flute,pipe	-rattle	currency	transport	headrest	mat	basket	bag	box
OCEANIA UN.																																					
AUSTRALIA	102																3					1			1	1	1										
MELA.UNPROV.																																					
Admiralty																																					
Banks																																					
Bismarck																																					
D'Entrecast.																																					
Fiji	63	1		1*				2			4	17	6	3												2									1		
Louisiade																																					
Loyalty																																					
N. Britain																																					
N. Caledonia																																					
N. Guinea	52		1		3	1*					1	1														2	3	1								2	
N. Hebrides	76			2		1		4	1		4			1		1								1				1						2		2*	
N. Ireland																																					
Santa Cruz																																					
Solomon	5											1												1													
Trobriand																																					
MICRO.UNPROV																																					
Caroline																																					
Gilbert																																					
Mariana																																					
Marshall																																					
POLY.UNPROV.	51		13	1																														20*	3	X	
Austral																																					
Chatham																																					
Cook																																					
Easter																																					
Hawaii	1																							1													
Marquesas	2								1																												
New Zealand	54	2					1	2			1	6																	2								7
Niue																																					
Pitcairn																																					
Samoa																																					
Society																																					
Tokelau																																					
Tonga	11												5	1										1									2				
Tuamotu																																					
Tuvalu																																					
Tahiti	1																						1														

Anthropological Museum

ABERDEEN

3

Artefact → / Provenance ↓	lime cont.	dish,vesse	lime spat.	utensil	pottery	smokng pi	fire,ligh	TOOL	-adze	-pounding	-grinding	-rasp	-chisel	-needle,aw	-weaving	-barkcloth	NAVIGATION	-paddle	-ornament	-model	hunting	FISHING	-fishhook	-spear	-net	-float,sin	WEAPON	-club	-spear	-spearthro	-dagger	-shield	-bow	-arrow	-sling,sto	raw mater	cord
OCEANIA UN.																																					
AUSTRALIA		1		1			1	3	40	3	1																	21	2	3		8				1	
MELA.UNPROV.																																					
Admiralty																																					
Banks																																					
Bismarck																																					
D'Entrecast.																																					
Fiji		9			4				1					1														10								1	
Louisiade																																					
Loyalty																																					
N. Britain																																					
N. Caledonia																																					
N. Guinea		1				1			3								1*	6	1							2	5	13	4								
N. Hebrides		3		3	3				2																		1	5					2	36		2	
N. Ireland																																					
Santa Cruz																																					
Solomon																											1	1	1								
Trobriand																																					
MICRO.UNPROV																																					
Caroline																																					
Gilbert																																					
Mariana																																					
Marshall																																					
POLY.UNPROV.																												2	4					8			
Austral																																					
Chatham																																					
Cook																																					
Easter																																					
Hawaii																																					
Marquesas																												1									
New Zealand									4				3					2					5				1	11	3	2	2						
Niue																																					
Pitcairn																																					
Samoa																																					
Society																																					
Tokelau																																					
Tonga.																												2									
Tuamotu																																					
Tuvalu																																					
Tahiti																																					
Rotuma									13																												

Name	Regimental Headquarters Royal Corps of Transport	ALDERSHOT
Address	Buller Barracks Aldershot Hampshire	Sources & Dates of Information R. Hutchings 1966 Visit MEG 1978 Letter
Telephone		
Contact	Regimental Secretary	

Notes

New Zealand: club 1

Dates of Collection/Acquisition	Donors/Collectors/Former Owners

Documentation

Comment

ARBROATH

Name	Arbroath Museum
Address	Signal Tower Ladyloan Arbroath DD11 1PU Angus
Telephone	0241-75598
Contact	Angus District Curator, c/o Montrose Museum, Panmure Place, Montrose, Angus, Scotland (tel. 0674-3232)

Sources & Dates of Information

R. Hutchings 1966

Visit

MEG 1978

Letter 1979

Notes

*Oceania unprovenanced-- paddle: in Brechin Museum
*Australia-- other: boomerang
*New Hebrides-- other: cloth
*Santa Cruz-- weaving tool: loom
*New Zealand-- tools: textile tools

Dates of Collection/Acquisition	Donors/Collectors/Former Owners
Acquired mainly 1840-80	about 40% of donors known

Documentation

Comment

Arbroath Museum

ARBROAT

Artefact → / Provenance ↓	TOTAL	OTHER	barkcloth	CLOTHING	-skirt	-belt	-cloak	PERS. ORN.	-head	-ear,nose	-arm	-neck,breast	comb	fan	toilet app.	staff,stick	CERE. OBJ.	-mask	-board	-adze	-paddle	-bullroarer	carving	fig.,image	magic,med.	charm	MUSICAL INS.	-drum,gong	-flute,pipe	-rattle	currency	transport	headrest	mat	basket	bag	box
OCEANIA UN.	4		1								1															1											
AUSTRALIA	17+	1										1																									
MELA.UNPROV.																																					
Admiralty																																					
Banks																																					
Bismarck																																					
D'Entrecast.																																					
Fiji	25			1										1																							
Louisiade																																					
Loyalty																																					
N. Britain	2																																				
N. Caledonia																																					
N. Guinea	2											1																									
N. Hebrides	1	1																																			
N. Ireland																																					
Santa Cruz	9+																																		2	1	
Solomon	9+										X																										
Trobriand																																					
MICRO.UNPROV.																																					
Caroline																																					
Gilbert																																					
Mariana																																					
Marshall																																					
POLY.UNPROV.																																					
Austral																																					
Chatham																																					
Cook																																					
Easter																																					
Hawaii																																					
Marquesas																																					
New Zealand	2+																																				
Niue																																					
Pitcairn																																					
Samoa																																					
Society																																					
Tokelau																																					
Tonga																																					
Tuamotu																																					
Tuvalu																																					
Tahiti	1																																				

ARBROATH

Arbroath Museum

Provenance ↓ / Artefact →	lime cont.	dish,vesse	lime spat.	utensil	pottery	smokng pip	fire,light	TOOL	-adze	-pounding	-grinding	-rasp	-chisel	-needle,aw	-weaving	-barkcloth	NAVIGATION	-paddle	-ornament	-model	hunting	FISHING	-fishhook	-spear	-net	-float,sin	WEAPON	-club	-spear	-spearthro	-dagger	-shield	-bow	-arrow	-sling,sto	raw mater.	cord
OCEANIA UN.																		1*										1									
AUSTRALIA																												7		2		6+					
MELA.UNPROV.																																					
Admiralty																																					
Banks																																					
Bismarck																																					
D'Entrecast.																																					
Fiji																												23									
Louisiade																																					
Loyalty																																					
N. Britain																												2									
N. Caledonia																																					
N. Guinea				1																																	
N. Hebrides																																					
N. Ireland																																					
Santa Cruz															1*										2			2						X			
Solomon																												6+				1		X			
Trobriand																																					
MICRO.UNPROV																																					
Caroline																																					
Gilbert																																					
Mariana																																					
Marshall																																					
POLY.UNPROV.																																					
Austral																																					
Chatham																																					
Cook																																					
Easter																																					
Hawaii																																					
Marquesas																																					
New Zealand															X																					X	
Niue																																					
Pitcairn																																					
Samoa																																					
Society																																					
Tokelau																																					
Tonga																																					
Tuamotu																																					
Tuvalu																																					
Tahiti																1																					

Name	Potter's Museum of Curiousity
Address	6 High Street Arundel Sussex
Telephone	0903-882420
Contact	

ARUNDEL

Sources & Dates of Information

R. Hutchings	1966
Visit	
MEG	1978
Letter	1979

Notes

- Probable, but collection unsorted and uncatalogued.

Dates of Collection/Acquisition

1860-1930; 1970+

Donors/Collectors/Former Owners

Documentation

Comment

An unknown quantity. Needs to be contacted later on progress.

AYLESBURY

Name	Buckinghamshire County Museum	
Address	Church Street Aylesbury HP20 2QP	
Telephone	0296-82158/88849	
Contact	Senior Curator of Archaeology and History	

Sources & Dates of Information

R. Hutchings	1966
Visit	
MEG	1978
Letter	1979

Notes

Numbers of artefacts and provenances uncertain. About 40 items unidentified.

Disposals: 1934, about 50 items to British Museum
1955, about 10 disposed of
1950's, some to school service, included in table

*Australia-- other: boomerangs 2

Dates of Collection/Acquisition	Donors/Collectors/Former Owners
Acquired 1860's-1920's	L. Payne, collected 1860, Fiji, Oceania A.M. Cocks, Fiji, Admiralty, Caroline Is., New Guinea Rev. R. Ussher, Fiji Rev. Claxton, Hambledon Collection Mr. Millburn, New Zealand Mrs. W. Sturge, Marquesas

Documentation

Documentation fragmentary.

Comment

1860's material to be seen (at least!).

County Museum

AYLESBURY

Provenance ↓ / Artefact →	TOTAL	OTHER	barkcloth	CLOTHING	-skirt	-belt	-cloak	PERS. ORN.	-head	-ear,nose	-arm	-neck,breast	comb	fan	toilet app.	staff,stick	CERE. OBJ.	-mask	-board	-adze	-paddle	-bullroarer	carving	fig.,image	magic,med.	charm	MUSICAL INS.	-drum,gong	-flute,pipe	-rattle	currency	transport	headrest	mat	basket	bag	box
OCEANIA UN.	4																1						2											1		1	
AUSTRALIA	4	2														2																					
MELA.UNPROV.	1							1																													
Admiralty	5																																				
Banks																																					
Bismarck	1										1																										
D'Entrecast.																																					
Fiji	5		1																																		
Louisiade																																					
Loyalty																																					
N. Britain																																					
N. Caledonia																																					
N. Guinea	1			1																																	
N. Hebrides																																					
N. Ireland																																					
Santa Cruz																																					
Solomon																																					
Trobriand																																					
MICRO.UNPROV.																																					
Caroline	2																																				
Gilbert																																					
Mariana																																					
Marshall																																					
POLY.UNPROV.																																					
Austral																																					
Chatham																																					
Cook																																					
Easter																																					
Hawaii																																					
Marquesas	2							1		1																											
New Zealand	1				1																																
Niue																																					
Pitcairn																																					
Samoa	3																											1									
Society																																					
Tokelau																																					
Tonga																																					
Tuamotu																																					
Tuvalu																																					

County Museum

AYLESBURY

Artefact → / Provenance ↓	lime cont.	dish,vesse.	lime spat.	utensil	pottery	smokng pip	fire,light	TOOL	-adze	-pounding	-grinding	-rasp	-chisel	-needle,aw	-weaving	-barkcloth	NAVIGATION	-paddle	-ornament	-model	hunting	FISHING	-fishhook	-spear	-net	-float,si	WEAPON	-club	-spear	-spearthr	-dagger	-shield	-bow	-arrow	-sling,st	raw mater	cord
OCEANIA UN.								1														1					6		27	1							
AUSTRALIA																																					
MELA.UNPROV.																																					
Admiralty																													5								
Banks																																					
Bismarck																																					
D'Entrecast.																																					
Fiji					1																							3									
Louisiade																																					
Loyalty																																					
N. Britain																																					
N. Caledonia																																					
N. Guinea																																					
N. Hebrides																																					
N. Ireland																																					
Santa Cruz																																					
Solomon																																					
Trobriand																																					
MICRO.UNPROV																																					
Caroline																													1						1		
Gilbert																																					
Mariana																																					
Marshall																																					
POLY.UNPROV.																																					
Austral																																					
Chatham																																					
Cook																																					
Easter																																					
Hawaii																																					
Marquesas																																					
New Zealand																																					
Niue																																					
Pitcairn																																					
Samoa																												2									
Society																																					
Tokelau																																					
Tonga																																					
Tuamotu																																					
Tuvalu																																					

Name	Kyle and Carrick District Library and Museum Service	AYR
Address	Carnegie Library 12 Main Street Ayr KA8 8ED Scotland	**Sources & Dates of Information** R. Hutchings 1966 Visit MEG 1978 Letters 1979
Telephone	0292-81511	
Contact	Museums Organiser	

Notes

Material in store.

Australia: weapons.

Dates of Collection/Acquisition	Donors/Collectors/Former Owners
Acquired mainly 1930-68	Hugh Hamilton (1822-1900)

Documentation

Oceanic uncatalogued.

Library, archival, photographic, iconographic.

Comment

BARNET

Name: The Abbey Art Centre and Museum

Address: 89 Park Road
New Barnet
Hertfordshire

Telephone: Barnet 3991

Contact: Director

Sources & Dates of Information

R. Hutchings 1966

Visit

MEG 1978

Letter 1979

Notes

A few "South Sea objects" reported in 1966. Museum now disbanded; location of objects not known.

Dates of Collection/Acquisition	Donors/Collectors/Former Owners

Documentation

Comment

BARROW

Name: The Furness Museum

Address: Ramsden Square
Barrow-in-Furness LA14 1LL

Telephone: 0229-20650

Contact: Curator

Sources & Dates of Information

R. Hutchings 1966
Visit

MEG 1978
Letter

Notes

Less than 100 Oceanic, total.

*Australia-- other: boomerangs

Dates of Collection/Acquisition	Donors/Collectors/Former Owners
Acquired mainly 1900-50	

Documentation

Comment

No comment yet possible.

The Furness Museum

BARROW

Artefact → / Provenance ↓	OCEANIA UN.	AUSTRALIA	MELA.UNPROV.	Admiralty	Banks	Bismarck	D'Entrecast.	Fiji	Louisiade	Loyalty	N. Britain	N. Caledonia	N. Guinea	N. Hebrides	N. Ireland	Santa Cruz	Solomon	Trobriand	MICRO.UNPROV.	Caroline	Gilbert	Mariana	Marshall	POLY.UNPROV.	Austral	Chatham	Cook	Easter	Hawaii	Marquesas	New Zealand	Niue	Pitcairn	Samoa	Society	Tokelau	Tonga	Tuamotu	Tuvalu
box																																							
bag																																							
basket																																							
mat																																							
headrest																																							
transport																																							
currency																																							
-rattle																																							
-flute,pipe																																							
-drum,gong																																							
MUSICAL INS.																																							
charm																																							
magic,med.																																							
fig.,image																																							
carving																																							
-bullroarer																														/									
-paddle																																							
-adze																																							
-board																																							
-mask																																							
CERE. OBJ.																																							
staff,stick																																							
toilet app.																																							
fan																																							
comb																																							
-neck,breast																																							
-arm																																							
-ear,nose																																							
-head																																							
PERS. ORN.																																							
-cloak																																							
-belt																																							
-skirt																																							
CLOTHING																																							
barkcloth																																							
OTHER		X																																					
TOTAL	X	X																													X								

The Furness Museum BARROW

Artefact ⟶ / Provenance	OCEANIA UN.	AUSTRALIA	MELA.UNPROV.	Admiralty	Banks	Bismarck	D'Entrecast.	Fiji	Louisiade	Loyalty	N. Britain	N. Caledonia	N. Guinea	N. Hebrides	N. Ireland	Santa Cruz	Solomon	Trobriand	MICRO.UNPROV	Caroline	Gilbert	Mariana	Marshall	POLY.UNPROV.	Austral	Chatham	Cook	Easter	Hawaii	Marquesas	New Zealand	Niue	Pitcairn	Samoa	Society	Tokelau	Tonga	Tuamotu	Tuvalu
cord																																							
raw mater																																							
-sling,st																																							
-arrow																																							
-bow																																							
-shield																																							
-dagger																																							
-spearthr																																							
-spear																																							
-club																																							
WEAPON																																							
-float,si																																							
-net																																							
-spear																																							
-fishhook																																							
FISHING																																							
hunting																																							
-model																																							
-ornament																																							
-paddle																																							
NAVIGATIO																																							
-barkclot																																							
-weaving																																							
-needle,aw																																							
-chisel																																							
-rasp																																							
-grinding																																							
-pounding																																							
-adze																								X															
TOOL																																							
fire,ligh																																							
smoking pi																																							
pottery																																							
utensil																																							
lime spat.																																							
dish,vesse																																							
lime cont.																																							

BATA

Name: Geology Museum

Address: 18 Queen Square
Bath BA1 2EW

Telephone: 0225-28144

Contact: Curatorial Assistant, Geology

Sources & Dates of Information

R. Hutchings 1966
Visit PG 1977
MEG 1978
Letter

Notes

*Australia-- other: boomerangs
*Marquesas-- carving: stilt step
*New Zealand-- other: heads 2

Dates of Collection/Acquisition

Donors/Collectors/Former Owners

Documentation

Limited (much lost, 1939-45)

Comment

Collection's future uncertain.

Geology Museum

BATH

Provenance	TOTAL	OTHER	barkcloth	CLOTHING	-skirt	-belt	-cloak	PERS. ORN.	-head	-ear,nose	-arm	-neck,breast	comb	fan	toilet app.	staff,stick	CERE. OBJ.	-mask	-board	-adze	-paddle	-bullroarer	carving	fig.,image	magic,med.	charm	MUSICAL INS.	-drum,gong	-flute,pipe	-rattle	currency	transport	headrest	mat	basket	bag	box
OCEANIA UN.	2																																				
AUSTRALIA	30	X																																			
MELA.UNPROV.	9																																				
Admiralty																																					
Banks																																					
Bismarck																																					
D'Entrecast.																																					
Fiji	10																																				
Louisiade																																					
Loyalty																																					
N. Britain	1																																				
N. Caledonia	3																																				
N. Guinea	34							6																													
N. Hebrides	1										1																										
N. Ireland																																					
Santa Cruz	2																																				
Solomon	37							2																													
Trobriand																																					
MICRO.UNPROV.																																					
Caroline																																					
Gilbert	1																																				
Mariana																																					
Marshall																																					
POLY.UNPROV.	3																																				
Austral	4																																				
Chatham																																					
Cook	4																																				
Easter																																					
Hawaii																																					
Marquesas	1																						1*														
New Zealand	6	2																																			
Niue																																					
Pitcairn																																					
Samoa																																					
Society																																					
Tokelau																																					
Tonga	5																																				
Tuamotu																																					
Tuvalu																																					

Geology Museum

BATH

Provenance ↓ / Artefact →	lime cont.	dish,vesse	lime spat	utensil	pottery	smokng pi	fire,ligh	TOOL	-adze	-pounding	-grinding	-rasp	-chisel	-needle,a	-weaving	-barkclot	NAVIGATIO	-paddle	-ornament	-model	hunting	FISHING	-fishhook	-spear	-net	-float,si	WEAPON	-club	-spear	-spearthr	-dagger	-shield	-bow	-arrow	-sling,st	raw mater	cord
OCEANIA UN.																																					
AUSTRALIA																																					
MELA.UNPROV.																																					
Admiralty																																					
Banks																																					
Bismarck																																					
D'Entrecast.																																					
Fiji																												10									
Louisiade																																					
Loyalty																																					
N. Britain																																					
N. Caledonia																																					
N. Guinea																													2			5					
N. Hebrides																																					
N. Ireland																																					
Santa Cruz																																					
Solomon																												6	4				5	17			
Trobriand																																					
MICRO.UNPROV																																					
Caroline																																					
Gilbert																															1						
Mariana																																					
Marshall																																					
POLY.UNPROV.																													2								
Austral																	4																				
Chatham																																					
Cook																												3									
Easter																																					
Hawaii																																					
Marquesas																																					
New Zealand																																					
Niue																																					
Pitcairn																																					
Samoa																																					
Society																																					
Tokelau																																					
Tonga																												2									
Tuamotu																																					
Tuvalu																																					

Name Bagshaw Museum

Address Wilton Park
Batley WF17 0AS

Telephone 0924-472514

Contact Assistant Curator

BATLEY

Sources & Dates of Information

R. Hutchings 1966

Visit Sp 1975

MEG 1978

Letter 1979

Notes

Data from entire Kirklees Libraries and Museums Service was collected at one time, so Batley entry includes material from Tolson Memorial Museum, Huddersfield, and Dewsbury Galleries, Dewsbury. For further details contact Principal Assistant (Museums), Headquarters, Kirklees Libraries and Museums Service, Princess Alexandra Walk, Huddersfield, HD1 2SU (tel. 0484-21356).

Total Oceanic collection: about 500 items (around half at Huddersfield).

*Australia-- other: boomerangs 3
*Melanesia-- utensils: sago scoops possibly New Britain or Admiralty
spears: 1 possibly New Hebrides
*New Zealand-- other: meeting house model, hook

Dates of Collection/Acquisition

Donors/Collectors/Former Owners

Walter Bagshaw, 1900-11
Church Missionary Society

Documentation

Library.

Collections are being catalogued, but documentation is uneven; attributions may be uncertain in some cases.

Comment

Bagshaw Museum

BATLEY

Provenance ↓ / Artefact →	TOTAL	OTHER	barkcloth	CLOTHING	-skirt	-belt	-cloak	PERS. ORN.	-head	-ear,nose	-arm	-neck,breast	comb	fan	toilet app.	staff,stick	CERE. OBJ.	-mask	-board	-adze	-paddle	-bullroarer	carving	fig.,image	magic,med.	charm	MUSICAL INS.	-drum,gong	-flute,pipe	-rattle	currency	transport	headrest	mat	basket	bag	box
OCEANIA UN.	5				2							2																									
AUSTRALIA	64	3																				1															
MELA.UNPROV.	10																																				
Admiralty																																					
Banks																																					
Bismarck																																					
D'Entrecast.																																					
Fiji	18		5		3									2																							
Louisiade																																					
Loyalty																																					
N. Britain																																					
N. Caledonia																																					
N. Guinea	13																																				
N. Hebrides	X																																				
N. Ireland																																					
Santa Cruz																																					
Solomon	45																																				
Trobriand	1										1																										
MICRO.UNPROV																																					
Caroline																																					
Gilbert	3																																				
Mariana																																					
Marshall																																					
POLY.UNPROV.																																					
Austral	X																				1																
Chatham																																					
Cook	1		1																																		
Easter																																					
Hawaii																																					
Marquesas																																					
New Zealand	7	2					1																	2												1	
Niue																																					
Pitcairn																																					
Samoa																																					
Society	2		2																																		
Tokelau																																					
Tonga	3																																				
Tuamotu																																					
Tuvalu																																					

Bagshaw Museum

BATLEY

Artefact → / Provenance ↓	OCEANIA UN.	AUSTRALIA	MELA.UNPROV.	Admiralty	Banks	Bismarck	D'Entrecast.	Fiji	Louisiade	Loyalty	N. Britain	N. Caledonia	N. Guinea	N. Hebrides	N. Ireland	Santa Cruz	Solomon	Trobriand	MICRO.UNPROV	Caroline	Gilbert	Mariana	Marshall	POLY.UNPROV.	Austral	Chatham	Cook	Easter	Hawaii	Marquesas	New Zealand	Niue	Pitcairn	Samoa	Society	Tokelau	Tonga	Tuamotu	Tuvalu
cord																																							
raw mater																																							
-sling,sto																																							
-arrow			4										9				25																						
-bow			3														2																						
-shield		2																																					
-dagger																																							
-spearthro		3																																					
-spear		45	~~27~~														10																						
-club		10						6					1				5																				3		
WEAPON																					3																		
-float,sin																																							
-net																																							
-spear																																							
-fishhook																																							
FISHING																																							
hunting																																							
-model								1																							1								
-ornament																																							
-paddle																	2																						
NAVIGATION	1																																						
-barkcloth								1																															
-weaving																																							
-needle,aw.																																							
-chisel																																							
-rasp																																							
-grinding																																							
-pounding																																							
-adze			1										1																										
TOOL																																							
fire,light																																							
smoking pip																																							
pottery																																							
utensil													~~27~~																										
lime spat.																																							
dish,vesse.																																							
lime cont.																	1																						

Name: Ulster Museum Address: Botanic Gardens Belfast BT9 5AB Telephone: 0232-668251 Contact: Research Assistant, Antiquities	BELFAST Sources & Dates of Information R. Hutchings 1966 Visit MEG 1978 Letters 1977, 1979

Notes

*Oceania unprovenanced-- belts: bark 1, woven 4
toilet apparatus: tattooing
sticks: walking
mus. instrument: shell trumpets
tool: 1 from "Oyster Harbour"
adze: possibly Hawaiian
weapons: all sharkstooth- Gilberts?
*Admiralty-- mus. instrument: shell trumpet
*New Guinea--tool: digging stick
*Solomons-- navigation: 40' war canoe, brought by Capt. Casement, c. 1896
*Easter-- figure: tapa figure c. 1840
*Hawaii-- staves, sticks: 2 walking, 1 whisk/sceptre
*New Zealand-- mus. instrument: shell trumpet
other: head 1, oil painting of Kuha (Robley; original in National Museum, Wellington)

Dates of Collection/Acquisition	Donors/Collectors/Former Owners
↔	G.A. Thomson (1799-1886) collected in Pacific c. 1841; collection acquired 1843.
	Canon Grainger (d. c.1902 aged 60).
↔	G.C. Hyndman (1796-1867) collection acquired in 1859.
↔	Robert Patterson donated Earl of Dudley collection which was collected between 1815 & 1872.

Documentation

Supporting documentation for individual specimens often sparse.

Comment

Contains some very good early material.

Ulster Museum

BELFAST

Provenance	TOTAL	OTHER	barkcloth	CLOTHING	-skirt	-belt	-cloak	PERS. ORN.	-head	-ear,nose	-arm	-neck,breast	comb	fan	toilet app.	staff,stick	CERE. OBJ.	-mask	-board	-adze	-paddle	-bullroarer	carving	fig.,image	magic,med.	charm	MUSICAL INS.	-drum,gong	-flute,pipe	-rattle	currency	transport	headrest	mat	basket	bag	box
OCEANIA UN.	90		16			1		1			2	9	4		1*	4*											2*										
AUSTRALIA																																					
MELA.UNPROV.	6					6																															
Admiralty	9																										1*						1				
Banks																																					
Bismarck																																					
D'Entrecast.																																					
Fiji	29											2																									
Louisiade																																					
Loyalty																																					
N. Britain	2																																				
N. Caledonia	1																																				
N. Guinea	67			1		1		2	2*	1	2	2	2			1								3				1			1					2	
N. Hebrides	43										2		1											1													
N. Ireland	2																							2													
Santa Cruz	2											1																									
Solomon	113							12		3	9	1	2			2	1				1			2							1						
Trobriand	1																																				
MICRO.UNPROV.																																					
Caroline																																					
Gilbert	4																																				
Mariana																																					
Marshall																																					
POLY.UNPROV.																																					
Austral	7																																				
Chatham	1																																				
Cook	13																			3																	
Easter	4																							4*													
Hawaii	67+		6	1			1	6	1	1	2	3	1		1	3*	4*							1*													
Marquesas	8							1		3			2	1																							
New Zealand	38	3					3			1		3					1						2				1*								1	2	
Niue																																					
Pitcairn																																					
Samoa	16					1			1*																												
Society																																					
Tokelau																																					
Tonga	13+		2*										1																				2				
Tuamotu																																					
Tuvalu																																					
Tahiti	8+														X*	2																					

Ulster Museum

BELFAST

Provenance ↓ / Artefact →	lime cont.	dish,vesse	lime spat.	utensil	pottery	smokng pip	fire,light	TOOL	-adze	-pounding	-grinding	-rasp	-chisel	-needle,aw	-weaving	-barkcloth	NAVIGATION	-paddle	-ornament	-model	hunting	FISHING	-fishhook	-spear	-net	-float,sin	WEAPON	-club	-spear	-spearthro	-dagger	-shield	-bow	-arrow	-sling,sto	raw mater.	cord
OCEANIA UN.		5		4				2*	1*									4						6			3*	3	5							12	
AUSTRALIA																																					
MELA.UNPROV.																																					
Admiralty		2																											5								
Banks																																					
Bismarck																																					
D'Entrecast.																																					
Fiji		4		2	2				1																			17	1								
Louisiade																																					
Loyalty																																					
N. Britain																												2									
N. Caledonia																												1									
N. Guinea			6	1			1	1*		1						2												12						21		1	
N. Hebrides																												8	4					2			
N. Ireland																																					
Santa Cruz																												1									
Solomon		1															1*	1	3				11					1	3				1	53		7	
Trobriand	1																																				
MICRO.UNPROV.																																					
Caroline																																					
Gilbert																											4										
Mariana																																					
Marshall																																					
POLY.UNPROV.																																					
Austral		1																1																			
Chatham									1																												
Cook		1																										1	7					1			
Easter																																					
Hawaii		23		1		1		1	1	1						2							3				X										
Marquesas																												1									
New Zealand									8				1				1	1		2			3					5									
Niue																																					
Pitcairn																																					
Samoa																3								5				5	1								
Society																																					
Tokelau																																					
Tonga																							X					9									
Tuamotu																																					
Tuvalu																																					
Tahiti																							5														
Rotuma																																					

BELSAY

		Sources & Dates of Information	
Name	Wallington Hall (National Trust)		
Address	Cambo Belsay Northumberland	R. Hutchings	1966
		Visit	
Telephone		MEG	1978
Contact	Regional Historic Buildings Representative, National Trust, Blagdon House, Seaton Burn, Northumberland (tel.067089-235)	Letter ✓ Natl. Trust Guide	1974 1979

Notes

Dates of Collection/Acquisition	Donors/Collectors/Former Owners
	Some on loan from British Museum

Documentation

Some of collection has been catalogued with help from Newcastle & Durham Universities and the British Museum.

Comment

Lady Wilson's "Cabinet of Curiousities", which originally came from Charlton Park, Greenwich (cf. Hodgson, History of Northumberland, 1927). Also contains natural history material.

Wallington Hall BELSAY

Artefact → / Provenance ↓	OCEANIA UN.	AUSTRALIA	MELA. UNPROV.	Admiralty	Banks	Bismarck	D'Entrecast.	Fiji	Louisiade	Loyalty	N. Britain	N. Caledonia	N. Guinea	N. Hebrides	N. Ireland	Santa Cruz	Solomon	Trobriand	MICRO. UNPROV	Caroline	Gilbert	Mariana	Marshall	POLY. UNPROV.	Austral	Chatham	Cook	Easter	Hawaii	Marquesas	New Zealand	Niue	Pitcairn	Samoa	Society	Tokelau	Tonga	Tuamotu	Tuvalu
box																																							
bag																																							
basket	/																																						
mat																																							
headrest																																							
transport																																							
currency																																							
-rattle																																							
-flute, pipe																																							
-drum, gong																																							
MUSICAL INS.																																							
charm	X																																						
magic, med.																																							
fig., image																																							
carving																																							
-bullroarer																																							
-paddle																																							
-adze																																							
-board																																							
-mask																																							
CERE. OBJ.																																							
staff, stick																																							
toilet app.																																							
fan																																							
comb																																							
-neck, breast																																							
-arm																																							
-ear, nose																																							
-head																																							
PERS. ORN.																																							
-cloak																																							
-belt																																							
-skirt																																							
CLOTHING																																							
barkcloth																																							
OTHER																																							
TOTAL	X	X						/									/																						

BELSAY

Wallington Hall

Artefact → / Provenance →	OCEANIA UN.	AUSTRALIA	MELA.UNPROV.	Admiralty	Banks	Bismarck	D'Entrecast.	Fiji	Louisiade	Loyalty	N. Britain	N. Caledonia	N. Guinea	N. Hebrides	N. Ireland	Santa Cruz	Solomon	Trobriand	MICRO.UNPROV	Caroline	Gilbert	Mariana	Marshall	POLY.UNPROV.	Austral	Chatham	Cook	Easter	Hawaii	Marquesas	New Zealand	Niue	Pitcairn	Samoa	Society	Tokelau	Tonga	Tuamotu	Tuvalu
cord																																							
raw mate	X	X																																					
-sling,s																																							
-arrow																	/																						
-bow																																							
-shield																																							
-dagger																																							
-spearthr																																							
-spear	X																																						
-club								-																															
WEAPON	X																																						
-float,s																																							
-net																																							
-spear	/																																						
-fishhook																																							
FISHING																																							
hunting																																							
-model																																							
-ornament																																							
-paddle																																							
NAVIGATIO																																							
-barkclo																																							
-weaving																																							
-needle,a																																							
-chisel																																							
-rasp																																							
-grinding																																							
-pounding																																							
-adze																																							
TOOL																																							
fire,ligh																																							
smoking pi																																							
pottery																																							
utensil																																							
lime spat																																							
dish,vess																																							
lime cont																																							

Name Libraries and Museums

Address (contact Area Librarian)

Telephone

Contact Area Librarian, Area Library, Barnstaple, Devon
(tel. 0271-71886)

BIDEFORD

Sources & Dates of Information

R. Hutchings 1966

Visit PG 1978

MEG 1978

Letter 1978

Notes

Objects not easily accessible, being in 4 locations: Bideford Library, Borough Library, Appledore Maritime Museum, Burton Art Gallery.

Collection under the jurisdiction of Area Library.

*Fiji-- vessel: 1 kava bowl possibly Tongan
*Samoa-- barkcloth: 1 possibly Fijian
clubs: possible Tongan

Dates of Collection/Acquisition

Donors/Collectors/Former Owners

Borough Library

Documentation

Comment

Barkcloth is large and good.

Libraries and Museums

BIDEFORD

Artefact → / Provenance ↓	OCEANIA UN.	AUSTRALIA	MELA.UNPROV.	Admiralty	Banks	Bismarck	D'Entrecast.	Fiji	Louisiade	Loyalty	N. Britain	N. Caledonia	N. Guinea	N. Hebrides	N. Ireland	Santa Cruz	Solomon	Trobriand	MICRO.UNPROV.	Caroline	Gilbert	Mariana	Marshall	POLY.UNPROV.	Austral	Chatham	Cook	Easter	Hawaii	Marquesas	New Zealand	Niue	Pitcairn	Samoa	Society	Tokelau	Tonga	Tuamotu	Tuvalu
box																																							
bag																																							
basket																																							
mat																																							
headrest													1																										
transport																																							
currency																																							
-rattle																																							
-flute,pipe																																							
-drum,gong																																							
MUSICAL INS.																																							
charm																																							
magic,med.																																							
fig.,image																																							
carving																																							
-bullroarer																																							
-paddle																																							
-adze																																							
-board																																							
-mask																																							
CERE. OBJ.																																							
staff,stick																																							
toilet app.																																							
fan																																							
comb																								1															
-neck,breast																																							
-arm																															2								
-ear,nose																																							
-head																																							
PERS. ORN.																																							
-cloak																																							
-belt																																							
-skirt																																							
CLOTHING																																							
barkcloth	4							3																										4*					
OTHER																																							
TOTAL	4	1						8					2											X							2			6+			X?		

Libraries and Museums BIDEFORD

Artefact ↑ / Provenance →	OCEANIA UN.	AUSTRALIA	MELA.UNPROV.	Admiralty	Banks	Bismarck	D'Entrecast.	Fiji	Louisiade	Loyalty	N. Britain	N. Caledonia	N. Guinea	N. Hebrides	N. Ireland	Santa Cruz	Solomon	Trobriand	MICRO.UNPROV.	Caroline	Gilbert	Mariana	Marshall	POLY.UNPROV.	Austral	Chatham	Cook	Easter	Hawaii	Marquesas	New Zealand	Niue	Pitcairn	Samoa	Society	Tokelau	Tonga	Tuamotu	Tuvalu		
cord																																									
raw mater																																									
-sling,st																																									
-arrow																																									
-bow																																									
-shield		/																																							
-dagger																																									
-spearthro																																									
-spear																																									
-club																							X											X							
WEAPON																																									
-float,si																																									
-net																																									
-spear																																									
-fishhook																																									
FISHING																																									
hunting																																									
-model																																									
-ornament																																									
-paddle																																									
NAVIGATIO																																									
-barkclot																																									
-weaving																																									
-needle,aw																																									
-chisel																																									
-rasp																																									
-grinding																																									
-pounding																																									
-adze																																									
TOOL																																									
fire,ligh																																									
smokng pi													/																												
pottery																																									
utensil																																									
lime spat																																									
dish,vesse								5*																																	
lime cont.																																									

BIRCHINGTON

Name: The Powell-Cotton Museum

Address: Quex Park
Birchington
Kent CT7 OBH

Telephone: 0843-42168

Contact: Director

Sources & Dates of Information

R. Hutchings 1966

Visit GSP 1974

MEG 1978

Letters 1974, 1979

Notes

*Marquesas-- musical instrument: shell trumpet

Dates of Collection/Acquisition	Donors/Collectors/Former Owners
Acquired mainly 1896-1938, much from naval officers by purchase.	Archdeacon Walker, collected by Miss M. Coombs, Church Missionary Society, 1908 Pinfold Collection, acquired 1926 Capt. Mackay, RN, 1896 - early 1900's Admiral E.H.M. Davis, 1892

Documentation

Collections catalogued. Documentation lacking in some cases.

Comment

Important family museum with wide ranging ethnographic collections.

BIRCHINGTON

Provenance ↓ / Artefact →	TOTAL	OTHER	barkcloth	CLOTHING	-skirt	-belt	-cloak	PERS. ORN.	-head	-ear,nose	-arm	-neck,breast	comb	fan	toilet app.	staff,stick	CERE. OBJ.	-mask	-board	-adze	-paddle	-bullroarer	carving	fig.,image	magic,med.	charm	MUSICAL INS.	-drum,gong	-flute,pipe	-rattle	currency	transport	headrest	mat	basket	bag	box
OCEANIA UN.																																					
AUSTRALIA	50																																				
MELA.UNPROV.																																					
Admiralty																																					
Banks	x							x																											X		
Bismarck																																					
D'Entrecast.																																					
Fiji	x		x																																		
Louisiade																																					
Loyalty																																					
N. Britain																																					
N. Caledonia																																					
N. Guinea	100													1																							
N. Hebrides	X							X																													
N. Ireland																																					
Santa Cruz	12+								1	2		2				1																					
Solomon	70+			1		1				9	9	21	4																					1			
Trobriand																																				2	
MICRO.UNPROV.																																					
Caroline																																					
Gilbert																																					
Mariana																																					
Marshall	X							x																											X		
POLY.UNPROV.																																					
Austral																																					
Chatham																																					
Cook	X							X																											X		
Easter																																					
Hawaii	X																																				
Marquesas	X																																				
New Zealand	7																						7				1										
Niue																																					
Pitcairn																																					
Samoa																																					
Society																																					
Tokelau																																					
Tonga																																					
Tuamotu																																					
Tuvalu																																					

Powell-Cotton Museum BIRCHINGTON

Artefact ⟶ / Provenance ⟶	OCEANIA UN.	AUSTRALIA	MELA.UNPROV.	Admiralty	Banks	Bismarck	D'Entrecast.	Fiji	Louisiade	Loyalty	N. Britain	N. Caledonia	N. Guinea	N. Hebrides	N. Ireland	Santa Cruz	Solomon	Trobriand	MICRO.UNPROV.	Caroline	Gilbert	Mariana	Marshall	POLY.UNPROV.	Austral	Chatham	Cook	Easter	Hawaii	Marquesas	New Zealand	Niue	Pitcairn	Samoa	Society	Tokelau	Tonga	Tuamotu	Tuvalu
cord																	1																						
raw mater																																							
-sling,st																																							
-arrow														X																									
-bow														X																									
-shield		X															X																						
-dagger																																							
-spearthro																																							
-spear		X		X												X	1																						
-club		X						X						X		1	3																				—		
WEAPON																																							
-float,si																																							
-net																																							
-spear																																							
-fishhook					X												10						X				X		X										
FISHING																																							
hunting																																							
-model																																							
-ornament																																							
-paddle					X												1						X		X		X												
NAVIGATIO																																							
-barkcloth						—																																	
-weaving																																							
-needle,aw																																							
-chisel																																							
-rasp																																							
-grinding																																							
-pounding																																							
-adze																	X																						
TOOL																																							
fire,light																																							
smoking pip																																							
pottery																																							
utensil																5	3																						
lime spat.																																							
dish,vesse																	3																						
lime cont.																	1																						

BIRMINGHAM (H)

Name	Birmingham Museums and Art Gallery
Address	Chamberlain Square Birmingham B3 3DH
Telephone	021-235 2834
Contact	Assistant Keeper of Archaeology

Sources & Dates of Information

R. Hutchings 1966

Visit

MEG 1978

Letter 1977

Notes

Contains less than 100 archaeological items.

Dates of Collection/Acquisition

Main period of acquisition:
1912-33

Donors/Collectors/Former Owners

A.W. Wilkins 1930
Birmingham University Medical School 1973
Wellcome Collection 1951

Documentation

Being catalogued.

Photographic.

Comment

Recently sorted.

Birmingham Museums and Art Gallery

BIRMINGHA

Provenance ↓ / Artefact →	TOTAL	OTHER	barkcloth	CLOTHING	-skirt	-belt	-cloak	PERS. ORN.	-head	-ear,nose	-arm	-neck,breast	comb	fan	toilet app.	staff,stick	CERE. OBJ.	-mask	-board	-adze	-paddle	-bullroarer	carving	fig.,image	magic,med.	charm	MUSICAL INS.	-drum,gong	-flute,pipe	-rattle	currency	transport	headrest	mat	basket	bag	box
OCEANIA UN.																																					
AUSTRALIA	180																																				
MELA.UNPROV.	111																																				
Admiralty																																					
Banks																																					
Bismarck																																					
D'Entrecast.																																					
Fiji	153		X					X																													
Louisiade																																					
Loyalty																																					
N. Britain																																					
N. Caledonia																																					
N. Guinea	367		X					X																													
N. Hebrides																																					
N. Ireland																																					
Santa Cruz																																					
Solomon	336		X					X																													
Trobriand																																					
MICRO.UNPROV	25																																				
Caroline																																					
Gilbert																																					
Mariana																																					
Marshall																																					
POLY.UNPROV.	179																																				
Austral																																					
Chatham																																					
Cook																								1													
Easter																																					
Hawaii																																					
Marquesas																																					
New Zealand	79						1	1																1													1
Niue																																					
Pitcairn																																					
Samoa																																					
Society																																					
Tokelau																																					
Tonga																																					
Tuamotu																																					
Tuvalu																																					

Birmingham Museums and Art Gallery BIRMINGHAM(H

Artefact → / Provenance →	OCEANIA UN.	AUSTRALIA	MELA.UNPROV.	Admiralty	Banks	Bismarck	D'Entrecast.	Fiji	Louisiade	Loyalty	N. Britain	N. Caledonia	N. Guinea	N. Hebrides	N. Ireland	Santa Cruz	Solomon	Trobriand	MICRO.UNPROV	Caroline	Gilbert	Mariana	Marshall	POLY.UNPROV.	Austral	Chatham	Cook	Easter	Hawaii	Marquesas	New Zealand	Niue	Pitcairn	Samoa	Society	Tokelau	Tonga	Tuamotu	Tuvalu
cord																																							
raw mater.																																							
-sling,sto.																																							
-arrow																																							
-bow																																							
-shield																																							
-dagger																																							
-spearthro.																																							
-spear																																							
-club																																							
WEAPON																																							
-float,sin								X					X				X																						
-net																																							
-spear																																							
-fishhook																																							
FISHING																																							
hunting																																							
-model																																							
-ornament								X					X				X																						
-paddle																																							
NAVIGATION																																							
-barkcloth																																							
-weaving																																							
-needle,aw.																																							
-chisel																																							
-rasp																																							
-grinding																																							
-pounding																																							
-adze																																							
TOOL																																							
fire,light																																							
smokng pip																																							
pottery																																							
utensil																																							
lime spat.																																							
dish,vesse																																							
lime cont.																																							

Name — Museum of Department of Geological Sciences

BIRMINGHAM (UNI)

Address — University of Birmingham
P.O. Box 363
Birmingham B15 2TT

Telephone — 021-472 1301

Contact — Curator

Sources & Dates of Information

R. Hutchings 1966

Visit

MEG 1978

Letter 1979

Notes

Fiji: axe, bought 1887
New Zealand: collection of modern flints

Dates of Collection/Acquisition

Acquired mainly 1900-30

Donors/Collectors/Former Owners

Wallis Collection, New Zealand

Documentation

Comment
If this is a sample collection of Maori stone technology, it is the only one of its kind in the U.K.

BLACKBURN (M+AG)

Name Blackburn Museum and Art Gallery

Address Library Street
Blackburn BB1 7AJ

Telephone 0254-667130

Contact Curator

Sources & Dates of Information

R. Hutchings 1966

Visit GSP 1974

MEG 1978

Letter

Notes

Table is incomplete.

Dates of Collection/Acquisition	Donors/Collectors/Former Owners

Documentation

Comment

Museum and Art Gallery

BLACKBURN (M+A

Provenance / Artifact	TOTAL	OTHER	barkcloth	CLOTHING	-skirt	-belt	-cloak	PERS. ORN.	-head	-ear,nose	-arm	-neck,breast	comb	fan	toilet app.	staff,stick	CERE. OBJ.	-mask	-board	-adze	-paddle	-bullroarer	carving	fig.,image	magic,med.	charm	MUSICAL INS.	-drum,gong	-flute,pipe	-rattle	currency	transport	headrest	mat	basket	bag	box
OCEANIA UN.	X																																				
AUSTRALIA																																					
MELA. UNPROV.																																					
Admiralty																																					
Banks																																					
Bismarck																																					
D'Entrecast.																																					
Fiji	X																																				
Louisiade																																					
Loyalty																																					
N. Britain																																					
N. Caledonia																																					
N. Guinea	X																																				
N. Hebrides																																					
N. Ireland																																					
Santa Cruz																																					
Solomon	X																																				
Trobriand																																					
MICRO. UNPROV.																																					
Caroline																																					
Gilbert	X																																				
Mariana																																					
Marshall																																					
POLY. UNPROV.																																					
Austral																																					
Chatham																																					
Cook																																					
Easter																																					
Hawaii																																					
Marquesas																																					
New Zealand	X																																				
Niue																																					
Pitcairn																																					
Samoa																																					
Society																																					
Tokelau																																					
Tonga																																					
Tuamotu																																					
Tuvalu																																					

Museum and Art Gallery

BLACKBURN CM+AG

Artefact → / Provenance →	OCEANIA UN.	AUSTRALIA	MELA.UNPROV.	Admiralty	Banks	Bismarck	D'Entrecast.	Fiji	Louisiade	Loyalty	N. Britain	N. Caledonia	N. Guinea	N. Hebrides	N. Ireland	Santa Cruz	Solomon	Trobriand	MICRO.UNPROV.	Caroline	Gilbert	Mariana	Marshall	POLY.UNPROV.	Austral	Chatham	Cook	Easter	Hawaii	Marquesas	New Zealand	Niue	Pitcairn	Samoa	Society	Tokelau	Tonga	Tuamotu	Tuvalu
cord																																							
raw mater																																							
-sling,st																																							
-arrow																																							
-bow																																							
-shield																																							
-dagger																																							
-spearthr																																							
-spear																																							
-club																																							
WEAPON																																							
-float,sl																																							
-net																																							
-spear																																							
-fishhook																																							
FISHING																																							
hunting																																							
-model																																							
-ornament																																							
-paddle																																							
NAVIGATIO																																							
-barkclot																																							
-weaving																																							
-needle,a																																							
-chisel																																							
-rasp																																							
-grinding																																							
-pounding																																							
-adze																																							
TOOL																																							
fire,ligh																																							
smoking pi																																							
pottery																																							
utensil																																							
lime spat																																							
dish,vess																																							
lime cont																																							

BLACKBURN (SC)

Name Stonyhurst College

Address Blackburn, Lancashire BB6 9PZ

Telephone 025486-345

Contact Andrew Henderson

Sources & Dates of Information

R. Hutchings 1966

Visit

MEG 1978

Letter 1979

Notes

Oceania: clubs, possibly other.

Dates of Collection/Acquisition	Donors/Collectors/Former Owners
1800-1900	Donors known.

Documentation

Library, archival.

Comment

Needs identification and help in cataloguing.

Name: Central Museum and Art Gallery	BOLTON
Address: Le Mans Crescent Bolton BL1 1SA	Sources & Dates of Information R. Hutchings 1966 Visit MEG 1978 Letters 1979
Telephone: 0204-22311	
Contact: Keeper of Archaeology	

Notes

More material may be identified as sorting continues.

Disposal: Samoan chief's house model disposed of in 1978 due to condition.

*Oceania-- barkcloth: possibly 2
club & paddles: possibly those listed under Solomons
other: "native screen"
*Australia-- other: boomerangs 2
*Gilberts-- weapon: armour suit
*Samoa-- musical instrument: shell trumpet

Dates of Collection/Acquisition	Donors/Collectors/Former Owners
Mainly acquired during 19th Century, some 20th.	

Documentation

Good progress in cataloguing.

Library, photographic.

Comment

Not seen. (Recent display.)

Central Museum and Art Gallery

BOLTON

Provenance ↓ / Artefact →	TOTAL	OTHER	barkcloth	CLOTHING	-skirt	-belt	-cloak	PERS. ORN.	-head	-ear,nose	-arm	-neck,breast	comb	fan	toilet app.	staff,stick	CERE. OBJ.	-mask	-board	-adze	-paddle	-bullroarer	carving	fig.,image	magic,med.	charm	MUSICAL INS.	-drum,gong	-flute,pipe	-rattle	currency	transport	headrest	mat	basket	bag	box
OCEANIA UN.	X	1	1+*		1																																
AUSTRALIA	8	2														1																					
MELA.UNPROV.																																					
Admiralty	2																																				
Banks	1																																				
Bismarck																																					
D'Entrecast.																																					
Fiji	5		1																																		
Louisiade																																					
Loyalty																																					
N. Britain																																					
N. Caledonia	1					1																															
N. Guinea	4+	X	1																																		
N. Hebrides	3											1																								1	
N. Ireland																																					
Santa Cruz																																					
Solomon	3																																				
Trobriand																																					
MICRO.UNPROV.																																					
Caroline																																					
Gilbert	2																																				
Mariana																																					
Marshall																																					
POLY.UNPROV.																																					
Austral	1																																				
Chatham																																					
Cook	2		1																	1																	
Easter																																					
Hawaii																																					
Marquesas																																					
New Zealand	12				1		1																1												1		
Niue																																					
Pitcairn																																					
Samoa	10		8																								1*										
Society																																					
Tokelau																																					
Tonga	1		1																																		
Tuamotu																																					
Tuvalu																																					
Tahiti	10		1	1							1	5											1												1		

Central Museum and Art Gallery BOLTON

Artefact → / Provenance ↓	OCEANIA UN.	AUSTRALIA	MELA.UNPROV.	Admiralty	Banks	Bismarck	D'Entrecast.	Fiji	Louisiade	Loyalty	N. Britain	N. Caledonia	N. Guinea	N. Hebrides	N. Ireland	Santa Cruz	Solomon	Trobriand	MICRO.UNPROV.	Caroline	Gilbert	Mariana	Marshall	POLY.UNPROV.	Austral	Chatham	Cook	Easter	Hawaii	Marquesas	New Zealand	Niue	Pitcairn	Samoa	Society	Tokelau	Tonga	Tuamotu	Tuvalu	Tahiti
cord		1																																						
raw mater																															2									
-sling,st																																								
-arrow																																								
-bow	1																																							
-shield																																								
-dagger				1																																				
-spearthro																																								
-spear		2																			1																			
-club	1*							2									1				1*										3									
WEAPON																																								
-float,si																																								
-net																																								
-spear																																								
-fishhook																															1									
FISHING																																								
hunting																																								
-model																																		1						
-ornament																																								
-paddle	2*																2														1									
NAVIGATIO																																								
-barkclot																																								
-weaving																																								
-needle,aw																																								
-chisel																																								
-rasp																																								
-grinding																																								
-pounding																																								
-adze		1		1	1			1					3	1																	1									
TOOL		1																																						
fire,ligh																																								
smokng pi																																								
pottery																																								
utensil																										1														
lime spat.																																								
dish,vesse								1																																
lime cont.																																								

Name	Russell-Cotes Art Gallery and Museum
Address	East Cliff Bournemouth BH1 3AA
Telephone	0202-21009
Contact	Curator

BOURNEMOUTH

Sources & Dates of Information

R. Hutchings 1969

Visits PG + ALK 1976, DRS 1978; GSP 197-

MEG 1978

Letters 1976, 1979

Notes

*Australia-- other: boomerangs 5
*New Guinea-- head ornament: headdress
*Austral-- and/or Cook
*New Zealand-- cloaks: 1 1920
clubs: taiaha 4, tewhatewha 2, patu 7
other: 5 kauri gum trade objects
*Samoa-- toilet apparatus: tattooing

Dates of Collection/Acquisition	Donors/Collectors/Former Owners
Acquired mainly 1921-22 (see also comment below)	

Documentation

Iconographic (5 oil paintings of Maoris by C.F. Goldie).
Museum publications: Bournemouth Museums Bulletin, c. 130 issues, 25p each (some out of print)

Reference: Barrow, 1959, Anthropology in the South Seas, esp. Maori figure.

Comment

Very interesting "late" collection acquired by Russell-Cotes, some in Pacific c. 1900. New Zealand carving is thus late. Two Beasley items (New Guinea) listed in his manuscript catalogue.

Russell-Cotes Art Gallery and Museum

BOURNEMOUTH

Provenance ↓ / Artefact →	TOTAL	OTHER	barkcloth	CLOTHING	-skirt	-belt	-cloak	PERS. ORN.	-head	-ear,nose	-arm	-neck,breast	comb	fan	toilet app.	staff,stick	CERE. OBJ.	-mask	-board	-adze	-paddle	-bullroarer	carving	fig.,image	magic,med.	charm	MUSICAL INS	-drum,gong	-flute,pipe	-rattle	currency	transport	headrest	mat	basket	bag	box
OCEANIA UN.	9											5																									
AUSTRALIA	11+	5																																			
MELA.UNPROV.																																					
Admiralty	1																																				
Banks																																					
Bismarck																																					
D'Entrecast.																																					
Fiji	6																																				
Louisiade																																					
Loyalty																																					
N. Britain																																					
N. Caledonia	1																																				
N. Guinea	26							5																													
N. Hebrides	2																																				
N. Ireland																																					
Santa Cruz																																					
Solomon	10																																				
Trobriand																																					
MICRO.UNPROV.																																					
Caroline																																					
Gilbert																																					
Mariana																																					
Marshall																																					
POLY.UNPROV.	1																																				
Austral	8*																																				
Chatham																																					
Cook																																					
Easter																																					
Hawaii	2											1																									
Marquesas	1																																				
New Zealand	54	5			1		3*	6				2											3					1									2
Niue																																					
Pitcairn																																					
Samoa	2														1*																						
Society																																					
Tokelau																																					
Tonga																																					
Tuamotu																																					
Tuvalu																																					

Russell-Cotes Art Gallery and Museum BOURNEMOUTH

Artefact → / Provenance ↓	OCEANIA UN.	AUSTRALIA	MELA.UNPROV.	Admiralty	Banks	Bismarck	D'Entrecast.	Fiji	Louisiade	Loyalty	N. Britain	N. Caledonia	N. Guinea	N. Hebrides	N. Ireland	Santa Cruz	Solomon	Trobriand	MICRO.UNPROV	Caroline	Gilbert	Mariana	Marshall	POLY.UNPROV.	Austral	Chatham	Cook	Easter	Hawaii	Marquesas	New Zealand	Niue	Pitcairn	Samoa	Society	Tokelau	Tonga	Tuamotu	Tuvalu
cord																																							
raw mater																																							
-sling,sto																																							
-arrow																																							
-bow														1																									
-shield																																							
-dagger																																							
-spearthro		3																																					
-spear		X		1													2								5														
-club	2							5					2	1			4													1	13			1			3		
WEAPON												1																											
-float,si																																							
-net																																							
-spear																																							
-fishhook	1																																						
FISHING																																							
hunting																															5								
-model	1																														2								
-ornament																																							
-paddle																	2								2						5								
NAVIGATIO																																							
-barkclot																																							
-weaving																																							
-needle,a																																							
-chisel																															2								
-rasp																																							
-grinding																																							
-pounding																													1										
-adze													2											1	1						2								
TOOL		1																													1								
fire,ligh		1																																					
smokng pi																																							
pottery																																							
utensil																																							
lime spat																																							
dish,vess																															1								
lime cont																																							

Name	Tong Hall	BRADFORD
Address	Tong Village Bradford BD4 ORR	Sources & Dates of Information R. Hutchings 1966 Visit SP 1975
Telephone	0532-852356	MEG 1978
Contact	Museums Officer, Cartwright Hall Art Gallery and Museum, Lister Park, Bradford BD9 4NS (tel. 0274-493313)	Letter Schools Loan Service List

Notes

Total Oceanic collection: about 200; also, some unidentified material. Listings overleaf incomplete.

Disposals: Most ethnographic collections transferred to Leeds City Museum.

*Gilbert-- these items apply to "Gilbert and Ellice"- not distinguished.
*Tuvalu-- see Gilbert.

Dates of Collection/Acquisition	Donors/Collectors/Former Owners
Mainly acquired 1945-60.	

Documentation

Comment

Limited opening hours (summer weekends): Museums Officer must be contacted.

Tong Hall

BRADFORD

Provenance	TOTAL	OTHER	barkcloth	CLOTHING	-skirt	-belt	-cloak	PERS. ORN.	-head	-ear,nose	-arm	-neck,breast	comb	fan	toilet app.	staff,stick	CERE. OBJ.	-mask	-board	-adze	-paddle	-bullroarer	carving	fig.,image	magic,med.	charm	MUSICAL INS.	-drum,gong	-flute,pipe	-rattle	currency	transport	headrest	mat	basket	bag	box
OCEANIA UN.	3					1					1																										
AUSTRALIA	X																																				
MELA.UNPROV.	-																																				
Admiralty																																					
Banks																																					
Bismarck																																					
D'Entrecast.																																					
Fiji	24	4									1			2																				5	1		
Louisiade																																					
Loyalty																																					
N. Britain																																					
N. Caledonia																																					
N. Guinea	X																																				
N. Hebrides																																					
N. Ireland																																					
Santa Cruz																																					
Solomon	5																1																				
Trobriand																																					
MICRO.UNPROV																																					
Caroline																																					
Gilbert *	7				1																														1		
Mariana																																					
Marshall																																					
POLY.UNPROV.																																					
Austral																																					
Chatham																																					
Cook																																					
Easter																																					
Hawaii																																					
Marquesas																																					
New Zealand																																					
Niue																																					
Pitcairn																																					
Samoa																																					
Society																																					
Tokelau																																					
Tonga	X		X																																		
Tuamotu																																					
Tuvalu	*																																				

Tong Hall

BRADFORD

Artefact → / Provenance ↓	OCEANIA UN.	AUSTRALIA	MELA.UNPROV.	Admiralty	Banks	Bismarck	D'Entrecast.	Fiji	Louisiade	Loyalty	N. Britain	N. Caledonia	N. Guinea	N. Hebrides	N. Ireland	Santa Cruz	Solomon	Trobriand	MICRO.UNPROV	Caroline	Gilbert	Mariana	Marshall	POLY.UNPROV.	Austral	Chatham	Cook	Easter	Hawaii	Marquesas	New Zealand	Niue	Pitcairn	Samoa	Society	Tokelau	Tonga	Tuamotu	Tuvalu
cord																																							
raw mater																																							
-sling,st																																							
-arrow																																							
-bow								1																															
-shield																																							
-dagger																																							
-spearthr																																							
-spear																					2																		
-club	1							2									3																						
WEAPON																																							
-float,si																																							
-net																																							
-spear																																							
-fishhook																																							
FISHING																																							
hunting																																							
-model																																							
-ornament								2									1																						
-paddle																																							
NAVIGATIO																																							
-barkclot																																							
-weaving																																							
-needle,a																																							
-chisel																																							
-rasp																																							
-grinding																																							
-pounding																																							
-adze																																							
TOOL																																							
fire,ligh																																							
smoking pi																																							
pottery																																							
utensil																																							
lime spat																																							
dish,vesse								6													3																		
lime cont.																																							

BRIGHTON

Name Royal Pavilion, Art Gallery and Museums

Address Church Street
Brighton BN1 1UE

Telephone 0273-603005

Contact Keeper of Ethnography

Sources & Dates of Information

R. Hutchings 1966

Visits PG 1976, DRS 1978

MEG 1978

Letters 1978-9

Notes

Total about 1660 items.

*Fiji-- toilet apparatus: tattooing
*New Zealand-- other: kauri gum heads 2, stone implements.

Dates of Collection/Acquisition	Donors/Collectors/Former Owners
Main period of acquisition: 1870-1940	

Documentation

Photographic, archival, iconographic.

Museum publications: Handbook and Brief Guide; Treasures from the Commonwealth Exhibition 1965.

Comment

Re-displayed in 1975. Well catalogued and stored. Important.

Royal Pavilion, Art Gallery and Museums

BRIGHTO

Artefact → / Provenance ↓	TOTAL	OTHER	barkcloth	CLOTHING	-skirt	-belt	-cloak	PERS. ORN.	-head	-ear,nose	-arm	-neck,breast	comb	fan	toilet app.	staff,stick	CERE. OBJ.	-mask	-board	-adze	-paddle	-bullroarer	carving	fig.,image	magic,med.	charm	MUSICAL INS.	-drum,gong	-flute,pipe	-rattle	currency	transport	headrest	mat	basket	bag	box
OCEANIA UN.																																					
AUSTRALIA	314																					2															
MELA.UNPROV.																																					
Admiralty	94																																				
Banks																																					
Bismarck																																					
D'Entrecast.																																					
Fiji	126		28	3		5						3	2		2*													1			13		3	1			
Louisiade																																					
Loyalty																																					
N. Britain	39					6		2			3	2					3							1						1	1						
N. Caledonia	34																																				
N. Guinea	298																																				
N. Hebrides	84				1																																
N. Ireland	43																	X																			
Santa Cruz	42																																				
Solomon	210																																				
Trobriand	8																																				
MICRO.UNPROV.																																					
Caroline																																					
Gilbert																																					
Mariana																																					
Marshall																																					
POLY.UNPROV.																																					
Austral																																					
Chatham																																					
Cook	33		4	1		3	1					1								5	10																
Easter	3																																				
Hawaii	10		1																					1													
Marquesas	12																1																				
New Zealand	186	25		8	1		6	1	1	1		6				11					1		3	2													
Niue	19													4															1						12		
Pitcairn																																					
Samoa	34		12	3	1		1					4																						1			
Society																																					
Tokelau																																					
Tonga	24		6	1								2	4																					1			
Tuamotu	4																																				
Tuvalu																																					
[illegible]	[illegible]																																			1	

Royal Pavilion, Art Gallery and Museums

BRIGHTON

Provenance ↓ / Artefact →	lime cont	dish,vess	lime spat	utensil	pottery	smokng pi	fire,ligh	TOOL	-adze	-pounding	-grinding	-rasp	-chisel	-needle,a	-weaving	-barkcloth	NAVIGATIO	-paddle	-ornament	-model	hunting	FISHING	-fishhook	-spear	-net	-float,si	WEAPON	-club	-spear	-spearthr	-dagger	-shield	-bow	-arrow	-sling,st	raw mate	cord
OCEANIA UN.																																					
AUSTRALIA																																					
MELA.UNPROV.																																					
Admiralty																																					
Banks																																					
Bismarck																																					
D'Entrecast.																																					
Fiji		4		4	4				4											1		8						3	3							3	
Louisiade																																					
Loyalty																																					
N. Britain		1																						1				8	9				1				
N. Caledonia																																					
N. Guinea																																					
N. Hebrides																																					
N. Ireland																																					
Santa Cruz																																					
Solomon																																					
Trobriand																																					
MICRO.UNPROV.																																					
Caroline																																					
Gilbert																																					
Mariana																																					
Marshall																																					
POLY.UNPROV.																																					
Austral																		6																			
Chatham																																					
Cook		3							2							1		3		1								1					1	2			1
Easter																													3								
Hawaii									5	1													2												1		
Marquesas									1				1										2					5									
New Zealand									38								1	4	2	2			7			27		22	6							3	
Niue																				2							2	2								1	
Pitcairn																																					
Samoa																													9	2							
Society																																					
Tokelau																												3									
Tonga					1																	1	1						4				1				
Tuamotu																							4														
Tuvalu																																					
Tahiti		1				1			1													2	3														

BRISTOL

Name: City Museum and Art Gallery

Address: Queen's Road
Clifton
Bristol BS8 1RL

Telephone: 0272-299771

Contact: Curator of Archaeology

Sources & Dates of Information

R. Hutchings 1966

Visits PG 1973, ALKS, DRS 1978

MEG 1978

Letters 1970-1979

Notes

Small amounts disposed of.

Dates of Collection/Acquisition	Donors/Collectors/Former Owners
Main period of acquisition: 1823-1940	Lt. Riske acquired 1840's Dr. S Stutchbury early 19th century Robertson, New Zealand Armitage, New Zealand John White, New Zealand

Documentation

Catalogue in good order.

Library, archival, photographic, iconographic.

Comment: Much work done on catalogue and display since 1973 visit (PG made brief visit May 1979)
Needs another visit to bring lists up to date and fill in details.

City Museum and Art Gallery BRISTOL

Provenance \ Artefact	TOTAL	OTHER	barkcloth	CLOTHING	-skirt	-belt	-cloak	PERS. ORN.	-head	-ear,nose	-arm	-neck,breast	comb	fan	toilet app.	staff,stick	CERE. OBJ.	-mask	-board	-adze	-paddle	-bullroarer	carving	fig.,image	magic,med.	charm	MUSICAL INS.	-drum,gong	-flute,pipe	-rattle	currency	transport	headrest	mat	basket	bag	box
OCEANIA UN.	14																																				
AUSTRALIA																																					
MELA.UNPROV.	212																																				
Admiralty																																					
Banks																																					
Bismarck																																					
D'Entrecast.																																					
Fiji																																					
Louisiade																																					
Loyalty																																					
N. Britain																																					
N. Caledonia																																					
N. Guinea	269																																				
N. Hebrides																																					
N. Ireland																																					
Santa Cruz																																					
Solomon																																					
Trobriand																																					
MICRO.UNPROV	6																																				
Caroline																																					
Gilbert																																					
Mariana																																					
Marshall																																					
POLY.UNPROV.	94																																				
Austral																							1														
Chatham																																					
Cook									1																												
Easter																																					
Hawaii																																					
Marquesas																																					
New Zealand	180	X		1	2		16	1				4	1			1	1							1											2	5	3
Niue																																					
Pitcairn																																					
Samoa																																					
Society																																					
Tokelau																																					
Tonga																																					
Tuamotu																																					
Tuvalu																																					

City Museum and Art Gallery

BRISTOL

Artefact → / Provenance →	OCEANIA UN.	AUSTRALIA	MELA.UNPROV.	Admiralty	Banks	Bismarck	D'Entrecast.	Fiji	Louisiade	Loyalty	N. Britain	N. Caledonia	N. Guinea	N. Hebrides	N. Ireland	Santa Cruz	Solomon	Trobriand	MICRO.UNPROV	Caroline	Gilbert	Mariana	Marshall	POLY.UNPROV.	Austral	Chatham	Cook	Easter	Hawaii	Marquesas	New Zealand	Niue	Pitcairn	Samoa	Society	Tokelau	Tonga	Tuamotu	Tuvalu
cord																																							
raw mate																															5								
-sling,st																																							
-arrow																																							
-bow																																							
-shield																																							
-dagger																																							
-spearthr																																							
-spear																																							
-club																															20								
WEAPON																															1								
-float,si																																							
-net																																							
-spear																																							
-fishhook																															2								
FISHING																															5								
hunting																																							
-model																															1								
-ornament																															2								
-paddle																															2								
NAVIGATIO																															2								
-barkclot																																							
-weaving																																							
-needle,aw																																							
-chisel																																							
-rasp																																							
-grinding																																							
-pounding																																							
-adze																																							
TOOL																																							
fire,light																																							
smoking pi																																							
pottery																																							
utensil																																							
lime spat.																																							
dish,vesse																																							
lime cont.																																							

BURNLEY

Name Towneley Hall Art Gallery and Museums
Burnley BB1 3RQ

Address Burnley BB1 3RQ

Telephone 0282-24213

Contact Curator

Sources & Dates of Information

R. Hutchings 1966

Visit

MEG 1978

Letter 1979

Notes

*Australia-- other: boomerang
*New Guinea-- weapon: basketwork breast plate
other: head

Dates of Collection/Acquisition	Donors/Collectors/Former Owners
Main period of acquisition: 1910-20	

Documentation

Archival, photographic.
Clear and accessible.

Comment

Towneley Hall

BURNLEY

Provenance ↓ / Artefact →	box	bag	basket	mat	headrest	transport	currency	-rattle	-flute,pipe	-drum,gong	MUSICAL INS.	charm	magic,med.	fig.,image	carving	-bullroarer	-paddle	-adze	-board	-mask	CERE. OBJ.	staff,stick	toilet app.	fan	comb	-neck,breast	-arm	-ear,nose	-head	PERS. ORN.	-cloak	-belt	-skirt	CLOTHING	barkcloth	OTHER	TOTAL
OCEANIA UN.																																					2
AUSTRALIA																																				1	1
MELA.UNPROV.																																					
Admiralty																																					
Banks																																					
Bismarck																																					
D'Entrecast.																																					
Fiji																																					
Louisiade																																					
Loyalty																																					
N. Britain																																					
N. Caledonia																																					
N. Guinea																																				1	5
N. Hebrides																																					
N. Ireland																																					
Santa Cruz																																					
Solomon																																					
Trobriand																																					
MICRO.UNPROV																																					
Caroline																																					
Gilbert																																					
Mariana																																					
Marshall																																					
POLY.UNPROV.																																					
Austral																																					
Chatham																																					
Cook																																					
Easter																																					
Hawaii																																					
Marquesas																																					
New Zealand																																					1
Niue																																					
Pitcairn																																					
Samoa																																					
Society																																					
Tokelau																																					
Tonga																																					
Tuamotu																																					
Tuvalu																																					

Towneley Hall BURNLEY

Artefact → / Provenance ↓	OCEANIA UN.	AUSTRALIA	MELA.UNPROV.	Admiralty	Banks	Bismarck	D'Entrecast.	Fiji	Louisiade	Loyalty	N. Britain	N. Caledonia	N. Guinea	N. Hebrides	N. Ireland	Santa Cruz	Solomon	Trobriand	MICRO.UNPROV.	Caroline	Gilbert	Mariana	Marshall	POLY.UNPROV.	Austral	Chatham	Cook	Easter	Hawaii	Marquesas	New Zealand	Niue	Pitcairn	Samoa	Society	Tokelau	Tonga	Tuamotu	Tuvalu
cord																																							
raw mate																																							
-sling,st																																							
-arrow																																							
-bow																																							
-shield																																							
-dagger																																							
-spearthr																																							
-spear																																							
-club																																							
WEAPON	2												1*3																										
-float,si																																							
-net																																							
-spear																																							
-fishhook																																							
FISHING																																							
hunting																																							
-model																																							
-ornament																															1								
-paddle																																							
NAVIGATIO																																							
-barkclot																																							
-weaving																																							
-needle,a																																							
-chisel																																							
-rasp																																							
-grinding																																							
-pounding																																							
-adze																																							
TOOL																																							
fire,ligh																																							
smoking pr																																							
pottery																																							
utensil																																							
lime spa																																							
dish,vess																																							
lime cont																																							

BURY

Name Bury Art Gallery and Museum

Address Moss Street
Bury

Telephone 061-764 4110

Contact Assistant Director, Leisure Services Dept., Manchester Road, Bury BL9 ODJ

Sources & Dates of Information

R. Hutchings 1966
Visit

MEG 1978
Letter

Notes

*Australia-- other: boomerangs

Dates of Collection/Acquisition

Main period of acquisition:
1907-30

Donors/Collectors/Former Owners

Documentation

Collection being catalogued.

Comment

Other items may be found.

Bury Art Gallery and Museum

BURY

Artefact → / Provenance →	OCEANIA UN.	AUSTRALIA	MELA.UNPROV.	Admiralty	Banks	Bismarck	D'Entrecast.	Fiji	Louisiade	Loyalty	N. Britain	N. Caledonia	N. Guinea	N. Hebrides	N. Ireland	Santa Cruz	Solomon	Trobriand	MICRO.UNPROV	Caroline	Gilbert	Mariana	Marshall	POLY.UNPROV.	Austral	Chatham	Cook	Easter	Hawaii	Marquesas	New Zealand	Niue	Pitcairn	Samoa	Society	Tokelau	Tonga	Tuamotu	Tuvalu
box																																							
bag																														1								
basket																																							
mat																																							
headrest																																							
transport																																							
currency																																							
-rattle																																							
-flute,pipe																																							
-drum,gong																																							
MUSICAL INS.																																							
charm																																							
magic,med.																																							
fig.,image																																							
carving																																							
-bullroarer																																							
-paddle																																							
-adze																																							
-board																																							
-mask																																							
CERE. OBJ.																																							
staff,stick																																							
toilet app.																																							
fan																																							
comb																																							
-neck,breast																																							
-arm																																							
-ear,nose																																							
-head																																							
PERS. ORN.																																							
-cloak																																							
-belt																																							
-skirt																																							
CLOTHING																																							
barkcloth																																							
OTHER		2																																					
TOTAL	8	2																													X								

Bury Art Gallery and Museum

BURY

Artefact → / Provenance	OCEANIA UN.	AUSTRALIA	MELA.UNPROV.	Admiralty	Banks	Bismarck	D'Entrecast.	Fiji	Louisiade	Loyalty	N. Britain	N. Caledonia	N. Guinea	N. Hebrides	N. Ireland	Santa Cruz	Solomon	Trobriand	MICRO.UNPROV	Caroline	Gilbert	Mariana	Marshall	POLY.UNPROV.	Austral	Chatham	Cook	Easter	Hawaii	Marquesas	New Zealand	Niue	Pitcairn	Samoa	Society	Tokelau	Tonga	Tuamotu	Tuvalu
cord																																							
raw mater																																							
-sling,st																																							
-arrow																																							
-bow																																							
-shield																																							
-dagger																																							
-spearthr																																							
-spear	1																																						
-club	6																																						
WEAPON																																							
-float,si																																							
-net																																							
-spear																																							
-fishhook																																							
FISHING																																							
hunting																																							
-model																																							
-ornament																																							
-paddle																																							
NAVIGATIO																																							
-barkclot	1																																						
-weaving																																							
-needle,a																																							
-chisel																																							
-rasp																																							
-grinding																																							
-pounding																																							
-adze																																							
TOOL																															4								
fire,ligh																																							
smoking pi																																							
pottery																																							
utensil																																							
lime spat																																							
dish,vess																																							
lime cont.																																							

Name	Moyse's Hall Museum
Address	Cornhill Bury St. Edmunds Suffolk
Telephone	0284-63233
Contact	Curator

BURY ST. EDMUNDS (M)

Sources & Dates of Information

R. Hutchings 1966

Visit

MEG 1978

Letter

Notes

Disposals ; Material from Australia, New Zealand and the Pacific disposed of between 1903 and 1955, much by sale, with no records.

Dates of Collection/Acquisition	Donors/Collectors/Former Owners

Documentation

Comment

BURY ST. EDMUNDS (REG

Name Suffolk Regiment Museum

Address The Keep
Gibralter Barracks
Bury St. Edmunds IP33 3RN

Telephone 0284-5371

Contact Curator

Sources & Dates of Information

R. Hutchings 1966

Visit

MEG 1978

Letter 1979

Notes

*New Zealand-- other: misc. 1

Dates of Collection/Acquisition

Donors/Collectors/Former Owners

Documentation

Comment

Suffolk Regiment Museum

BURY ST. EDMUNDS(?)

Provenance / Artifact	box	bag	basket	mat	headrest	transport	currency	-rattle	-flute,pipe	-drum,gong	MUSICAL INS.	charm	magic,med.	fig.,image	carving	-bullroarer	-paddle	-adze	-board	-mask	CERE. OBJ.	staff,stick	toilet app.	fan	comb	-neck,breast	-arm	-ear,nose	-head	PERS. ORN.	-cloak	-belt	-skirt	CLOTHING	barkcloth	OTHER	TOTAL
OCEANIA UN.																																					
AUSTRALIA																																					
MELA.UNPROV.																																					
Admiralty																																					
Banks																																					
Bismarck																																					
D'Entrecast.																																					
Fiji																																					1
Louisiade																																					
Loyalty																																					
N. Britain																																					
N. Caledonia																																					
N. Guinea																																					
N. Hebrides																																					
N. Ireland																																					
Santa Cruz																																					
Solomon																																					
Trobriand																																					
MICRO.UNPROV.																																					
Caroline																																					
Gilbert																																					
Mariana																																					
Marshall																																					
POLY.UNPROV.																																					
Austral																																					
Chatham																																					
Cook																																					
Easter																																					
Hawaii																																					
Marquesas																																					
New Zealand																										1											5+1
Niue																																					
Pitcairn																																					
Samoa																																					
Society																																					
Tokelau																																					
Tonga																																					
Tuamotu																																					
Tuvalu																																					

Suffolk Regiment Museum

BURY ST. EDMUNDS (RE

Artefact → / Provenance ↓	OCEANIA UN.	AUSTRALIA	MELA.UNPROV.	Admiralty	Banks	Bismarck	D'Entrecast.	Fiji	Louisiade	Loyalty	N. Britain	N. Caledonia	N. Guinea	N. Hebrides	N. Ireland	Santa Cruz	Solomon	Trobriand	MICRO.UNPROV.	Caroline	Gilbert	Mariana	Marshall	POLY.UNPROV.	Austral	Chatham	Cook	Easter	Hawaii	Marquesas	New Zealand	Niue	Pitcairn	Samoa	Society	Tokelau	Tonga	Tuamotu	Tuvalu
cord																																						
raw mater																																						
-sling,st																																						
-arrow																																						
-bow																																						
-shield																																						
-dagger																																						
-spearthr																																						
-spear																															X								
-club								/																							/								
WEAPON																																						
-float,sl																																						
-net																																						
-spear																																						
-fishhook																																						
FISHING																																						
hunting																																						
-model																																						
-ornament																																						
-paddle																															/								
NAVIGATIO																																						
-barkclot																																						
-weaving																																						
-needle,aw																																						
-chisel																																						
-rasp																																						
-grinding																																						
-pounding																																						
-adze																																						
TOOL																																						
fire,ligh																																						
smoking pi																																						
pottery																																						
utensil																																						
lime spat																																						
dish,vesse																																						
lime cont.																																						

CAMPBELTOWN

Name	Public Library and Museum
Address	Hall Street Campbeltown, Argyll PA28 6BJ
Telephone	0586-2367
Contact	Branch Librarian (Museums)

Sources & Dates of Information

R. Hutchings 1966
Visit

MEG 1978
Letter

Notes

Oceania: 2 objects

Disposals: Much was discarded in 1950's reorganisation, mostly in tourist, souvenir class.

Dates of Collection/Acquisition

Donors/Collectors/Former Owners

Documentation

Comment

No comment yet possible!

Name: Camborne Public Library and Museum	CAMBORNE
Address: Cross Street Camborne Cornwall	Sources & Dates of Information R. Hutchings 1966 Visit PG } ALK } 1973 MEG 1978 Letter
Telephone: 0209-713544	
Contact: Manager of Leisure Services	

Notes

Fiji: clubs 2

Dates of Collection/Acquisition	Donors/Collectors/Former Owners

Documentation

Comment

My favorite collection. Clubs were used by police against Camborne rioters 1830, thus early. (Collected by Cornish whalers?)

CAMBRIDGE

Name: University Museum of Archaeology & Anthropology

Address: Downing Street
Cambridge CB2 3DZ

Telephone: 0223-59714

Contact: Curator

Sources & Dates of Information

R. Hutchings 1966
Visit

MEG 1978
Letter
AC inventory, 1979

Notes

For table explanatory notes, see UMAA (D).

Dates of Collection/Acquisition	Donors/Collectors/Former Owners
Acquisition: 1884+ Some material collected in late 18th, but most in 19th and early 20th.	See UMAA (E)

Documentation

Documentation variable; Haddon Library; archival; photographic (inter alia Haddon Collection); iconographic; sound recordings (Layard - Malekula); films (copy of 3-4 min. silent film Torres Straits, 1898; Trobriands).
Geographically arranged card index being updated during reorganisation.

Museum publications: E.S. Fegan & J.D. Pickles, Bibliography of A.C. Haddon, 1978.
F.J. Hayter, Catalogue of Australian Exhibits, 1930.
Annual Reports (1885+)

Also works by: Bateson, Gathercole (1976), Haddon, Harrisson, Kaeppler (1978), Landtmann, Layard, Moore (on Torres Straits - forthcoming), Rivers, Shawcross, A. and M. Strathern, etc.

Comment

Important collection, notably Massim, N. Hebrides, N. Britain, Solomons, Santa Cruz, Torres Straits, Cook collections. UMAA in midst of large-scale physical renovation starting with storage and study facilities,and ultimately, displays. Parts of collection inaccessible from time to time; e.g. Oceanic collection will be largely unavailable until mid-1980.
Figures in tables are provisional, subject to upward revision as sorting cataloguing continue.

UMAA

CAMBRIDGE

Provenance ↓ / Artefact →	TOTAL	OTHER	-barkcloth	CLOTHING	-skirt	-belt	-cloak	PERS. ORN.	-head	-ear,nose	-arm	-neck,breast	comb	fan	toilet app.	staff,stick	CERE. OBJ.	-mask	-board	-adze	-paddle	-bullroarer	carving	fig.,image	magic,med.	charm	MUSICAL IN.	-drum,gong	-flute,pipe	-rattle	currency	transport	headrest	mat	basket	bag	box
OCEANIA UN.	110	5	6		1			13	2			2			2														1	1	1			16	4	2	1
AUSTRALIA	see attached																																				
MELA.UNPROV.	33+																														1						
Admiralty	110			5	4			11	6		5		2											1							1	1					
Banks	494+	3	2	11*		27		10	1+	35	30	5	2			1	30	1						1		4		2	5	1	5	1		1	37	26	
Bismarck	105			2	3	2		1			2		2				4	4					2						1		2				4		
D'Entrecast.	233				1	1		8	1	3	41	4	6															7							1		
Fiji	2373+	57	200	10	65	2		39	14	22	36	92	15	40	7	11	42*						1	5		1	16	7	20			4	43	98	79		14
Louisiade	141	3				1				7	3	4	4				2									1					25				16		
Loyalty	4																3									1											
N. Britain	413	17	12	12*	5	4	2	6	4		21	5	2			4	9	19	5		7	9	1	9		3	5	1	5	2	11	1			14	16	
N. Caledonia	452	3	6	2	4	4	2	5	2		15	6	5		1		5	5		4			2	1	39	3	4		4		7			2	6	11	4
N. Guinea	see attached																																				
N. Hebrides	1539+		11	40+	24	80+		21	34	44	111	12	42		5*	7	81	26		4		5	8	21	35	16	12	4	14	8+	10+			24	26	8	
N. Ireland	60							1										1					2	2				1			14						
Santa Cruz	869+		10	30	7	24		29	3	52+	58+	36+	1	3	2*	4	16						4	8	3	5	12		3	3	11		6	21	18+	75	2
Solomon	see attached																																				
Trobriand	84	1			1							1	5			2	2		3	1			4	3				4									
MICRO.UNPROV	5				1	1						1																									
Caroline	70					5		3	1		3	14	7		1						3										5						1
Gilbert	105	2		1	1	2		1				8					1						2								5						
Mariana	1																																	1			
Marshall	19			3		1						1		2																	4			2			
POLY.UNPROV.	13		2					1																										2			
Austral	23															3	4				10		1					2									
Chatham	94	1						2															1														
Cook	79		1	1					2			4		3		2	1			22				5													
Easter	30							1				1					1				4		1	6													
Hawaii	99	6	2				5	2	1		4	13			2*									2		2		1		1		1				2	
Marquesas	90+		2		5			2	3	7		6		1		3	6						4*	2		1	2										
New Zealand	676+	12	1	2	3	6	26	51		22		29	6		3	8	14						5	15+		1	6		7			1		10	1	2	17
Niue	22												1																						1		
Pitcairn	21	14	2																																		
Samoa	227+	4	32+	1				1	3			5	12	33+	1	2					4		1											2	13	2	
Society	38	3	1						1																		1	2					1				
Tokelau	1																																				1
Tonga	194+	3	6+		5	1			2	3		10	19	1		2	4				1												4		12		1
Tuamotu	1								1																												
Tuvalu	122			5		2			6		1	8		2	4										1			1			1	3	1	8	4		1
Tahiti	142	4	4					1	2*	4		2			8		1							1			1	1	4				4			1	

UMAA

CAMBRIDGE

Artefact → / Provenance ↓	lime cont.	dish, vesse	lime spat	utensil	pottery	smokng pi	fire, ligh	TOOL	-adze	-pounding	-grinding	-rasp	-chisel	-needle, a	-weaving	-barkclot	NAVIGATIO	-paddle	-ornament	-model	hunting	FISHING	-fishhook	-spear	-net	-float, si	WEAPON	-club	-spear	-spearthr	-dagger	-shield	-bow	-arrow	-sling, st	raw mater	cord
OCEANIA UN.	1	4						2				2	1	1			3	2		1			25					1								9	1
AUSTRALIA																																					
MELA. UNPROV.								2	1														2				2		1				7	17+			
Admiralty	2	22		4				3	2									1										1	38		1						
Banks		18		97			3		8	1		3						1			6	1			4			19	1				5	77+		9	
Bismarck	2	2	2	2*	1			1	3	2					3*							2				1	1	7	44					1	2		
D'Entrecast.	7	7	32	12	9			4	8	1	1			1			1	1	2	1		7	13	1	3	3		27	14				1			2	1
Fiji		321		38	190		5	93	75+	3				33		32	3	2		5	3	4	8	2	4			40 2*	100				7	4	2	64+	23
Louisiade		5	1	8		2		8	16	12							3	5							2		3	4	2						2	3	
Loyalty																																					
N. Britain	4	10		5	1*	3	1	9	17	4				1		9		3			8	1			4		9	30	27		2	4		8	12	12	3
N. Caledonia		10			7		1	12	30					3	3	11						5			2		1	60	64	5			1	3	74	7	1
N. Guinea																																					
N. Hebrides		11		27	33		5+	9	97+	2				1			2	3+	2	4	6	3	1	6	5		3	127+	34+				32	349+	3	35	6
N. Ireland									2									2										13	22								
Santa Cruz	15+	27	2	24+		1	1	17	8	10		5	1	3	20*	1	7	9+	1	10	7	9	11	5	5	12		6+	1				16+	15+	1	27+	8
Solomon																																					
Trobriand	3	14	8					3	1	2								2	1			2			5			10				2					
MICRO. UNPROV								1																			1										
Caroline		2		3				1	11	2					2								4			1									1		
Gilbert								2	5											2			9				27*	1	13		13					6	4
Mariana																																					
Marshall										1													5														
POLY. UNPROV.		2							2														1					1	2								
Austral										1																			2								
Chatham								14	57				4	2									5					4						2		2	
Cook									6								1	16					2	7			1	3	1		1						
Easter								2	1																			3	10								
Hawaii		11		1				2	9	2	3					4	1					1	11						1		5				1	2	
Marquesas		4		4				1	8	2						6+	2	7		1		2	3					5								1	
New Zealand		3		2*			1	33	167	8	3		9	3			9	10	10	3	4	1	51			7	2	80+	7							15	
Niue									1							1								2				7	6						3		
Pitcairn								3	2																												
Samoa		1							25													1	26					55	1							2	
Society									5	3		1				2							17						1								
Tokelau																																					
Tonga							1		4	1		1				2		3		2			14					88					3				1
Tuamotu																																					
Tuvalu		4		7			1	3	6	1		1	1	3			2			2	2	5	20		2											10	4
Tahiti		1		4			1		7	7		1	2			4	1			1		6	14				1		4				2	15		1	24

CONT. NEXT PAGE

UMAA (B)

CAMBRIDGE

Provenance (Artefact →)	TOTAL	OTHER	barkcloth	CLOTHING	-skirt	-belt	-cloak	PERS. ORN.	-head	-ear,nose	-arm	-neck,breast	comb	fan	toilet app.	staff,stick	CERE. OBJ.
Futuna (E)	2		2														
Mangareva	2																
Anuta	29	1				2				4		5					
Bellona	145							1		6					2	3	
Fila	2																1
Mae	2					2											
Hele	6																
Ontong Java	4																
Rennell	99		1	2				1	1	4		3	2	3		9	1
Rotuma	29	3						4			1	1					2
Sikiana	25					3						2					
Tikopia	71	7	2			2		1		1	9	7		6	2		1
Ninigo	61			1				1			2	2				4	
Woodlark	18	1														3	
Marshall Bennett	21					1											
Torres Strait*	1356+	86		3	15	23		173+	62	44	75	82	6			2	57
New Guinea un.	512+					8		8	12	6	15	39	15	1		1	2
West Irian	503+	6		8	3	10+	2	32	5	5	22	16	10			1	2
MT unprov.	527	11	6	16		19		15	16	3	39	45	5			14	1
Highlands	677+		1	8	8	22	3	58	61	15	21	36			1	2	16
Sepik	801+	54	2	5	18	8	6	18	17	2	7	7	2			1	29
Ramu	53			2		4		1	2		2	11	3				
other Madang	6		2										1				
Huon + Tami	72			2			1		1		6						
other Morobe	23				3			2	2			5					
Papua unprov.	286			6	2	5		10	9	1	3	27				1	
Fly	1081+	2		26	12	41		63+	82	34	39	30	24		3*	4	22
Gulf	469		2	3	1	27		32	9	4	4	1	10		1		18
Massim *	1661+	27+	9	13	12	21		69	40	75	57	64	21		11+	7	9
other Papuan	216	1	13			6		3	3	1	3	10	2	2			2

Provenance (Artefact →)	-mask	-board	-adze	-paddle	-bullroarer	carving	fig.,image	magic,med.	charm	MUSICAL INS.	-drum,gong	-flute,pipe	-rattle	currency	transport	headrest	mat	basket	bag	box
Futuna (E)																				
Mangareva																				
Anuta				1												4	1			
Bellona										2				2		3	1		2	
Fila																				
Mae																				
Hele																				
Ontong Java																				1
Rennell				1						2						4	8	1	4	
Rotuma									1											
Sikiana							1													
Tikopia										1						1		5	2	
Ninigo														1						
Woodlark							1													
Marshall Bennett																				
Torres Strait*	18	3			20	1	19	33	74	25	11	23+	25		4		29	32	2	
New Guinea un.	1	1				3	3		4	2	6					1	1	7		1
West Irian	1	6				3	12	2		1	5	1		1		2		2	8	
MT unprov.	11					1	15	1		4	4		2			2	3	12	27	
Highlands			3				3	81	1	2	2	10	9	11	2		1		17	
Sepik	20	12			1	36	23	1	36	13	16	3		21	1	18*	1	18	31	1
Ramu											1	1				1			3	
other Madang																			1	
Huon + Tami	2				1						2				6	2			1	
other Morobe						1														
Papua unprov.					1		1		3		4					4	1	5	4	
Fly	12	20			13		16		4	16	29	9	2		15	12	1	20	1	1
Gulf	22	26			22	4	14	1	7	2	9				2	3		6	2	
Massim *	1	3	2			4		4	16	6	16	9	2	7	3+	5	7	6	21	
other Papuan					1		2	4	1		4	3			1	3		6	6	

UMAA (B)

CAMBRIDGE

Provenance ↓ / Artefact →	lime cont.	dish,vesse	lime spat.	utensil	pottery	smokng pi	fire,ligh	TOOL	-adze	-pounding	-grinding	-rasp	-chisel	-needle,a	-weaving	-barkclót	NAVIGATIO	-paddle	-ornament	-model	hunting	FISHING	-fishhook	-spear	-net	-float,si	WEAPON	-club	-spear	-spearthr	-dagger	-shield	-bow	-arrow	-sling,st	raw mate	cord
Futuna (E)																																					
Mangareva																		2																			
Anuta		2														1									4			2	1								1
Bellona	3	3	3	1				1						2								4	1	1	2		1	14	15				6	63			3
Fila																	1																				
Mac																																					
Mele									2																			1						3			
Ontong Java									3																												
Rennell	2		10	2					1													4	2		2			15	4				2	6			2
Rotuma									12	2			1			1												1									
Sikiana															1*					1			17														
Tikopia	1	3		4					1	1						1	1					4	3		3			1									1
Ninigo		6						6	2									5		2		4	10	2					11				1			1	
Woodlark			2						5				5									1															
Marshall Bennett			6					1	3	6									3				1														
Torres Strait		37		24	1	9	2	86	4	3	2	2		7			1		10		10	6	6+	12		1	1	30	5				9	12		108	21
New Guinea un.	3	14	47	12	3	16		16	34	9						3		11	4		4	6		2	10	4	1	29	49	4	5+	13	11	65+			
West Irian	6	19	1	17		3	5	13+	18	10				1	1*		1*	6	7	1	4			11	4			23	11		3	5	18	146+		2	1
MT unprov.	6	5	2	13	5			20	10	4				13		3	1	3				1			15		2	9	40	1	22	5	5	56		12	2
Highlands		20		31		6	2	39+	85		3			8		2						2			2		7		13		1	4	6	25+		16	11
Sepik	57	24	18	8	40*	6	13	19	8					20				6	16		1	2		7	2		4	6	38	29	13	17	2	7+		16	
Ramu					4	1			2									1									1		1			3	1	8			
other Madang					1																											1					
Huon + Tami		9		3				2	4		1							1			11							2				1	1	11		2	
other Morobe						3																						2					1	4			
Papua unprov.		11	5	8	5	14		7	21	2						1			1		3							6					2+	110		3	
Fly	5	25	4	34		60	2	17	53	4		3						10	3		7	5		1	4	1	14	18	2		3	2	10	198		31	12
Gulf	1	3	2	20		23	3	9	2	5						1	3	5		1		2			5		1	19	1		4	6	9	107		5	
Massim	94	46	190	58	33	116	2	74	118	15+	13	7	2	5+	1	10	6	25	18	1	16	17	1	3	13	8	2	84	59		2	19	5+	5+	1	48	2
other Papuan	5	19	9	26		31		3	9	5						2											3	7	3			6			13		

Provenance ↓ / Artefact →	TOTAL	OTHER	barkcloth	CLOTHING	-skirt	-belt	-cloak	PERS. ORN.	-head	-ear,nose	-arm	-neck,breast	comb	fan	toilet app.	staff,stick	CERE. OBJ.	-mask	-board	-adze	-paddle	-bullroarer	carving	fig.,image	magic,med.	charm	MUSICAL INS.	-drum,gong	-flute,pipe	-rattle	currency	transport	headrest	mat	basket	bag	box
Australia un.	237	64				2		1	4		7	27			1*	3*	4					11			15										1	2	
Central	338	72		3		2		4	16	3	4	6			3*		8					69			27	2	1		1							3	
N. Territories	137	1		2		2		1	1	2	7	1					2																			1	
Arnhemland*	42	2		2		1											1					1		2	1												
Queensland	130	19		4					1			4					10					5														3	
Cape York*	46					1		4	1	1		4					7					2			4												
New S. Wales	96	36								2		1					7					2															
Victoria	52	3																																			
Western	127	24		1		1		5	3	3	7	8			1*	17*						9			2							1*					
Northwestern*	45	3								1		2										19															
South Australia	30											2				2*						2			3										2		
Tasmania	4											1							1																	2	
Solomons un.	1301	7	6	14	8	12		39	5	67+	89+	80	57	2	2*	5	17		1	2	3		6	6	3	2	1		4	2	8			3	11	16	
Buka + Bougainville	160	3							2	1	1	1	5				1				1										2				1	1	
Central	966	7	29	1	5	6		30	15	56+	65+	30	25	2	5*	5	24+			1			9	4		18	10		9	1	20+			2	7	7	2

UMAA (C)

CAMBRIDGE

Artefact → / Provenance ↓	Australia ua.	Central	N. Territories	Arnhemland	Queensland	Cape York	New S. Wales	Victoria	Western	Northwestern	South Australia	Tasmania	Solomons ua.	Buka + Bougain.	Central
cord	5	1		2			1		1				1	1	
raw mater	6	7		1	1.	2	1		10		3		6+		24
-sling,st															
-arrow													33+	32	31+
-bow													19	4	11
-shield	2	12	1	1	6		10	14	7	3	1		8		14
-dagger		1													
-spearthr	5	6	2	2	19	6	2	6	2	12	3				
-spear	44	26	102	18	32	7	1		6	3	8		129	78	33
-club	18	4	7	3	13		20	25	4		1		46+	2	42
WEAPON		2								1			1		14
-float,st													5		3
-net		1			1				1						3
-spear	1					4	2						3		2
-fishhook	1+												71	10	157
FISHING													7	2	8
hunting									1		1		3		
-model				1									2		3
-ornament													13		11
-paddle													32	7	19
NAVIGATIO													2*		
-barkclo													1		2
-weaving	2			2											
-needle,a		1											2		
-chisel		6	1						3				9		18
-rasp															2
-grinding					1		8		1		1				2
-pounding	1												5	1	18+
-adze	3	3			4		3		3		1		39	2	79
TOOL	6	23	2	1	1	1		4	4*	1			4		16
fire,lig		6	1		2										2
smoking pi			1										1		1
pottery															1
utensil		3				2			1				5		30
lime spa															3
dish,vess	1	12		1	4				1				42		30
lime cont													37	2	14

CAMBRIDGE

UMAA CAMBRIDGE (D)

Table Explanatory Notes

Torres Strait includes Mawata, on Papuan coast.
Northwestern Australia covers the area north of the Fitzroy, Mary & Elvira Rivers.
Arnhemland covers the area north of the Roper River and east of the Mary River.
Cape York covers the area north of the Gulf Highway and west of Cairns.
Massim indicates mainland Massim only, including the coastal peoples from Kukipi to Cape Nelson.
For Hermit, see Admiralty.
For Wuvulu, see Ninigo.
For Aua, see Ninigo.

Banks--	clothing:	includes ceremonial costumes 3
Bismarck--	utensil:	1 spoon traded from Tami Is.
	weaving:	3 looms, 2 from Emirau
Fiji--	ceremonial objects:	include 36 tambua
	clubs:	pineapple 51, throwing 76, horned 60, paddle 31, root 56, gunstock 1, sword 2, asparagus 7, rounded 2, mushroom 1, pole (cylindrical) 76, lotus 13, indeterminate 26
	other:	sunshades 17, flywhisks 10, toys 8, hooks 12, "ash trays" 5, house models 4, door screen 1, plus iconographic (Gordon-Cumming) and archival material
Louisiade--	other:	misc. 3
New Britain--	clothing:	includes 6 costume peices
	pottery:	pot traded from Huon Gulf
	other:	cloth 7, toys 2, physical anthropology 2, misc. 6
New Caledonia--	other:	misc. 3
New Hebrides--	toilet apparatus:	deformation 4, surgical 1
	other:	modelled heads 11, modelled animals 4, house finials 4, toys 51, stone yoke, physical anthropology 1, misc. 6
	Note:	effigies, composition & tree fern figures under figures
Santa Cruz--	toilet apparatus:	shaving 1, backscratcher 1
	weaving:	looms 14
	other:	toys 7, bamboo tubes 7, physical anthropology 1, misc. 7
Trobriand--	other:	misc. 1
Gilbert--	weapons:	include 9 armour (1 complete)
	other:	misc. 2
Chatham--	other:	misc. 1
Hawaii--	toilet apparatus:	includes 1 mirror
	other:	toys 5, misc. 1
Marquesas--	carvings:	stilt 3
	other:	misc. 1
New Zealand--	utensil:	feeding funnel 1
	clubs:	tewhatewha 15, taiaha/hani 18, patu onewa 15, patu pounamu 3, patu kotiate 5, patu paraoa 8, wood patu 1, wahaika 8, patuki 3, pouwhenua 2, unspecified 2
	other:	preserved heads 8, toy, archaeological material, misc. 2

CAMBRID

UMAA Cambridge (D) ii

Pitcairn-- other: archaeological 14

Samoa-- other: flywhisks 3, misc. 1

Society-- other: flywhisk 1, portrait of Omai, misc. 1

Tonga-- other other: flywhisks 2, misc. 1

Tuvalu-- toilet apparatus: includes surgical 1
other: eyeshades 2, toys 3, flywhisk (Samoan) 1, misc. 1

Tahiti-- head ornament: includes 1 mourning headdress

Anuta-- other: toy

Rotuma-- other: European 3

Sikiana-- weaving: loom

Tikopia-- other: toys 2, physical anthropology 1, misc. 4

Woodlark-- other: misc. 1

Torres Strait-- other: toys 74, misc. 11, physical anthropology 1

West Irian-- weaving: loom
navigation: canoe 14.8 m.
other: physical anthropology 5, "model" 1

MT-- other: flywhisk, hook, house model, toy, misc. 7

Highlands-- other decorated bamboo 1, toy

Sepik-- headrests: include 7 stools
pottery: includes 1 modelled head, 4 house ornaments
other: hooks 36, flywhisks 7, toys 7, physical anthropology 2, sleeping bags 2

Papua unprovenanced-- toilet apparatus: razor 1 surgical 1, tattooing 1

Fly-- other: physical anthropology 1, hook

Massim-- other: toys 21+, scarecrows 3, hooks 3

other Papuan-- other: hook

Australia-- Note: A number of stone implements from Australia & Tasmania, not included in these totals.
toilet apparatus: surgical 1
sticks: message 3
other: boomerangs 57, misc. 7

Central-- toilet apparatus: deformation 1, surgical 2
other: toys 32, boomerangs 40

N. Territories-- other: boomerang 1

Arnhemland-- other: 1 Groote Eylandt painting, 1 boomerang. All items except for painting & cord made for sale.

Queensland-- other: boomerangs 13, toys 6

New South Wales-- other: toy, boomerangs 35

Victoria-- other: boomerangs 3

Western-- toilet apparatus: surgical
sticks: message 13
transport: camel halter 1
tool: digging stick/weapon
other: boomerangs 24

CAMBRIDGE

UMAA Cambridge (D) iii

Northwestern--	other: boomerangs 3
Solomon unprovenanced--	toilet apparatus: depilatory 1, tattoing 1 navigation: includes 1 canoe (15 ft.) other: eyeshade, toys 3, misc. 3
Buka & Bougainville--	other: umbrella, eyeshades 2
Central--	toilet apparatus: surgical 5 other: toy, flywhisk, misc. 5

CAMBRIDG.

UMAA CAMBRIDGE (E)

Donors/Collectors/Former Owners

W.E. Armstrong	Louisiade Archipelago	1922
G. Bateson	Bismarck Archipelago, Sepik River	1930+
I.M. Beasley	New Guinea, Melanesia, Caroline Is., Samoa	1954
G. Brady	Polynesia, Melanesia	1891
J.B. Buchanan	Challenger Expedition; West Irian, Samoa	1875
E. Cheesman	New Hebrides, West Irian	1916+
E.W.P. Chinnery	New Guinea, New Britain	1930+
L.C.G. Clarke	Polynesia	1932
Capt. Cook	Cook Is., New Zealand	
W.A. Cooke-Daniels	Papua, island Massim	1898+
T. Crocker	Solomon Is., Santa Cruz, Melanesia	1934
Rev. F.H. Drew	New Hebrides, Solomon Is., Santa Cruz	1909+
W.L.H. Duckworth	Melanesia	1900+
R.E. Froude	Ruddock Collection; Melanesia	1890
J.S. Gardiner	Tuvalu, Polynesia	1897
A.C. Haddon	Papua, Torres Strait	1898
T. Harrisson	New Hebrides	1937
A.M. Hocart	Polynesia, Fiji	1914
G. Horne	Australia	1920's
C.B. Humphreys	Sepik River, New Hebrides	1921+
A. von Hügel	Fiji	1875
A.S. Kenyon	Australia	1915
G. Landtman	Papua	1912
J.W. Layard	New Hebrides	1914
W. MacGregor	New Guinea	1896
R.H. Marten	Australia	1904
A.P. Maudslay	Fiji	1877
E.G. McAfee	New Hebrides	1919
Lord Moyne	Papua New Guinea, West Irian, Bismarck Archipelago	1936
Rev. W. O'Ferrall	New Hebrides, Solomon Is., Santa Cruz	1920
Portsmouth Dockyard Museum	Polynesia, Melanesia	1947
A. Radcliffe-Brown	Australia, New Britain, Louisiade Archipelago	1914
W. Rivers	Solomon Is., Melanesia, Polynesia	1910
G.F. Rogers	New Guinea	1915
G.K. Roth	Fiji	1930's
Admiral A.C. Scott	Polynesia, Santa Cruz	1938
P. Scratchley	New Guinea	1889

CAMBRIDGE

UMAA Cambridge (E) ii

C.G. Seligmann	Papua	1898
Bishop Selwyn	New Hebrides, Solomon Is., Santa Cruz	1901+
Sheffield Museum	Bennet & Williams Collections; Polynesia	1890
Lord Stanmore	Fiji, Melanesia, Polynesia	1880+
Sir Everard im Thurn	Polynesia, Melanesia	1912
A.F.R. Wollaston	West Irian	1912
Admiral Gordon	Polynesia	1922

Photographs in the Haddon Photo Archive from:

Australia
Admiralty Is.
Banks Is.
Fiji
New Britain
New Caledonia
New Guinea
New Ireland
Santa Cruz
Solomon Is.
Trobriand Is.
Caroline Is.
Gilbert Is.
Marshall Is.
Cook Is.
Easter Is.
Hawaii
Marquesas Is.
New Zealand
Pitcairn Is.
Samoa
Society Is.
Tonga
Tuamotu Is.
Tuvalu
Anuta
Bellona
Rennell
Rotuma
Sikiana
Tikopia
Tasmania
Torres Strait Is.

CANTERBURY (CITY)

Name: Canterbury City Museums

Address: High Street
Canterbury CT1 2JF

Telephone: 0227-52747

Contact: Curator

Sources & Dates of Information

R. Hutchings 1966

Visits: PG 1976, GSP 197-

MEG 1978

Letter 1979

Notes

Disposals: Some loaned to Birchington. A Polynesian tapa manuscript book given to Cambridge.
Not accessible.

*Oceania-- other: stone implements

Dates of Collection/Acquisition	Donors/Collectors/Former Owners
1825 Crow Collection acquired by Literary & Philosophical Society	Canterbury Literary and Philosophical Society, collected 1825-46, when taken over by City Museum, which collected until c. 1940

Documentation

Comment

Not yet possible to distinguish early from late material.

City Museums CANTERBURY (CITY

Provenance ↓ / Artefact →	box	bag	basket	mat	headrest	transport	currency	-rattle	-flute,pipe	-drum,gong	MUSICAL INS.	charm	magic,med.	fig.,image	carving	-bullroarer	-paddle	-adze	-board	-mask	CERE. OBJ.	staff,stick	toilet app.	fan	comb	-neck,breast	-arm	-ear,nose	-head	PERS. ORN.	-cloak	-belt	-skirt	CLOTHING	barkcloth	OTHER	TOTAL
OCEANIA UN.																																				x	X
AUSTRALIA																																					
MELA.UNPROV.																																					
Admiralty																																					
Banks																																					
Bismarck																																					
D'Entrecast.																																					
Fiji																																					
Louisiade																																					
Loyalty																																					
N. Britain																																					
N. Caledonia																																					
N. Guinea																																					
N. Hebrides																																					
N. Ireland																																					
Santa Cruz																																					
Solomon																	1																				X
Trobriand																																					
MICRO.UNPROV.																																					X
Caroline																																					
Gilbert																																					
Mariana																																					
Marshall																																					
POLY.UNPROV.																																					
Austral																																					7
Chatham																																					
Cook																																					
Easter																																					
Hawaii																																			x		X
Marquesas																																					
New Zealand																										1										X	25
Niue																																					
Pitcairn																																					
Samoa																																					
Society																																			x		
Tokelau																																					
Tonga					1																														x		1
Tuamotu																																					
Tuvalu																																					

City Museums

CANTERBURY (CITY)

Artefact → / Provenance ↓	lime cont	dish,vess	lime spat	utensil	pottery	smokng pi	fire,ligh	TOOL	-adze	-pounding	-grinding	-rasp	-chisel	-needle,aw	-weaving	-barkclot	NAVIGATIO	-paddle	-ornament	-model	hunting	FISHING	-fishhook	-spear	-net	-float,si	WEAPON	-club	-spear	-spearthr	-dagger	-shield	-bow	-arrow	-sling,st	raw mater	cord
OCEANIA UN.																																					
AUSTRALIA																																					
MELA.UNPROV.																																					
Admiralty																																					
Banks																																					
Bismarck																																					
D'Entrecast.																																					
Fiji																																					
Louisiade																																					
Loyalty																																					
N. Britain																																					
N. Caledonia																																					
N. Guinea																																					
N. Hebrides																																					
N. Ireland																																					
Santa Cruz																																					
Solomon																							X														
Trobriand																																					
MICRO.UNPROV																							X														
Caroline																																					
Gilbert																																					
Mariana																																					
Marshall																																					
POLY.UNPROV.																																					
Austral																		7																			
Chatham																																					
Cook																																					
Easter																																					
Hawaii																							X														
Marquesas																																					
New Zealand									19																												
Niue																																					
Pitcairn																																					
Samoa																																					
Society																																					
Tokelau																																					
Tonga																																					
Tuamotu																																					
Tuvalu																																					

CANTERBURY (REG)

Name Queen's Regiment Museum

Address Regimental Headquarters
The Queen's Regiment
Howe Barracks
Canterbury CT1 1JY

Telephone 0227-65281

Contact Regimental Secretary

Sources & Dates of Information

R. Hutchings 1966

Visit

MEG 1978

Letter

Notes

*Australia-- other: hawkspear, gooseball (both Tiwi, Melville Island)

Dates of Collection/Acquisition

Australian items acquired 1974.
New Zealand items collected during 1863 campaign.

Donors/Collectors/Former Owners

Documentation

Comment Queen's Own Royal West Kent Regiment (antecedent to Queen's Regiment) had detatchment in NZ 1834, and was there also 1863-67 as 50th (West Kent) Regiment

Queen's Regiment Museum CANTERBURY (Re

Artefact → / Provenance →	OCEANIA UN.	AUSTRALIA	MELA.UNPROV.	Admiralty	Banks	Bismarck	D'Entrecast.	Fiji	Louisiade	Loyalty	N. Britain	N. Caledonia	N. Guinea	N. Hebrides	N. Ireland	Santa Cruz	Solomon	Trobriand	MICRO.UNPROV.	Caroline	Gilbert	Mariana	Marshall	POLY.UNPROV.	Austral	Chatham	Cook	Easter	Hawaii	Marquesas	New Zealand	Niue	Pitcairn	Samoa	Society	Tokelau	Tonga	Tuamotu	Tuvalu
box																																							
bag																																							
basket																																							
mat																																							
headrest																																							
transport																																							
currency																																							
-rattle																																							
-flute,pipe																																							
-drum,gong																																							
MUSICAL INS.																																							
charm																																							
magic,med.																																							
fig.,image																																							
carving																																							
-bullroarer																																							
-paddle																																							
-adze																																							
-board																																							
-mask																																							
CERE. OBJ.																																							
staff,stick																																							
toilet app.																																							
fan																																							
comb																																							
-neck,breast																																							
-arm																																							
-ear,nose																																							
-head																																							
PERS. ORN.																																							
-cloak																																							
-belt																																							
-skirt																																							
CLOTHING																																							
barkcloth																																							
OTHER		2																																					
TOTAL		2																													4								

Queen's Regiment Museum CANTERBURY (REG)

Artefact → / Provenance	OCEANIA UN.	AUSTRALIA	MELA.UNPROV.	Admiralty	Banks	Bismarck	D'Entrecast.	Fiji	Louisiade	Loyalty	N. Britain	N. Caledonia	N. Guinea	N. Hebrides	N. Ireland	Santa Cruz	Solomon	Trobriand	MICRO.UNPROV.	Caroline	Gilbert	Mariana	Marshall	POLY.UNPROV.	Austral	Chatham	Cook	Easter	Hawaii	Marquesas	New Zealand	Niue	Pitcairn	Samoa	Society	Tokelau	Tonga	Tuamotu	Tuvalu
cord																																							
raw mater																																							
-sling,st																																							
-arrow																																							
-bow																																							
-shield																																							
-dagger																																							
-spearthr																																							
-spear																																							
-club																															2								
WEAPON																																							
-float,si																																							
-net																																							
-spear																																							
-fishhook																															1								
FISHING																																							
hunting																																							
-model																																							
-ornament																																							
-paddle																															1								
NAVIGATIO																																							
-barkclot																																							
-weaving																																							
-needle,a																																							
-chisel																																							
-rasp																																							
-grinding																																							
-pounding																																							
-adze																																							
TOOL																																							
fire,ligh																																							
smoking pi																																							
pottery																																							
utensil																																							
lime spat																																							
dish,vess																																							
lime cont.																																							

Name	National Museum of Wales	CARDIFF
Address	Cathays Park Cardiff CF1 3NP	**Sources & Dates of Information** R. Hutchings 1966 Visit MEG 1978 Letter 1976-7
Telephone	0222-397951-9	
Contact	Assistant Keeper, Archaeology	

Notes

Disposals: Some to Horniman. Most ethnographic disposed of.

Fiji: adzes 2
Gilbert: skirt 1
Polynesia: a number of stone implements

Dates of Collection/Acquisition	Donors/Collectors/Former Owners
	Cardiff Municipal Museum (before World War I)

Documentation

Comment

CARMARTHEN

Name: Carmarthen County Museum

Address: Abergwili
Carmarthen
Dyfed
Wales

Telephone: 0267-31691

Contact: Curator

Sources & Dates of Information

R. Hutchings 1966

Visit

MEG 1978

Letters 1979

Notes

*Australia-- clubs, axes and shield made by an aborigine at Dandaloo c. 1938

Dates of Collection/Acquisition

Acquired mainly 1905-39

Donors/Collectors/Former Owners

Lt. Col. William Gwynne-Hughes donated New Zealand nephrite club brought back by his father Capt. William Garnons Hughes c. 1820.

Documentation

Photographic.

Comment

Garnons Hughes material may be important.

Carmarthen County Museum CARMARTHEN

Artefact → / Provenance	OCEANIA UN.	AUSTRALIA	MELA.UNPROV.	Admiralty	Banks	Bismarck	D'Entrecast.	Fiji	Louisiade	Loyalty	N. Britain	N. Caledonia	N. Guinea	N. Hebrides	N. Ireland	Santa Cruz	Solomon	Trobriand	MICRO.UNPROV.	Caroline	Gilbert	Mariana	Marshall	POLY.UNPROV.	Austral	Chatham	Cook	Easter	Hawaii	Marquesas	New Zealand	Niue	Pitcairn	Samoa	Society	Tokelau	Tonga	Tuamotu	Tuvalu
box																																							
bag																																							
basket																																							
mat																																							
headrest																																							
transport																																							
currency																																							
-rattle																																							
-flute,pipe																																							
-drum,gong																																							
MUSICAL IN.																																							
charm																																							
magic,med.																																							
fig.,image																																							
carving																																							
-bullroarer																																							
-paddle																																							
-adze																																							
-board																																							
-mask																																							
CERE. OBJ.																																							
staff,stick																																							
toilet app.																																							
fan																																							
comb																																							
-neck,breast																																							
-arm		/																																					
-ear,nose																																							
-head																																							
PERS. ORN.																																							
-cloak																																							
-belt																																							
-skirt																																							
CLOTHING																																							
barkcloth																																							
OTHER																																							
TOTAL		//																													/								

Carmarthen County Museum

CARMARTHEN

Artefact → / Provenance →	OCEANIA UN.	AUSTRALIA	MELA.UNPROV.	Admiralty	Banks	Bismarck	D'Entrecast.	Fiji	Louisiade	Loyalty	N. Britain	N. Caledonia	N. Guinea	N. Hebrides	N. Ireland	Santa Cruz	Solomon	Trobriand	MICRO.UNPROV.	Caroline	Gilbert	Mariana	Marshall	POLY.UNPROV.	Austral	Chatham	Cook	Easter	Hawaii	Marquesas	New Zealand	Niue	Pitcairn	Samoa	Society	Tokelau	Tonga	Tuamotu	Tuvalu
cord																																							
raw mate																																							
-sling,st																																							
-arrow																																							
-bow																																							
-shield		1																																					
-dagger																																							
-spearthr																																							
-spear		3*																																					
-club		4																													1								
WEAPON																																							
-float,si																																							
-net																																							
-spear																																							
-fishhook																																							
FISHING																																							
hunting																																							
-model																																							
-ornament																																							
-paddle																																							
NAVIGATIO																																							
-barkclot																																							
-weaving																																							
-needle,a																																							
-chisel																																							
-rasp																																							
-grinding																																							
-pounding																																							
-adze		2																																					
TOOL																																							
fire,ligh																																							
smokng pi																																							
pottery																																							
utensil																																							
lime spat																																							
dish,vess																																							
lime cont																																							

Name	Royal Engineers Museum
Address	Brompton Barracks Chatham ME4 4UG
Telephone	0634-44555
Contact	Curator

CHATHAM

Sources & Dates of Information

R. Hutchings 1966

Visit

MEG 1978

Letter

Notes

Oceania: less than 10 objects

Dates of Collection/Acquisition	Donors/Collectors/Former Owners

Documentation

Comment

No comment yet possible.

Name	Chelmsford and Essex Museum (including the Essex Regiment Museum)	CHELMSFORD	
Address	Oakland Park Moulsham Street Chelmsford CM2 9AQ	Sources & Dates of Information	
		R. Hutchings	1966
		Visit	
Telephone	0245-53066/60614	MEG	1978
Contact	Curator	Letter	

Notes

Disposals : In 1963 transferred 31 objects to Liverpool. In the correspondence were references to other material to be disposed of, including Oceanic. Some to Saffron Walden, 1961-3.

Dates of Collection/Acquisition	Donors/Collectors/Former Owners

Documentation

Comment

Name	Cheltenham Art Gallery and Museum
Address	Clarence Street Cheltenham GL50 3JT
Telephone	0242-37431
Contact	Keeper

CHELTENHAM

Sources & Dates of Information

R. Hutchings 1966
Visit

MEG 1978
Letter

Notes

Objects from Australia, Fiji, and Solomons. Total about 65, plus 10 archaeological.

Dates of Collection/Acquisition	Donors/Collectors/Former Owners
Acquired 1900-50	Mrs. Irving, 1940, Australia L. Scaley, 1931, Fiji Capt. C.A. Stokes, 1927, Solomons

Documentation

Catalogued.

Comment

No comment yet possible.

CHERTSEY

Name: Chertsey Museum

Address: The Cedars
Windsor Street
Chertsey KT16 8AT

Telephone: 09328-65764

Contact: Curator

Sources & Dates of Information

R. Hutchings 1966

Visit

MEG 1978

Letter 1979

Notes

Australia: boomerang 1
parrying shields 3 (on long-term loan to John McDouall Stuart Museum, Dysart, Kirkcaldy)

Dates of Collection/Acquisition	Donors/Collectors/Former Owners

Documentation

Comment

Museum opened in 1965. Collection probably acquired 1938-39 for projected museum.

CHRISTCHURCH

Name: Red House Museum

Address: Quay Road
Christchurch
Dorset

Telephone: 02015-2860

Contact: Hampshire County Museum Service, Chilcomb House, Chilcomb Lane, Bar End, Winchester SO23 8RD (tel. 0962-66242)

Sources & Dates of Information

R. Hutchings 1966

Visit GSP 1974

MEG 1978

Letter

Notes

Objects from Oceania, including New Zealand. Comprises some good material.

Dates of Collection/Acquisition	Donors/Collectors/Former Owners
Acquired 1920+	Beasley

Documentation

Comment

Name	Clandon House
Address	Clandon Park West Clandon Guildford Surrey
Telephone	0483-222482
Contact	Administrator (National Trust)

CLANDON

Sources & Dates of Information

R. Hutchings 1966

Visit

MEG 1978

Letter 1976

Notes

Maori [meeting] house erected in grounds of family house. Purchased by Lord Onslow when Governor General, 1892.

Dates of Collection/Acquisition	Donors/Collectors/Former Owners

Documentation

Photographed by Axel Poignant (cf. R. Poignant, 1967, Oceanic Mythology).

Comment

House is receiving attention by National Trust.

Name	Castle Museum
Address	Castle Hill Clitheroe BB7 1BA
Telephone	0200-24635
Contact	Keeper of Social History, c/o Lancashire County Museum Service, Stanley Street, Preston PR1 4YP (tel. 0772-56397)

CLITHEROE

Sources & Dates of Information

R. Hutchings	1966
Visit	
MEG	1978
Letter	1979

Notes

Dates of Collection/Acquisition

Donors/Collectors/Former Owners

Documentation

Comment

Castle Museum CLITHEROE

Artefact ↑ / Provenance →	OCEANIA UN.	AUSTRALIA	MELA.UNPROV.	Admiralty	Banks	Bismarck	D'Entrecast.	Fiji	Louisiade	Loyalty	N. Britain	N. Caledonia	N. Guinea	N. Hebrides	N. Ireland	Santa Cruz	Solomon	Trobriand	MICRO.UNPROV	Caroline	Gilbert	Mariana	Marshall	POLY.UNPROV.	Austral	Chatham	Cook	Easter	Hawaii	Marquesas	New Zealand	Niue	Pitcairn	Samoa	Society	Tokelau	Tonga	Tuamotu	Tuvalu
box																																							
bag																																							
basket																																							
mat																																							
headrest																																							
transport																																							
currency																																							
-rattle																																							
-flute,pipe																																							
-drum,gong																																							
MUSICAL INS.																																							
charm																																							
magic,med.																																							
fig.,image																																							
carving																																							
-bullroarer																																							
-paddle																																							
-adze																																							
-board																																							
-mask																																							
CERE. OBJ.																																							
staff,stick																																							
toilet app.																																							
fan																																							
comb																																							
-neck,breast																																							
-arm																																							
-ear,nose																																							
-head																																							
PERS. ORN.																																							
-cloak																																							
-belt																																							
-skirt																																							
CLOTHING																																							
barkcloth																																							
OTHER																																							
TOTAL	X	X																																					

Castle Museum

CLITHEROE

Artefact → / Provenance →	OCEANIA UN.	AUSTRALIA	MELA.UNPROV.	Admiralty	Banks	Bismarck	D'Entrecast.	Fiji	Louisiade	Loyalty	N. Britain	N. Caledonia	N. Guinea	N. Hebrides	N. Ireland	Santa Cruz	Solomon	Trobriand	MICRO.UNPROV.	Caroline	Gilbert	Mariana	Marshall	POLY.UNPROV.	Austral	Chatham	Cook	Easter	Hawaii	Marquesas	New Zealand	Niue	Pitcairn	Samoa	Society	Tokelau	Tonga	Tuamotu	Tuvalu
cord																																							
raw mater																																							
-sling,st																																							
-arrow																																							
-bow																																							
-shield																																							
-dagger																																							
-spearthr																																							
-spear																																							
-club																																							
WEAPON																																							
-float,si																																							
-net																																							
-spear																																							
-fishhook																																							
FISHING																																							
hunting																																							
-model																																							
-ornament																																							
-paddle																																							
NAVIGATIO																																							
-barkclot																																							
-weaving																																							
-needle,a																																							
-chisel																																							
-rasp																																							
-grinding																																							
-pounding																																							
-adze																																							
TOOL																																							
fire,ligh																																							
smoking pi																																							
pottery																																							
utensil																																							
lime spat																																							
dish,vess																																							
lime cont																																							

Name	Colchester and Essex Museum
Address	The Castle Colchester CO1 1TJ
Telephone	0206-76071/77475
Contact	Curator

COLCHESTER

Sources & Dates of Information

R. Hutchings 1966

Visit D. Jones 1977

MEG 1978

Letter

Notes

Disposals: Some to Cambridge; photographs to Pitt Rivers Museum, Oxford.

*New Hebrides-- club: or Collingwood Bay

Dates of Collection/Acquisition	Donors/Collectors/Former Owners
1860-1900	

Documentation

Comment

A typical local museum collection.

Colchester and Essex Museum

COLCHESTER

Artefact → / Provenance ↓	OCEANIA UN.	AUSTRALIA	MELA.UNPROV.	Admiralty	Banks	Bismarck	D'Entrecast.	Fiji	Louisiade	Loyalty	N. Britain	N. Caledonia	N. Guinea	N. Hebrides	N. Ireland	Santa Cruz	Solomon	Trobriand	MICRO.UNPROV	Caroline	Gilbert	Mariana	Marshall	POLY.UNPROV.	Austral	Chatham	Cook	Easter	Hawaii	Marquesas	New Zealand	Niue	Pitcairn	Samoa	Society	Tokelau	Tonga	Tuamotu	Tuvalu	[illegible]
box																																								
bag																																								
basket																																								
mat																																								
headrest																																								
transport																																								
currency																																								
-rattle																																								
-flute,pipe																																								
-drum,gong																																								
MUSICAL INS.																																								
charm																																								
magic,med.																																								
fig.,image																																								
carving																																								
-bullroarer		1																																						
-paddle																																								
-adze																																								
-board																																								
-mask																																								
CERE. OBJ.																																								
staff,stick																																								
toilet app.																																				1			
fan																																								
comb																																	1						
-neck,breast																																								
-arm																																								
-ear,nose																																								
-head																																								
PERS. ORN.																																								
-cloak																																								
-belt																																								
-skirt																																								1
CLOTHING																																								
barkcloth																																								
OTHER		3																																						
TOTAL	2	10	6								1		4	1		1	13																	1			1			2

Colchester and Essex Museum

COLCHESTER

Artefact → / Provenance →	OCEANIA UN.	AUSTRALIA	MELA.UNPROV.	Admiralty	Banks	Bismarck	D'Entrecast.	Fiji	Louisiade	Loyalty	N. Britain	N. Caledonia	N. Guinea	N. Hebrides	N. Ireland	Santa Cruz	Solomon	Trobriand	MICRO.UNPROV
cord																			
raw mater																			
-sling,st																			
-arrow			3										2			1	4		
-bow			2														1		
-shield		1															1		
-dagger																			
-spearthro		2																	
-spear			1										2				6		
-club		2									1			1*					
WEAPON																			
-float,si																			
-net																			
-spear																			
-fishhook																			
FISHING																			
hunting																			
-model																			
-ornament																			
-paddle																	1		
NAVIGATIO																			
-barkclot																			
-weaving																			
-needle,aw																			
-chisel																			
-rasp																			
-grinding																			
-pounding																			
-adze		1																	
TOOL																			
fire,ligh																			
smoking pi																			
pottery																			
utensil																			
lime spat																			
dish,vesse																			
lime cont																			

Artefact → / Provenance →	Caroline	Gilbert	Mariana	Marshall	POLY.UNPROV.	Austral	Chatham	Cook	Easter	Hawaii	Marquesas	New Zealand	Niue	Pitcairn	Samoa	Society	Tokelau	Tonga	Tuamotu	Tuvalu	Tahiti
cord																					
raw mater																					
-sling,st																					
-arrow																					
-bow																					
-shield																					
-dagger																					
-spearthro																					
-spear																					2
-club																					
WEAPON																					
-float,si																					
-net																					
-spear																					
-fishhook																					
FISHING																					
hunting																					
-model																					
-ornament																					
-paddle																					
NAVIGATIO																					
-barkclot																					
-weaving																					
-needle,aw																					
-chisel																					
-rasp																					
-grinding																					
-pounding																					
-adze																					
TOOL																					
fire,ligh																					
smoking pi																					
pottery																					
utensil																					
lime spat																					
dish,vesse																					
lime cont																					

COVENTRY

Name: Libraries, Arts and Museums Department

Address: Bayley Lane
Coventry CV1 5RG

Telephone: 0203-25555

Contact: Keeper of Folk Life

Sources & Dates of Information

R. Hutchings 1966

Visit

MEG 1978

Letters 1979

Notes

Australia: axe

Disposals: 23 items on long-term loan to Nuneaton Museum (see Nuneaton entry).

Dates of Collection/Acquisition	Donors/Collectors/Former Owners

Documentation

Comment

No comment yet possible.

Name	Queen's Hall	CUCKFIELD
Address	Mid-Sussex District Council Cuckfield Sussex	**Sources & Dates of Information** R. Hutchings 1966 Visit MEG 1978 Letter, 1979, from G. Bankes
Telephone	0444-50301	
Contact	Mr. Wall, Mid-Sussex District Council Administrative Offices, Oaklands, Oaklands Rd., Haywards Heath	

Notes

*Australia-- other: boomerang

Dates of Collection/Acquisition	Donors/Collectors/Former Owners
	Cuckfield Historical Society

Documentation

Comment

No comment yet possible.

CUCKFIELD

Artefact →

Provenance ↓

Provenance	TOTAL	OTHER	barkcloth	CLOTHING	-skirt	-belt	-cloak	PERS. ORN.	-head	-ear,nose	-arm	-neck,breast	comb	fan	toilet app.	staff,stick	CERE. OBJ.	-mask	-board	-adze	-paddle	-bullroarer	carving	fig.,image	magic,med.	charm	MUSICAL INS.	-drum,gong	-flute,pipe	-rattle	currency	transport	headrest	mat	basket	bag	box
OCEANIA UN.	4																																				
AUSTRALIA	1	1																																			
MELA.UNPROV.																																					
Admiralty																																					
Banks																																					
Bismarck																																					
D'Entrecast.																																					
Fiji																																					
Louisiade																																					
Loyalty																																					
N. Britain																																					
N. Caledonia																																					
N. Guinea																																					
N. Hebrides																																					
N. Ireland																																					
Santa Cruz																																					
Solomon																																					
Trobriand																																					
MICRO.UNPROV																																					
Caroline																																					
Gilbert																																					
Mariana																																					
Marshall																																					
POLY.UNPROV.																																					
Austral																																					
Chatham																																					
Cook																																					
Easter																																					
Hawaii																																					
Marquesas																																					
New Zealand	2																																				
Niue																																					
Pitcairn																																					
Samoa																																					
Society																																					
Tokelau																																					
Tonga																																					
Tuamotu																																					
Tuvalu																																					

CUCKFIELD

Artefact → / Provenance ↓	lime cont.	dish,vesse	lime spat	utensil	pottery	smokng pi	fire,ligh	TOOL	-adze	-pounding	-grinding	-rasp	-chisel	-needle,a	-weaving	-barkclot	NAVIGATIO	-paddle	-ornament	-model	hunting	FISHING	-fishhook	-spear	-net	-float,si	WEAPON	-club	-spear	-spearthr	-dagger	-shield	-bow	-arrow	-sling,st	raw mater	cord
OCEANIA UN.																											2		x			1					
AUSTRALIA																																					
MELA.UNPROV.																																					
Admiralty																																					
Banks																																					
Bismarck																																					
D'Entrecast.																																					
Fiji																																					
Louisiade																																					
Loyalty																																					
N. Britain																																					
N. Caledonia																																					
N. Guinea																																					
N. Hebrides																																					
N. Ireland																																					
Santa Cruz																																					
Solomon																																					
Trobriand																																					
MICRO.UNPROV.																																					
Caroline																																					
Gilbert																																					
Mariana																																					
Marshall																																					
POLY.UNPROV.																																					
Austral																																					
Chatham																																					
Cook																																					
Easter																																					
Hawaii																																					
Marquesas																																					
New Zealand																		2																			
Niue																																					
Pitcairn																																					
Samoa																																					
Society																																					
Tokelau																																					
Tonga																																					
Tuamotu																																					
Tuvalu																																					

DARLINGTON

Name Darlington Museum

Address Tubwell Row
Darlington DL1 1PD

Telephone 0325-3795

Contact Curator

Sources & Dates of Information

R. Hutchings 1966

Visit

MEG 1978

Letter 1979

Notes

*Oceania-- models: dugout 2, outrigger 1
*Australia-- other: boomerangs 2

Dates of Collection/Acquisition

Acquired mainly 1921-39

Donors/Collectors/Former Owners

Lucas, Australia

Documentation

Identification and cataloguing continuing.

Comment

Darlington Museum

DARLINGTON

Provenance / Artefact	TOTAL	OTHER	barkcloth	CLOTHING	-skirt	-belt	-cloak	PERS. ORN.	-head	-ear,nose	-arm	-neck,breast	comb	fan	toilet app.	staff,stick	CERE. OBJ.	-mask	-board	-adze	-paddle	-bullroarer	carving	fig.,image	magic,med.	charm	MUSICAL INS.	-drum,gong	-flute,pipe	-rattle	currency	transport	headrest	mat	basket	bag	box
OCEANIA UN.	3																																				
AUSTRALIA	9	2																																			
MELA.UNPROV.																																					
Admiralty																																					
Banks																																					
Bismarck																																					
D'Entrecast.																																					
Fiji	22											1																									
Louisiade																																					
Loyalty																																					
N. Britain	2																																				
N. Caledonia																																					
N. Guinea	1																																				
N. Hebrides	1																																				
N. Ireland																																					
Santa Cruz	1															1																					
Solomon	9																																				
Trobriand																																					
MICRO.UNPROV.																																					
Caroline																																					
Gilbert																																					
Mariana																																					
Marshall																																					
POLY.UNPROV.																																					
Austral	1																			1																	
Chatham																																					
Cook																																					
Easter																																					
Hawaii																																					
Marquesas																																					
New Zealand	2																																				
Niue																																					
Pitcairn																																					
Samoa	1																																				
Society																																					
Tokelau																																					
Tonga																																					
Tuamotu																																					
Tuvalu																																					

DARLINGTON

Darlington Museum

Artefact → / Provenance ↓	lime cont.	dish,vesse	lime spat	utensil	pottery	smokng pi	fire,ligh	TOOL	-adze	-pounding	-grinding	-rasp	-chisel	-needle,aw	-weaving	-barkclot	NAVIGATIO	-paddle	-ornament	-model	hunting	FISHING	-fishhook	-spear	-net	-float,si	WEAPON	-club	-spear	-spearthro	-dagger	-shield	-bow	-arrow	-sling,sto	raw mater	cord
OCEANIA UN.																			3*																		
AUSTRALIA		1																										1	4								
MELA.UNPROV.																																					
Admiralty																																					
Banks																																					
Bismarck																																					
D'Entrecast.																																					
Fiji																	2											19									
Louisiade																																					
Loyalty																																					
N. Britain																												2									
N. Caledonia																																					
N. Guinea																																		1			
N. Hebrides																												1									
N. Ireland																																					
Santa Cruz																																					
Solomon																												9									
Trobriand																																					
MICRO.UNPROV.																																					
Caroline																																					
Gilbert																																					
Mariana																																					
Marshall																																					
POLY.UNPROV.																																					
Austral																																					
Chatham																																					
Cook																																					
Easter																																					
Hawaii																																					
Marquesas																																					
New Zealand																			1									1									
Niue																																					
Pitcairn																																					
Samoa																												1									
Society																																					
Tokelau																																					
Tonga																																					
Tuamotu																																					
Tuvalu																																					

Name	Derby Museums and Art Gallery
Address	Strand Derby DE1 1BS
Telephone	0332-31111
Contact	Keeper of Antiquities

DERBY (M + AG)

Sources & Dates of Information

R. Hutchings 1966

Visit PG 1970

MEG 1978

Letter

Notes

Total Oceanic around 40 items, plus 14 archaeological.

Dates of Collection/Acquisition	Donors/Collectors/Former Owners
20th Century	

Documentation

Comment

There was a collection in Derby in 1843 ("Town and Country Museum"), but none of these objects are in the Museum and Art Gallery. Present data inadequate.

Museums and Art Gallery DERBY (M+A

Artefact ↑ / Provenance →	OCEANIA UN.	AUSTRALIA	MELA.UNPROV.	Admiralty	Banks	Bismarck	D'Entrecast.	Fiji	Louisiade	Loyalty	N. Britain	N. Caledonia	N. Guinea	N. Hebrides	N. Ireland	Santa Cruz	Solomon	Trobriand	MICRO.UNPROV	Caroline	Gilbert	Mariana	Marshall	POLY.UNPROV.	Austral	Chatham	Cook	Easter	Hawaii	Marquesas	New Zealand	Niue	Pitcairn	Samoa	Society	Tokelau	Tonga	Tuamotu	Tuvalu
box																																							
bag																																							
basket																																							
mat																																							
headrest																																							
transport																																							
currency																																							
-rattle																																							
-flute,pipe																																							
-drum,gong																																							
MUSICAL INS.																																							
charm																																							
magic,med.																																							
fig.,image																																							
carving																																							
-bullroarer																																							
-paddle																																							
-adze																																							
-board																																							
-mask																																							
CERE. OBJ.																																							
staff,stick																																							
toilet app.																																							
fan																																							
comb																																							
-neck,breast																																							
-arm																																							
-ear,nose																																							
-head																																							
PERS. ORN.																																							
-cloak													X																										
-belt																																							
-skirt																																							
CLOTHING																																							
barkcloth																																							
OTHER																																							
TOTAL	X												X																										

Museums and Art Gallery

DERBY CM.AG

Artefact → / Provenance →	OCEANIA UN.	AUSTRALIA	MELA.UNPROV.	Admiralty	Banks	Bismarck	D'Entrecast.	Fiji	Louisiade	Loyalty	N. Britain	N. Caledonia	N. Guinea	N. Hebrides	N. Ireland	Santa Cruz	Solomon	Trobriand	MICRO.UNPROV	Caroline	Gilbert	Mariana	Marshall	POLY.UNPROV.	Austral	Chatham	Cook	Easter	Hawaii	Marquesas	New Zealand	Niue	Pitcairn	Samoa	Society	Tokelau	Tonga	Tuamotu	Tuvalu
cord																																						
raw mate																																						
-sling,st																																						
-arrow																																						
-bow																																						
-shield																																						
-dagger																																						
-spearthr																																						
-spear																																						
-club																																						
WEAPON																																						
-float,si																																						
-net																																						
-spear																																						
-fishhook																																						
FISHING																																						
hunting																																						
-model																																						
-ornament																																						
-paddle																																						
NAVIGATIO																																						
-barkclot																																						
-weaving																																						
-needle,a																																						
-chisel																																						
-rasp																																						
-grinding																																						
-pounding																																						
-adze																																						
TOOL																																						
fire,ligh																																						
smoking pi																																						
pottery																																						
utensil																																						
lime spat																																						
dish,vess																																						
lime cont																																						

DERBY (SCHOOLS)

Name: Schools Resources Centre (Derbyshire Museum Service)

Address: Kedlestone Road
Derby DE3 1GT

Telephone: 0332-371921

Contact: County Museums Officer

Sources & Dates of Information

R. Hutchings	1966
Visit	
MEG	1978
Letter	1979

Notes

*Australia-- other: boomerangs 4, bark paintings
*New Guinea-- other: hook

Dates of Collection/Acquisition

Acquired mainly 1950-65

Donors/Collectors/Former Owners

Documentation

Archival, iconographic.

Publication: Geography Catalogue of Schools Loans (out of print).

Comment

This material may have come in part from the collection in Derby in the 1840's.

Schools Resources Centre

DERBY (SCHOOL

Provenance ↓ / Artefact →	TOTAL	OTHER	barkcloth	CLOTHING	-skirt	-belt	-cloak	PERS. ORN.	-head	-ear,nose	-arm	-neck,breast	comb	fan	toilet app.	staff,stick	CERE. OBJ.	-mask	-board	-adze	-paddle	-bullroarer	carving	fig.,image	magic,med.	charm	MUSICAL INS.	-drum,gong	-flute,pipe	-rattle	currency	transport	headrest	mat	basket	bag	box
OCEANIA UN.	5																					1							1							1	
AUSTRALIA	17+	5+																																			
MELA.UNPROV.																																					
Admiralty																																					
Banks																																					
Bismarck																																					
D'Entrecast.																																					
Fiji	12		4													2					1																
Louisiade																																					
Loyalty																																					
N. Britain																																					
N. Caledonia	2																																				
N. Guinea	27	1				5						1					2					1		2													
N. Hebrides	4																																				
N. Ireland																																					
Santa Cruz																																					
Solomon	5																														2						
Trobriand																																					
MICRO.UNPROV.																																					
Caroline																																					
Gilbert																																					
Mariana																																					
Marshall																																					
POLY.UNPROV.																																					
Austral																																					
Chatham																																					
Cook																																					
Easter																																					
Hawaii																																					
Marquesas																																					
New Zealand	13							1		1																											1
Niue																																					
Pitcairn																																					
Samoa	2																																				
Society																																					
Tokelau																																					
Tonga	5		1														1																				
Tuamotu																																					
Tuvalu																																					
[illegible]	1																																				

Schools Resources Centre

DERBY SCHOOLS

Provenance ↓ / Artefact →	lime cont.	dish,vess	lime spat	utensil	pottery	smokng pi	fire,ligh	TOOL	-adze	-pounding	-grinding	-rasp	-chisel	-needle,a	-weaving	-barkclot	NAVIGATIO	-paddle	-ornament	-model	hunting	FISHING	-fishhook	-spear	-net	-float,si	WEAPON	-club	-spear	-spearthro	-dagger	-shield	-bow	-arrow	-sling,st	raw mater	cord
OCEANIA UN.							2																														
AUSTRALIA																												5	1	4		2					
MELA.UNPROV.																																					
Admiralty																																					
Banks																																					
Bismarck																																					
D'Entrecast.																																					
Fiji				1																								4									
Louisiade																																					
Loyalty																																					
N. Britain																																					
N. Caledonia																												2									
N. Guinea		2	4	2					2																				1						4		
N. Hebrides																1												3									
N. Ireland																																					
Santa Cruz																																					
Solomon																						1							2								
Trobriand																																					
MICRO.UNPROV.																																					
Caroline																																					
Gilbert																																					
Mariana																																					
Marshall																																					
POLY.UNPROV.																																					
Austral																																					
Chatham																																					
Cook																																					
Easter																																					
Hawaii																																					
Marquesas																																					
New Zealand									2	1													2					5									
Niue																																					
Pitcairn																																					
Samoa																												2									
Society																																					
Tokelau																																					
Tonga																												3									
Tuamotu																																					
Tuvalu																																					
Torres Strait						1																															

Name	Museum of the Wiltshire Archaeological Society	DEVIZES	
Address	41 Long Street Devizes SN10 1NS	Sources & Dates of Information	
		R. Hutchings	1966
		Visit	
Telephone	0380-2765	MEG	1978
Contact		Letter	
		Museum catalogue	1911
		Personal communication,	1977

Notes

Disposals : Pacific material present 1911, dispersed in 1920's, and recent transfer to Exeter Museum.

Dates of Collection/Acquisition	Donors/Collectors/Former Owners

Documentation

Comment

Wilts. Archaeological Society DEVIZES

Artefact ↓ / Provenance →	OCEANIA UN.	AUSTRALIA	MELA.UNPROV.	Admiralty	Banks	Bismarck	D'Entrecast.	Fiji	Louisiade	Loyalty	N. Britain	N. Caledonia	N. Guinea	N. Hebrides	N. Ireland	Santa Cruz	Solomon	Trobriand	MICRO.UNPROV	Caroline	Gilbert	Mariana	Marshall	POLY.UNPROV.	Austral	Chatham	Cook	Easter	Hawaii	Marquesas	New Zealand	Niue	Pitcairn	Samoa	Society	Tokelau	Tonga	Tuamotu	Tuvalu
cord																																							
raw mater.																																							
-sling,stone																																							
-arrow																																							
-bow	X																																						
-shield																																							
-dagger																																							
-spearthrower		2																																					
-spear								X																															
-club	X							X																							4								
WEAPON	X																																						
-float,sinker																																							
-net																																							
-spear																																							
-fishhook																																							
FISHING																																							
hunting																																							
-model																																							
-ornament																																							
-paddle	X																																						
NAVIGATION																																							
-barkcloth	X																																						
-weaving																																							
-needle,awl																																							
-chisel																																							
-rasp																																							
-grinding																																							
-pounding																																							
-adze	X	X																													1								
TOOL		X																																					
fire,light																																							
smoking pipe																																							
pottery																																							
utensil																																							
lime spat.																																							
dish,vessel																																							
lime cont.																																							

DONCASTER

Name: Doncaster Museum and Art Gallery

Address: Chequer Road
Doncaster DN1 2AE

Telephone: 0302-62095

Contact: Curator

Sources & Dates of Information

R. Hutchings 1966

Visit SP 1975

MEG 1978

Letter

Notes

Table incomplete.
Disposals: some material loaned to Bagshaw Museum, Batley.

*Australia-- other: boomerang
*New Guinea-- figures: Tami Island 5, Sepik (?) 1

Dates of Collection/Acquisition

Acquired mainly 1912-63

Donors/Collectors/Former Owners

Woodend Museum, Scarborough, loan
Buckingham Palace, permanent loan

Documentation

Photographic.

Comment

Collection being sorted.

Museum and Art Gallery

DONCASTER

Artcfact → / Provenance ↓	TOTAL	OTHER	barkcloth	CLOTHING	-skirt	-belt	-cloak	PERS. ORN.	-head	-ear,nose	-arm	-neck,breast	comb	fan	toilet app.	staff,stick	CERE. OBJ.	-mask	-board	-adze	-paddle	-bullroarer	carving	fig.,image	magic,med.	charm	MUSICAL INS.	-drum,gong	-flute,pipe	-rattle	currency	transport	headrest	mat	basket	bag	box
OCEANIA UN.	2																																				
AUSTRALIA	1	1																																			
MELA.UNPROV.																																					
Admiralty																																					
Banks																																					
Bismarck																																					
D'Entrecast.																																					
Fiji																																					
Louisiade																																					
Loyalty																																					
N. Britain																																					
N. Caledonia																																					
N. Guinea	7																							6*				1									
N. Hebrides	1						1																														
N. Ireland																																					
Santa Cruz																																					
Solomon	14						1			1		8																									
Trobriand	2																																				
MICRO.UNPROV.																																					
Caroline																																					
Gilbert																																					
Mariana																																					
Marshall																																					
POLY.UNPROV.																																					
Austral																																					
Chatham																																					
Cook																																					
Easter																																					
Hawaii	1																																				
Marquesas																																					
New Zealand	6																							1												1	1
Niue																																					
Pitcairn																																					
Samoa																																					
Society																																					
Tokelau																																					
Tonga																																					
Tuamotu																																					
Tuvalu																																					

Museum and Art Gallery

DONCASTER

Artefact → / Provenance →	OCEANIA UN.	AUSTRALIA	MELA.UNPROV.	Admiralty	Banks	Bismarck	D'Entrecast.	Fiji	Louisiade	Loyalty	N. Britain	N. Caledonia	N. Guinea	N. Hebrides	N. Ireland	Santa Cruz	Solomon	Trobriand	MICRO.UNPROV	Caroline	Gilbert	Mariana	Marshall	POLY.UNPROV.	Austral	Chatham	Cook	Easter	Hawaii	Marquesas	New Zealand	Niue	Pitcairn	Samoa	Society	Tokelau	Tonga	Tuamotu	Tuvalu
cord																																							
raw mater																																							
-sling,st																																							
-arrow																																							
-bow																																							
-shield																																							
-dagger																																							
-spearthr																																							
-spear																																							
-club																	2	1													2						1		
WEAPON																																							
-float,si																																							
-net																																							
-spear																																							
-fishhook																																							
FISHING																																							
hunting																																							
-model																																							
-ornament																																							
-paddle																															1								
NAVIGATIO																																							
-barkclot																																							
-weaving																																							
-needle,a																																							
-chisel																																							
-rasp																																							
-grinding																																							
-pounding																																							
-adze	2																																						
TOOL																																							
fire,ligh																																							
smokng pi																																							
pottery																																							
utensil																		1																					
lime spat																																							
dish,vess																														1									
lime cont																	2																						

Name Dorset Military Museum

Address The Keep
Bridport Road
Dorchester DT1 1RN

Telephone 0305-4066

Contact Curator

DORCHESTER

Sources & Dates of Information

R. Hutchings 1966

Visit

MEG 1978

Letters 1979

Notes

Australia: 2 manuscript diaries of two officiers of the 39th Regiment who explored in New South Wales and the Bathurst area (Capt. John Forbes and Lt. Maule).

Dates of Collection/Acquisition	Donors/Collectors/Former Owners

Documentation

Reference: P. Mander-Jones, 1972, Manuscripts in the British Isles relating to Australia, New Zealand and the Pacific, ANU Press, Canberra, p. 421.

Comment

DOVER

Name Dover Museum

Address Ladywell
Dover CT16 1DQ

Telephone 0304-201066

Contact Curator

Sources & Dates of Information

R. Hutchings 1966
Visit

MEG 1978
Letter

Notes

Gilbert: spear 1
Cook: adze 1

Disposal: In 1948, 2 Hawaiian cloaks, 1 feather & 1 barkcloth, to James Hooper.

Dates of Collection/Acquisition	Donors/Collectors/Former Owners

Documentation

Comment

Name National Museum of Ireland Address Kildare Street Dublin 2 Eire 10 Telephone 0001-765521 Contact Director	DUBLIN Sources & Dates of Information R. Hutchings 1966 Visits ALK 1977 1978 PG + ALK 1975 MEG 1978 Letter

Notes

For table explanatory notes, see Dublin (C).

Dates of Collection/Acquisition	Donors/Collectors/Former Owners

Documentation

References: Collection of Weapons (Science and Art Museum, Dublin), 1894 Deposit by Trinity College, 1894.
J.D. Freeman, 1949, "The Polynesian Collection of Trinity College, Dublin and the National Museum of Ireland," J. of the Polynesian Society, 58:1-18.
Art of the Pacific, catalogue of exhibition at the Douglas Hyde Art Gallery, Trinity College, 1978.
List of 1883 Trinity College loan to National Museum (mostly Oceanic).
See also Freeman bibliography.
Photographic, iconographic.

Comment

Very important collections requiring detailed examination, treatment, listing, sorting.

National Museum of Ireland

DUBLIN

Artefact → / Provenance ↓	TOTAL	OTHER	barkcloth	CLOTHING	-skirt	-belt	-cloak	PERS. ORN.	-head	-ear,nose	-arm	-neck,breast	comb	fan	toilet app.	staff,stick
OCEANIA UN.																
AUSTRALIA	336*	48+		1		3		8	5	1	1	7				12*
MELA.UNPROV.	16+	1			X	X		X								
Admiralty																
Banks																
Bismarck																
D'Entrecast.																
Fiji	128	1	11		6				1			5	4	5	3*	
Louisiade																
Loyalty																
N. Britain																
N. Caledonia																
N. Guinea	13					1										
N. Hebrides	1															
N. Ireland	8															
Santa Cruz	2															
Solomon	11															
Trobriand	4															
MICRO.UNPROV.																
Caroline	6					1										
Gilbert	20					1						2				
Mariana																
Marshall																
POLY.UNPROV.	5															
Austral	11	1	1													
Chatham																
Cook	18		1													
Easter	5	1														
Hawaii	3	1										1				
Marquesas	8							2		1				2		
New Zealand	212	5		1	5		16	29				7	1		1	4
Niue	3		1													
Pitcairn																
Samoa	14												1			
Society																
Tokelau																
Tonga	45	4				1						2	4		3*	
Tuamotu																
Tuvalu																
Tahiti	31+	1	2												1*	

Artefact → / Provenance ↓	CERE. OBJ.	-mask	-board	-adze	-paddle	-bullroarer	carving	fig.,image	magic,med.	charm	MUSICAL INS.	-drum,gong	-flute,pipe	-rattle	currency	transport	headrest	mat	basket	bag	box
OCEANIA UN.																					
AUSTRALIA	5		1			12	1		2				1			1			4	4	
MELA.UNPROV.	1											4									
Admiralty																					
Banks																					
Bismarck																					
D'Entrecast.																					
Fiji																	4		4		
Louisiade																					
Loyalty																					
N. Britain																					
N. Caledonia																					
N. Guinea		2	6				2	1													
N. Hebrides		1																			
N. Ireland		2						6													
Santa Cruz													2								
Solomon																					
Trobriand																					
MICRO.UNPROV.																					
Caroline																					
Gilbert																					
Mariana																					
Marshall																					
POLY.UNPROV.																					
Austral					1							1*									
Chatham																					
Cook				1														2			
Easter							1	3													
Hawaii								2													
Marquesas							1*														
New Zealand							4	7					4							1	5
Niue																					
Pitcairn																					
Samoa																		1	1		
Society																					
Tokelau																					
Tonga																	7		1		
Tuamotu																					
Tuvalu																					
Tahiti																					

Artefact → / Provenance ↓	lime cont.	dish,vesse	lime spat	utensil	pottery	smoking pi	fire,ligh	TOOL	-adze	-pounding	-grinding	-rasp	-chisel	-needle,aw	-weaving	-barkclot	NAVIGATIO	-paddle	-ornament	-model	hunting	FISHING	-fishhook	-spear	-net	-float,si	WEAPON	-club	-spear	-spearthro	-dagger	-shield	-bow	-arrow	-sling,st	raw mater	cord
OCEANIA UN.																																					
AUSTRALIA		4				1	8	21	11	1	2		2	1	2						1			1			1	39	58	24		24		5		11	2
MELA.UNPROV.									X									X					X					X	X				X	X			
Admiralty																																					
Banks																																					
Bismarck																																					
D'Entrecast.																												1									
Fiji		9			15				10						4													36	7							4	2
Louisiade																																					
Loyalty																																					
N. Britain																																					
N. Caledonia																																					
N. Guinea																			1																		
N. Hebrides																																					
N. Ireland																																					
Santa Cruz																																					
Solomon		1																4	1	1								1				3					
Trobriand																												2				2					
MICRO.UNPROV																																					
Caroline									5																												
Gilbert																											16*				1						
Mariana																																					
Marshall																																					
POLY.UNPROV.								3												2																	
Austral																		7																			
Chatham																																					
Cook		1							10											1								2									
Easter																																					
Hawaii																																					
Marquesas																												2									
New Zealand									29	1			2			2		7	1	3			31				2	31	3								
Niue									1																			1									
Pitcairn																																					
Samoa		3																										8									
Society																																					
Tokelau																																					
Tonga		1						1	1						2			1				2	11					4									
Tuamotu																																					
Tuvalu																																					
Tahiti									3	3					3	3						X	11+														
Torres Straits																																					

National Museum of Ireland (B)

DUBLIN

Provenance ↓ / Artefact →	TOTAL	OTHER	barkcloth	CLOTHING	-skirt	-belt	-cloak	PERS. ORN.	-head	-ear,nose	-arm	-neck,breas;	comb	fan	toilet app.	staff,stick	CERE. OBJ.	-mask	-board	-adze	-paddle	-bullroarer	carving	fig.,image	magic,med.	charm	MUSICAL INS.	-drum,gong	-flute,pipe	-rattle	currency	transport	headrest	mat	basket	bag	box
OCEANIA UN.	21				9																							3									
AUSTRALIA																																					
MELA.UNPROV.	2																																				
Admiralty																																					
Banks																																					
Bismarck																																					
D'Entrecast.																																					
Fiji	56																3												3								
Louisiade																																					
Loyalty																																					
N. Britain																																					
N. Caledonia	3																																				
N. Guinea	42																																				
N. Hebrides	44																																				
N. Ireland																																					
Santa Cruz																																					
Solomon	14																																				
Trobriand																																					
MICRO.UNPROV																																					
Caroline																																					
Gilbert	1																																				
Mariana																																					
Marshall																																					
POLY.UNPROV.																																					
Austral	3																																				
Chatham																																					
Cook	10																			3																	
Easter																																					
Hawaii	28	5	4	1					1*		2	1												2										6			
Marquesas												2																									
New Zealand	27	2		1			3	1				1																	3								
Niue	11																																				
Pitcairn																																					
Samoa	1																																				
Society																																					
Tokelau																																					
Tonga	44	3			10				1			2															1		1				7	3			
Tuamotu	5																																				
Tuvalu																																					
Tahiti	37+	6	7	2*	1				1*			2												1				5									

National Museum of Ireland (B)

DUBLIN

Provenance ↓ / Artefact →	lime cont	dish,vess	lime spa	utensil	pottery	smokng pi	fire,lig	TOOL	-adze	-pounding	-grinding	-rasp	-chisel	-needle,a	-weaving	-barkclot	NAVIGATIO	-paddle	-ornament	-model	hunting	FISHING	-fishhook	-spear	-net	-float,si	WEAPON	-club	-spear	-spearthr	-dagger	-shield	-bow	-arrow	-sling,st	raw mater	cord
OCEANIA UN.									1																		1										
AUSTRALIA																																					
MELA.UNPROV.																													2								
Admiralty																																					
Banks																																					
Bismarck																																					
D'Entrecast.																																					
Fiji									1							1								1				36	6				2	3			
Louisiade																																					
Loyalty																																					
N. Britain																																					
N. Caledonia																												3									
N. Guinea				1																								25					5	11			
N. Hebrides																								1				2	3				2	36			
N. Ireland																																					
Santa Cruz																																					
Solomon																						1						2					1	10			
Trobriand																																					
MICRO.UNPROV																																					
Caroline																																					
Gilbert																											1										
Mariana																																					
Marshall																																					
POLY.UNPROV.																																					
Austral																		3																			
Chatham																																					
Cook																												7									
Easter																																					
Hawaii		1																									1		4								
Marquesas																												2									
New Zealand									2					1			1	3										7	2								
Niue																												4	7								
Pitcairn																																					
Samoa																												1									
Society																																					
Tokelau																																					
Tonga		1																				5					14	11									
Tuamotu																													5								
Tuvalu																																					
Tahiti								X	3			1				4										1			1		1						
Torres Straits																																		10			

DUBLIN

National Museum of Ireland (C)

NOTE: Sheets A and Sheets B show information derived from different sources.

A: -visits by PG and ALK. Only material on display is listed.
-exhibition catalogue from Art of the Pacific (1978).

B: -1894 Weapons Catalogue
-1882 list of Trinity College Ethnographic Loan
-Polynesian items listed by Freeman in J.P.S.
Objects listed in the latter two were cited only when they had not already been cited in the Weapons Catalogue.

Only the material on Sheets A is known still to be in Dublin. Sheets B are included to give an inkling of the full range which, however, will be a matter for conjecture until the collection can be sorted.

*Oceania-- headrests: Tongan? -identified later? See Tonga entry.

*Australia-- sticks: message 3
other: boomerangs 41+; stone tools; misc. 6
Photographs

*Melanesia unprovenanced-- other: modelled skull

*Fiji-- toilet apparatus: tatooing
other: misc. 1

*Gilberts-- weapon: armour 1

	(A)	(B)
*Australs--	drum: or Society other: flywhisk	
*Easter--	other: misc. 1	
*Hawaii--		head ornament: helmet other: royal spittoon, cloth, mourning cloth, flywhisks
*New Zealand--	other: toys 2, heads 2, illustrations	other: cloth 2
*Tahiti--	toilet apparatus: tatooing other: eyeshade	clothing: mourning dress head ornament: headdress other: flywhisks 3, eyeshades 2, cloth
*Tonga--	toilet apparatus: tatooing other: flywhisks 2, hook, misc. 1	weapon: possibly Futuna other: flywhisks 2

Name	Dumfries Museum	DUMFRIES
Address	The Observatory Dumfires DG2 7SW	**Sources & Dates of Information** R. Hutchings 1966 Visit MEG 1978 Letters 1979
Telephone	0387-3374	
Contact	Curator	

Notes

Disposals: some to Liverpool

*Australia-- other: boomerangs 3, stone tools, whip. Hairbelt collected between 1840 & 1860.
*Gilberts-- weapon: armour suit
*Tonga-- club: 18th Century

Dates of Collection/Acquisition	Donors/Collectors/Former Owners
Acquired mainly mid-1960's	Dr. Grierson, collected between 1860 & 1889 Royal Scottish Museum, 1960's British Museum Dumfries & Maxwelltown Astronomical Society, 1835-1934

Documentation

Library, archival, photographic.
Dr. Grierson's manuscript catalogue.
1894 Catalogue of Dr. Grierson's Museum at Thornhill, Dumfriesshire, written by Black of The National Museum of Antiquities, Edinburgh.

Comment

Note early material.

Dumfries Museum

DUMFRIES

Provenance ↓ / Artefact →	TOTAL	OTHER	barkcloth	CLOTHING	-skirt	-belt	-cloak	PERS. ORN.	-head	-ear,nose	-arm	-neck,breast	comb	fan	toilet app.	staff,stick	CERE. OBJ.	-mask	-board	-adze	-paddle	-bullroarer	carving	fig.,image	magic,med.	charm	MUSICAL INS.	-drum,gong	-flute,pipe	-rattle	currency	transport	headrest	mat	basket	bag	box
OCEANIA UN.	5+		X																																		
AUSTRALIA	9+	5+				1						1																									
MELA.UNPROV.																																					
Admiralty																																					
Banks																																					
Bismarck																																					
D'Entrecast.																																					
Fiji	3																																				
Louisiade																																					
Loyalty																																					
N. Britain																																					
N. Caledonia	2																																				
N. Guinea	1																																				
N. Hebrides	1																																				
N. Ireland	2																																				
Santa Cruz																																					
Solomon																																					
Trobriand																																					
MICRO.UNPROV.	X																																				
Caroline																																					
Gilbert	1																																				
Mariana																																					
Marshall																																					
POLY.UNPROV.																																					
Austral																																					
Chatham																																					
Cook																																					
Easter																																					
Hawaii	1		1																																		
Marquesas																																					
New Zealand	4+											1				1																					
Niue																																					
Pitcairn																																					
Samoa																																					
Society	X																																				
Tokelau																																					
Tonga	1																																				
Tuamotu																																					
Tuvalu																																					

Dumfries Museum

DUMFRIES

Artefact → / Provenance →	OCEANIA UN.	AUSTRALIA	MELA.UNPROV.	Admiralty	Banks	Bismarck	D'Entrecast.	Fiji	Louisiade	Loyalty	N. Britain	N. Caledonia	N. Guinea	N. Hebrides	N. Ireland	Santa Cruz	Solomon	Trobriand	MICRO.UNPROV	Caroline	Gilbert	Mariana	Marshall	POLY.UNPROV.	Austral	Chatham	Cook	Easter	Hawaii	Marquesas	New Zealand	Niue	Pitcairn	Samoa	Society	Tokelau	Tonga	Tuamotu	Tuvalu
cord																																							
raw mate																																							
-sling,st	1																																						
-arrow	1																																						
-bow																																							
-shield																																							
-dagger																																							
-spearthr																																							
-spear																																							
-club		1	1					2					1																		X						1*		
WEAPON																				X	1*																		
-float,si																																							
-net																																							
-spear																				X																			
-fishhook	1							1				2			2																				X				
FISHING																																							
hunting																																							
-model																																							
-ornament																															1								
-paddle	X																																						
NAVIGATIO																																							
-barkclot																																							
-weaving																																							
-needle,a																																							
-chisel																																							
-rasp																																							
-grinding																																							
-pounding																																							
-adze		X																																					
TOOL																																							
fire,lig																																							
smoking p																																							
pottery																																							
utensil																																							
lime spa																																							
dish,vess														1																									
lime con																																							

DUNDEE

Name Central Museum and Art Gallery

Address Albert Square
Dundee DD1 1DA

Telephone 0382-25492/3

Contact Keeper of Antiquities

Sources & Dates of Information

R. Hutchings 1966

Visit GSP 1974

MEG 1978

Letter

Notes

Dates of Collection/Acquisition	Donors/Collectors/Former Owners
Acquired mainly 1870-1970	

Documentation

Library, archival, photographic.

Comment

Central Museum

DUNDEE

Artefact → / Provenance ↓	TOTAL	OTHER	barkcloth	CLOTHING	-skirt	-belt	-cloak	PERS. ORN.	-head	-ear,nose	-arm	-neck,breast	comb	fan	toilet app.	staff,stick	CERE. OBJ.	-mask	-board	-adze	-paddle	-bullroarer	carving	fig.,image	magic,med.	charm	MUSICAL IN.	-drum,gong	-flute,pipe	-rattle	currency	transport	headrest	mat	basket	bag	box
OCEANIA UN.	20																																				
AUSTRALIA																																					
MELA. UNPROV.																																					
Admiralty																																					
Banks																																					
Bismarck																																					
D'Entrecast.																																					
Fiji																																					
Louisiade																																					
Loyalty																																					
N. Britain																																					
N. Caledonia																																					
N. Guinea	X																																				
N. Hebrides																																					
N. Ireland																																					
Santa Cruz																																					
Solomon																																					
Trobriand																																					
MICRO. UNPROV																																					
Caroline																																					
Gilbert																																					
Mariana																																					
Marshall																																					
POLY. UNPROV.																																					
Austral																																					
Chatham																																					
Cook	8																																				
Easter																																					
Hawaii	10																																				
Marquesas																																					
New Zealand	9																																				
Niue																																					
Pitcairn																																					
Samoa																																					
Society																																					
Tokelau																																					
Tonga																																					
Tuamotu																																					
Tuvalu																																					

Central Museum DUNDEE

Artefact ↑ / Provenance →	OCEANIA UN.	AUSTRALIA	MELA.UNPROV.	Admiralty	Banks	Bismarck	D'Entrecast.	Fiji	Louisiade	Loyalty	N. Britain	N. Caledonia	N. Guinea	N. Hebrides	N. Ireland	Santa Cruz	Solomon	Trobriand	MICRO.UNPROV	Caroline	Gilbert	Mariana	Marshall	POLY.UNPROV.	Austral	Chatham	Cook	Easter	Hawaii	Marquesas	New Zealand	Niue	Pitcairn	Samoa	Society	Tokelau	Tonga	Tuamotu	Tuvalu
cord																																							
raw mater																																							
-sling,st																																							
-arrow																																							
-bow																																							
-shield																																							
-dagger																																							
-spearthr																																							
-spear																																							
-club																																							
WEAPON																																							
-float,si																																							
-net																																							
-spear																																							
-fishhook																																							
FISHING																																							
hunting																																							
-model																																							
-ornament																																							
-paddle																																							
NAVIGATIO																																							
-barkclot																																							
-weaving																																							
-needle,a																																							
-chisel																																							
-rasp																																							
-grinding																																							
-pounding																																							
-adze																																							
TOOL																																							
fire,ligh																																							
smoking pi																																							
pottery																																							
utensil																																							
lime spat																																							
dish,vess																																							
lime cont.																																							

Name	D.L.I. Museum and Arts Centre
Address	Aykley Heads Durham DH1 5TU
Telephone	0385-2214
Contact	Keeper

DURHAM (DLI)

Sources & Dates of Information

R. Hutchings 1966

Visit

MEG 1978

Letters 1979

Notes

New Zealand: tewhatewha 1, collected 1864-66
photo album (Maori portraits, Tauranga, etc.)
watercolours by Lt. Horatio Gordon Robley (1864)

Dates of Collection/Acquisition	Donors/Collectors/Former Owners
	Durham Light Infantry Regiment

Documentation

Archival, photographic, iconographic.

Catalogue.

Comment

Robley material interesting and important.

Name	Gulbenkian Museum of Oriental Art
Address	Elvet Hill Durham DH1 3TH
Telephone	0385-66711
Contact	Curator

DURHAM (GULB)

Sources & Dates of Information

R. Hutchings 1966

Visit

MEG 1978

Letter 1979

Notes

Dates of Collection/Acquisition

Acquired mainly 1952+

Donors/Collectors/Former Owners

Documentation

Library, archival, photographic, iconographic.

Comment

Gulbenkian Museum of Oriental Art

DURHAM (GULB.

Artefact → / Provenance	OCEANIA UN.	AUSTRALIA	MELA.UNPROV.	Admiralty	Banks	Bismarck	D'Entrecast.	Fiji	Louisiade	Loyalty	N. Britain	N. Caledonia	N. Guinea	N. Hebrides	N. Ireland	Santa Cruz	Solomon	Trobriand	MICRO.UNPROV	Caroline	Gilbert	Mariana	Marshall	POLY.UNPROV.	Austral	Chatham	Cook	Easter	Hawaii	Marquesas	New Zealand	Niue	Pitcairn	Samoa	Society	Tokelau	Tonga	Tuamotu	Tuvalu
box																																							
bag																																							
basket																																							
mat																																							
headrest																																							
transport																																							
currency																																							
-rattle																																							
-flute,pipe																																							
-drum,gong																																							
MUSICAL INST.																																							
charm																																							
magic,med.																																							
fig.,image																																							
carving																																							
-bullroarer																																							
-paddle																																							
-adze																											/												
-board																																							
-mask																																							
CERE. OBJ.																																							
staff,stick																																							
toilet app.																																		—					
fan																																							
comb																																							
-neck,breast																																							
-arm																																							
-ear,nose																																							
-head																																							
PERS. ORN.																																							
-cloak																																							
-belt																																							
-skirt																																							
CLOTHING																																							
barkcloth																																							
OTHER																																							
TOTAL								/																			/			/				/					

 DURHAM(GULB

Artefact → / Provenance	OCEANIA UN.	AUSTRALIA	MELA.UNPROV.	Admiralty	Banks	Bismarck	D'Entrecast.	Fiji	Louisiade	Loyalty	N. Britain	N. Caledonia	N. Guinea	N. Hebrides	N. Ireland	Santa Cruz	Solomon	Trobriand	MICRO.UNPROV	Caroline	Gilbert	Mariana	Marshall	POLY.UNPROV.	Austral	Chatham	Cook	Easter	Hawaii	Marquesas	New Zealand	Niue	Pitcairn	Samoa	Society	Tokelau	Tonga	Tuamotu	Tuvalu
cord																																							
raw mater																																							
-sling,st																																							
-arrow																																							
-bow																																							
-shield																																							
-dagger																																							
-spearthr																																							
-spear																																							
-club																																							
WEAPON								/																							/								
-float,si																																							
-net																																							
-spear																																							
-fishhook																																							
FISHING																																							
hunting																																							
-model																																							
-ornament																																							
-paddle																																							
NAVIGATI																																							
-barkclot																																							
-weaving																																							
-needle,a																																							
-chisel																																							
-rasp																																							
-grinding																																							
-pounding																																							
-adze																																							
TOOL																																							
fire,ligh																																							
smoking p																																							
pottery																																							
utensil																																							
lime spa																																							
dish,vess																																							
lime con																																							

Name	Osborne House
Address	East Cowes Isle of Wight PO32 6JY
Telephone	098382-292511
Contact	Steward

EAST COWES

Sources & Dates of Information

R. Hutchings 1966

Visit

MEG 1978

Letter 1979

Notes

Some articles made for presentation.

*Oceania-- other: 4 other items presented to Queen Victoria.

Dates of Collection/Acquisition	Donors/Collectors/Former Owners
	Collected by Queen'Victoria's children.

Documentation

Comment

Osborne House

EAST COWES

Artefact → / Provenance ↓	OCEANIA UN.	AUSTRALIA	MELA.UNPROV.	Admiralty	Banks	Bismarck	D'Entrecast.	Fiji	Louisiade	Loyalty	N. Britain	N. Caledonia	N. Guinea	N. Hebrides	N. Ireland	Santa Cruz	Solomon	Trobriand	MICRC.UNPROV	Caroline	Gilbert	Mariana	Marshall	POLY.UNPROV.	Austral	Chatham	Cook	Easter	Hawaii	Marquesas	New Zealand	Niue	Pitcairn	Samoa	Society	Tokelau	Tonga	Tuamotu	Tuvalu
box																																							
bag																																							
basket																																							
mat																																	1						
headrest																																							
transport																																							
currency																																							
-rattle																																							
-flute,pipe																																							
-drum,gong																																							
MUSICAL INS.																																							
charm																																							
magic,med.																																							
fig.,image																																							
carving																																							
-bullroarer																																							
-paddle																																							
-adze																																							
-board																																							
-mask																																							
CERE. OBJ.																																							
staff,stick																																							
toilet app.																																							
fan																																							
comb																																							
-neck,breast																																							
-arm																																							
-ear,nose																																							
-head																																							
PERS. ORN																																							
-cloak																															2								
-belt																															1								
-skirt																																							
CLOTHING																																							
barkcloth																																							
OTHER	4																																						
TOTAL	5+	1																													11+		1						

Osborne House

EAST COWES

Artefact → / Provenance →	OCEANIA UN.	AUSTRALIA	MELA.UNPROV.	Admiralty	Banks	Bismarck	D'Entrecast.	Fiji	Louisiade	Loyalty	N. Britain	N. Caledonia	N. Guinea	N. Hebrides	N. Ireland	Santa Cruz	Solomon	Trobriand	MICRO.UNPROV.	Caroline	Gilbert	Mariana	Marshall	POLY.UNPROV.	Austral	Chatham	Cook	Easter	Hawaii	Marquesas	New Zealand	Niue	Pitcairn	Samoa	Society	Tokelau	Tonga	Tuamotu	Tuvalu
cord	X																																						
raw mater		1																													X								
-sling,st																																							
-arrow																																							
-bow																																							
-shield																																							
-dagger																																							
-spearthr																																							
-spear																																							
-club																															2								
WEAPON																																							
-float,sa																																							
-net																																							
-spear																																							
-fishhook																															5								
FISHING																																							
hunting																																							
-model																																							
-ornament																																							
-paddle																																							
NAVIGATIO																																							
-barkclot																																							
-weaving																																							
-needle,a																																							
-chisel																																							
-rasp																																							
-grinding																																							
-pounding																																							
-adze																																							
TOOL																																							
fire,ligh																																							
smoking pi																																							
pottery																																							
utensil																																							
lime spat																																							
dish,vess																																							
lime cont																																							

Name: Edinburgh University Collection of Historic Musical Instruments

Address: Faculty of Music
Reid School of Music
Teviot Row
Edinburgh EH8

Telephone: 031-667 1011 (ext. 2573)

Contact: Faculty of Music, Alison House, Nicolson Square, Edinburgh EH8 9BH (tel. 031-6671011, ext. 2572)

EDINBURGH (MUSIC)

Sources & Dates of Information

R. Hutchings 1966
Visit

MEG 1978
Letter

Notes

Oceania: 2 objects

Disposals: Some pre-1900 instruments given to Royal Scottish Museum at end of last century.

Dates of Collection/Acquisition	Donors/Collectors/Former Owners
Collected from 1860 Acquired before 1900	Galpin Collection

Documentation

Comment

Name Royal Scottish Museum	EDINBURGH (RSM)
Address Chambers Street Edinburgh EH1 1JF	Sources & Dates of Information R. Hutchings 1969 Visits PG 1970, DRS 1978 MEG 1978
Telephone 031-225 7534	Letter
Contact Assistant Keeper of Ethnography	UNESCO I questionnaire 1970

Notes

400 of Oceanic specimens are pre-1850.

*New Guinea-- includes 35 West Irian, that is, the detailed objects under New Guinea on table, excepting 1 figure; and 165 Papua.
*New Zealand-- mus. instrument: shell trumpet
utensil: funnel
tools: agricultural 1, stone implements 2
navigation: uncertain whether 2 canoes included here are models or full size, but probably models.
clubs: patu (unspecified) 3,paraoa 6, onewa 6, tewhatewha 4, pounamu 3, wahaika 6, hoeroa 2, patuki 1, kotiate 2, hani/taiaha 12.

Dates of Collection/Acquisition	Donors/Collectors/Former Owners
	Society of Antiquaries of Scotland Cook Sir Thomas Brisbane, 1826, Australia Beechey, expedition, 1825-6

Documentation

Library, photographic.

Comment

Important collection. Good display.

Royal Scottish Museum

EDINBURGH (RS.

Provenance ↓ / Artefact →	TOTAL	OTHER	barkcloth	CLOTHING	-skirt	-belt	-cloak	PERS. ORN.	-head	-ear,nose	-arm	-neck,breast	comb	fan	toilet app.	staff,stick	CERE. OBJ.	-mask	-board	-adze	-paddle	-bullroarer	carving	fig.,image	magic,med.	charm	MUSICAL INS.	-drum,gong	-flute,pipe	-rattle	currency	transport	headrest	mat	basket	bag	box
OCEANIA UN.																																					
AUSTRALIA																																					
MELA.UNPROV.	39																																				
Admiralty	8																																				
Banks																																					
Bismarck																																					
D'Entrecast.																																					
Fiji	380																																				
Louisiade																																					
Loyalty	45																																				
N. Britain	31																																				
N. Caledonia	163																																				
N. Guinea	308*												1											2		1		1	1				1				
N. Hebrides	410																																				
N. Ireland	44																																				
Santa Cruz																																					
Solomon	417																																				
Trobriand	488																																				
MICRO.UNPROV.	26																																				
Caroline	63																																				
Gilbert	56																																				
Mariana																																					
Marshall																																					
POLY.UNPROV.	131																																				
Austral	20																																				
Chatham																																					
Cook	77																																				
Easter	28																																				
Hawaii	82																																				
Marquesas	59																																				
New Zealand	190	6	1	3			11	11		6		10				4	1						12			5	1*		4						7	1	15
Niue	41																																				
Pitcairn																																					
Samoa	88																																				
Society	99																																				
Tokelau																																					
Tonga	73																																				
Tuamotu	12																																				
Tuvalu	22																																				

Royal Scottish Museum

EDINBURGH (RSM)

Provenance ↓ / Artefact →	lime cont	dish,vess	lime spa	utensil	pottery	smokng p	fire,lig	TOOL	-adze	-pounding	-grinding	-rasp	-chisel	-needle,a	-weaving	-barkclot	NAVIGATIO	-paddle	-ornamen	-model	hunting	FISHING	-fishhook	-spear	-net	-float,s	WEAPON	-club	-spear	-spearthr	-dagger	-shield	-bow	-arrow	-sling,s	raw mate	cord
OCEANIA UW.																																					
AUSTRALIA																																					
MELA.UNPROV.																																					
Admiralty																																					
Banks																																					
Bismarck																																					
D'Entrecast.																																					
Fiji																																					
Louisiade																																					
Loyalty																																					
N. Britain																																					
N. Caledonia																																					
N. Guinea									1									2	2			1							2			1	1	21			
N. Hebrides																																					
N. Ireland																																					
Santa Cruz																																					
Solomon																																					
Trobriand																																					
MICRO.UNPROV																																					
Caroline																																					
Gilbert																																					
Mariana																																					
Marshall																																					
POLY.UNPROV.																																					
Austral																																					
Chatham																																					
Cook																																					
Easter																																					
Hawaii																																					
Marquesas																																					
New Zealand		1		1*				3	7	3			1	1	1		6*	5	2	1	3	2	9			4	1	45*	1								1
Niue																																					
Pitcairn																																					
Samoa																																					
Society																																					
Tokelau																																					
Tonga																																					
Tuamotu																																					
Tuvalu																																					

Name	Elgin Museum (Moray Society)	ELGIN
Address	1 High Street Elgin Morayshire IV30 1EQ	**Sources & Dates of Information** R. Hutchings 1966 Visit MEG 1978 Letters 1979
Telephone	0343-3675	
Contact	Curator	

Notes

Disposals: Much to other museums, and private collector. No records found.

*Australia-- other: boomerang 1, "bone stake & kangaroo sinew- garotte"- trapping device?

Dates of Collection/Acquisition	Donors/Collectors/Former Owners
Mainly 19th Century	Natives of Morayshire travelling abroad as missionaries, tourists, governors, etc.

Documentation

Comment

The best items are clubs, adzes and some Fijian.

Artefact → / Provenance ↓	TOTAL	OTHER	barkcloth	CLOTHING	-skirt	-belt	-cloak	PERS. ORN.	-head	-ear,nose	-arm	-neck,breast	comb	fan	toilet app.	staff,stick	CERE. OBJ.	-mask	-board	-adze	-paddle	-bullroarer	carving	fig.,image	magic,med.	charm	MUSICAL INS.	-drum,gong	-flute,pipe	-rattle	currency	transport	headrest	mat	basket	bag	box
OCEANIA UN.	2																																				
AUSTRALIA	3	2																																			
MELA.UNPROV.																																					
Admiralty																																					
Banks																																					
Bismarck																																					
D'Entrecast.																																					
Fiji	15											2																					2				
Louisiade																																					
Loyalty																																					
N. Britain																																					
N. Caledonia																																					
N. Guinea																																					
N. Hebrides	1																																				
N. Ireland																																					
Santa Cruz																																					
Solomon	2																																				
Trobriand																																					
MICRO.UNPROV.																																					
Caroline																																					
Gilbert																																					
Mariana																																					
Marshall																																					
POLY.UNPROV.																																					
Austral																																					
Chatham																																					
Cook	6																			5																	
Easter																																					
Hawaii																																					
Marquesas																																					
New Zealand	6+		1	2			1																												X		
Niue																																					
Pitcairn																																					
Samoa	1		1																																		
Society																																					
Tokelau																																					
Tonga																																					
Tuamotu																																					
Tuvalu																																					
Tahiti	4		1																															1			

Elgin Museum

ELGIN

Provenance ↓ / Artefact →	lime cont.	dish, vesse.	lime spat.	utensil	pottery	smokng pip	fire, light	TOOL	-adze	-pounding	-grinding	-rasp	-chisel	-needle, aw	-weaving	-barkcloth	NAVIGATION	-paddle	-ornament	-model	hunting	FISHING	-fishhook	-spear	-net	-float, sin	WEAPON	-club	-spear	-spearthro	-dagger	-shield	-bow	-arrow	-sling, sto	raw mater	cord
OCEANIA UN.		1		1																																	
AUSTRALIA																																1					
MELA. UNPROV.																																					
Admiralty																																					
Banks																																					
Bismarck																																					
D'Entrecast.																																					
Fiji		2			5											1												2									1
Louisiade																																					
Loyalty																																					
N. Britain																																					
N. Caledonia																																					
N. Guinea																																					
N. Hebrides																												1									
N. Ireland																																					
Santa Cruz																																					
Solomon																												2									
Trobriand																																					
MICRO. UNPROV.																																					
Caroline																																					
Gilbert																																					
Mariana																																					
Marshall																																					
POLY. UNPROV.																																					
Austral																																					
Chatham																																					
Cook									1																												
Easter																																					
Hawaii																																					
Marquesas																																					
New Zealand																				1																	
Niue																																					
Pitcairn																																					
Samoa																																					
Society																																					
Tokelau																																					
Tonga																																					
Tuamotu																																					
Tuvalu																																					
Tahiti																							2														
Rotuma																																					

Name	Exeter Maritime Museum	EXETER (MM)
Address	ISCA Ltd. The Quay Exeter EX2 4AN	Sources & Dates of Information
		R. Hutchings 1966
		Visit
Telephone	0392-58075/36031	MEG 1978
Contact	Director	Letters 1979

Notes

*Australia-- surfing boat 1, post-European
*New Guinea-- Papuan outrigger 1
*Fiji-- outrigger (proa) 1
*Gilberts-- outrigger (proa) 1, built for & donated by Dr. Denny, Gloucester
*Tonga-- canoe 1, collected 1977
*Tuvalu-- te baobao 1, shows European influence
*Samoa-- outrigger from Upola(?)

Dates of Collection/Acquisition	Donors/Collectors/Former Owners
Acquired 1966-78+	

Documentation

Library, sound recordings, films, photographic.

Museum publication: Catalogue (list of boats), 20p.
Brochure, 60p.

Comment

Exeter Maritime Museum

EXETER (MM,

Provenance \ Artefact	TOTAL	OTHER	barkcloth	CLOTHING	-skirt	-belt	-cloak	PERS. ORN.	-head	-ear,nose	-arm	-neck,breast	comb	fan	toilet app.	staff,stick	CERE. OBJ.	-mask	-board	-adze	-paddle	-bullroarer	carving	fig.,image	magic,med.	charm	MUSICAL INS.	-drum,gong	-flute,pipe	-rattle	currency	transport	headrest	mat	basket	bag	box
OCEANIA UN.																																					
AUSTRALIA	/																																				
MELA.UNPROV.																																					
Admiralty																																					
Banks																																					
Bismarck																																					
D'Entrecast.																																					
Fiji	/																																				
Louisiade																																					
Loyalty																																					
N. Britain																																					
N. Caledonia																																					
N. Guinea	/																																				
N. Hebrides																																					
N. Ireland																																					
Santa Cruz																																					
Solomon																																					
Trobriand																																					
MICRO.UNPROV																																					
Caroline																																					
Gilbert	/																																				
Mariana																																					
Marshall																																					
POLY.UNPROV.																																					
Austral																																					
Chatham																																					
Cook																																					
Easter																																					
Hawaii																																					
Marquesas																																					
New Zealand																																					
Niue																																					
Pitcairn																																					
Samoa	/																																				
Society																																					
Tokelau																																					
Tonga	/																																				
Tuamotu																																					
Tuvalu	/																																				

Exeter Maritime Museum

EXETER (MM)

Artefact → / Provenance	OCEANIA UN.	AUSTRALIA	MELA.UNPROV.	Admiralty	Banks	Bismarck	D'Entrecast.	Fiji	Louisiade	Loyalty	N. Britain	N. Caledonia	N. Guinea	N. Hebrides	N. Ireland	Santa Cruz	Solomon	Trobriand	MICRO.UNPROV.	Caroline	Gilbert	Mariana	Marshall	POLY.UNPROV.	Austral	Chatham	Cook	Easter	Hawaii	Marquesas	New Zealand	Niue	Pitcairn	Samoa	Society	Tokelau	Tonga	Tuamotu	Tuvalu
cord																																							
raw mater.																																							
-sling,sto																																							
-arrow																																							
-bow																																							
-shield																																							
-dagger																																							
-spearthro																																							
-spear																																							
-club																																							
WEAPON																																							
-float,sin																																							
-net																																							
-spear																																							
-fishhook																																							
FISHING																																							
hunting																																							
-model																																							
-ornament																																							
-paddle																																							
NAVIGATION																																							
-barkcloth		1*						1*					1*								1*													1*			1*		1*
-weaving																																							
-needle,aw.																																							
-chisel																																							
-rasp																																							
-grinding																																							
-pounding																																							
-adze																																							
TOOL																																							
fire,light																																							
smoking pip																																							
pottery																																							
utensil																																							
lime spat.																																							
dish,vesse																																							
lime cont.																																							

EXETER (RAMM)

Name Royal Albert Memorial Museum

Address Queen Street
Exeter EX4 3RX

Telephone 0392-56724

Contact Curator of Antiquities

Sources & Dates of Information

R. Hutchings 1966

Visit {PG 1978+ / ALK

MEG 1978

Letters 1975

Catalogue 1973

Notes

Possibly more Melanesian arrows, paddles and clubs than recorded here.

*Oceania-- figure: "Tarri" Island: possibly Tami Island? (New Guinea)
*Fiji-- toilet apparatus: tattooing
other: misc. 1
Gilberts-- weapons: 3 coconut fibre tunics, helmet
*Hawaii-- spear: spear rest
*Marquesas-- carvings: stilt steps
ceremonial objects: clubs

*Tahiti-- clothing: incomplete mourning dress; dance costume
toilet apparatus: tattooing
fishooks: 8 unfinished
physical anthropology: 2
*Polynesia unprovenanced-- other: flywhisk
*New Zealand-- other: misc. 1
clubs: taiaha/hani 15, patu paraoa 3, patu onewa 4, wood patu 4

Dates of Collection/Acquisition

1868-1930 (main period of acquisition), 1977+

Donors/Collectors/Former Owners

Devon Institute Collection (1813-1868)
Plymouth City Museum
F.W. Ross
L.D. Montague
Royal Navy officers
Cook

Documentation

Library, archival, photographic, iconographic, records, films.

Museum publication: Pearce, 1973, Arts of Polynesia (40p).

Comment

Good, well-maintained collection, including some Cook (Vaughan). Not sure what derives from Devon Institute.

Royal Albert Memorial Museum

EXETER (R

Artefact → / Provenance →

Artefact	OCEANIA UN.	AUSTRALIA	MELA. UNPROV.	Admiralty	Banks	Bismarck	D'Entrecast.	Fiji	Louisiade	Loyalty	N. Britain	N. Caledonia	N. Guinea	N. Hebrides	N. Ireland	Santa Cruz	Solomon	Trobriand
box																		
bag																		
basket																		
mat																		
headrest								1										
transport																		
currency																		
-rattle				1														
-flute, pipe																		
-drum, gong													6					
MUSICAL INS.																		
charm																		
magic, med.																		
fig., image	1*												1					
carving																		
-bullroarer													1					
-paddle																		
-adze																		
-board													4					
-mask													1	2				
CERE. OBJ.													2					
staff, stick																		
toilet app.								2*										
fan																		
comb				1										1			4	
-neck, breast				2				1									3	
-arm								8						1			1	
-ear, nose																		
-head								1						4				
PERS. ORN.								5						1			1	
-cloak																		
-belt													1					
-skirt											2			1				
CLOTHING								1						2				
barkcloth																		
OTHER								1										
TOTAL	1			28				79			29							

Artefact	MICRO. UNPROV.	Caroline	Gilbert	Mariana	Marshall	POLY. UNPROV.	Austral	Chatham	Cook	Easter	Hawaii	Marquesas	New Zealand	Niue	Pitcairn	Samoa	Society	Tokelau	Tonga	Tuamotu	Tuvalu
box													1								
bag													1			1					
basket																1					
mat													1			1					
headrest																			1		
transport																					
currency																					
-rattle																					
-flute, pipe																1					
-drum, gong																1					
MUSICAL INS.																					
charm																					
magic, med.																					
fig., image										2											
carving												3*	1								
-bullroarer																					
-paddle																					
-adze									3												
-board																					
-mask																					
CERE. OBJ.												2*				1					
staff, stick										3	2		4								
toilet app.																					
fan																5					
comb																			2		
-neck, breast										1	3					3					
-arm											1					1					
-ear, nose													4								
-head											1										
PERS. ORN.						8					2		2			2					
-cloak											1		3								
-belt																					
-skirt																2					
CLOTHING													1			2					
barkcloth									1		1		1			4			3		
OTHER						1							2								
TOTAL																					

Royal Albert Memorial Museum

EXETER (RAMM

Artefact → / Provenance →	OCEANIA UN.	AUSTRALIA	MELA.UNPROV.	Admiralty	Banks	Bismarck	D'Entrecast.	Fiji	Louisiade	Loyalty	N. Britain	N. Caledonia	N. Guinea	N. Hebrides	N. Ireland	Santa Cruz	Solomon	Trobriand	MICRO.UNPROV.	Caroline	Gilbert	Mariana	Marshall	POLY.UNPROV.	Austral	Chatham	Cook	Easter	Hawaii	Marquesas	New Zealand	Niue	Pitcairn	Samoa	Society	Tokelau	Tonga	Tuamotu	Tuvalu	Tahiti	Torres Strait
cord																																								7	
raw mate																										1				2											
-sling,s										1																															
-arrow-												SD 300																												X
-bow-																																				2				
-shield-																	1																							
-dagger-				6								1																1												
-spearth																																									
-spear				7																				1		3		1*		1										
-club-				7				52			25		57	1		5	15							1				2		2	32*			10			13				
WEAPON																					4*																			2	
-float,s																																									
-net-																																									
-spear-								1																							2										
-fishhoo																	1						1	1					4		1				1*		1			4	
FISHING																																		1							
hunting																																									
-model-																															1			3							
-ornamen				2													1														1										
-paddle-																	5								13					3											
NAVIGAT																															2										
-barkclo																													2											2	
-weaving																																									
-needle,																																									
-chisel-																												1			4						1				
-rasp-				1																																					
-grindin																																									
-poundin																																									
-adze-				1				3			1		4	5			2							4			2		2		21						2			5	
TOOL													x				1											4			2									1	
fire,lig																																									
smoking p													2																												1
pottery														1																											
utensil																															1									2	
lime spa													12																												
dish,ves								3					3																					1							
lime con																																									

FORRES

Name: Falconer Museum

Address: Tolbooth Street
Forres
Morayshire IV36 OPH

Telephone: 0309-73701

Contact: District Curator

Sources & Dates of Information

R. Hutchings 1966

Visit

MEG 1978

Letter 1979

Notes

Dates of Collection/Acquisition	Donors/Collectors/Former Owners
	Constance Gordon-Cumming, collected 1868-1880, Fiji

Documentation

Archival, iconographic.

Comment

Note link with C. Gordon-Cumming, who was in Fiji with Sir Arthur Gordon and Anatole von Hügel (1875-77?), and also in New Zealand.

Falconer Museum

FORRES

Artifact → / Provenance →	OCEANIA UN.	AUSTRALIA	MELA.UNPROV.	Admiralty	Banks	Bismarck	D'Entrecast.	Fiji	Louisiade	Loyalty	N. Britain	N. Caledonia	N. Guinea	N. Hebrides	N. Ireland	Santa Cruz	Solomon	Trobriand	MICRO.UNPROV.	Caroline	Gilbert	Mariana	Marshall	POLY.UNPROV.	Austral	Chatham	Cook	Easter	Hawaii	Marquesas	New Zealand	Niue	Pitcairn	Samoa	Society	Tokelau	Tonga	Tuamotu	Tuvalu
box																																							
bag																																							
basket																																							
mat																																							
headrest								X																															
transport																																							
currency																																							
-rattle																																							
-flute,pipe																																							
-drum,gong																																							
MUSICAL IN.																																							
charm																																							
magic,med.																																							
fig.,image																																							
carving																																							
-bullroarer																																							
-paddle																																							
-adze																																							
-board																																							
-mask																																							
CERE. OBJ.																																							
staff,stick																																							
toilet app.																																							
fan																																							
comb																																							
-neck,breast																																							
-arm																																							
-ear,nose																																							
-head																																							
PERS. ORN																																							
-cloak																																							
-belt																																							
-skirt																																							
CLOTHING																																							
barkcloth																																							
OTHER																																							
TOTAL								18																															

Falconer Museum

FORRES

Artefact → / Provenance →	OCEANIA UN.	AUSTRALIA	MELA.UNPROV.	Admiralty	Banks	Bismarck	D'Entrecast.	Fiji	Louisiade	Loyalty	N. Britain	N. Caledonia	N. Guinea	N. Hebrides	N. Ireland	Santa Cruz	Solomon	Trobriand	MICRO.UNPROV	Caroline	Gilbert	Mariana	Marshall	POLY.UNPROV.	Austral	Chatham	Cook	Easter	Hawaii	Marquesas	New Zealand	Niue	Pitcairn	Samoa	Society	Tokelau	Tonga	Tuamotu	Tuvalu
cord																																							
raw mater								X																															
-sling,sto																																							
-arrow																																							
-bow																																							
-shield																																							
-dagger																																							
-spearthro																																							
-spear																																							
-club																																							
WEAPON																																							
-float,si																																							
-net																																							
-spear																																							
-fishhook																																							
FISHING																																							
hunting																																							
-model																																							
-ornament																																							
-paddle																																							
NAVIGATIO																																							
-barkclot								X																															
-weaving																																							
-needle,a																																							
-chisel																																							
-rasp																																							
-grinding																																							
-pounding																																							
-adze								X																															
TOOL																																							
fire,ligh								X																															
smoking pi																																							
pottery								X																															
utensil																																							
lime spat																																							
dish,vess								X																															
lime cont																																							

GLASGOW (H)

Name Hunterian Museum and Art Gallery

Address University of Glasgow
Glasgow G12 8QQ

Telephone 041-339 8855

Contact Director

Sources & Dates of Information

R. Hutchings 1966

Visits ALK) PGS 1977
DRS 1978

MEG 1978

Letters 1976, 1979

Notes

For table explanatory notes, see Hunterian (B).

Dates of Collection/Acquisition	Donors/Collectors/Former Owners
	Cook, Hunter

Documentation

Comment

Important collection. Recently re-organised.

Hunterian Museum and Art Gallery

GLASGOW

Provenance \ Artefact	TOTAL	OTHER	barkcloth	CLOTHING	-skirt	-belt	-cloak	PERS. ORN.	-head	-ear,nose	-arm	-neck,breast	comb	fan	toilet app.	staff,stick	CERE. OBJ.	-mask	-board	-adze	-paddle	-bullroarer	carving	fig.,image	magic,med.	charm	MUSICAL INS.	-drum,gong	-flute,pipe	-rattle	currency	transport	headrest	mat	basket	bag	box
OCEANIA UN.	111				4	7		1	5	1	4	2						1									1*	1						19	2		
AUSTRALIA	217	22				4		10	1	2		3				4*						32	8		6		2										
MELA.UNPROV.	37			1					1				1															1								1	
Admiralty																																					
Banks																																					
Bismarck																																					
D'Entrecast.																																					
Fiji	54	1			1						1					1	2													1							
Louisiade																																					
Loyalty	7				1																								3								
N. Britain																																					
N. Caledonia	20										1																									2	
N. Guinea	104			2	2	5		1	5	7	11	11	3					2									2*								2	9	
N. Hebrides	37										9*	3	1		1																					1	
N. Ireland																																					
Santa Cruz	1																													1							
Solomon	53				4	1		1																2												2	
Trobriand																																					
MICRO.UNPROV.	1																																				
Caroline	1																																				
Gilbert	6																																				
Mariana																																					
Marshall																																					
POLY.UNPROV.	16												1		1*	1													3								
Austral	3																											1									
Chatham																																					
Cook	55	2																		1				4													
Easter	1																																				
Hawaii	13				3																			1				1							4		
Marquesas																																					
New Zealand	53	11															11						9	3			1*							1			
Niue	9																												4*								
Pitcairn																																					
Samoa	75	1		1		2							2	2			4										1*						4			3	
Society																																					
Tokelau	1																																				
Tonga	20	1		4		1	1						2																							1	
Tuamotu																																					
Tuvalu																																					
Kermadec	1																																				

Hunterian Museum and Art Gallery

GLASGOW (H)

Provenance ↓ / Artefact →	cord	raw mater	-sling,st	-arrow	-bow	-shield	-dagger	-spearthr	-spear	-club	WEAPON	-float,si	-net	-spear	-fishhook	FISHING	hunting	-model	-ornament	-paddle	NAVIGATIO	-barkclot	-weaving	-needle,a	-chisel	-rasp	-grinding	-pounding	-adze	TOOL	fire,ligh	smoking pi	pottery	utensil	lime spat	dish,vess	lime cont.
OCEANIA UN.	1		1		2				38	4	5											2							4	1					5		
AUSTRALIA		1			11	6		34	33	18	1			2			1							2	1				6	4						3	
MELA.UNPROV.	1			12	1	1				14										1										1		1					
Admiralty							2																														
Banks																																					
Bismarck															3																						
D'Entrecast.																																					
Fiji	1	2								15																			6				23				
Louisiade																																					
Loyalty										3*																											
N. Britain																																					
N. Caledonia										14																			1						1		1
N. Guinea				X	2			2		3	10		1		1								2*						4	2		1	1	1	2*		
N. Hebrides				2	17					3																											
N. Ireland																																					
Santa Cruz																																					
Solomon				28	5					3	3		1					3																			
Trobriand																																					
MICRO.UNPROV.																																					1
Caroline	1																																				
Gilbert									1		54																										
Mariana																																					
Marshall																																					
POLY.UNPROV.										7										1.		1*							1								
Austral																				1														1			
Chatham																																					
Cook			3	X							2				3					32*								3	3					1		2	
Easter																				1																	
Hawaii																													2							2	
Marquesas																																					
New Zealand							1			8																		1	7								
Niue										1										2									2								
Pitcairn																																					
Samoa	5	3							21	1*					19			1		1								1		2							
Society																																					
Tokelau																														1							
Tonga	3									4			1			1													1								
Tuamotu																																					
Tuvalu																																					
Kermadec																															1						
Tah.it.							2								1													3	1								

GLASGOW (A

Hunterian Museum and Art Gallery (B)

*Oceania-- mus. instrument: jewsharp
other: cloth sample

*Australia-- sticks: message
other: boomerangs 19, toy, flint implements, misc. 1

*Fiji-- other: cloth

*New Guinea-- lime spatulae: 3 also combination pounders
weaving: 1 tool also spatula
mus. instrument: jewsharps

*Loyalty-- clubs: Fijian origin

*New Hebrides-- arm ornaments: 2 Hawaiian?

*Gilberts-- weapons: 1 armour

*Polynesia unprovenanced-- toilet apparatus: tattooing
barkcloth tool: Polynesia or Fiji

*Cook-- paddles: 3 possibly Australs
other: flywhisks (or Australs?), cloth 1

*New Zealand-- mus. instrument: 'bugle'
other: heads 11

*Niue-- flute, pipe: 1 possibly Admiralty

*Samoa-- mus. instrument: shell trumpet
club: or Marquesas
other: flywhisk

*Tonga-- other: hammock

Name Glasgow Museums and Art Galleries	BLASGOW (M+AG)
Address Art Gallery and Museum Kelvingrove Glasgow G3 8AG	Sources & Dates of Information
	R. Hutchings 1966
	Visit PG 1970
Telephone 041-334 1134	MEG 1978
Contact Keeper, Archaeology, Ethnography and History	Letter Questionnaire 1970

Notes

*New Guinea-- includes 579 from Papua.
*Gilberts-- weapons: includes armour.

Dates of Collection/Acquisition	Donors/Collectors/Former Owners
	Bloxam 1825

Documentation

Reference: Barrow, 1959, Anthropology in the South Seas, esp. Maori human figure.

Comment

Important. Coupled with Hunterian, this makes Glasgow important centre for Scotland. Note Bloxam (HMS Blonde 1825) material from Hawaii.

Art Gallery and Museum

GLASGOW (H+A

Provenance ↓ / Artefact →	TOTAL	OTHER	barkcloth	CLOTHING	-skirt	-belt	-cloak	PERS. ORN.	-head	-ear,nose	-arm	-neck,breast	comb	fan	toilet app.	staff,stick	CERE. OBJ.	-mask	-board	-adze	-paddle	-bullroarer	carving	fig.,image	magic,med.	charm	MUSICAL INS.	-drum,gong	-flute,pipe	-rattle	currency	transport	headrest	mat	basket	bag	box
OCEANIA UN.																																					
AUSTRALIA																																					
MELA.UNPROV.																																					
Admiralty																																					
Banks																																					
Bismarck																																					
D'Entrecast.																																					
Fiji	190																																				
Louisiade																																					
Loyalty																																					
N. Britain																																					
N. Caledonia	79																																				
N. Guinea	1169*																																				
N. Hebrides	200+																																				
N. Ireland																																					
Santa Cruz																																					
Solomon	323																																				
Trobriand																																					
MICRO.UNPROV.																																					
Caroline	4			X		1							X																								
Gilbert	14																																				
Mariana																																					
Marshall	6											X																									
POLY.UNPROV.																																					
Austral																																					
Chatham																																					
Cook	8											X		X																				X			
Easter	1																							1													
Hawaii	16		X																																		
Marquesas	16			X																																	
New Zealand	143																							1													
Niue																																					
Pitcairn	3		X																																		
Samoa	29		X										X	X																							
Society	5																																				
Tokelau																																					
Tonga	64																																				
Tuamotu																																					
Tuvalu	28			X									X																						X		

Art Gallery and Museum

GLASGOW (M+AG)

Artefact → / Provenance ↓	OCEANIA UN.	AUSTRALIA	MELA.UNPROV.	Admiralty	Banks	Bismarck	D'Entrecast.	Fiji	Louisiade	Loyalty	N. Britain	N. Caledonia	N. Guinea	N. Hebrides	N. Ireland	Santa Cruz	Solomon	Trobriand	MICRO.UNPROV.	Caroline	Gilbert	Mariana	Marshall	POLY.UNPROV.	Austral	Chatham	Cook	Easter	Hawaii	Marquesas	New Zealand	Niue	Pitcairn	Samoa	Society	Tokelau	Tonga	Tuamotu	Tuvalu
cord																																							
raw mater																																							
-sling,sto																																							
-arrow																																							
-bow																																							
-shield																																							
-dagger																																							
-spearthro																																							
-spear																																							
-club																														/				X					
WEAPON													X				X				X																		
-float,si																																							
-net																																							
-spear																																		X					
-fishhook																							X																X
FISHING																																							
hunting																																							
-model																																							
-ornament																															3								
-paddle																											X												
NAVIGATIO																																							
-barkclot																																							
-weaving																																							
-needle,aw																																							
-chisel																																							
-rasp																																							
-grinding																																							
-pounding																														X									
-adze																																							
TOOL																														X									
fire,ligh																																							
smoking pi																																							
pottery																																							
utensil																																							
lime spat																																							
dish,vess																																		X					
lime cont																																							

GODALMING

Name	Charterhouse (School) Museum
Address	High Street Godalming GU7 2DX Surrey
Telephone	04868-4104
Contact	Curator

Sources & Dates of Information

R. Hutchings 1966

Visit

MEG 1978

Letter 1979

Notes

Total between 50 & 100 objects.

Dates of Collection/Acquisition

Donors/Collectors/Former Owners

Documentation

Comment

Comment not yet possible.

Charterhouse(School) Museum GODALMING

Artifact →

Provenance →

Provenance	box	bag	basket	mat	headrest	transport	currency	rattle	-flute,pipe	-drum,gong	MUSICAL INS.	charm	magic,med.	fig.,image	carving	-bullroarer	-paddle	-adze	-board	-mask	CERE. OBJ.	staff,stick	toilet app.	fan	comb	-neck,breast	-arm	-ear,nose	-head	PERS. ORN.	-cloak	-belt	-skirt	CLOTHING	barkcloth	OTHER	TOTAL
OCEANIA UN.																																					100
AUSTRALIA																																					
MELA. UNPROV.																																					
Admiralty																																					
Banks																																					
Bismarck																																					
D'Entrecast.																																					
Fiji																																					
Louisiade																																					
Loyalty																																					
N. Britain																																					
N. Caledonia																																					
N. Guinea																																					
N. Hebrides																																					
N. Ireland																																					
Santa Cruz																																					
Solomon																																					
Trobriand																																					
MICRO. UNPROV																																					
Caroline																																					
Gilbert																																					
Mariana																																					
Marshall																																					
POLY. UNPROV.																																					
Austral																																					
Chatham																																					
Cook																																					
Easter																																					
Hawaii																																					
Marquesas																																					
New Zealand																																					
Niue																																					
Pitcairn																																					
Samoa																																					
Society																																					
Tokelau																																					
Tonga																																					
Tuamotu																																					
Tuvalu																																					

Charterhouse(School) Museum

GODALMING

Artefact → / Provenance →	OCEANIA UN.	AUSTRALIA	MELA.UNPROV.	Admiralty	Banks	Bismarck	D'Entrecast.	Fiji	Louisiade	Loyalty	N. Britain	N. Caledonia	N. Guinea	N. Hebrides	N. Ireland	Santa Cruz	Solomon	Trobriand	MICRO.UNPROV	Caroline	Gilbert	Mariana	Marshall	POLY.UNPROV.	Austral	Chatham	Cook	Easter	Hawaii	Marquesas	New Zealand	Niue	Pitcairn	Samoa	Society	Tokelau	Tonga	Tuamotu	Tuvalu
cord																																							
raw mate																																							
-sling,st																																							
-arrow																																							
-bow																																							
-shield																																							
-dagger																																							
-spearthr																																							
-spear																																							
-club																																							
WEAPON																																							
-float,si																																							
-net																																							
-spear																																							
-fishhook																																							
FISHING																																							
hunting																																							
-model																																							
-ornament																																							
-paddle																																							
NAVIGATIO																																							
-barkclot																																							
-weaving																																							
-needle,a																																							
-chisel																																							
-rasp																																							
-grinding																																							
-pounding																																							
-adze																																							
TOOL																																							
fire,ligh																																							
smoking pi																																							
pottery																																							
utensil																																							
lime spat																																							
dish,vess																																							
lime cont.																																							

Name: Thurrock Local History Museum	GRAYS
Address: Orsett Road Grays Thurrock Essex RM17 5DX	Sources & Dates of Information R. Hutchings 1966 Visit MEG 1978 Letter 1979
Telephone: 0375-76826	
Contact: Curator	

Notes

Disposals : Collections destroyed by bombing in 1944 and flooding in 1953. Some transfers probable too.

Dates of Collection/Acquisition	Donors/Collectors/Former Owners
Acquired 1927-34,	Sir Fielding Clarke, South Seas & Samoa, acquired 1930

Documentation

Museum publication: Revised catalogue of 1957 lists specimens, then no longer present.

Comment

Thurrock Local History Museum GRAYS

Artefact → / Provenance →	OCEANIA UN.	AUSTRALIA	MELA.UNPROV.	Admiralty	Banks	Bismarck	D'Entrecast.	Fiji	Louisiade	Loyalty	N. Britain	N. Caledonia	N. Guinea	N. Hebrides	N. Ireland	Santa Cruz	Solomon	Trobriand	MICRO.UNPROV	Caroline	Gilbert	Mariana	Marshall	POLY.UNPROV.	Austral	Chatham	Cook	Easter	Hawaii	Marquesas	New Zealand	Niue	Pitcairn	Samoa	Society	Tokelau	Tonga	Tuamotu	Tuvalu
cord																																							
raw mater.																																							
-sling,stone																																							
-arrow																																							
-bow																																							
-shield																																							
-dagger																																							
-spearthrowr																																							
-spear																																							
-club																																							
WEAPON	X																																	X					
-float,sinkr																																							
-net																																							
-spear																																		X					
-fishhook																																							
FISHING																																							
hunting																																							
-model																																							
-ornament																																							
-paddle																																							
NAVIGATION																																							
-barkcloth																																							
-weaving																																							
-needle,awl																																							
-chisel																																							
-rasp																																							
-grinding																																							
-pounding																																							
-adze																																							
TOOL																																							
fire,light																																							
smoking pipe																																							
pottery																																							
utensil																																							
lime spat.																																							
dish,vessel																																							
lime cont.																																							

Name McLean Museum and Art Gallery

Address 9 Union Street
Greenock PA16 9JH

Telephone 0475-23741

Contact Curator

GREENOCK

Sources & Dates of Information

R. Hutchings 1966

Visit

MEG 1978

Letters 1979

Notes

Total Oceanic roughly 200, plus about 300 unidentified ethnographic specimens.

*Australia-- other: boomerangs 4
*New Britain-- head ornaments: headdresses
weaving tools: loom 1, weaving sample 1

Dates of Collection/Acquisition

Acquired 1875-1925

New Britain items presented in 1894.

Donors/Collectors/Former Owners

The museum made a practice of inviting visiting ship captains to collect and deposit artefacts from voyages.

Documentation

Cataloguing begun in 1976. Previously objects catalogued without being numbered, so there is something of a muddle.

Comment

New Britain collection is clearly important.

McLean Museum and Art Gallery GREENOCK

Provenance ↓ / Artcfact →	box	bag	basket	mat	headrest	transport	currency	-rattle	-flute,pipe	-drum,gong	MUSICAL INS.	charm	magic,med.	fig.,image	carving	-bullroarer	-paddle	-adze	-board	-mask	CERE. OBJ.	staff,stick	toilet app.	fan	comb	neck,breast	-arm	-ear,nose	-head	PERS. ORN.	-cloak	-belt	-skirt	CLOTHING	barkcloth	OTHER	TOTAL
OCEANIA UN.																																					X
AUSTRALIA		X																																		4	X
MELA.UNPROV.																																					
Admiralty																																					
Banks																																					
Bismarck																																					
D'Entrecast.																																					
Fiji																																					X
Louisiade																																					
Loyalty																																					
N. Britain														1	1											X	X		4*			X					14+
N. Caledonia																																					
N. Guinea																																					
N. Hebrides																																					
N. Ireland																																					
Santa Cruz																																					
Solomon																																					
Trobriand																																					
MICRO.UNPROV.																																					
Caroline																																					
Gilbert																																					
Mariana																																					
Marshall																																					
POLY.UNPROV.																																					
Austral																																					
Chatham																																					
Cook																																					
Easter																																					
Hawaii																																					
Marquesas																																					
New Zealand																																					
Niue																																					
Pitcairn																																					
Samoa																																					
Society																																					
Tokelau																																					
Tonga																																					
Tuamotu																																					
Tuvalu																																					

McLean Museum and Art Gallery GREENOCK

Artefact → / Provenance →	OCEANIA UN.	AUSTRALIA	MELA.UNPROV.	Admiralty	Banks	Bismarck	D'Entrecast.	Fiji	Louisiade	Loyalty	N. Britain	N. Caledonia	N. Guinea	N. Hebrides	N. Ireland	Santa Cruz	Solomon	Trobriand	MICRO.UNPROV	Caroline	Gilbert	Mariana	Marshall	POLY.UNPROV.	Austral	Chatham	Cook	Easter	Hawaii	Marquesas	New Zealand	Niue	Pitcairn	Samoa	Society	Tokelau	Tonga	Tuamotu	Tuvalu
cord																																							
raw mate																																							
-sling,s																																							
-arrow																																							
-bow																																							
-shield		2									2																												
-dagger																																							
-spearth		1																																					
-spear																																							
-club		2						X			X																												
WEAPON																																							
-float,s.																																							
-net																																							
-spear																																							
-fishhoo																																							
FISHING																																							
hunting																																							
-model																																							
-ornamen																																							
-paddle																																							
NAVIGATI																																							
-barkclo																																							
-weaving											2*																												
-needle,e																																							
-chisel																																							
-rasp																																							
-grinding																																							
-pounding																																							
-adze																																							
TOOL																																							
fire,lig																																							
smokng p																																							
pottery																																							
utensil	X																																						
lime spa																																							
dish,vess																																							
lime con																																							

Name	Guernsey Museum and Art Gallery
Address	Candie Gardens St. Peter Port Guernsey Channel Islands
Telephone	0481-26518
Contact	Curator

GUERNSEY

Sources & Dates of Information

R. Hutchings 1966

Visit

MEG 1978

Letters 1976, 1977, 1979

Notes

Jurisdiction now includes Guille Allès Museum which contains a large amount of ethnographic material donated by local collectors in the 19th Century.

Material from Lukis & Island Museum (now Guernsey Museum & Art Gallery) contains several hundred totally unprovenanced ethnographic items.

*Tahiti-- other: flywhisk

Dates of Collection/Acquisition	Donors/Collectors/Former Owners
1791-95	Capt. Le Messurier (Vancouver Expedition)
1894	Capt. Le Sauvage
	J. Fallaize
1890's	F.M. Allès
	Sir E. MacCullock
	G.T. Sullock
	D. Mollet & other local collectors

Documentation

No catalogue as yet.
Guille Allès uncatalogued; list started.

Comment

Tahitian material appears to be important.

Museum and Art Gallery GUERNSEY

Artefact → / Provenance →

Artefact	OCEANIA UN.	AUSTRALIA	MELA.UNPROV.	Admiralty	Banks	Bismarck	D'Entrecast.	Fiji	Louisiade	Loyalty	N. Britain	N. Caledonia	N. Guinea	N. Hebrides	N. Ireland	Santa Cruz	Solomon	Trobriand
box	X																	
bag	X																	
basket	X							X										
mat																		
headrest																		
transport																		
currency																		
-rattle																		
-flute,pipe																		
-drum,gong																		
MUSICAL INS.																		
charm																		
magic,med.																		
fig.,image								X					X	1				
carving								X										
-bullroarer																		
-paddle	X																	
-adze																		
-board																		
-mask																		
CERE. OBJ.																		
staff,stick	X																	
toilet app.																		
fan																		
comb								X										
-neck,breast	X												X				X	
-arm	X												X					
-ear,nose	X																	
-head																		
PERS. ORN.																		
-cloak																		
-belt								X										
-skirt																		
CLOTHING																		
barkcloth								X										
OTHER																		
TOTAL																		

Artefact	MICRO.UNPROV	Caroline	Gilbert	Mariana	Marshall	POLY.UNPROV.	Austral	Chatham	Cook	Easter	Hawaii	Marquesas	New Zealand	Niue	Pitcairn	Samoa	Society	Tokelau	Tonga	Tuamotu	Tuvalu
box																					
bag													X								
basket																					
mat																					
headrest																			X		
transport																					
currency																					
-rattle																					
-flute,pipe																					
-drum,gong																					
MUSICAL INS.																					
charm																					
magic,med.																					
fig.,image																					
carving													X								
-bullroarer																					
-paddle							X		X												
-adze						X															
-board																					
-mask																					
CERE. OBJ.												2									
staff,stick													X								
toilet app.																					
fan							X														
comb																					
-neck,breast													X								
-arm													X								
-ear,nose													X								
-head													X								
PERS. ORN.																					
-cloak											1										
-belt																					
-skirt																					
CLOTHING																					
barkcloth																					
OTHER																					
TOTAL						X															

Museum and Art Gallery

GUERNSEY

Artefact → / Provenance ↓	OCEANIA UN.	AUSTRALIA	MELA.UNPROV.	Admiralty	Banks	Bismarck	D'Entrecast.	Fiji	Louisiade	Loyalty	N. Britain	N. Caledonia	N. Guinea	N. Hebrides	N. Ireland	Santa Cruz	Solomon	Trobriand	MICRO.UNPROV	Caroline	Gilbert	Mariana	Marshall	POLY.UNPROV.	Austral	Chatham	Cook	Easter	Hawaii	Marquesas	New Zealand	Niue	Pitcairn	Samoa	Society	Tokelau	Tonga	Tuamotu	Tuvalu	Tahiti
cord	X												X																											
raw mater																																								
sling,sto																																								
arrow	X							X																																
bow	X							X																																
shield		X																																						
dagger																					X																			
spearthro		X																																						
spear																																								
club	X	X						X																						X	X			X			X			
WEAPON																					X																			
float,si	X																																							
net	X																												X											
spear	X																																							
fishhook	X																							X							X									
FISHING																																								
hunting																																								
model								X									X							X																
ornament																															X									
paddle		X																						X																
NAVIGATIO																																								
barkclot								X																																
weaving																																								
needle,aw																																								
chisel																																								
rasp																																								
grinding																																								
pounding																																								
adze	X																																							
TOOL																																								
fire,ligh																																								
smoking pi																																								
pottery																																								
utensil	X												X																											
lime spat.																		X																						
dish,vesse	X							X																																
lime cont.																																								

HALIFAX

Name Bankfield Museum

Address Akroyd Park
Halifax HX3 6HG

Telephone 0422-54823

Contact Keeper, Textiles and Costume

Sources & Dates of Information

R. Hutchings 1966

Visit SP 1975

MEG 1978

Letter

Notes

Disposals: Pacific non-textile collection exchanged with Manchester Museum in 1950's. Some also in Ohly and Hooper Collections.

A few more pieces possibly in store.

Dates of Collection/Acquisition	Donors/Collectors/Former Owners
1897+	

Documentation

Library, archival, photographic, iconographic.

Reference: H. Ling Roth, 1918, Studies in Primitive Looms, £2.40 (reprinted 1977).

Comment

Association with H. Ling Roth, previous curator and prolific writer.

Bankfield Museum

HALIFAX

Artefact → / Provenance ↓	TOTAL	OTHER	barkcloth	CLOTHING	-skirt	-belt	-cloak	PERS. ORN.	-head	-ear,nose	-arm	-neck,breast	comb	fan	toilet app.	staff,stick	CERE. OBJ.	-mask	-board	-adze	-paddle	-bullroarer	carving	fig.,image	magic,med.	charm	MUSICAL INS.	-drum,gong	-flute,pipe	-rattle	currency	transport	headrest	mat	basket	bag	box
OCEANIA UN.																																					
AUSTRALIA																																					
MELA.UNPROV.																																					
Admiralty																																					
Banks																																					
Bismarck																																					
D'Entrecast.																																					
Fiji	22		8										2	1																							
Louisiade																																					
Loyalty																																					
N. Britain																																					
N. Caledonia																																					
N. Guinea																																					
N. Hebrides																																					
N. Ireland																																					
Santa Cruz																																					
Solomon																																					
Trobriand																																					
MICRO.UNPROV.	1																																			1	
Caroline																																					
Gilbert																																					
Mariana																																					
Marshall																																					
POLY.UNPROV.	3		3																																		
Austral																																					
Chatham																																					
Cook																																					
Easter																																					
Hawaii																																					
Marquesas																																					
New Zealand	1						1																														
Niue																																					
Pitcairn																																					
Samoa																																					
Society																																					
Tokelau																																					
Tonga																																					
Tuamotu																																					
Tuvalu																																					
Tahiti	4		3																																		

Bankfield Museum

HALIFAX

Artefact → / Provenance ↓	lime cont	dish,vess	lime spa	utensil	pottery	smokng p	fire,lig	TOOL	-adze	-pounding	-grinding	-rasp	-chisel	-needle,a	-weaving	-barkclot	NAVIGATIO	-paddle	-ornament	-model	hunting	FISHING	-fishhook	-spear	-net	-float,s	WEAPON	-club	-spear	-spearthr	-dagger	-shield	-bow	-arrow	-sling,st	raw mate	cord
OCEANIA UN.																																					
AUSTRALIA																																					
MELA.UNPROV.																																					
Admiralty																																					
Banks																																					
Bismarck																																					
D'Entrecast.																																					
Fiji		2													3				2					1													3
Louisiade																																					
Loyalty																																					
N. Britain																																					
N. Caledonia																																					
N. Guinea																																					
N. Hebrides																																					
N. Ireland																																					
Santa Cruz																																					
Solomon																																					
Trobriand																																					
MICRO.UNPROV.																																					
Caroline																																					
Gilbert																																					
Mariana																																					
Marshall																																					
POLY.UNPROV.																																					
Austral																																					
Chatham																																					
Cook																																					
Easter																																					
Hawaii																																					
Marquesas																																					
New Zealand																																					
Niue																																					
Pitcairn																																					
Samoa																																					
Society																																					
Tokelau																																					
Tonga																																					
Tuamotu																																					
Tuvalu																																					
Tahiti															1																						

HARTLEPOOL

Name: Gray Art Gallery and Museum

Address: Clarence Road
Hartlepool TS26 8BT

Telephone: 0429-68916

Contact: Curator

Sources & Dates of Information

R. Hutchings 1966
Visit

MEG 1978
Letter

Notes

Dates of Collection/Acquisition	Donors/Collectors/Former Owners
Acquired 1930-40	

Documentation

Comment

Gray Art Gallery and Museum

HARTLEPOO

Provenance → / Artefact →	TOTAL	OTHER	barkcloth	CLOTHING	-skirt	-belt	-cloak	PERS. ORN.	-head	-ear,nose	-arm	-neck,breast	comb	fan	toilet app.	staff,stick	CERE. OBJ.	-mask	-board	-adze	-paddle	-bullroarer	carving	fig., image	magic,med.	charm	MUSICAL INS.	-drum,gong	-flute,pipe	-rattle	currency	transport	headrest	mat	basket	bag	box
OCEANIA UN.	7																																				
AUSTRALIA																																					
MELA.UNPROV.																																					
Admiralty																																					
Banks																																					
Bismarck																																					
D'Entrecast.																																					
Fiji																																					
Louisiade																																					
Loyalty																																					
N. Britain																																					
N. Caledonia																																					
N. Guinea																																					
N. Hebrides																																					
N. Ireland																																					
Santa Cruz																																					
Solomon																																					
Trobriand																																					
MICRO.UNPROV.																																					
Caroline																																					
Gilbert																																					
Mariana																																					
Marshall																																					
POLY.UNPROV.																																					
Austral																																					
Chatham																																					
Cook																																					
Easter																																					
Hawaii																																					
Marquesas																																					
New Zealand																																					
Niue																																					
Pitcairn																																					
Samoa																																					
Society																																					
Tokelau																																					
Tonga																																					
Tuamotu																																					
Tuvalu																																					

Gray Art Gallery and Museum

HARTLEPOOL

Artefact → / Provenance ↓	OCEANIA UN.	AUSTRALIA	MELA.UNPROV.	Admiralty	Banks	Bismarck	D'Entrecast.	Fiji	Louisiade	Loyalty	N. Britain	N. Caledonia	N. Guinea	N. Hebrides	N. Ireland	Santa Cruz	Solomon	Trobriand	MICRO.UNPROV.	Caroline	Gilbert	Mariana	Marshall	POLY.UNPROV.	Austral	Chatham	Cook	Easter	Hawaii	Marquesas	New Zealand	Niue	Pitcairn	Samoa	Society	Tokelau	Tonga	Tuamotu	Tuvalu
cord																																							
raw mater.																																							
-sling,sto																																							
-arrow																																							
-bow																																							
-shield																																							
-dagger																																							
-spearthro																																							
-spear																																							
-club																																							
WEAPON																																							
-float,si																																							
-net																																							
-spear																																							
-fishhook																																							
FISHING																																							
hunting																																							
-model																																							
-ornament																																							
-paddle																																							
NAVIGATION																																							
-barkcloth																																							
-weaving																																							
-needle,aw																																							
-chisel																																							
-rasp																																							
-grinding																																							
-pounding																																							
-adze																																							
TOOL																																							
fire,ligh																																							
smokng pip																																							
pottery																																							
utensil																																							
lime spat																																							
dish,vesse																																							
lime cont.																																							

HASTINGS

Name Hastings Museum and Art Gallery

Address John's Place
Cambridge Road
Hastings
E. Sussex

Telephone 0424-435952

Contact Curator

Sources & Dates of Information

R. Hutchings 1966

Visits PG, ALK 1974

MEG 1978

Letter 1979

List of Cullen Collection

Notes

Disposals: British Museum, Liverpool and sales (post WWII).

Table does not show complete holdings.

*Fiji-- toilet apparatus: tatooing
*New Guinea-- headrests: from Tami Is.
mus. instrument: shell trumpet
other: heddle, misc. 1
*Carolines-- mus. instrument: shell trumpet
*Cook-- tools: stone tools from Mangaia & Aitutaki

Dates of Collection/Acquisition

Donors/Collectors/Former Owners

Brassey c. 1870
Rev. J.H. Cullen (about 50 objects)

Documentation

Library, archival, photographic, iconographic.

Comment

Very interesting. Brassey Collection mostly obtained during personal visits in 1870's, and Cullen Collection acquired before 1914 by donor when missionary. Both collections reflect objects available 1870.

Hastings Museum and Art Gallery

HASTING

Provenance ↓ / Artefact →	TOTAL	OTHER	barkcloth	CLOTHING	-skirt	-belt	-cloak	PERS. ORN.	-head	-ear,nose	-arm	-neck,breast	comb	fan	toilet app.	staff,stick	CERE. OBJ.	-mask	-board	-adze	-paddle	-bullroarer	carving	-fig.,image	magic,med.	charm	MUSICAL INS.	-drum,gong	-flute,pipe	-rattle	currency	transport	headrest	mat	basket	bag	bcx
OCEANIA UN.	8+	1											X											1					2								
AUSTRALIA	2																																				
MELA.UNPROV.	3																																				
Admiralty	2																																				
Banks																																					
Bismarck																																					
D'Entrecast.																																					
Fiji	19+							X							1*																						
Louisiade																																					
Loyalty																																					
N. Britain	X							X																													
N. Caledonia	1																																				
N. Guinea	86+	2			1	1		X	1		2		X			1				1			1	1		1	1*	1					2*				
N. Hebrides	4																												1								
N. Ireland	6																1	1						1													
Santa Cruz	1																	1																			
Solomon	26+							X		1			X				2																				
Trobriand	25+							X												1																	
MICRO.UNPROV.	4+					1						1																									
Caroline	19+	X						1								1	1										1*										
Gilbert	6+							X				1																									
Mariana																																					
Marshall	3+							X																													
POLY.UNPROV.	2																																				
Austral	2																				1																
Chatham																																					
Cook	54+																											1									
Easter	1																							1													
Hawaii	7						1					5																									1
Marquesas																																					
New Zealand	9																																				1
Niue	5	1											1																								
Pitcairn																																					
Samoa	6											1	1																								
Society																																					
Tokelau																																					
Tonga	5		1																																		
Tuamotu																																					
Tuvalu	4																																				
Duke of York	1																																				

Hastings Museum and Art Gallery

HASTINGS

Artefact → / Provenance ↓	lime cont	dish,vess	lime spa	utensil	pottery	smokng pi	fire,lig	TOOL	-adze	-pounding	-grinding	-rasp	-chisel	-needle,a	-weaving	-barkclo	NAVIGATIO	-paddle	-ornamen
OCEANIA UN.	1																		
AUSTRALIA														1					
MELA.UNPROV.	1			1					1										
Admiralty																			
Banks																			
Bismarck																			
D'Entrecast.																			
Fiji		1			7				1										
Louisiade																			
Loyalty																			
N. Britain																			
N. Caledonia																			
N. Guinea	X	2		1		2	1		11+										1
N. Hebrides																			
N. Ireland																			
Santa Cruz																			
Solomon		X		1														4+	
Trobriand		X	20						1										
MICRO.UNPROV.									1										
Caroline		4+		4	1		1		2										
Gilbert																			
Mariana																			
Marshall				1					1										
POLY.UNPROV.										1									
Austral																		1	
Chatham																			
Cook		3						31*	6+	3						1		2	
Easter																			
Hawaii																			
Marquesas																			
New Zealand									1				1						
Niue									1										
Pitcairn																			
Samoa																			
Society																			
Tokelau																			
Tonga																			
Tuamotu																			
Tuvalu																			
Duke of York																			
Tahiti									X										

Artefact → / Provenance ↓	-model	hunting	FISHING	-fishhook	-spear	-net	-float,s	WEAPON	-club	-spear	-spearthr	-dagger	-shield	-bow	-arrow	-sling,s	raw mate	cord
OCEANIA UN.									X			X					1	
AUSTRALIA								1										
MELA.UNPROV.																		
Admiralty										2								
Banks																		
Bismarck																		
D'Entrecast.																		
Fiji	1								7									
Louisiade																		
Loyalty																		
N. Britain																		
N. Caledonia									1									
N. Guinea								10	2	2		X		2	32			
N. Hebrides								1	2									
N. Ireland									3									
Santa Cruz																		
Solomon				2	2				8	3								
Trobriand													X					
MICRO.UNPROV.				X														
Caroline										2								
Gilbert								1	1	2								
Mariana																		
Marshall																		
POLY.UNPROV.																1		
Austral																		
Chatham																		
Cook				5						1						X		
Easter																		
Hawaii																		
Marquesas																		
New Zealand				2					4									
Niue	1															1		
Pitcairn																		
Samoa				1					2	1								
Society																		
Tokelau																		
Tonga				2					2									
Tuamotu																		
Tuvalu				4														
Duke of York			1															
Tahiti																		

Name: Hatfield House	HATFIELD
Address: Hatfield Hertfordshire	Sources & Dates of Information R. Hutchings 1966 Visit ALK 1970 MEG 1978 Letter
Telephone:	
Contact: Agent to Lord Salisbury	

Notes

Hawaii: feather cloak, latter half of the 18th Century, 126 cm. x 226 cm.

Dates of Collection/Acquisition	Donors/Collectors/Former Owners
Acquired perhaps around 1820	Capt. Josceline Percy ? (d. 1856)

Documentation

Reference: Christie's catalogue, Important Tribal Art, of sale of June 19, 1979.

Comment

Withdrawn from sale by vendor.

Name	Hertford Museum
Address	18 Bull Plain Hertford SG14 1DT
Telephone	0992-52686
Contact	Curator

HERTFORD

Sources & Dates of Information

R. Hutchings 1966

Visit

MEG 1978

Letter

personal communication 1979

Notes

Around 100 total; includes many weapons.

*Australia-- other: boomerangs

Dates of Collection/Acquisition	Donors/Collectors/Former Owners
Acquired from 1888	

Documentation

Needs identification and cataloguing.

Comment

May include ex-Haileybury School. To be examined summer 1979.

Hertford Museum

HERTFORD

Artifact → / Provenance →	OCEANIA UN.	AUSTRALIA	MELA.UNPROV.	Admiralty	Banks	Bismarck	D'Entrecast.	Fiji	Louisiade	Loyalty	N. Britain	N. Caledonia	N. Guinea	N. Hebrides	N. Ireland	Santa Cruz	Solomon	Trobriand	MICRO.UNPROV.	Caroline	Gilbert	Mariana	Marshall	POLY.UNPROV.	Austral	Chatham	Cook	Easter	Hawaii	Marquesas	New Zealand	Niue	Pitcairn	Samoa	Society	Tokelau	Tonga	Tuamotu	Tuvalu
box																																							
bag																														/								
basket																																							
mat																																							
headrest																																							
transport																																							
currency																																							
-rattle																																							
-flute,pipe																																							
-drum,gong																																							
MUSICAL INS.																																							
charm																																							
magic,med.																																							
fig.,image																																							
carving																																							
-bullroarer																																							
-paddle																																							
-adze																																							
-board																																							
-mask																																							
CERE. OBJ.																																							
staff,stick																																							
toilet app.	X																																						
fan																																							
comb																																							
-neck,breast																														/								
-arm																														/								
-ear,nose																																							
-head																																							
PERS. ORN.																																							
-cloak																																							
-belt																																							
-skirt																																							
CLOTHING																																							
barkcloth																																							
OTHER		X																																					
TOTAL		X	X																											X								

Hertford Museum

HERTFORD

Artefact → / Provenance →	OCEANIA UN.	AUSTRALIA	MELA.UNPROV.	Admiralty	Banks	Bismarck	D'Entrecast.	Fiji	Louisiade	Loyalty	N. Britain	N. Caledonia	N. Guinea	N. Hebrides	N. Ireland	Santa Cruz	Solomon	Trobriand	MICRO.UNPROV	Caroline	Gilbert	Mariana	Marshall	POLY.UNPROV.	Austral	Chatham	Cook	Easter	Hawaii	Marquesas	New Zealand	Niue	Pitcairn	Samoa	Society	Tokelau	Tonga	Tuamotu	Tuvalu
cord																																							
raw mater.																																							
-sling,sto																																							
-arrow																																							
-bow	X		X																																				
-shield			X																																				
-dagger																															/								
-spearthro																																							
-spear																																							
-club	X																																						
WEAPON																																							
-float,sin																																							
-net																																							
-spear																																							
-fishhook																																							
FISHING																																							
hunting																																							
-model																																							
-ornament																																							
-paddle																																							
NAVIGATION																															X								
-barkcloth																																							
-weaving																																							
-needle,aw																																							
-chisel																																							
-rasp																																							
-grinding																																							
-pounding																																							
-adze																																							
TOOL																																							
fire,ligh																																							
smoking pi																																							
pottery																																							
utensil																																							
lime spat																																							
dish,vess																																							
lime cont.																																							

HORSHAM

Name: Horsham Museum

Address: 9, The Causeway
Horsham
West Sussex RH12 1HE

Telephone: 0403-4959

Contact: Curator

Sources & Dates of Information

R. Hutchings 1966

Visit

MEG 1978

Letter 1979

Notes

Oceania: food bowl
Austral: ceremonial paddle

Dates of Collection/Acquisition

Donors/Collectors/Former Owners

Documentation

Comment

Unsorted material in store.

Name	Town Docks Museum	HULL	
Address	Queen Victoria Square Kingston upon Hull HU1 3RA	Sources & Dates of Information	
		R. Hutchings	1966
		Visit	
Telephone	0482-22311	MEG	1978
Contact	Keeper of Archaeology	Letter	1979

Notes

*Australia--other: boomerangs 5

Dates of Collection/Acquisition	Donors/Collectors/Former Owners
Mainly post-1945	

Documentation

Comment

Town Docks Museum

HULL

Provenance ↓ / Artefact →	TOTAL	OTHER	barkcloth	CLOTHING	-skirt	-belt	-cloak	PERS. ORN.	-head	-ear,nose	-arm	-neck,breast	comb	fan	toilet app.	staff,stick	CERE. OBJ.	-mask	-board	-adze	-paddle	-bullroarer	carving	fig.,image	magic,med.	charm	MUSICAL INS.	-drum,gong	-flute,pipe	-rattle	currency	transport	headrest	mat	basket	bag	box
OCEANIA UN.	1																						1														
AUSTRALIA	11	5														1						3															
MELA.UNPROV.																																					
Admiralty																																					
Banks																																					
Bismarck																																					
D'Entrecast.																																					
Fiji	1		1																																		
Louisiade																																					
Loyalty																																					
N. Britain																																					
N. Caledonia																																					
N. Guinea																																					
N. Hebrides																																					
N. Ireland																																					
Santa Cruz																																					
Solomon																																					
Trobriand																																					
MICRO.UNPROV.																																					
Caroline																																					
Gilbert																																					
Mariana																																					
Marshall																																					
POLY.UNPROV.																																					
Austral																																					
Chatham																																					
Cook																																					
Easter																																					
Hawaii																																					
Marquesas																																					
New Zealand																																					
Niue																																					
Pitcairn																																					
Samoa																																					
Society																																					
Tokelau																																					
Tonga																																					
Tuamotu																																					
Tuvalu																																					

Town Docks Museum

HULL

Artefact → / Provenance ↓	OCEANIA UN.	AUSTRALIA	MELA.UNPROV.	Admiralty	Banks	Bismarck	D'Entrecast.	Fiji	Louisiade	Loyalty	N. Britain	N. Caledonia	N. Guinea	N. Hebrides	N. Ireland	Santa Cruz	Solomon	Trobriand	MICRO.UNPROV	Caroline	Gilbert	Mariana	Marshall	POLY.UNPROV.	Austral	Chatham	Cook	Easter	Hawaii	Marquesas	New Zealand	Niue	Pitcairn	Samoa	Society	Tokelau	Tonga	Tuamotu	Tuvalu
cord																																							
raw mater																																							
-sling,sto																																							
-arrow																																							
-bow																																							
-shield																																							
-dagger																																							
-spearthro																																							
-spear		/																																					
-club																																							
WEAPON																																							
-float,si																																							
-net																																							
-spear																																							
-fishhook																																							
FISHING																																							
hunting																																							
-model																																							
-ornament																																							
-paddle																																							
NAVIGATIO																																							
-barkclot																																							
-weaving																																							
-needle,aw																																							
-chisel																																							
-rasp																																							
-grinding																																							
-pounding																																							
-adze		/																																					
TOOL																																							
fire,ligh																																							
smokng pi																																							
pottery																																							
utensil																																							
lime spat																																							
dish,vesse																																							
lime cont.																																							

Name	Ilfracombe Museum	ILFRACOMBE
Address	Wilder Road Ilfracombe, Devon EX34 8AF	Sources & Dates of Information
		R. Hutchings 1966
		Visit
Telephone	0271-63541	MEG 1978
Contact	Honorary Curator	Letter 1979

Notes

*Australia-- other: emu egg decorated by a European

Dates of Collection/Acquisition	Donors/Collectors/Former Owners
Mainly 1939+	M. McKissack donated 6 items from Fiji, 1951 J. Chapple donated 2 ula clubs " " , 1937

Documentation

Comment

ILFRACOMBE

Ilfracombe Museum

Provenance ↓ / Artefact →	TOTAL	OTHER	barkcloth	CLOTHING	-skirt	-belt	-cloak	PERS. ORN.	-head	-ear,nose	-arm	-neck,breast	comb	fan	toilet app.	staff,stick	CERE. OBJ.	-mask	-board	-adze	-paddle	-bullroarer	carving	fig.,image	magic,med.	charm	MUSICAL IN.	-drum,gong	-flute,pipe	-rattle	currency	transport	headrest	mat	basket	bag	box
OCEANIA UN.																																					
AUSTRALIA	2	1																																			
MELA.UNPROV.																																					
Admiralty																																					
Banks																																					
Bismarck																																					
D'Entrecast.																																					
Fiji	8																																1				
Louisiade																																					
Loyalty																																					
N. Britain																																					
N. Caledonia																																					
N. Guinea																																					
N. Hebrides																																					
N. Ireland																																					
Santa Cruz																																					
Solomon																																					
Trobriand																																					
MICRO.UNPROV.																																					
Caroline																																					
Gilbert																																					
Mariana																																					
Marshall																																					
POLY.UNPROV.																																					
Austral																																					
Chatham																																					
Cook																																					
Easter																																					
Hawaii	2																																				
Marquesas																																					
New Zealand																																					
Niue																																					
Pitcairn																																					
Samoa																																					
Society																																					
Tokelau																																					
Tonga																																					
Tuamotu																																					
Tuvalu																																					

Ilfracombe Museum

ILFRACOMBE

Artefact → / Provenance →	OCEANIA UN.	AUSTRALIA	MELA.UNPROV.	Admiralty	Banks	Bismarck	D'Entrecast.	Fiji	Louisiade	Loyalty	N. Britain	N. Caledonia	N. Guinea	N. Hebrides	N. Ireland	Santa Cruz	Solomon	Trobriand	MICRO.UNPROV.	Caroline	Gilbert	Mariana	Marshall	POLY.UNPROV.	Austral	Chatham	Cook	Easter	Hawaii	Marquesas	New Zealand	Niue	Pitcairn	Samoa	Society	Tokelau	Tonga	Tuamotu	Tuvalu
cord																																							
raw mate																																							
-sling,s																																							
-arrow																																							
-bow																																							
-shield																																							
-dagger																																							
-spearth																																							
-spear		1																																					
-club								2																															
WEAPON																																							
-float,s.																																							
-net																																							
-spear																																							
-fishhoo																																							
FISHING																																							
hunting																																							
-model								2																															
-ornamen																																							
-paddle																																							
NAVIGATIO																																							
-barkclo																																							
-weaving																																							
-needle,a																																							
-chisel																																							
-rasp																																							
-grinding																																							
-pounding																																							
-adze																																							
TOOL																																							
fire,lig																																							
smoking pr																																							
pottery								1																															
utensil								1																															
lime spa																																							
dish,vess								1																					2										
lime cont																																							

IPSWICH

Name Ipswich Museums and Art Galleries

Address The Museum
High Street
Ipswich IP1 3QH

Telephone 0473-213761/2

Contact Assistant Curator of Human History (Ethnography)

Sources & Dates of Information

R. Hutchings 1966

Visits PG, ALK 1977

MEG 1978

Letters 1976, 1979

Notes

*Easter-- other: moai kavakava, rongo-rongo tablet (fake?)

Dates of Collection/Acquisition

Main periods of acquisition:
1840's-1860's, 1920-1930's

Donors/Collectors/Former Owners

Admiral B.W. Page 1790-1840
Layard and Routledge
E. Clement

Documentation

Reference: Barrow, 1961 (esp. New Zealand godstick).

Comment

Some excellent early material. Collection now being studied carefully. Compares well with Saffron Walden, Exeter, Aberdeen, Glasgow (M & AG), Glasgow (Hunterian).

Ipswich Museums and Art Galleries

IPSWI

Provenance / Artefact →	TOTAL	OTHER	barkcloth	CLOTHING	-skirt	-belt	-cloak	PERS. ORN.	-head	-ear,nose	-arm	-neck,breast	comb	fan	toilet app.	staff,stick	CERE. OBJ.	-mask	-board	-adze	-paddle	-bullroarer	carving	fig.,image	magic,med.	charm	MUSICAL INS.	-drum,gong	-flute,pipe	-rattle	currency	transport	headrest	mat	basket	bag	box
OCEANIA UN.																																					
AUSTRALIA	X					2				6		5							3			2														2	
MELA.UNPROV.	X																																				
Admiralty																																					
Banks																																					
Bismarck																																					
D'Entrecast.																																					
Fiji	X		6			1			2			2	4	1															1		2			1	1		
Louisiade																																					
Loyalty																																					
N. Britain																																					
N. Caledonia	X																			2											1						
N. Guinea	X					2				1	1	1												1													
N. Hebrides	X				2	2			1	1	2	2	1					1								1					1						
N. Ireland	1																							1													
Santa Cruz	X					1																															
Solomon	X										3	2	1				2	1			1		X	3	1												
Trobriand	X										2		1			1				1		1		2				3									
MICRO.UNPROV																																					
Caroline	X								1																												
Gilbert	X																																				
Mariana																																					
Marshall																																					
POLY.UNPROV.																																					
Austral	X													1							8																
Chatham																																					
Cook	X		1											1						2																	
Easter	X	2																					1														
Hawaii	X		1				1	1																													
Marquesas	1																																				
New Zealand	X				2							1											1						3								4
Niue	X																																				
Pitcairn																																					
Samoa	X																																				
Society	X																																				
Tokelau																																					
Tonga	X																																				
Tuamotu	1																																1				
Tuvalu																																					

Ipswich Museums and Art Galleries

IPSWICH

Provenance ↓ / Artefact →	cord	raw mater	-sling,sto	-arrow	-bow	-shield	-dagger	-spearthro	-spear	-club	WEAPON	-float,sin	-net	-spear	-fishhook	FISHING	hunting	-model	-ornament	-paddle	NAVIGATIO	-barkclot	-weaving	-needle,aw	-chisel	-rasp	-grinding	-pounding	-adze	TOOL	fire,ligh	smoking pi	pottery	utensil	lime spat	dish,vesse	lime cont.
OCEANIA UN.																																					
AUSTRALIA						10		11	17	32														1	1	1					2					1	
MELA.UNPROV.							2		10																												
Admiralty																																					
Banks																																					
Bismarck																																					
D'Entrecast.																																					
Fiji									[illegible]	1								1									1						10	3		2	
Louisiade																																					
Loyalty																																					
N. Britain																																					
N. Caledonia			1							3																			1								
N. Guinea										3																			2			2					
N. Hebrides									2	2																1			2								
N. Ireland																																					
Santa Cruz				20						1																											
Solomon				20					9	6										3									2								
Trobriand						X				5																									6	1	1
MICRO.UNPROV																																					
Caroline																				1																	
Gilbert							7				1																										
Mariana																																					
Marshall																																					
POLY.UNPROV.																																					
Austral																																					
Chatham																																					
Cook									X																				1								
Easter																																					
Hawaii																																					
Marquesas										1																											
New Zealand									3	[illegible]						3				2								1	4		1						
Niue										2								1																			
Pitcairn																																					
Samoa									1	2																											
Society			1						1			1			3														1								
Tokelau																																					
Tonga										4																											
Tuamotu																																					
Tuvalu																																					

Name	The Museum (Société Jersaise)	**JERSEY**
Address	9 Pier Road St. Helier Jersey Channel Isles	Sources & Dates of Information R. Hutchings 1966 Visit MEG 1978 Letter 1979
Telephone	0534-22133	
Contact	Curator	

Notes

Disposals : A large collection (1912 Catalogue lists 17 cases including Oceanic) was dispersed between 1912 and 1968, some to a local dealer, but without records.

Dates of Collection/Acquisition	Donors/Collectors/Former Owners
Acquired 1873-1912	

Documentation

Reference : R.G. Warton, 1912, Catalogue of the Museum of the Société Jersaise, p. 73-78.

Comment

Name Fitz Park Museum and Art Gallery

KESWICK

Address Station Road
Keswick CA12 4NF

Sources & Dates of Information

R. Hutchings 1966

Visit

MEG 1978

Letter 1979

Telephone 0596-73263

Contact Curator

Notes

Oceania: fishing arrows 4
fishing spear 1

Dates of Collection/Acquisition	Donors/Collectors/Former Owners
	possibly P. Croathwaite, collected around 1760 while workin for East India Company, opened a museum in 1780 (many of th objects were from the Pacific) which was auctioned in 1870.

Documentation

Comment

KEW

Name	Museums of Economic Botany Royal Botanic Gardens
Address	Kew Richmond TW9 3AB
Telephone	01-940 1171
Contact	Officer in Charge, Museums Division

Sources & Dates of Information

R. Hutchings	1966
Visit	
MEG	1978
Letter	1979

Notes

RBG ". . .concerned with economic plants and their uses and this has always been interpreted widely to include materials of plant origin used by man in different parts of the world. . . ethnographic material from Australia, New Zealand and Oceania, partly collected on voyages such as HMS Challenger, Herald, etc., and also by botanic collectors such as Seeman, by missionaries such as Powell in Hawaii, and also donations by Edward VII (when Prince of Wales) . . .little displayed, not yet catalogued, arranged systematically from the botanical viewpoint quite a large amount, mainly dicotyledonous. Monocotyledonous mostly distributed to other museums in 1960." (information from Rosemary Angel)

Disposals: small amount of material manufactured from monocotyledonous plants donated to British Museum, Horniman Museum, Luton Museum.

Dates of Collection/Acquisition	Donors/Collectors/Former Owners
Mainly 1840-1900	

Documentation

Library, archival, photographic, iconographic.

Comment

Material from 19th Century scientific expeditions important as they have dates of collection and attribution.

Royal Botanic Gardens

KEW

Artifact / Provenance	OCEANIA UN.	AUSTRALIA	MELA.UNPROV.	Admiralty	Banks	Bismarck	D'Entrecast.	Fiji	Louisiade	Loyalty	N. Britain	N. Caledonia	N. Guinea	N. Hebrides	N. Ireland	Santa Cruz	Solomon	Trobriand	MICRO.UNPROV.	Caroline	Gilbert	Mariana	Marshall	POLY.UNPROV.	Austral	Chatham	Cook	Easter	Hawaii	Marquesas	New Zealand	Niue	Pitcairn	Samoa	Society	Tokelau	Tonga	Tuamotu	Tuvalu
box																																							
bag																																							
basket																																							
mat																																							
headrest	X																																						
transport																																							
currency																																							
-rattle																																							
-flute,pipe																																							
-drum,gong																																							
MUSICAL INS.																																							
charm																																							
magic,med.																																							
fig.,image																																							
carving																																							
-bullroarer																																							
-paddle																																							
-adze																																							
-board																																							
-mask																																							
CERE. OBJ.																																							
staff,stick																																							
toilet app.																																							
fan																																							
comb																																							
-neck,breast																																							
-arm																																							
-ear,nose																																							
-head																																							
PERS. ORN.																																							
-cloak																																							
-belt																																							
-skirt																																							
CLOTHING																																							
barkcloth	X																																						
OTHER		X																																					
TOTAL	X	X																											X		X								

Royal Botanic Gradens KEW

Artefact → / Provenance →	OCEANIA UN.	AUSTRALIA	MELA.UNPROV.	Admiralty	Banks	Bismarck	D'Entrecast.	Fiji	Louisiade	Loyalty	N. Britain	N. Caledonia	N. Guinea	N. Hebrides	N. Ireland	Santa Cruz	Solomon	Trobriand	MICRO.UNPROV	Caroline	Gilbert	Mariana	Marshall	POLY.UNPROV.	Austral	Chatham	Cook	Easter	Hawaii	Marquesas	New Zealand	Niue	Pitcairn	Samoa	Society	Tokelau	Tonga	Tuamotu	Tuvalu
cord																																							
raw mater																																							
-sling,st																																							
-arrow																																							
-bow																																							
-shield																																							
-dagger																																							
-spearthro																																							
-spear																																							
-club																																							
WEAPON																																							
-float,si																																							
-net																																							
-spear																																							
-fishhook																																							
FISHING																																							
hunting																																							
-model																																							
-ornament																																							
-paddle																																							
NAVIGATIO																																							
-barkclot																																							
-weaving	X																																						
-needle,a																																							
-chisel																																							
-rasp																																							
-grinding																																							
-pounding																																							
-adze																																							
TOOL																																							
fire,ligh																																							
smoking pi																																							
pottery																																							
utensil																																							
lime spat																																							
dish,vess	X																																						
lime cont																																							

Name	Dick Institute
Address	Elmbank Avenue Kilmarnock KA1 3BU
Telephone	0563-26401
Contact	Curator

KILMARNOCK

Sources & Dates of Information

R. Hutchings 1967

Visit GSP 1974

MEG 1978

Letter

Notes

Total collection 400-500 items, plus some unidentified material.

Dates of Collection/Acquisition	Donors/Collectors/Former Owners
acquired 1900, 1946	Mrs. Tim Betts (Ursula Graham-Bower)

Documentation

Photographic.

Comment

Dick Institute

KILMARNOCK

Provenance ↓ / Artefact →	box	bag	basket	mat	headrest	transport	currency	-rattle	-flute,pipe	-drum,gong	MUSICAL INS.	charm	magic,med.	fig.,image	carving	-bullroarer	-paddle	-adze	-board	-mask	CERE. OBJ.	staff,stick	toilet app.	fan	comb	-neck,breast	-arm	-ear,nose	-head	PERS. ORN.	-cloak	-belt	-skirt	CLOTHING	barkcloth	OTHER	TOTAL
OCEANIA UN.																X																					X
AUSTRALIA																X																					X
MELA.UNPROV.																																					
Admiralty																																					
Banks																																					
Bismarck																																					
D'Entrecast.																																					
Fiji																																					2+
Louisiade																																					
Loyalty																																					
N. Britain																																					
N. Caledonia																																					
N. Guinea																																					1+
N. Hebrides																																					
N. Ireland																																					
Santa Cruz																																					
Solomon																																					
Trobriand																																					
MICRO.UNPROV.																																					
Caroline																																					
Gilbert																																					
Mariana																																					
Marshall																																					
POLY.UNPROV.																																					
Austral																																					
Chatham																																					
Cook																																					
Easter																																					
Hawaii																																					
Marquesas																																					
New Zealand																																					
Niue																																					
Pitcairn																																					
Samoa																																					
Society																																					
Tokelau																																					
Tonga																																					
Tuamotu																																					
Tuvalu																																					

Dick Institute KILMARNOCK

Artefact → / Provenance →	OCEANIA UN.	AUSTRALIA	MELA.UNPROV.	Admiralty	Banks	Bismarck	D'Entrecast.	Fiji	Louisiade	Loyalty	N. Britain	N. Caledonia	N. Guinea	N. Hebrides	N. Ireland	Santa Cruz	Solomon	Trobriand	MICRO.UNPROV.	Caroline	Gilbert	Mariana	Marshall	POLY.UNPROV.	Austral	Chatham	Cook	Easter	Hawaii	Marquesas	New Zealand	Niue	Pitcairn	Samoa	Society	Tokelau	Tonga	Tuamotu	Tuvalu
cord																																							
raw mate																																							
-sling,st																																							
-arrow																																							
-bow																																							
-shield																																							
-dagger																																							
-spearthr																																							
-spear																																							
-club																																							
WEAPON																																							
-float,si																																							
-net																																							
-spear																																							
-fishhook																																							
FISHING																																							
hunting																																							
-model																																							
-ornament																																							
-paddle													X																										
NAVIGATIO																																							
-barkclot																																							
-weaving																																							
-needle,a																																							
-chisel																																							
-rasp																																							
-grinding																																							
-pounding																																							
-adze																																							
TOOL																																							
fire,ligh																																							
smokng pi																																							
pottery																																							
utensil																																							
lime spat																																							
dish,vess																																							
lime cont																																							

KING'S LYNN

Name The Lynn Museum

Address Old Market Street
King's Lynn PE30 1NL

Telephone 0553-5001

Contact Curator

Sources & Dates of Information

R. Hutchings 1966

Visit (ALK) P6/1974

MEG 1978

Letter 1979

Notes

Disposals: Some lost before 1958.

Dates of Collection/Acquisition

1840-1930

Donors/Collectors/Former Owners

Thomas Baines, "Australasia"
Admiral Swaine

Documentation

Archival (including Baines), iconographic.

Comment

Vancouver was born in King's Lynn, but had no connexion with this material (his collection in the Museum of Mankind). Swaine was a lieutenant with Vancouver 1794-98 in the Pacific and Northwest Coast of America.

Lynn Museum

KING'S LYNN

Artefact → / Provenance →	OCEANIA UN.	AUSTRALIA	MELA.UNPROV.	Admiralty	Banks	Bismarck	D'Entrecast.	Fiji	Louisiade	Loyalty	N. Britain	N. Caledonia	N. Guinea	N. Hebrides	N. Ireland	Santa Cruz	Solomon	Trobriand	MICRO.UNPROV	Caroline	Gilbert	Mariana	Marshall	POLY.UNPROV.	Austral	Chatham	Cook	Easter	Hawaii	Marquesas	New Zealand	Niue	Pitcairn	Samoa	Society	Tokelau	Tonga	Tuamotu	Tuvalu	Tahiti
box																																								
bag																																								
basket																																								
mat																																								
headrest																																								
transport																																								
currency																																								
-rattle																																								
-flute,pipe																																								
-drum,gong																																								
MUSICAL INS																																								
charm																																								
magic,med.																																								
fig.,image																																								
carving																																								
-bullroarer																																								
-paddle																																								
-adze																																								
-board																																								
-mask																																								
CERE. OBJ.																																								
staff,stick																																								
toilet app.																																								
fan																																								
comb																																								
-neck,breast																																								
-arm																																								
-ear,nose																																								
-head																																								
PERS. ORN.																																								
-cloak																																								
-belt																																								
-skirt																																								
CLOTHING																																								
barkcloth																																								
OTHER																																								
TOTAL													1																4								1			1

Lynn Museum

KING'S LYNN

Artefact → / Provenance →	OCEANIA UN.	AUSTRALIA	MELA.UNPROV.	Admiralty	Banks	Bismarck	D'Entrecast.	Fiji	Louisiade	Loyalty	N. Britain	N. Caledonia	N. Guinea	N. Hebrides	N. Ireland	Santa Cruz	Solomon	Trobriand	MICRO.UNPROV	Caroline	Gilbert	Mariana	Marshall	POLY.UNPROV.	Austral	Chatham	Cook	Easter	Hawaii	Marquesas	New Zealand	Niue	Pitcairn	Samoa	Society	Tokelau	Tonga	Tuamotu	Tuvalu	Tahiti
cord																																								
raw mater.																																								
-sling,sto																																								
-arrow																																								
-bow																																								
-shield																																								
-dagger																																								
-spearthro																																								
-spear																																								
-club																																								
WEAPON																																					1			
-float,sin																																								
-net																																								
-spear																																								
-fishhook																																								
FISHING																													4								1			1
hunting																																								
-model																																								
-ornament																																								
-paddle																																								
NAVIGATION																																								
-barkcloth																																								
-weaving																																								
-needle,aw.																																								
-chisel																																								
-rasp																																								
-grinding																																								
-pounding																																								
-adze																																								
TOOL																																								
fire,light																																								
smoking pip													1																											
pottery																																								
utensil																																								
lime spat.																																								
dish,vesse																																								
lime cont.																																								

KINGSTON

Name: Museum and Art Gallery

Address: Fairfield Road
Kingston upon Thames KT1 2PS

Telephone: 01-546 5386

Contact: Curator

Sources & Dates of Information

R. Hutchings 1966

Visit

MEG 1978

Letters 1979

Notes

Australia: boomerangs 3
spearthrower 1

Dates of Collection/Acquisition

Acquired 1969+

Donors/Collectors/Former Owners

Documentation

Comment

Name	John McDouall Stuart Museum	KIRKCALDY (JMS)
Address	Rectory Lane Dysart Kirkcaldy Fife	**Sources & Dates of Information** R. Hutchings 1966 Visit MEG 1978
Telephone	0592-53118	
Contact	Assistant Curator, c/o Kirkcaldy Museum & Art Gallery, War Memorial Grounds, Kirkcaldy, KY1 1YG (tel. 0592-60732)	Letter 1979 Letter from J. Bentley 19[illegible]

Notes

Australia: club, boomerang

Dates of Collection/Acquisition	Donors/Collectors/Former Owners
Collected early 20th Century	

Documentation

Comment

KIRKCALDY (M.AG)

Name	Kirkcaldy Museum and Art Gallery
Address	War Memorial Grounds Kirkcaldy Fife KY1 1YG
Telephone	0592-60732
Contact	Assistant Curator

Sources & Dates of Information

R. Hutchings 1966

Visit

MEG 1978

Letter 1979

Notes

Dates of Collection/Acquisition

Acquired 1925-29

Donors/Collectors/Former Owners

Australian material on loan from other museums.

Documentation

Catalogued. Collectors unknown, but probably 19th Century.

Comment

Tongan headrest sounds interesting.

Museum and Art Gallery

KIRKCALD

Provenance ↓ / Artcfact →	TOTAL	OTHER	barkcloth	CLOTHING	-skirt	-belt	-cloak	PERS. ORN.	-head	-ear,nose	-arm	-neck,breast	comb	fan	toilet app.	staff,stick	CERE. OBJ.	-mask	-board	-adze	-paddle	-bullroarer	carving	fig.,image	magic,med.	charm	MUSICAL INS.	-drum,gong	-flute,pipe	-rattle	currency	transport	headrest	mat	basket	bag	box
OCEANIA UN.																																					
AUSTRALIA	6																																				
MELA.UNPROV.																																					
Admiralty																																					
Banks																																					
Bismarck																																					
D'Entrecast.																																					
Fiji	4																																				
Louisiade																																					
Loyalty																																					
N. Britain																																					
N. Caledonia																																					
N. Guinea																																					
N. Hebrides																																					
N. Ireland																																					
Santa Cruz																																					
Solomon																																					
Trobriand																																					
MICRO.UNPROV.																																					
Caroline																																					
Gilbert																																					
Mariana																																					
Marshall																																					
POLY.UNPROV.																																					
Austral																																					
Chatham																																					
Cook	2																		2																		
Easter																																					
Hawaii																																					
Marquesas																																					
New Zealand																																					
Niue																																					
Pitcairn																																					
Samoa																																					
Society																																					
Tokelau																																					
Tonga	1																																1				
Tuamotu																																					
Tuvalu																																					

Museum and Art Gallery

KIRKCALDY (M&AG

Artefact → / Provenance →	OCEANIA UN.	AUSTRALIA	MELA.UNPROV.	Admiralty	Banks	Bismarck	D'Entrecast.	Fiji	Louisiade	Loyalty	N. Britain	N. Caledonia	N. Guinea	N. Hebrides	N. Ireland	Santa Cruz	Solomon	Trobriand	MICRO.UNPROV	Caroline	Gilbert	Mariana	Marshall	POLY.UNPROV.	Austral	Chatham	Cook	Easter	Hawaii	Marquesas	New Zealand	Niue	Pitcairn	Samoa	Society	Tokelau	Tonga	Tuamotu	Tuvalu
cord																																							
raw mater.																																							
-sling,ston																																							
-arrow																																							
-bow																																							
-shield																																							
-dagger																																							
-spearthrow																																							
-spear																																							
-club																																							
WEAPON								4*																															
-float,sin																																							
-net																																							
-spear																																							
-fishhook																																							
FISHING																																							
hunting																																							
-model																																							
-ornament																																							
-paddle																																							
NAVIGATION																																							
barkcloth																																							
-weaving																																							
-needle,aw																																							
-chisel																																							
-rasp																																							
-grinding																																							
-pounding																																							
-adze																																							
TOOL																																							
fire,light																																							
smoking pip																																							
pottery																																							
utensil																																							
lime spat.																																							
dish,vesse																																							
lime cont.																																							

Name	Leeds City Museum
Address	Municipal Buildings Leeds LS1 3AA
Telephone	0532-462630
Contact	Assistant Keeper of Ethnography

LEEDS

Sources & Dates of Information

R. Hutchings 1966

Visit SP/1975

MEG 1978

Letter 1979

Notes

Disposals: most Oceanic disposed of late 40's, much in U.S.A. via Mr. K. Webster, no record. George Bennet material: some destroyed in war, much went to Hooper Collection, some probably in Webster Collection, New Zealand. A few pieces remain in Leeds.

*Oceania unprovenanced-- skirts: 1 Christmas Island?
*Australia-- bullroarers: churinga 5
other: toy
*Santa Cruz-- other: cloth
*Solomons-- ceremonial objects: grave ornaments
*Micronesia-- adze: 1 Nauru? (Gilberts)
*Carolines-- other: cloth
*Hawaii-- other: toy
*Marquesas-- carving: stilt step
*New Zealand-- figures: 3 are casts, 1 is modern
other: kauri gum heads 2
*Society-- adzes: 8 hafted

Dates of Collection/Acquisition

Mainly since 1960

Donors/Collectors/Former Owners

Eyres, 1881, Polynesia
Leeds Literary & Philosophical Society 1820-1921
Cullingworth, 1846, New Zealand
Williamson, 1869, Hawaii (most went to Hooper Collection)
Bedford, 1901, New Guinea
Whitehead, 1977-78, New Guinea

Documentation

A virtually complete card index.

Library, photographic.

Comment

Literary and Philosophical Society material needs to be disentangled. Research under way on Bennet.

Leeds City Museum

LEEDS

Artefact → / Provenance ↓	TOTAL	OTHER	barkcloth	CLOTHING	-skirt	-belt	-cloak	PERS. ORN.	-head	-ear,nose	-arm	-neck,breast	comb	fan	toilet app.	staff,stick	CERE. OBJ.	-mask	-board	-adze	-paddle	-bullroarer	carving	fig.,image	magic,med.	charm	MUSICAL INS.	-drum,gong	-flute,pipe	-rattle	currency	transport	headrest	mat	basket	bag	box
OCEANIA UN.	61		1		1*							3											1												1		
AUSTRALIA	75	1						2	1													7			4												
MELA.UNPROV.	34					2					16																										
Admiralty																																					
Banks	2																																				
Bismarck																																					
D'Entrecast.																																					
Fiji	26																1																				
Louisiade																																					
Loyalty																																					
N. Britain	8										2																										
N. Caledonia	3															2																					
N. Guinea	212		3		1			12	19	2	5	6		2				1					1	3				5	2				2		8		
N. Hebrides	5							1																1													
N. Ireland																																					
Santa Cruz	29	1*				3																												1		1	
Solomon	126							5			3	2	5				3*						3						1								
Trobriand																																					
MICRO.UNPROV.																																					
Caroline	2	1*										1																									
Gilbert	14																																				
Mariana																																					
Marshall	1																																				
POLY.UNPROV.	12		2																																		
Austral																																					
Chatham																																					
Cook	1																																				
Easter																																					
Hawaii	5	1																																			
Marquesas	1																						1*														
New Zealand	69	2					2	2		1		2	1				2							5*												6	2
Niue	3																																				
Pitcairn																																					
Samoa	16		5											2																						1	
Society	18		X																																	1	
Tokelau																																					
Tonga	10																				4																
Tuamotu																																					
Tuvalu																																					

LEEDS

Leeds City Museum

Provenance ↓ / Artefact →	lime con	dish,vess	lime spa	utensil	pottery	smokng p	fire,lig	TOOL	-adze	-pounding	-grinding	-rasp	-chisel	-needle,a	-weaving	-barkclo	NAVIGATI	-paddle
OCEANIA UN.									1									
AUSTRALIA								3	11									
MELA.UNPROV.		2																
Admiralty																		
Banks				1														
Bismarck																		
D'Entrecast.																		
Fiji		2			2													
Louisiade																		
Loyalty																		
N. Britain																		
N. Caledonia									2									
N. Guinea	X	6	2			8			1									1
N. Hebrides																		
N. Ireland																		
Santa Cruz		1																
Solomon																		4
Trobriand																		
MICRO.UNPROV									3*									
Caroline																		
Gilbert																		
Mariana																		
Marshall																		
POLY.UNPROV.																		
Austral																		
Chatham																		
Cook									1	1								
Easter																		
Hawaii									1	1								
Marquesas																		
New Zealand						2			6									
Niue																		
Pitcairn																		
Samoa		1																
Society									11*									
Tokelau																		
Tonga																		
Tuamotu																		
Tuvalu																		

Provenance ↓ / Artefact →	-ornamen	-model	hunting	FISHING	-fishhoo	-spear	-net	-float,s	WEAPON	-club	-spear	-spearth	-dagger	-shield	-bow	-arrow	-sling,s	raw mate	cord
OCEANIA UN.					5						52				5	2			2
AUSTRALIA									11	10	5	11		2					
MELA.UNPROV.																		X	
Admiralty																			
Banks													1						
Bismarck																			
D'Entrecast.																			
Fiji		1					1			7	1							1	
Louisiade																			
Loyalty																			
N. Britain										1	4								
N. Caledonia																			
N. Guinea							1			1	1			1	2	1			
N. Hebrides											1								
N. Ireland																			
Santa Cruz														4		20			
Solomon	1	2			7				2	41	8				13	6			
Trobriand																			
MICRO.UNPROV																	2		
Caroline																			
Gilbert									6		5								
Mariana																			
Marshall																			
POLY.UNPROV.																			
Austral																			
Chatham																			
Cook																			
Easter																			
Hawaii		2			3														
Marquesas																			
New Zealand	1	1			11					7									
Niue		3																	
Pitcairn																			
Samoa					1					1									
Society																			
Tokelau																			
Tonga					2					3									
Tuamotu																			
Tuvalu																			

LEICESTER

Name: Education and Interpretation Division (Loan Service)
Leicestershire Museums, Art Gallery and Record Service

Address: 96 New Walk
Leicester LE1 6TD

Telephone: 0533-554100

Contact: Assistant Director, Education and Interpretation

Sources & Dates of Information

R. Hutchings	1966
Visit	
MEG	1978
Letter	1979

Notes

Disposals: some material dispersed post-war

*Australia-- other: boomerang

Dates of Collection/Acquisition

Donors/Collectors/Former Owners

Documentation

Comment

Schools' teaching collection.

Loan Service

LEICESTER

Artefact → / Provenance ↓	TOTAL	OTHER	barkcloth	CLOTHING	-skirt	-belt	-cloak	PERS. ORN.	-head	-ear,nose	-arm	-neck,breast	comb	fan	toilet app.	staff,stick	CERE. OBJ.	-mask	-board	-adze	-paddle	-bullroarer	carving	fig.,image	magic,med.	charm	MUSICAL INS.	-drum,gong	-flute,pipe	-rattle	currency	transport	headrest	mat	basket	bag	box
OCEANIA UN.	1																																				
AUSTRALIA	2	1																																			
MELA.UNPROV.																																					
Admiralty																																					
Banks																																					
Bismarck																																					
D'Entrecast.																																					
Fiji	1													1																							
Louisiade																																					
Loyalty																																					
N. Britain	1																												1								
N. Caledonia																																					
N. Guinea	1																											1									
N. Hebrides																																					
N. Ireland																																					
Santa Cruz																																					
Solomon	1							1																													
Trobriand																																					
MICRO.UNPROV																																					
Caroline																																					
Gilbert																																					
Mariana																																					
Marshall																																					
POLY.UNPROV.																																					
Austral																																					
Chatham																																					
Cook																																					
Easter																																					
Hawaii																																					
Marquesas																																					
New Zealand	3						1														1																
Niue																																					
Pitcairn																																					
Samoa																																					
Society																																					
Tokelau																																					
Tonga																																					
Tuamotu																																					
Tuvalu																																					

Loan Service

LEICESTER

Artefact → / Provenance	OCEANIA UN.	AUSTRALIA	MELA.UNPROV.	Admiralty	Banks	Bismarck	D'Entrecast.	Fiji	Louisiade	Loyalty	N. Britain	N. Caledonia	N. Guinea	N. Hebrides	N. Ireland	Santa Cruz	Solomon	Trobriand	MICRO.UNPROV.	Caroline	Gilbert	Mariana	Marshall	POLY.UNPROV.	Austral	Chatham	Cook	Easter	Hawaii	Marquesas	New Zealand	Niue	Pitcairn	Samoa	Society	Tokelau	Tonga	Tuamotu	Tuvalu
cord																																						
raw mater																																						
-sling,sto																																						
-arrow																																						
-bow																																						
-shield		/																																				
-dagger	/																																					
-spearthro																																						
-spear																																						
-club																																						
WEAPON																																						
-float,si																																						
-net																																						
-spear																																						
-fishhook																																						
FISHING																																						
hunting																																						
-model																																						
-ornament																																						
-paddle																																						
NAVIGATIO																																						
-barkclot																																						
-weaving																																						
-needle,aw																																						
-chisel																																						
-rasp																																						
-grinding																																						
-pounding																																						
-adze																														/								
TOOL																																						
fire,ligh																																						
smoking pi																																						
pottery																																						
utensil																																						
lime spat																																						
dish,vess																																						
lime cont																																						

LEWES

Name	Museum of Sussex Archaeology
Address	Barbican House High Street Lewes BN7 1YE
Telephone	07916-4379
Contact	Curator

Sources & Dates of Information

R. Hutchings 1966

Visit

MEG 1978

Letter 1979

Notes

Disposals: Museum of Local History (Lewes) sold at auction spears "etc."- not known if include Oceanic. No details.

Dates of Collection/Acquisition	Donors/Collectors/Former Owners
	Bartlett, Australia, 30 stone implements Mr. Alban Head, Australian stone implement (saw?) F.J. Tritton, Queensland knife Dr. E.C. Curwen, Admiralty obsidian knife

Documentation

Records in order. Bartlett Collection well documented.

Comment

Basically comparative ethnographic collection for local archaeologists (e.g. Curwen who was a very able local archaeologist).

Museum of Sussex Archaeology

LEWES

Provenance \ Artifact	TOTAL	OTHER	barkcloth	CLOTHING	-skirt	-belt	-cloak	PERS. ORN.	-head	-ear,nose	-arm	-neck,breast	comb	fan	toilet app.	staff,stick	CERE. OBJ.	-mask	-board	-adze	-paddle	-bullroarer	carving	fig.,image	magic,med.	charm	MUSICAL INST	-drum,gong	-flute,pipe	-rattle	currency	transport	headrest	mat	basket	bag	box
OCEANIA UN.																																					
AUSTRALIA	32																																				
MELA. UNPROV.																																					
Admiralty	1																																				
Banks																																					
Bismarck																																					
D'Entrecast.																																					
Fiji																																					
Louisiade																																					
Loyalty																																					
N. Britain																																					
N. Caledonia																																					
N. Guinea	1																																				
N. Hebrides																																					
N. Ireland																																					
Santa Cruz																																					
Solomon																																					
Trobriand																																					
MICRO. UNPROV.																																					
Caroline																																					
Gilbert																																					
Mariana																																					
Marshall																																					
POLY. UNPROV.																																					
Austral																																					
Chatham																																					
Cook																																					
Easter																																					
Hawaii																																					
Marquesas																																					
New Zealand																																					
Niue																																					
Pitcairn																																					
Samoa																																					
Society																																					
Tokelau																																					
Tonga																																					
Tuamotu																																					
Tuvalu																																					

Museum of Sussex Archaeology

LEWES

Artefact → / Provenance ↓	OCEANIA UN.	AUSTRALIA	MELA.UNPROV.	Admiralty	Banks	Bismarck	D'Entrecast.	Fiji	Louisiade	Loyalty	N. Britain	N. Caledonia	N. Guinea	N. Hebrides	N. Ireland	Santa Cruz	Solomon	Trobriand	MICRO.UNPROV	Caroline	Gilbert	Mariana	Marshall	POLY.UNPROV.	Austral	Chatham	Cook	Easter	Hawaii	Marquesas	New Zealand	Niue	Pitcairn	Samoa	Society	Tokelau	Tonga	Tuamotu	Tuvalu		
cord																																									
raw mater																																									
-sling,st																																									
-arrow																																									
-bow																																									
-shield																																									
-dagger																																									
-spearthr				1																																					
-spear																																									
-club																																									
WEAPON																																									
-float,sl																																									
-net																																									
-spear																																									
-fishhook																																									
FISHING																																									
hunting																																									
-model																																									
-ornament																																									
-paddle																																									
NAVIGATIO																																									
-barkclot																																									
-weaving																																									
-needle,a																																									
-chisel																																									
-rasp																																									
-grinding																																									
-pounding																																									
-adze																																									
TOOL													1																												
fire,ligh		32																																							
smoking pi																																									
pottery																																									
utensil																																									
lime spat																																									
dish,vess																																									
lime cont																																									

LINCOLN (CCM)

Name: City and County Museum

Address: Greyfriars
Broadgate
Lincoln LN2 1EZ

Telephone: 0522-30401

Contact: Keeper of Archaeology

Sources & Dates of Information

R. Hutchings 1966

Visit SP 1975

MEG 1978

Letter

Notes

Total Oceanic about 110.
Material in store.

Dates of Collection/Acquisition	Donors/Collectors/Former Owners
Acquired mainly 1906-30	J.T. White, donated 1860's-80's

Documentation

Comment

City and County Museum LINCOLN(

Artefact →
Provenance ↓

Provenance	TOTAL	OTHER	barkcloth	CLOTHING	-skirt	-belt	-cloak	PERS. ORN.	-head	-ear,nose	-arm	-neck,breast	comb	fan	toilet app.	staff,stick	CERE. OBJ.	-mask	-board	-adze	-paddle	-bullroarer	carving	fig.,image	magic,med.	charm	MUSICAL INS.	-drum,gong	-flute,pipe	-rattle	currency	transport	headrest	mat	basket	bag	box
OCEANIA UN.	5							1																				1									
AUSTRALIA	25																				9																
MELA.UNPROV.	1																																				
Admiralty																																					
Banks																																					
Bismarck																																					
D'Entrecast.																																					
Fiji	3																																				
Louisiade																																					
Loyalty																																					
N. Britain																																					
N. Caledonia																																					
N. Guinea	12				2								3																								
N. Hebrides																																					
N. Ireland																																					
Santa Cruz																																					
Solomon	3																																				
Trobriand	4																																				
MICRO.UNPROV.																																					
Caroline																																					
Gilbert																																					
Mariana																																					
Marshall																																					
POLY.UNPROV.																																					
Austral																				1																	
Chatham																																					
Cook																																					
Easter																																					
Hawaii																																					
Marquesas																																					
New Zealand	6												1																								1
Niue																																					
Pitcairn																																					
Samoa	1		1																																		
Society																																					
Tokelau																																					
Tonga																																					
Tuamotu																																					
Tuvalu																																					

City and County Museum

LINCOLN (CCM)

Artefact → / Provenance ↓	OCEANIA UN.	AUSTRALIA	MELA.UNPROV.	Admiralty	Banks	Bismarck	D'Entrecast.	Fiji	Louisiade	Loyalty	N. Britain	N. Caledcnia	N. Guinea	N. Hebrides	N. Ireland	Santa Cruz	Solomon	Trobriand	MICRO.UNPROV.	Caroline	Gilbert	Mariana	Marshall	POLY.UNPROV.	Austral	Chatham	Cook	Easter	Hawaii	Marquesas	New Zealand	Niue	Pitcairn	Samoa	Society	Tokelau	Tonga	Tuamotu	Tuvalu
cord	1																																						
raw mater.																																							
-sling,sto																																							
-arrow																	2																						
-bow																																							
-shield		4																																					
-dagger																																							
-spearthro		4																																					
-spear		11	1																																				
-club		7						3					2				1	3													3								
WEAPON																																							
-float,sin																																							
-net																																							
-spear																																							
-fishhook																																							
FISHING																																							
hunting																																							
-model																																							
-ornament																																							
-paddle																																							
NAVIGATION																																							
-barkcloth																																							
-weaving																																							
-needle,aw																																							
-chisel																																							
-rasp																																							
-grinding																																							
-pounding																																							
-adze	2												1																		1								
TOOL																																							
fire,light																																							
smoking pip																																							
pottery																																							
utensil																																							
lime spat.																																							
dish,vesse																																							
lime cont.																	1																						

LINCOLN (MLL)

Name: Museum of Lincolnshire Life

Address: Burton Road
Lincoln LN1 3LY

Telephone: 0522-28448

Contact: Keeper

Sources & Dates of Information

R. Hutchings 1966
Visit

MEG 1978
Letter

Notes

Dates of Collection/Acquisition

Donors/Collectors/Former Owners

Documentation

Some documentation relating to the discovery of Australia.

Comment

Museum of Lincolnshire Life

LINCOLN CML

Provenance / Artefact	box	bag	basket	mat	headrest	transport	currency	rattle	flute,pipe	drum,gong	MUSICAL INS.	charm	magic,med.	fig.,image	carving	bullroarer	paddle	adze	board	mask	CERE. OBJ.	staff,stick	toilet app.	fan	comb	neck,breast	arm	ear,nose	head	PERS. ORN.	cloak	belt	skirt	CLOTHING	barkcloth	OTHER	TOTAL
OCEANIA UN.																																				
AUSTRALIA																																				
MELA.UNPROV.																																				
Admiralty																																				
Banks																																				
Bismarck																																				
D'Entrecast.																																				
Fiji																																				12
Louisiade																																				
Loyalty																																				
N. Britain																																				
N. Caledonia																																				
N. Guinea																																				
N. Hebrides																																				
N. Ireland																																				
Santa Cruz																																				
Solomon																																				
Trobriand																																				
MICRO.UNPROV																																				
Caroline																																				
Gilbert																																				
Mariana																																				
Marshall																																				
POLY.UNPROV.																																				
Austral																																				
Chatham																																				
Cook																																				
Easter																																				
Hawaii																																				
Marquesas																																				
New Zealand																																				
Niue																																				
Pitcairn																																				
Samoa																																				
Society																																				
Tokelau																																				
Tonga																																				
Tuamotu																																				
Tuvalu																																				

Museum of Lincolnshire Life

LINCOLN (MLL)

Artefact → / Provenance ↓	OCEANIA UN.	AUSTRALIA	MELA.UNPROV.	Admiralty	Banks	Bismarck	D'Entrecast.	Fiji	Louisiade	Loyalty	N. Britain	N. Caledonia	N. Guinea	N. Hebrides	N. Ireland	Santa Cruz	Solomon	Trobriand	MICRO.UNPROV.	Caroline	Gilbert	Mariana	Marshall	POLY.UNPROV.	Austral	Chatham	Cook	Easter	Hawaii	Marquesas	New Zealand	Niue	Pitcairn	Samoa	Society	Tokelau	Tonga	Tuamotu	Tuvalu
cord																																							
raw mate																																							
-sling,s																																							
-arrow																																							
-bow																																							
-shield																																							
-dagger																																							
-spearth																																							
-spear																																							
-club																																							
WEAPON																																							
-float,s																																							
-net																																							
-spear																																							
-fishhoo																																							
FISHING																																							
hunting																																							
-model																																							
-ornamen																																							
-paddle																																							
NAVIGATI																																							
-barkclo																																							
-weaving																																							
-needle,																																							
-chisel																																							
-rasp																																							
-grinding																																							
-pounding																																							
-adze																																							
TOOL																																							
fire,lig																																							
smokng p																																							
pottery																																							
utensil																																							
lime spa																																							
dish,vess																																							
lime con																																							

LIVERPOOL (E)

Name Merseyside County Museums

Address William Brown Street
Liverpool L3 8EN

Telephone 051-207 0001

Contact Keeper of Ethnology

Sources & Dates of Information

R. Hutchings 1966

Visit SP 1975

MEG 1978

Letter 1974

Notes

Disposals: Chicago, Field Museum, 1899
Salford, Peel Park Museum
Rawtenstall Museum
East London Museum, South Africa, 1971
New York, Natural History Museum, 1900
fire, 1941, much Oceanic destroyed

For table explanatory notes, see Liverpool (C).

Dates of Collection/Acquisition	Donors/Collectors/Former Owners
	Joseph Mayer, acquired 1867 Liverpool Royal Institute, 1814-1894 (possible Cook) Norwich Castle Museum, 1950's Wellcome Collection, 1950's Beasley, 1950's ex-Holmes Collection, collected 1893-1900, New Guinea

Documentation

Library, archival, photographic, iconographic.

Reference: Kaeppler, 1974, "Cook Voyage Provenance of the 'Artificial Curiousities' of Bullock's Museum," Man, 9:68-92.

Comment

Very important. Recent display. Well curated. Need to separate early material (Mayer, Liverpool Royal Institute) from that obtained from Norwich, Wellcome, Beasley.

Merseyside County Museums

LIVERPOOL

Provenance ↓ / Artefact →	TOTAL	OTHER	barkcloth	CLOTHING	-skirt	-belt	-cloak	PERS. ORN.	-head	-ear,nose	-arm	-neck,breast	comb	fan	toilet app.	staff,stick	CERE. OBJ.	-mask	-board	-adze	-paddle	-bullroarer	carving	fig.,image	magic,med.	charm	MUSICAL INS.	-drum,gong	-flute,pipe	-rattle	currency	transport	headrest	mat	basket	bag	box
OCEANIA UN.																																					
AUSTRALIA	525	270		7													65																				
MELA.UNPROV.	107	5		11				59					7			5													1							6	
Admiralty	25					1		6																		1					2						
Banks	24+	1								20+																											
Bismarck																																					
D'Entrecast.																																					
Fiji	442	12	21					14	2				1	1	11	2	25											1		1			9		5		
Louisiade																																					
Loyalty	9										2															1										1	
N. Britain	51							5																					1						9		
N. Caledonia	50												1			1				3																	
N. Guinea	1396*		see next page (8)																																		
N. Hebrides	96	10	4					16					2					1																			
N. Ireland	16	1																4					3	2													
Santa Cruz	109	11						33					1			16															7				9	27	
Solomon	583	16	1	2				157*					135				8						2						5		X					9	
Trobriand																																					
MICRO.UNPROV																																					
Caroline	26				2	14		1			1	1	4																								
Gilbert	76+	4						2+																										10	3		
Mariana																																					
Marshall	5				1																														1		
POLY.UNPROV.	25		20																																5		
Austral	63																																				
Chatham	20*																																				
Cook	60		1									2												1													
Easter	9															1																					
Hawaii	47		3		2		1		1*		2	5																	2								
Marquesas	16								1							2							1*				1*										
New Zealand	371	4					28	5				4+			1	8	2						12	2					3							21	20
Niue																													4								
Pitcairn			8	1																															2		
Samoa	61	5	25					1					13																								
Society	39	4	1									2												1									2	2			
Tokelau																																					
Tonga	78	4						2					2			1																	4		2		
Tuamotu																																					
Tuvalu	2				1																																
[illegible]	[illegible]																																				

Provenance ↓ / Artefact →	lime cont.	dish,vesse.	lime spat.	utensil	pottery	smokng pip	fire,light	TOOL	-adze	-pounding	-grinding	-rasp	-chisel	-needle,awl	-weaving	-barkcloth	NAVIGATION	-paddle	-ornament	-model	hunting	FISHING	-fishhook	-spear	-net	-float,sink	WEAPON	-club	-spear	-spearthrow	-dagger	-shield	-bow	-arrow	-sling,stone	raw mater.	cord
OCEANIA UN.																																					
AUSTRALIA																											184										
MELA.UNPROV.		4							1														4					4									
Admiralty								15																													
Banks																															3						
Bismarck																																					
D'Entrecast.																																					
Fiji		33+		13	19				18					13		9				2								207	20+								
Louisiade																																					
Loyalty		1							2													1														1	
N. Britain								10*		1																		22							2	1	
N. Caledonia		1							5														3					28		4					1		
N. Guinea	see next page (B)																																				
N. Hebrides								3	9	1																		49						1			
N. Ireland																												6									
Santa Cruz									5																												
Solomon		8	3					2	58	1						2		10+	2	2		1	50				3	93*				11					
Trobriand																																					
MICRO.UNPROV																																					
Caroline									1														2														
Gilbert																							6				40*		11								
Mariana																																					
Marshall														1									2														
POLY.UNPROV.																																					
Austral									9									54																			
Chatham																																					
Cook									46	7										1																	
Easter									8																												
Hawaii									15	2						5							3			7	1										
Marquesas																1												10									
New Zealand								21*	88	2							2	8	1	7			29					92		1							
Niue																												6									
Pitcairn									4																												
Samoa								8								1						1						3									
Society									23	4													4														
Tokelau																																					
Tonga																												63									
Tuamotu																																					
Tuvalu									1																												
Torres Straits																								1				2				1					

CONT. NEXT PAGE (B)

Merseyside County Museums (B)

LIVERPOOL(

Provenance ↓ / Artefact →	TOTAL	OTHER	barkcloth	CLOTHING	-skirt	-belt	-cloak	PERS. ORN.	-head	-ear,nose	-arm	-neck,breast	comb	fan	toilet app.	staff,stick	CERE. OBJ.	-mask	-board	-adze	-paddle	-bullroarer	carving	fig.,image	magic,med.	charm	MUSICAL INS.	-drum,gong	-flute,pipe	-rattle	currency	transport	headrest	mat	basket	bag	box
NEWGUINEA:																																					
unprovenanced	396	7						136					8									2					2	11					2		13	X	
West Irian	122	6		7				52					9										3	5			1	2					1			5	
Sepik	47	4	1					6										1					11				1						2			4	
Highlands	29			7		6																														2	
NE	58	1		5				32					3																							4	
Papuan Gulf	461	16		26		27		43					21						10			29				37		7								19	
SE + Massim	289	14	2			6		72								12	1																2			4	
Phoenix	1													1																							
Mangareva	3																																				
Rotuma	4																																				

Merseyside County Museums (B)

LIVERPOOL (E

Artefact → / Provenance ↓	lime cont.	dish,vesse.	lime spat.	utensil	pottery	smokng pip	fire,light	TOOL	-adze	-pounding	-grinding	-rasp	-chisel	-needle,aw.	-weaving	-barkcloth	NAVIGATION	-paddle
NEW GUINEA:																		
unprovenanced		3	44			13		19	21						1	1		5
West Irian				3		1			7	1								2
Sepik ·			2	3				1	3	2								
Highlands						1		2	4									
N/E						1												
Papuan Gulf			1	35		10		13	6									
SE + Massim		1	39					4	28								1	2
Phoenix																		
Mangareva									1	1								1
Rotuma																		

Artefact → / Provenance ↓	-ornament	-model	hunting	FISHING	-fishhook	-spear	-net	-float,sink	WEAPON	-club	-spear	-spearthrow	-dagger	-shield	-bow	-arrow	-sling,ston	raw mater.	cord
NEW GUINEA:																			
unprovenanced					16		4		1	12	10		9	1	16	38		1	
West Irian	1										1		4			10			
Sepik ·												1	2						
Highlands											6			1					
N/E					3					5					1	131			4
Papuan Gulf										28				1					
SE + Massim							8			68	2			3	4		10		
Phoenix																			
Mangareva																			
Rotuma										4									

Merseyside County Museums (C)

*Australia-- other: includes 69 household objects

*Melanesia unprovenanced-- other: misc. 5

*Banks-- other: cloth

*New Hebrides-- other: hook 1, skull 1, misc. 8

*New Britain-- tools: stone implements

*Santa Cruz-- other: 'containers' 3, misc. 8

*Solomons-- ornaments: many armbands functioning as currency as well
clubs: includes some batons
other: 'containers' 16

*Gilberts-- weapons: includes armour suits 7, helmet 1, pair of gauntlets
other: misc. 4

*Fiji-- other: textiles 5, flywhisks 3, misc. 4

*Hawaii-- head ornament: helmet

*Marquesas-- mus. instrument: shell trumpet
carving: stilt step

*New Zealand-- tools: stone implements, ko steps 2
other: heads 4

*Samoa-- other: flywhick 1, printing tablet 1, misc. 3

*Tonga-- other: hooks

*Chathams-- includes stone artefacts

New Guinea

*unprovenanced-- other: suspension hook 1, 'containers' (unspecified) 6

*West Irian-- other: skulls 3, misc. 3

*Sepik-- other: containers 4, skull

*Northeast-- other: container

*Papuan Gulf-- other: containers 5, skulls 4, misc. 7

*Southeast & Massim-- other: containers 7, misc.

LIVERPOOL (MARITIME

Name	Maritime History Department Merseyside County Museums
Address	William Brown Street Liverpool L3 8EN
Telephone	051-2070001
Contact	Keeper, Maritime History Department

Sources & Dates of Information

R. Hutchings 1966

Visit

MEG 1978

Letter 1979

Notes

*Australia-- model: rigged fishing boat
*New Guinea-- model: outrigger
*Solomons-- navigation: canoe, 16 feet long
model: dugout canoe model
*Samoa-- models: outrigger 1, double-prowed (tanmulna) 1

Dates of Collection/Acquisition	Donors/Collectors/Former Owners
Acquired mainly 1929-39	

Documentation

Archival, photographic, iconographic, sound recordings, films.

Museum publication: R.B. Smith & E.W. Paget Tomlinson, 1967, Handlist of Ship Models.

Comment

Maritime History Dept., Merseyside County Museums

LIVERPOOL (MARITI

Artefact → / Provenance ↓	OCEANIA UN.	AUSTRALIA	MELA.UNPROV.	Admiralty	Banks	Bismarck	D'Entrecast.	Fiji	Louisiade	Loyalty	N. Britain	N. Caledonia	N. Guinea	N. Hebrides	N. Ireland	Santa Cruz	Solomon	Trobriand	MICRO.UNPROV.	Caroline	Gilbert	Mariana	Marshall	POLY.UNPROV.	Austral	Chatham	Cook	Easter	Hawaii	Marquesas	New Zealand	Niue	Pitcairn	Samoa	Society	Tokelau	Tonga	Tuamotu	Tuvalu
box																																							
bag																																							
basket																																							
mat																																							
headrest																																							
transport																																							
currency																																							
-rattle																																							
-flute,pipe																																							
-drum,gong																																							
MUSICAL INS.																																							
charm																																							
magic,med.																																							
fig.,image																																							
carving																																							
-bullroarer																																							
-paddle																																							
-adze																																							
-board																																							
-mask																																							
CERE. OBJ.																																							
staff,stick																																							
toilet app.																																							
fan																																							
comb																																							
-neck,breast																																							
-arm																																							
-ear,nose																																							
-head																																							
PERS. ORN.																																							
-cloak																																							
-belt																																							
-skirt																																							
CLOTHING																																							
barkcloth																																							
OTHER																																							
TOTAL		1											1				2																	2					

Maritime History Dept., Merseyside County Museums

LIVERPOOL (MARITIME

Artefact → / Provenance ↓	OCEANIA UN.	AUSTRALIA	MELA.UNPROV.	Admiralty	Banks	Bismarck	D'Entrecast.	Fiji	Louisiade	Loyalty	N. Britain	N. Caledonia	N. Guinea	N. Hebrides	N. Ireland	Santa Cruz	Solomon	Trobriand	MICRO.UNPROV	Caroline	Gilbert	Mariana	Marshall	POLY.UNPROV.	Austral	Chatham	Cook	Easter	Hawaii	Marquesas	New Zealand	Niue	Pitcairn	Samoa	Society	Tokelau	Tonga	Tuamotu	Tuvalu
cord																																							
raw mat																																							
-sling,s																																							
-arrow																																							
-bow																																							
-shield																																							
-dagger																																							
-speart																																							
-spear																																							
-club																																							
WEAPON																																							
-float,s																																							
-net																																							
-spear																																							
-fishho																																							
FISHING																																							
hunting																																							
-model		1*											1*				1*																	2*					
-ornamen																																							
-paddle																																							
NAVIGAT																	1*																						
-barkclo																																							
-weavin																																							
-needle,																																							
-chisel																																							
-rasp																																							
-grindin																																							
-poundin																																							
-adze																																							
TOOL																																							
fire,lig																																							
smokng p																																							
pottery																																							
utensil																																							
lime spa																																							
dish,ves																																							
lime con																																							

LONDON (ADMIRALTY)

Name: Admiralty House

Address: Ministry of Defence
Whitehall
London SW1

Telephone:

Contact: Board of Admiralty

Sources & Dates of Information

R. Hutchings 1966
Visit ALK? PG 1974
MEG 1978
Letter

Notes

Admiralty House is now used for receptions by HM Government. In two rooms hang 9 Hodges' oil paintings from Cook's 2nd Voyage.

Dates of Collection/Acquisition	Donors/Collectors/Former Owners

Documentation

Comment

Not open to public.

Name	Commonwealth Institute
Address	Kensington High Street London W8 6NQ
Telephone	01-602 3252
Contact	Deputy Director

LONDON (CI)

Sources & Dates of Information

R. Hutchings	1966
Visit	
MEG	1978
Letter	1979

Notes

Objects from Oceania, including Papua New Guinea. Most on exhibition, some in Education Department, some in store.

Disposals: When converted from Imperial Institute in 1961, large ethnographic collections disposed of.

Dates of Collection/Acquisition	Donors/Collectors/Former Owners
1900+	Commonwealth Governments Some individuals Royal Presents

Documentation

Library, sound recordings, photographic. 15000 slides of way of life in Commonwealth countries.
Catalogue not available.
Documentation of collections sparse.

Publication: CI Leaflet no. 6, "Books and Pamphlets" (0306-381X).
CI "List of Publications" (ISSN 0143-0882)

Comment

Name	Courtauld Institute Galleries	LONDON (COURTAULD)
Address	Woburn Square London WC1H OAA	**Sources & Dates of Information**
		R. Hutchings 1966
		Visit
Telephone	01-580 1015/636 2095	MEG 1978
Contact	Curatorial Assistant	Letter 1979

Notes

Admiralty: food bowl 1

Dates of Collection/Acquisition	Donors/Collectors/Former Owners
	Roger Fry donation (no collection data)

Documentation

Museum publication: General Catalogue of Courtauld Collection, 30p.

Comment

LONDON (CUMING)

Name Cuming Museum

Address 155-157 Walworth Road
London SE17 1RS

Telephone 01-7033324/5329/6514

Contact Keeper of Cuming Museum

Sources & Dates of Information

R. Hutchings 1966

Visit

MEG 1978

Letters 1979

Notes

Disposals: to Saffron Walden, Cambridge, London School of Economics, Horniman Museum (see these entries). Hooper acquired some.

NOTE: All items, now in museum, except Australian knife and Hawaiian dagger, have not been traced and may have been destroyed in war or lost their identification.

*Australs-- other: flywhisk
*Cook-- belt: of barkcloth
*Hawaii-- dagger: Cook (Leverian)
*Marquesas-- carving: stilt
*New Zealand-- musical intrument: shell trumpet
utensil: chief's feeding funnel
*Tahiti-- toilet apparatus: tatooing
*Tonga-- stick: "constable's staff"

Dates of Collection/Acquisition	Donors/Collectors/Former Owners
Acquired 1902	R. & H. Cuming, 1782-1902 Leverian Other donors, post-1912

Documentation

Archival, iconographic.

Cuming's manuscript catalogue of 1840-54.

Reference: see A.L. Kaeppler, forthcoming Bishop Museum (Honolulu) publication.

Comment

Cuming Museum

LONDON (CUMI

Provenance ↓ / Artefact →	TOTAL	OTHER	barkcloth	CLOTHING	-skirt	-belt	-cloak	PERS. ORN.	-head	-ear,nose	-arm	-neck,breast	comb	fan	toilet app.	staff,stick	CERE. OBJ.	-mask	-board	-adze	-paddle	-bullroarer	carving	fig.,image	magic,med.	charm	MUSICAL INS.	-drum,gong	-flute,pipe	-rattle	currency	transport	headrest	mat	basket	bag	box
OCEANIA UN.	1		1																																		
AUSTRALIA	5							1																													
MELA.UNPROV.																																					
Admiralty																																					
Banks																																					
Bismarck																																					
D'Entrecast.																																					
Fiji	3												1																								
Louisiade	1																																				1
Loyalty																																					
N. Britain																																					
N. Caledonia	2																							1													
N. Guinea																																					
N. Hebrides	3										1	1																									
N. Ireland																																					
Santa Cruz																																					
Solomon	3									1																		1									
Trobriand	1									1																											
MICRO.UNPROV.																																					
Caroline																																					
Gilbert																																					
Mariana																																					
Marshall	2																																				
POLY.UNPROV.																																					
Austral	3	1																																			
Chatham																																					
Cook	1					1*																															
Easter																																					
Hawaii	12										4	2																									
Marquesas	2																						1*														
New Zealand	14											3											1				1*		1							1	1
Niue																																					
Pitcairn																																					
Samoa																																					
Society	1																																				
Tokelau																																					
Tonga	9		1									3	1			1*																					
Tuamotu																																					
Tuvalu																																					
[illegible]	2		1												2*																						

Cuming Museum

LONDON (CUMIN

Artefact →

Provenance →

Provenance	cord	raw mater.	-sling,sto	-arrow	-bow	-shield	-dagger	-spearthro	-spear	-club	WEAPON	-float,sin	-net	-spear	-fishhook	FISHING	hunting	-model	-ornament	-paddle	NAVIGATION	-barkcloth	-weaving	-needle,aw	-chisel	-rasp	-grinding	-pounding	-adze	TOOL	fire,light	smoking pip	pottery	utensil	lime spat.	dish,vesse	lime cont.
OCEANIA UN.																																					
AUSTRALIA									1	1					1															1							
MELA.UNPROV.																																					
Admiralty																																					
Banks																																					
Bismarck																																					
D'Entrecast.																																					
Fiji										1																										1	
Louisiade																																					
Loyalty																																					
N. Britain																																					
N. Caledonia											1																										
N. Guinea																																					
N. Hebrides																				1																	
N. Ireland																																					
Santa Cruz																																					
Solomon				1																																	
Trobriand																																					
MICRO.UNPROV																																					
Caroline																																					
Gilbert																																					
Mariana																																					
Marshall															1									1													
POLY.UNPROV.																																					
Austral																				2																	
Chatham																																					
Cook																																					
Easter																																					
Hawaii			1				1		1						1																						
Marquesas															1																						
New Zealand		2													1					1				1										1+			
Niue																																					
Pitcairn																																					
Samoa																																					
Society										1																											
Tokelau																																					
Tonga	1									1					1																						
Tuamotu																																					
Tuvalu																																					
Tahiti																																					
Tasmania										1																											

Name	National Maritime Museum
Address	Romney Road Greenwich London SE10 9NF
Telephone	01-858 4422
Contact	Deputy Director

LONDON (GREENWICH

Sources & Dates of Information

R. Hutchings	1966
Visit	ALK, PG 1977
MEG	1978
Letter	1977

Notes

Total Oceanic: 80.

Dates of Collection/Acquisition	Donors/Collectors/Former Owners

Documentation

Archival, iconographic.

Comment

Some objects associated with Cook (see Kaeppler, Artificial Curiosities... 1978). Museum has outstanding collections relating to British naval history, navigation, etc. Of particular Pacific interest are Dance's portrait of Cook, Zoffany's 'Death of Capt. James Cook,' paintings and drawings by Hodges (2nd Voyage) and by Webber (3rd Voyage), and Kendall's Timekeepers Nos. 1 and 3 (a highly select list!).

National Maritime Museum

LONDON (GREENW

Artefact → / Provenance	OCEANIA UN.	AUSTRALIA	MELA.UNPROV.	Admiralty	Banks	Bismarck	D'Entrecast.	Fiji	Louisiade	Loyalty	N. Britain	N. Caledonia	N. Guinea	N. Hebrides	N. Ireland	Santa Cruz	Solomon	Trobriand	MICRO.UNPROV	Caroline	Gilbert	Mariana	Marshall	POLY.UNPROV.	Austral	Chatham	Cook	Easter	Hawaii	Marquesas	New Zealand	Niue	Pitcairn	Samoa	Society	Tokelau	Tonga	Tuamotu	Tuvalu	Tahiti
box																																								
bag																																								
basket																																								
mat																																								
headrest																																								
transport																																								
currency																																								
-rattle																																								
-flute,pipe																																								
-drum,gong																																								
MUSICAL INS.																																								
charm																																								
magic,med.																																								
fig.,image																																								
carving																												1												
-bullroarer																																								
-paddle																																								
-adze																																								
-board																																								
-mask																																								
CERE. OBJ.																																								
staff,stick																												1												
toilet app.																																								
fan																																								
comb																																								
-neck,breast																																							6	
-arm																																								
-ear,nose																																								
-head																																								
PERS. ORN.																																								
-cloak																																								
-belt																																								
-skirt																																								
CLOTHING																																								
barkcloth																																								
OTHER		2																																						
TOTAL		3	5					8						X			4							4				2	2		3						12		10+	1

National Maritime Museum — LONDON (GREENW...

Artefact → / Provenance →	OCEANIA UN.	AUSTRALIA	MELA.UNPROV.	Admiralty	Banks	Bismarck	D'Entrecast.	Fiji	Louisiade	Loyalty	N. Britain	N. Caledonia	N. Guinea	N. Hebrides	N. Ireland	Santa Cruz	Solomon	Trobriand	MICRO.UNPROV	Caroline	Gilbert	Mariana	Marshall	POLY.UNPROV.	Austral	Chatham	Cook	Easter	Hawaii	Marquesas	New Zealand	Niue	Pitcairn	Samoa	Society	Tokelau	Tonga	Tuamotu	Tuvalu	Tahiti
cord																																								
raw mate														X																										
-sling,s																																								
-arrow																																								
-bow																																								
-shield																																								
-dagger																																								
-spearth																																								
-spear																																								
-club																													1											
WEAPON		1						6					2																								10			
-float,s																																								
-net																																								
-spear																																								
-fishhoo																																								
FISHING																																							4	
hunting																																								
-model																																								
-ornamen																																								
-paddle																																								
NAVIGATI																	2																							
-barkclo																																								
-weaving																																								
-needle,e																																								
-chisel																																								
-rasp																																								
-grinding																																								
-pounding																																								1
-adze																																								
TOOL																													1											
fire,lig																																								
smoking p																																								
pottery																																								
utensil																																								
lime spa																																								
dish,vess													1																											
lime con																																								

LONDON (HENDON)

Name: Royal Air Force Museum

Address: Aerodrome Road
Hendon
London NW9 5LL

Telephone: 01-205 2266

Contact: Keeper of Art, Design and General Collections

Sources & Dates of Information

R. Hutchings 1966

Visit PG 1974

MEG 1978

Letter 1979

Notes

Dates of Collection/Acquisition

Donors/Collectors/Former Owners

Marshall of the RAF Sir Cyril L. Newall, former Governor-General of New Zealand, 1941-46

Documentation

Archival.

Comment

Good adze. Wood carvings interesting examples of 1940's styles.

RAF Museum

LONDON (HEND

Artefact → / Provenance →	OCEANIA UN.	AUSTRALIA	MELA.UNPROV.	Admiralty	Banks	Bismarck	D'Entrecast.	Fiji	Louisiade	Loyalty	N. Britain	N. Caledonia	N. Guinea	N. Hebrides	N. Ireland	Santa Cruz	Solomon	Trobriand	MICRO.UNPROV.	Caroline	Gilbert	Mariana	Marshall	POLY.UNPROV.	Austral	Chatham	Cook	Easter	Hawaii	Marquesas	New Zealand	Niue	Pitcairn	Samoa	Society	Tokelau	Tonga	Tuamotu	Tuvalu
box																															1								
bag																																							
basket																																							
mat																																							
headrest																																							
transport																																							
currency																																							
-rattle																																							
-flute,pipe																																							
-drum,gong																																							
MUSICAL INS.																																							
charm																																							
magic,med.																																							
fig.,image																																							
carving																																							
-bullroarer																																							
-paddle																																							
-adze																																							
-board																																							
-mask																																							
CERE. OBJ.																																							
staff,stick																																							
toilet app.																															2								
fan																																							
comb																																							
-neck,breast																																							
-arm																															1								
-ear,nose																																							
-head																																							
PERS. ORN.																																							
-cloak																																							
-belt																															1								
-skirt																																							
CLOTHING																																							
barkcloth																																							
OTHER																																							
TOTAL																															6								

RAF Museum LONDON (HENDON

Artefact → / Provenance →	OCEANIA UN.	AUSTRALIA	MELA.UNPROV.	Admiralty	Banks	Bismarck	D'Entrecast.	Fiji	Louisiade	Loyalty	N. Britain	N. Caledonia	N. Guinea	N. Hebrides	N. Ireland	Santa Cruz	Solomon	Trobriand	MICRO.UNPROV	Caroline	Gilbert	Mariana	Marshall	POLY.UNPROV.	Austral	Chatham	Cook	Easter	Hawaii	Marquesas	New Zealand	Niue	Pitcairn	Samoa	Society	Tokelau	Tonga	Tuamotu	Tuvalu		
cord																																									
raw mater																																									
-sling,sto																																									
-arrow																																									
-bow																																									
-shield																																									
-dagger																																									
-spearthro																																									
-spear																																									
-club																																									
WEAPON																																									
-float,sin																																									
-net																																									
-spear																																									
-fishhook																																									
FISHING																																									
hunting																																									
-model																																									
-ornament																																									
-paddle																																									
NAVIGATIO																																									
-barkclot																																									
-weaving																																									
-needle,aw																																									
-chisel																																									
-rasp																																									
-grinding																																									
-pounding																																									
-adze																																									
TOOL																															/										
fire,ligh																																									
smokng pi																																									
pottery																																									
utensil																																									
lime spat																																									
dish,vesse																																									
lime cont																																									

Name: Horniman Museum and Library Address: London Road Forest Hill London SE23 3PQ Telephone: 01-699 1872/2339/4911 Contact: Keeper of Ethnography Keeper of Musical Instruments (instruments only)	LONDON (HORNIMAN) Sources & Dates of Information R. Hutchings 1966 Visit PG 1977 MEG 1978 Letters 1977, 1979

Notes

Figures on table do not include all musical instruments.
Museum notes that "the total number and the subtotals represent those sections of the collection processed to date. There are still substantial sections that have not been processed and the present totals must be indicated as provisional."

*Oceania-- navigation: 23' canoe
*Banks-- includes Torres Island
*Fiji-- toilet apparatus: tattooing
ceremonial objects: fetish house, tambua
other: toys 2, hook 1
*New Zealand-- other: stone tools; misc. 6
*Tahiti-- other: flywhisk

Dates of Collection/Acquisition	Donors/Collectors/Former Owners
1860+	Haddon, Torres Straits Oldman

Documentation

Library, photographic, sound recordings, films. Separate card catalogue for musical instruments.

No Oceanic items appear on list of published specimens.

Museum publications: Horniman Museum Handbooks- Stone to Steel, Weapons of War and the Chase, Domestic Arts I, II, Travel and Transport (all out of print), Musical Instruments

Comment

Important and interesting collection. Information compiled from card index because collections not all easily accessible. Range of collection a tribute to Harrison, former Director.

Horniman Museum and Library

LONDON (HORNIMA

Provenance ↓ / Artefact →	TOTAL	OTHER	barkcloth	CLOTHING	-skirt	-belt	-cloak	PERS. ORN.	-head	-ear,nose	-arm	-neck,breast	comb	fan	toilet app.	staff,stick	CERE. OBJ.	-mask	-board	-adze	-paddle	-bullroarer	carving	fig.,image	magic,med.	charm	MUSICAL INS.	-drum,gong	-flute,pipe	-rattle	currency	transport	headrest	mat	basket	bag	box
OCEANIA UN.	43																																				
AUSTRALIA	350																																				
MELA.UNPROV.	2																																				
Admiralty	26							1					2																								
Banks *	13																																				
Bismarck																																					
D'Entrecast.																																					
Fiji	176+	4	27	9				4	1			8	2	1	1*	2	2*										3	4					8	4			
Louisiade	4																																				
Loyalty																																					
N. Britain	32+																																				
N. Caledonia	70																																				
N. Guinea	995																	1					1	1													
N. Hebrides	88																																				
N. Ireland	6																																				
Santa Cruz	14+																																				
Solomon	197+																																				
Trobriand	42																																				
MICRO.UNPROV.	1																																				
Caroline	30																																				
Gilbert	56																																				
Mariana																																					
Marshall	3																																				
POLY.UNPROV.	6																																				
Austral	17																				10																
Chatham	9																																				
Cook	39																																				
Easter	7															1					2			2													
Hawaii	17																																				
Marquesas	10																																				
New Zealand	213	7		X				1				8				2	1										1										3
Niue	11																																				
Pitcairn	9																																				
Samoa	51+		14																																		
Society	4			1				X																													
Tokelau																																					
Tonga	25		6					1	1				1																				1		1		
Puamotu																																					
Tuvalu	14+		X																																		
Tahiti	15	1							1			2		1																							

Horniman Museum and Library

LONDON (HORNIMAN)

Artefact → / Provenance ↓	lime cont	dish,vess	lime spat	utensil	pottery	smoking pi	fire,ligh	TOOL	-adze	-pounding	-grinding	-rasp	-chisel	-needle,a	-weaving	-barkclou	NAVIGATIO	-paddle	-ornament	-model	hunting	FISHING	-fishhook	-spear	-net	-float,si	WEAPON	-club	-spear	-spearthr	-dagger	-shield	-bow	-arrow	-sling,st	raw mater	cord
OCEANIA UN.																	1*																	X			
AUSTRALIA																																					
MELA.UNPROV.																																					
Admiralty		5	1	1																				X					10		6						
Banks																																					
Bismarck	12																			1																	
D'Entrecast.																																					
Fiji		13		3	10				11	2				1		1	1			1			1	6				45								2	
Louisiade																																					
Loyalty																																					
N. Britain																																					
N. Caledonia																																					
N. Guinea																																					
N. Hebrides																																					
N. Ireland																																					
Santa Cruz																																					
Solomon																																					
Trobriand			X																																		
MICRO.UNPROV.																																					
Caroline																																					
Gilbert																																					
Mariana																																					
Marshall																																					
POLY.UNPROV.																																					
Austral				1													1	3										2									
Chatham									3																												
Cook																				2																	
Easter									2																												
Hawaii																																					
Marquesas																																					
New Zealand									3	1									1	1							X										
Niue																																					
Pitcairn																																					
Samoa																																					
Society																																					
Tokelau																																					
Tonga																						2	1					10									1
Tuamotu																																					
Tuvalu																				2																	
Tahiti		1						3								3							1	1													
Torres Straits																																					

Horniman Museum and Library (B)

LONDON (HORNI

Artefact →

box, bag, basket, mat, headrest, transport, currency, rattle, flute, pipe, drum, gong, MUSICAL INS., charm, magic, med., fig., image, carving, bullroarer, paddle, adze, board, mask, CERE. OBJ., staff, stick, toilet app., fan, comb, neck, breast, arm, ear, nose, head, PERS. ORN., cloak, belt, skirt, CLOTHING, barkcloth, OTHER, TOTAL

Provenance	TOTAL
Ninigo	15
Woodlark	1
W. Futuna	2
Ontong Java	1
Wallis	1
"Sanwa" k	1

Horniman Museum and Library (B) LONDON (HORNIMAN

Artefact → / Provenance →	Ninigo	Woodlark	W. Futuna	Ontong Java	Wallis	"Sanwa"
cord						
raw mater						
-sling,st						
-arrow						
-bow						
-shield						
-dagger						
-spearthr					/	
-spear						
-club						
WEAPON						
-float,si						
-net						
-spear						
-fishhook						
FISHING						
hunting						
-model						
-ornament						
-paddle						
NAVIGATIO						
-barkclot						
-weaving						
-needle,a						
-chisel						
-rasp						
-grinding						
-pounding						
-adze	/					
TOOL						
fire,ligh						
smoking pi						
pottery						
utensil						
lime spat						
dish,vess						
lime cont						

LONDON (L.S.E.)

Name London School of Economics
Department of Anthropology

Address Houghton Street
London WC2

Telephone 01-405 7686

Contact Head of Department

Sources & Dates of Information

R. Hutchings 1966

Visit ALK, PG 1973-4

MEG 1978

Letter
Loan list, J. Woodburn, 1973

Notes

Hawaiian cloak is temporarily loaned to the Museum of Mankind.
Firth collection transferred to A.N.U., Canberra, June 1979

Dates of Collection/Acquisition

Donors/Collectors/Former Owners

Malinowski
Cuming Museum, 1973 (permanent loan)

Documentation

Comment

Important collection.

London School of Economics LONDON C.L.S.

Artefact ↓ / Provenance →	OCEANIA UN.	AUSTRALIA	MELA.UNPROV.	Admiralty	Banks	Bismarck	D'Entrecast.	Fiji	Louisiade	Loyalty	N. Britain	N. Caledonia	N. Guinea	N. Hebrides	N. Ireland	Santa Cruz	Solomon	Trobriand	MICRO.UNPROV.	Caroline	Gilbert	Mariana	Marshall	POLY.UNPROV.	Austral	Chatham	Cook	Easter	Hawaii	Marquesas	New Zealand	Niue	Pitcairn	Samoa	Society	Tokelau	Tonga	Tuamotu	Tuvalu	Tikopia
box																																								
bag	1																																							
basket																																								
mat																																								
headrest																																					1			
transport																																								
currency																																								
-rattle																																								
-flute,pipe																															2						1			
-drum,gong																																								
MUSICAL INS.																																								
charm																																								
magic,med.																																								
fig.,image																																								
carving																																								
-bullroarer																																								
-paddle																																								
-adze																																								
-board																																								
-mask																																								
CERE. OBJ.																																								
staff,stick																																								
toilet app.																																								
fan																																								
comb																																								
-neck,breast																																								
-arm														1																										
-ear,nose																																								
-head																																								
PERS. ORN.																																								
-cloak																													1											
-belt																																								
-skirt																																								
CLOTHING																																								
barkcloth																																								
OTHER																																					1			
TOTAL	1													1															2		X						9			2

London School of Economics

LONDON (L.S.E.

Artefact / Provenance	OCEANIA UN.	AUSTRALIA	MELA.UNPROV.	Admiralty	Banks	Bismarck	D'Entrecast.	Fiji	Louisiade	Loyalty	N. Britain	N. Caledonia	N. Guinea	N. Hebrides	N. Ireland	Santa Cruz	Solomon	Trobriand	MICRO.UNPROV	Caroline	Gilbert	Mariana	Marshall	POLY.UNPROV.	Austral	Chatham	Cook	Easter	Hawaii	Marquesas	New Zealand	Niue	Pitcairn	Samoa	Society	Tokelau	Tonga	Tuamotu	Tuvalu	T.kopia	Tahiti
cord																																									
raw mater.																																									
-sling,sto.																																									
-arrow																																									
-bow																																									
-shield																																									
-dagger																													1												
-spearthro.																																									
-spear																																									
-club																																					2				
WEAPON																															X										
-float,sin																																									
-net																																									
-spear																																									
-fishhook																																					1				
FISHING																																									1
hunting																																									
-model																																									
-ornament																																									
-paddle																																									
NAVIGATION																																									
-barkcloth																																									
-weaving																																									
-needle,aw																																									
-chisel																																									
-rasp																																									
-grinding																																									
-pounding																																									
-adze																																					1			350	
TOOL																																					1				
fire,light																																									
smoking pip																																									
pottery																																									
utensil																																									
lime spat.																																									
dish,vesse.																																					1				
lime cont.																																									

LONDON (MUSEUM OF

Sources & Dates of Information

R. Hutchings 1966

Visit

MEG 1978

Letters 1979

Name Museum of London

Address London Wall
London EC2Y 5HN

Telephone 01-600 3699

Contact Senior Assistant Keeper, Prehistoric and Roman Department

Notes

Oceanic about 40 items; some unidentified material. Data subject to update.

Dates of Collection/Acquisition	Donors/Collectors/Former Owners
Acquired mainly 1949-59	London & Guildhall Museums Thomas Layton (1819-1911) Collection, lent to London Museum by Layton Trustees in 1959. W.H. Lloyd Collection, lent to London Museum by Richmond upon Thames Borough Council in 1949.

Documentation

Manuscript catalogues of Layton and Lloyd Collections

Comment

Collection not yet sorted (museum opened in 1976 following merger of Guildhall and London Museums).

Museum of London

LONDON (MUSEUM

Provenance / Artefact →	box	bag	basket	mat	headrest	transport	currency	-rattle	-flute,pipe	-drum,gong	MUSICAL INS.	charm	magic,med.	fig.,image	carving	-bullroarer	-paddle	-adze	-board	-mask	CERE. OBJ.	staff,stick	toilet app.	fan	comb	-neck,breast	-arm	-ear,nose	-head	PERS. ORN.	-cloak	-belt	-skirt	CLOTHING	barkcloth	OTHER	TOTAL
OCEANIA UN.																																					X
AUSTRALIA																																					
MELA.UNPROV.																																					
Admiralty																																					
Banks																																					
Bismarck																																					
D'Entrecast.																																					
Fiji																																					
Louisiade																																					
Loyalty																																					
N. Britain																																					
N. Caledonia																																					
N. Guinea																																					
N. Hebrides																																					
N. Ireland																																					
Santa Cruz																						/															X
Solomon																																					
Trobriand																																					
MICRO.UNPROV.																																					
Caroline																																					
Gilbert																																					
Mariana																																					
Marshall																																					
POLY.UNPROV.																																					
Austral																																					
Chatham																																					
Cook																																					
Easter																																					
Hawaii																																					
Marquesas																																					
New Zealand	/																																				X
Niue																																					
Pitcairn																																					
Samoa																																					
Society																																					
Tokelau																																					
Tonga																																					X
Tuamotu																																					
Tuvalu																																					

Museum of London

LONDON (MUSEUM OF

Artefact → / Provenance →	OCEANIA UN.	AUSTRALIA	MELA.UNPROV.	Admiralty	Banks	Bismarck	D'Entrecast.	Fiji	Louisiade	Loyalty	N. Britain	N. Caledonia	N. Guinea	N. Hebrides	N. Ireland	Santa Cruz	Solomon	Trobriand	MICRO.UNPROV	Caroline	Gilbert	Mariana	Marshall	POLY.UNPROV.	Austral	Chatham	Cook	Easter	Hawaii	Marquesas	New Zealand	Niue	Pitcairn	Samoa	Society	Tokelau	Tonga	Tuamotu	Tuvalu
cord																																							
raw mate																																							
-sling,st																																							
-arrow																																							
-bow																																							
-shield	X																																						
-dagger																																							
-spearthr																																							
-spear	X																																						
-club		X																																			2		
WEAPON																																							
-float,si																																							
-net																																							
-spear																																							
-fishhook																																							
FISHING																																							
hunting																																							
-model																																							
-ornament																																							
-paddle	X																																						
NAVIGATIO																																							
-barkclot																																							
-weaving																																							
-needle,a																																							
-chisel																																							
-rasp																																							
-grinding																																							
-pounding																																							
-adze	X																																						
TOOL																																							
fire,ligh																																							
smoking pi																																							
pottery																																							
utensil																																							
lime spat																																							
dish,vesse																																							
lime cont																																							

Name: Museum of Mankind (Department of Ethnography, British Museum) to be transferred Address: 6 Burlington Gardens, London, W1X 2EX. Telephone: 01-437 2224 Contact: Dorota Starzecka (Assistant Keeper)	LONDON (MM) Sources & Dates of Information R. Hutchings 1966 Visit 1979 AC, 1978 DRS MEG 1978 Letter

Notes: See pages 1 - 14 attached. Note also:-

"Other" includes accessions to 1974, plus Sillitoe Collection, S. Highlands, PNG 1978 Royal loan collection excluded, except for 3 items; similarly excluded unsorted objects at Sheperdhess Walk store, and up to 2,000 archaeological objects (all not yet adequately catalogued).

Geographical boundaries in PNG, W. Irian, Solomon Is and some other island groups modified to suit recorded data. Ditto artefact categories.

Numbers of arrows approx, except for Solomon Is.

Arnhem Land not always distinguished from N. Territory (Australia).

Banks Is. not always distinguishable from N. Hebrides.

Dates of Collection/Acquisition	Donors/Collectors/Former Owners
See summary (p. 15) supplied by D. Starzecka	

Documentation: Extensive:
library, archive, photographs, films, sound recordings, catalogues.

BM publications on or connected with specific exhibitions. Note especially Handbook of Ethnographical Collections (1911, 1925 - still relevant), Melanesia (B.A.L. Cranstone, 1961), Cook's Voyages and Peoples of the Pacific (ed. H. Cobbe, 1979), Captain Cook and the South Pacific (BM Yearbook 3, ed. T. C. Mitchell, 1979).

Comment: Largest and single most important collection in U.K. Has at least 27,000 objects (previously roughly calculated at c. 50,000). But note that some archaeological and low quality ethnographical material still being catalogued, and therefore this survey will have to be updated in a few years' time. Impressive collection, well maintained, and continually increasing in significance. This survey done very expertly by Alison Clarke, with much help from Dorota Starzecka and Richard Proctor, whose co-operation is here happily recorded.

(PG).

A

LONDON (MM)

Artefact → / Provenance ↓	TOTAL	OTHER	barkcloth	CLOTHING	-skirt	-belt	-cloak	PERS. ORN.	-head	-ear,nose	-arm	-neck,breast	comb	fan	toilet app.	staff,stick	CERE. OBJ.	-mask	-board	-adze	-paddle	-bullroarer	carving	fig.,image	magic,med.	charm	MUSICAL INS.	-drum,gong	-flute,pipe	-rattle	currency	transport	headrest	mat	basket	bag	box
OCEANIA UN.	X	X	X		X			X								X																		X	X		
AUSTRALIA	See		'D'																																		
MELA.UNPROV.	4+		2																																		
Admiralty	481	1	2	14	1			8	9	4	29	4	14										1	2	1	9	1*	2*	2*						3	4	
Banks	167			14		3		1		22			1		1*	3*	1	1								8			1*				1		1	2	
Bismarck	63			1		1				1	2	3	8											2*					1*								
D'Entrecast.	113	1																		4							1*						1				
Fiji	1241+	36	107*		41	1		12	8*		12	43	10	20*	6	8	42*				5*			2	2		6*	1*	7*			2*	26	8	11		
Louisiade	190	1	3		1	1		1	7	6	16	16	8				1*											2	2*				4		7	2	2
Loyalty	61	1			3	5		6	1		5	1	2										1		1									1	1	1	
N. Britain	261+		2					6	18	4	16	21	5				4	11*	3	3	1		1	2		1		1	3*	1	12				10	4	
N. Caledonia	287	2	1		12	4	1	3	4*			5	17			11	3*	7	7	12			8	8	1		3				6				1	9	
N. Guinea	See	'C'																																			
N. Hebrides	984	3	8	42	13	22		23	6	31	79	7	15		7*	4	23*	12*					11*	9*		4	2*	3*	9*	1	5		1	7		10	
N. Ireland	249			2				4	9		30	1	1				3*	26*	1*		1		23*	31*			2*	3*			7				1		
Santa Cruz	489	4	9	9	1	4		15	5	16	8	16			5		21*						9	15*	2	12					13	2	6	11	2	6	
Solomon	See	'B'																																			
Trobriand	1315	11		1	36	11	1	39	5*	35	24	54	26	1*		4	1		1		39		34	12	4			20	8*			4*	1	1	20		
MICRO.UNPROV	37	4						6				8																						1			
Caroline	397	17		2	5	32		21	2	6	9	9	26	1	3	2	1*	1			7		1			1		2*			6			8			2
Gilbert	427	3		7	7	5		9	3*		1	49		3*	6*	2	1								1						8		1	24	4	2	2
Mariana	5	1																																			
Marshall	83	1							1*			16																1			1			10	1		
POLY.UNPROV.	143+	9	91*	1				2	2*			6	1											1											1		
Austral	147	6		2	1				9*			1		13*		3	9*				50			1			1	1									
Chatham	71	4						6																													
Cook	370	4	19*	9*	1	5		11	2*	4		6		2		7	4*			41	2			38*	1*			5*						1	2		
Easter	174+	8+	2	1		1		10+	6*	5		8				5		2			6		13	49*												2	
Hawaii	835+	15	282*	13*			17	18	8		20	64		11	7*	3	3*							21*			2	7*	6*	2	3	3*	1*	2	6		1
Marquesas	203		6		5			8	14*	29		9		7		7							17*	10*		1	1*	2				3*			2		
New Zealand	1529+	38+		9	11	15	104*	29*	2*	58		63*	11		30	19	14*			7*	3	2	59*	50		2	16*		50+			3		11		23	50+
Niue	151	3	10*		2	1		5				2	8	1		1	3											1*	10				1*	1		3	
Pitcairn	30		25																																		
Samoa	453	15	81*	3	1	3	2		7*			16	21	25*	26	2								1				1*	5				2	20	10		
Society	364+	5	29	10				2	4*			13*		22*	10	8	3							27*			5*	3	13			1*	5*	6	1	12	
Tokelau	19				1										1																						3
Tonga	394	17	21*			14		6		2	2	18	68	6*	1		1				1			5*			1		10*				17	6	24	1	2
Tuamotu	34			6		1	2	1	2*																												
Tuvalu	61			2	7			2	4			2												2									1	1			
Tahiti	302+	3	33	2*	3	1		1	4*			9*			25	5*							1	34*				6				5*	1			1	

A

LONDON (MM)

Provenance ↓ / Artefact →	lime cont.	dish,vesse	lime spat	utensil	pottery	smokng pi	fire,ligh	TOOL	-adze	-pounding	-grinding	-rasp	-chisel	-needle,aw	-weaving	-barkclot	NAVIGATIO	-paddle	-ornament	-model	hunting	FISHING	-fishhook	-spear	-net	-float,sin	WEAPON	-club	-spear	-spearthro	-dagger	-shield	-bow	-arrow	-sling,sto	raw mater	ccrd
OCEANIA UN.								x									4*				x	x					x		19					x		x	
AUSTRALIA	See	'D'																																			
MELA.UNPROV.																													2								
Admiralty	19	38*	15	12	3			3	17								1*	3	2				17		1		24		80*	1	115					15	4
Banks		10		41				2	28							2					1	1*						8					3	10		1	
Bismarck				1				2*	4									2					1			2		2	30								
D'Entrecast.		3	32	8	3	4			1	4			1						3			1*	1		1			43							1		
Fiji		139		35*	81+	4*	2	7*	107	4		1		39*		40*		3		18*		5*	2	8	1	1		249*	61				1	2		13	8
Louisiade	7	6	35		3	3		4*	5	1				3				2	3	6*		1	1		4	2		5	13							4	2
Loyalty		2							2							1					1		14					5	5						2		
N. Britain	1	3	2	2				1	20	3				1	1			1				1+						34	45			5		6	3	3+	
N. Caledonia		7			3+			1	11	1						5				1					2			73	18	8					30+		2
N. Guinea	See	'C'																																			
N. Hebrides		12			15			1	40	1							1*	6	1	1	2		1	8			2	115	58				31	322*	2	8	1
N. Ireland		1						4*										7		1			3					26*	58*			1			1	1	1
Santa Cruz	12	12*	1	6				40	8	6		3	1		17*	2	5*	6		2	1	3*	6			4			1				2	15	1	3	1
Solomon	See	'B'																																			
Trobriand	36	66	154	9	10	17	7	122*	45	90	3	1				2	6*	3	58	23*	1	4	23	4	22	14		48	111		2	19			1	15	6
MICRO.UNPROV		3						1							3			1		7				1													2
Caroline		33*		6*			2	75*	28	3					6*		1*		1	3			46		2		4	4	8		3			2	5	1	
Gilbert		10		12				5*	11	5		6		10			1		9	2	2	12*	50		5			105*	6	10	14				1	5	8
Mariana																																			4		
Marshall		1								2					1*		3*						37								1						7
POLY.UNPROV.		2						2*		2								2				1	7			1			4							7	1
Austral		4				1			8	8						9		1					10			3			6								
Chatham								17*	4		1			6									23	1				7	2								
Cook		11*		8				2	16	35				1		11	1	7		6*		1	64				4	22	8			2				6	1
Easter		2						17*	3	3												2	13		1	2		3								9	1
Hawaii		56*		3		7	3	5*	10	21			1			33	4*	1		2		1	99			2	28		14*		8			1	3	4+	14
Marquesas		15*				2			3	8							1	6	2	1*		2	4	1		1		28*							5	2	1
New Zealand		11		9*		5	1	32*	39	11	1		7	21	6*		12*	31	15	20*	16*	2	340		5	5	14*	205*	10		3			4		30+	
Niue									5							3				4		4	16		3		1	18	31				2		10		2
Pitcairn							1+	3		1																											
Samoa		9						6*	4			1				7*	1*	1		11	2	7	41	4	1			83	14							17	3
Society		2		8		2	1	9*	24	16		1	2			8	1	5	2	1	1*	4	53					1	10					22*		3	9
Tokelau									1														13														
Tonga		3		1					3			3				1							35		1			104	2				11	1		2	4
Tuamotu									3	1							1*						14					1								2	
Tuvalu									3													1	34				1										1
Tahiti		1		6			2	4*	5	3				3		3			1			2	66		1	3	2	1	7				6	42*		3	2

cont. next page

Provenance / Artefact	TOTAL	OTHER	barkcloth	CLOTHING	-skirt	-belt	-cloak	PERS. ORN.	-head	-ear,nose	-arm	-neck,breast	comb	fan	toilet app.	staff,stick	CERE. OBJ.	-mask	-board	-adze	-paddle	-bullroarer	carving	fig.,image	magic,med.	charm	MUSICAL INS.	-drum,gong	-flute,pipe	-rattle	currency	transport	headrest	mat	basket	bag	box
Torres Strait	581	10			12	12		57	31*	22	28*	23	13				4*	30				9	24	13	1	7	2*	7		7		5*		2	12		1
Ninigo	107		2								10		7																					2			
Rotuma	17				1	1		1	1*			1																						4			
Massim unprov.	594	4		1	3			24	11*	28	17	24	18			3	1*			3			6		2	1	2*	10	7*				1	14	33		
Engineer	214				2			6	1		5	5	3			1									6		2*	9	3*						12		
Marshall Bennett	220				1			12	2	5	10	2	1			1												1			1		2			2	
Woodlark	10+								1																			2									
Anuta	2												2																								
Bellona	33																2									1											
Kapingamarangi	4																				1																
Mele	1																												1								
Nukumanu	6																																				
Nukuoro	6																							1			1*										2
Ontong Java	86	1				2		2		29	1	2			6									1		1								2			1
Rennell	220		4					4		10	10	9	4	3	6	6	2*							1	1		1*	1					3	10	16	3	
Sikiana	15	4											1	1	3	1																		1			
Taku	1																																				
Tikopia	17							2	1																								1	2*			
Uvea	17	1		2	1						1		2														1								1		
Gambier	56		4																																		
Mangareva	12	1																						1													
Norfolk	1																																				
Line	6																																				
Phoenix	1							1																													
Futuna	21		21																																		
Wallis	90	2	6									6	9	7*							2						2*			2			2	2	11		
Solomon unprov.	921+	13+	17	1	4	16		84	9	43	119	53	23	4	1	6	4*		1*		4		27*	9		8	7*		6*		4	2*	1	3	17		
Buka + Bougainville	1021	5		1	1	3		14	33*	8	7	7	230			1	11*	4	1*				2			1	1*		3*	1	4	1*		1	17	12	
Central	332+	3	14	1		2		20	5	2	30	11	1				4*		2*				24*	2		4	1*		3*		2			2	5	1	1
South East	688	5		1	6	11		22	18*	31	18	24	24	3		7	21*		5*		2		11*	4	1	8	2*		2*	1	8			4	12	2	

Provenance ↓ / Artefact →	lime cont	dish,vess	lime spat	utensil	pottery	smokng pi	fire,ligh	TOOL	-adze	-pounding	-grinding	-rasp	-chisel	-needle,a	-weaving	-barkclot	NAVIGATIO	-paddle	-ornament	-model	hunting	FISHING	-fishhook	-spear	-net	-float,si	WEAPON	-club	-spear	-spearthr	-dagger	-shield	-bow	-arrow	-sling,st	raw mater	cord
Torres Strait		7	1	3		17		11*	1			1		4	7			1	8	1		7	9	4				11	1		3		1R	126+		4	4
Ninigo		5		2				2	2							1		5	2			2	22	2			7	10	12		10*		1				1
Rotuma									2														1					4							1		
Massim unprov.	10	4	141	6		5		11*	17	3							4*	34	33	2	2		8	2	6	8		36	35			5			5	1	3
Engineer	15	6	31	5		1		13*	2	20		1		7			4	4	7	7*		1*		1	4	8		4	3							10	5
Marshall Bennett		33	40			1		4*	2	39				3			4*		2	31*		3	10		1	4		2								1	
Woodlark			3	3																																x	
Anuta																																					
Bellona									2													1		2			1	3					2	17		1	1
Kapingamarangi		1																1		1																	
Mele																																					
Nukumanu									2														4														
Nukuoro		1																		1																	
Ontong Java		3							5						1*								27													2	
Rennell	3	2	5	13			2	9*	5		2					1				1	5	2*	2	2	2	6		33	19				2	5		6	
Sikiana									1						1*					1																	1
Taku																													1								
Tikopia		1													1*								4					5									
Uvea								1	1														1												4		1
Gambier								4*	10	12	2			7				1					2	2		7			2						2	1	
Mangareva										3	2			1										1					1						2		
Norfolk																																				1	
Line																						4	2														
Phoenix																																					
Futuna																																					
Wallis		2		1				10*	1			1				2	1*											5								15	1
Solomon unprov.	28	19*	4	10	1	2	1	28*	8*	5					1	1	8*	28	34	2		13*	6		10	5	1	30	78			10	23*	47		16	16
Buka+Bougainville	32	8		3	10	2		10*	6	2								16	4			10*	91		2			11	37				9*	398		1	
Central	15	4*	1	9				7*		9	2					2		10	9	3*		4*	51	1		4		9	14			9	5	19+	1	3	
South East	9	31*	6	10	1	3		17*	20	2	1							11	6	3*	2	2	95	1		7		37	38			5	5	121		1	1

cont next page

c

LONDON (MM)

Provenance ↓ / Artefact →	TOTAL	OTHER	barkcloth	CLOTHING	-skirt	-belt	-cloak	PERS. ORN.	-head	-ear,nose	-arm	-neck,breast	comb	fan	toilet app.	staff,stick	CERE. OBJ.	-mask	-board	-adze	-paddle	-bullroarer	carving	fig.,image	magic,med.	charm	MUSICAL INS.	-drum,gong	-flute,pipe	-rattle	currency	transport	headrest	mat	basket	bag	box
New Guinea unprov.	836+	21	8	2	23	5		61	10*	8	95	79	15	2*		10	2*		1				4	3	3	9+	5*	1	4*	10	1	3	2		4	18	
Westlrian unprov.	389					2		8	2		4	1	2										1	1			1*									3	
West unprov.	61		1					3			7		1				1							9									4				2
North unprov.	27					2		2	3			7																									1
South unprov.	168		3*	3		1		25	9*	4	18	11					3						3	1		8		15					2		3	10	
Geelvinck	57					2		4		4	6	1	4						1					12			1*						4				7
Humboldt + Sentani	113	1	2			4		5	1	2	8	5	4				1						3	4*				1	1							2	
Highlands	16				4				1		1	1																									
Mimika + Utakwa	234																																				
Tapira	51							10	1*	2	1	5	2		5*								1				1*									2	
Kampong + Eilanden	30															3	1*																				
Asmat	195	1			4	6		10	1*	6		1						3*					7*	13			10*	10								1	
Marind-Anim + Merauke	44			1													1*											1									
T.T. unprovenanced	184	2	15*	5	1	1		7	2*		10	9	2						2								1*	5	1				1			13	
Sepik	294	7			2			2			12	1*	2				18*	25					11*	17		3		7*	1*			2*	9			8	
Ramu	101			3		5		1			1	11	2		1*			5		5			2	5		1		1	2				1			7	
Sepik - Ramu	186	7		1	2	13		10	19*	2	10	10	6	1				4	4				5	12		1	3*	1	3*				7			3*	
Madang	44		1		3			3	3	1	7	8	1										2	4	1											3	
Highlands	587	26		8	11	6	1	30	34*	20	21	22	3		11*		5*	1	6	3					3	29	6*	1	6*	1		2*	1*			18	
Huon + Tami	78		1			2		3	1	6	3							1						5	1			1					11			9	
Morobe	20			5							1																										
Papua unprov.	269+	4	1	1.	3	6		56	19	2	6	14	2	6*			5*	2*	1			2	1		3	10	2	1						1	3	4	1
Western	470	5		2	15	8		53	35*	10	13	7	7			12	10*				1	17	3*	16		15	2*	7				7*	1	1	4	2	1
Gulf	983+	3	22*	5	7	33*		39	9*	4	25	27	20			3	10*	51*	68			18	4	3		32*	1*	16		2*		2				21*	
Central	1049+	13	44*	6	12	12		59	65*	43	68	61	17		2*	4	11*					5	3	1	3	22	4*	11	1	1		1*		1	1	35	
Mainland Massim	294+	1	23*		1	1		22	11	7	11	9	5			1							1			1	1*	3	2*	1			5	2	3	5	
North East	174		45	3	10	2		12	5	5	5	4	2															3	4							4	

Artefact → / Provenance ↓	lime cont	dish,vess	lime spat	utensil	pottery	smokng pi	fire,lig	TOOL	-adze	-pounding	-grinding	-rasp	-chisel	-needle,a	-weaving	-barkclot	NAVIGATIO	-paddle	-ornament	-model	hunting	FISHING	-fishhook	-spear	-net	-float,si	WEAPON	-club	-spear	-spearthr	-dagger	-shield	-bow	-arrow	-sling,st	raw mater	cord
New Guinea unprov.	6	29	2	20	7+		2	47*	18	7		6		6		4	3	8		3	1	3*	6	2	7	6	1	38	4		8	2	8	127	1	32	13
West Irian unprov.				1			1																	1			2	2	7				17	327		1	
West unprov.				22			1	1	1							3													2					1		1	
North unprov.	1		2	2	1	3																						1					2				
South unprov.	2	1	2	3					1							1			2					1			1*	6	13		3		2*			2	2
Geelvinck		1		1		1													3		1					2						1	1				
Humboldt + Sentani	6	2	4	4				1	6				1					5	7						1						2		1	25		3	1
Highlands									3																		3*										3
Mimika + Utakwa		2							15									5	1					3			1	31	16			1	4	155			
Tapiro				1		1	6	4*	1					1																			1			2	4
Kampong + Eilanden		1						1									1*	3							1			2	6			1	4	6			
Asmat	1	20	1			4			3	2	2		1					1	12					2					23		8	27	4*	10		1	
Marind-Anim + Merauke																						1*						1	1				3*	35			
T.T. unprovenanced		3		5	1			1*	5								2	4				2*	5					11	25*	5		3	15	20			
Sepik	1	4	7*	1	11*			1	9										2										3	1	1	15	1	109		1	
Ramu		2	1		5					2								4	1										4	4	2	6		17			
Sepik-Ramu	17	12	5	3	6		1			2	2			1		1			1*								1*		1		9						
Madang	1		1		1*															1												3					
Highlands		19		6		26*	5	13*	21	2	1			3							2						5*	3				18		151		37	1
Huon + Tami		16	1	4				1*	1								1*		3				4														
Morobe		1		3	3	1*		2*															4														
Papua unprov.		8	2	1	24	15		10*	14	1	1	1						2				2*						11					3	15		6	
Western		5		9		53	4	12*	1									1	4		5*						1	10*			1		4*	105		1	
Gulf	5	18	3	41	2	20	4	8*	3			1						1				3*		3	3	12	2	34	67		7	15	22*	281+*		4	1
Central	65	13	5	29	29+	78	4	34*	27							16		1		5	10	2*	13		11			17	33			13	7	122	1	5	3
Mainland Massim	3	40	34	4	1+*	5		19*	7	1		3	3			3	1*		1	1*		1*	1	3	4	8	1	5	11			3			9	6	
North East	2	1	2		7			4*	13	6												1*						20				14					

cont. next page

D

LONDON (M

Provenance ↓ / Artefact →	TOTAL	OTHER	barkcloth	CLOTHING	-skirt	-belt	-cloak	PERS. ORN.	-head	-ear,nose	-arm	-neck,breast	comb	fan	toilet app.	staff,stick	CERE. OBJ.	-mask	-board	-adze	-paddle	-bullroarer	carving	fig.,image	magic,med.	charm	MUSICAL INS.	-drum,gong	-flute,pipe	-rattle	currency	transport	headrest	mat	basket	bag	box
Australia unprov.	196+	37	1	1	1			20	1	12		13		1*	1							7*			2	4					1				6	2	
Queensland	495	19	1	2	1	2		17	29*	14		23		1*		26*	7			1		5	1			1									14	16	
Cape York	54				4			1	2*	1		2					1	1					1			1									2		
N. Territory	441	1		3	4	7		41	3	2	110	25				20*	10*					20*			10		3								1	14	
Arnhemland	179	13		6	1									1*		2*	12*					1			3		4						1*		5	34	
Western	461+	2		1		2		40	3	9	1	9				23*	6					45*	2		13										1	2	
Northwestern	126+	3		1		8		12		1	3	6				1*						10*													5	1	
Central	126	1		2	1			14	2*	1		4					.					24*			7											5	
South Australia	69					1		5		1		1					1					2*			13										2		
New South Wales	107	1			1	1	1	1				6					10*																		1	3	
Victoria	88	2		1													1*																		1	3	
South East	160																																		4	1	
Tasmania	54+	x						2				9					3																		31		

Artefact → / Provenance ↓	lime cont.	dish,vesse	lime spat	utensil	pottery	smokng pi	fire,ligh	TOOL	-adze	-pounding	-grinding	-rasp	-chisel	-needle,aw	-weaving	-barkcloti	NAVIGATIO	-paddle
Australia unprov.		2				1	2	17#	6	1	2			1				
Queensland		6				5	16	36*	11		4		2	6				1
Cape York							2	1			1							
N. Territory		13				1	1	17*	2		1				1*			
Arnhemland		7		2			1	7*										
Western		3		1			2	53*+			1			1	3*			
Northwestern		2					1	6+					1		1*		1*	
Central		2					2	12*	3				4					
South Australia		2		1				4*	1									
New South Wales		2						2*										
Victoria											1	1		1			1*	
South East				1			1		5					1				
Tasmania		1						6										

Artefact → / Provenance ↓	-ornament	-model	hunting	FISHING	-fishhook	-spear	-net	-float,sin	WEAPON	-club	-spear	-spearthro	-dagger	-shield	-bow	-arrow	-sling,sto	raw mater.	cord
Australia unprov.						1	2		1*	7	31			3				6	3
Queensland		2	1	5*	9	3	4		51*	45	35	15		30				17	12
Cape York						10			1*		18	5							
N. Territory		1		1	2	3			20*	8	66	19						7	4
Arnhemland						2			3*	23	40	7						1	3
Western						1	2		45*	15	84	47		24				15	5
Northwestern									1*	6	35	4		12				3	2
Central									18*	4	10	4		3				1	2
South Australia									7*	9	15			2				2	
New South Wales			1	1		2	2		25*	22	11	1		11				1	1
Victoria				1					10*	29	10	6		20					
South East						1			34*	64	6	17		24				1	
Tasmania		1								1									

Name	National Army Museum
Address	Royal Hospital Road London SW3 4HT
Telephone	01-730 0717
Contact	Research & Information Officer

LONDON (NAM)

Sources & Dates of Information

R. Hutchings 1966

Visit

MEG 1978

Letter 1979

Notes

New Zealand: nephrite club, presented to Gen. Lord Roberts by a Maori chief and friend, Tuta Nihoniho

Possibly other material.

Dates of Collection/Acquisition	Donors/Collectors/Former Owners

Documentation

Restricted access to catalogue.

Comment

Name	Royal Geographic Society	LONDON (RGS)
Address	Kensington Gore London SW7 2AR	Sources & Dates of Information
		R. Hutchings 1966
		Visit
Telephone	01-5895466	MEG 1978
Contact	Archivist	Letter 1979

Notes

Archive of 100,00 photographs and 50,000 slides, mainly from the period 1880-1920. Taken by British travellers; also, 19th Century prints by professional artists. A few artefacts.
(Not all Oceanic)

Dates of Collection/Acquisition	Donors/Collectors/Former Owners

Documentation

Reference: Handlist of documentary material in Geographical Journal, July 1976, March 1977 & July 1977.

Comment

LONDON(SCIENCE)Engineering

Name: Department of Mechanical and Civil Engineering (Hand and Machine Tool Collection)

Address: Science Museum
Exhibition Road
London SW7 2DD

Telephone: 01-589 3456

Contact: Keeper

Sources & Dates of Information

R. Hutchings 1966

Visit

MEG 1978

Letter 1979

Notes

Dates of Collection/Acquisition

Donors/Collectors/Former Owners

Documentation

Comment

Department of Mechanical and Civil Engineering LONDON (SCIENCE-Engineering

Provenance / Artfact →	TOTAL	OTHER	barkcloth	CLOTHING	-skirt	-belt	-cloak	PERS. ORN.	-head	-ear,nose	-arm	-neck,breast	comb	fan	toilet app.	staff,stick	CERE. OBJ.	-mask	-board	-adze	-paddle	-bullroarer	carving	fig.,image	magic,med.	charm	MUSICAL INS.	-drum,gong	-flute,pipe	-rattle	currency	transport	headrest	mat	basket	bag	box
OCEANIA UN.	1																																				
AUSTRALIA	1																																				
MELA.UNPROV.																																					
Admiralty																																					
Banks																																					
Bismarck																																					
D'Entrecast.																																					
Fiji	1																																				
Louisiade																																					
Loyalty																																					
N. Britain																																					
N. Caledonia																																					
N. Guinea	3																																				
N. Hebrides																																					
N. Ireland																																					
Santa Cruz																																					
Solomon	1																																				
Trobriand																																					
MICRO.UNPROV																																					
Caroline																																					
Gilbert																																					
Mariana																																					
Marshall																																					
POLY.UNPROV.																																					
Austral																																					
Chatham																																					
Cook																																					
Easter																																					
Hawaii																																					
Marquesas																																					
New Zealand																																					
Niue																																					
Pitcairn																																					
Samoa																																					
Society																																					
Tokelau																																					
Tonga																																					
Tuamotu																																					
Tuvalu																																					
T.A.I.	1																																				

Department of Mechanical and Civil Engineering LONDON (SCIENCE-Engineering)

Artefact → / Provenance ↓	OCEANIA UN.	AUSTRALIA	MELA.UNPROV.	Admiralty	Banks	Bismarck	D'Entrecast.	Fiji	Louisiade	Loyalty	N. Britain	N. Caledonia	N. Guinea	N. Hebrides	N. Ireland	Santa Cruz	Solomon	Trobriand	MICRO.UNPROV.	Caroline	Gilbert	Mariana	Marshall	POLY.UNPROV.	Austral	Chatham	Cook	Easter	Hawaii	Marquesas	New Zealand	Niue	Pitcairn	Samoa	Society	Tokelau	Tonga	Tuamotu	Tuvalu	Tahiti
cord																																								
raw mater																																								
-sling,st																																								
-arrow																																								
-bow																																								
-shield																																								
-dagger																																								
-spearthro																																								
-spear																																								
-club																																								
WEAPON																																								
-float,si																																								
-net																																								
-spear																																								
-fishhook																																								
FISHING																																								
hunting																																								
-model																																								
-ornament																																								
-paddle																																								
NAVIGATIO																																								
-barkclot																																								
-weaving																																								
-needle,a																																								
-chisel																																								
-rasp																																								
-grinding																																								
-pounding																																								
-adze	1							1					3																											1
TOOL		1															1																							
fire,ligh																																								
smokng pi																																								
pottery																																								
utensil																																								
lime spat																																								
dish,vess																																								
lime cont																																								

Name	Department of Earth and Space Sciences Science Museum	LONDON (SCIENCE - Naviga
Address	South Kensington London SW7 2DD	**Sources & Dates of Information** R. Hutchings 1966 Visit MEG 1978 Letters 1979
Telephone	01-589 3456	
Contact	Assistant Keeper, Navigation Collection	

Notes

Marshall: sailing charts 6: 3 mattang
1 medo
1 rebbelib
1 replica of rebbelib type in British Museum

Dates of Collection/Acquisition	Donors/Collectors/Former Owners
	Loaned by Royal Colonial Institute (now Royal Empire Society)

Documentation

Comment

LONDON (UCL)

Name University College of London
Department of Anthropology

Address Gower Street
London WC1

Telephone 01-387 7050

Contact Head of Department

Sources & Dates of Information

R. Hutchings 1966

Visit

MEG 1978

Letter

Notes

Total Oceanic collection: between 200 & 300 items. This is principally a teaching collection; there is no comprehensive collection either in terms of type or group. Some archaeology specimens.

*Melanesia unprovenanced-- other: cloth
*New Guinea-- other: Swart Valley collection
*Polynesia unprovenanced-- musical instrument: shell trumpet

Dates of Collection/Acquisition	Donors/Collectors/Former Owners
1945+	Working anthropologists have donated collections. Wellcome Collection Cuming Museum

Documentation

Not a lot of information on context.

Collection catalogued by area and function; cross-indexed.

Comment

University College of London

LONDON (UCL

Artefact → / Provenance ↓	TOTAL	OTHER	barkcloth	CLOTHING	-skirt	-belt	-cloak	PERS. ORN.	-head	-ear,nose	-arm	-neck,breast	comb	fan	toilet app.	staff,stick	CERE. OBJ.	-mask	-board	-adze	-paddle	-bullroarer	carving	fig.,image	magic,med.	charm	MUSICAL IN.	-drum,gong	-flute,pipe	-rattle	currency	transport	headrest	mat	basket	bag	box
OCEANIA UN.			X		/																													X	X		
AUSTRALIA	X																					X															
MELA.UNPROV.	X	X																																			
Admiralty	X																																				
Banks																																					
Bismarck																																					
D'Entrecast.																																					
Fiji	X		X																																		
Louisiade																																					
Loyalty																																					
N. Britain																																					
N. Caledonia	2						/																														
N. Guinea	X	X				X					X	X						X										/									
N. Hebrides	2					/																															
N. Ireland																																					
Santa Cruz	3					/																												/			
Solomon	X										X															/											
Trobriand	3										/	/								/																	
MICRO.UNPROV																																					
Caroline																																					
Gilbert	X																														X						
Mariana																																					
Marshall	2																																	/			
POLY.UNPROV.	X		X																								1*										
Austral																																					
Chatham																																					
Cook	X																																				
Easter																																					
Hawaii	X																																				
Marquesas																																					
New Zealand	X						/																X														
Niue																																					
Pitcairn																																					
Samoa	X																																				
Society													X																								
Tokelau																																					
Tonga	X																																				
Tuamotu																																					
Tuvalu																																					
Matty	1																																				

University College of London

LONDON UCL

Artefact → / Provenance ↓	OCEANIA UN.	AUSTRALIA	MELA.UNPROV.	Admiralty	Banks	Bismarck	D'Entrecast.	Fiji	Louisiade	Loyalty	N. Britain	N. Caledonia	N. Guinea	N. Hebrides	N. Ireland	Santa Cruz	Solomon	Trobriand	MICRO.UNPROV	Caroline	Gilbert	Mariana	Marshall	POLY.UNPROV.	Austral	Chatham	Cook	Easter	Hawaii	Marquesas	New Zealand	Niue	Pitcairn	Samoa	Society	Tokelau	Tonga	Tuamotu	Tuvalu	MaHy	Tasmania
cord																																									
raw mate																																									
-sling,st																																									
-arrow														/			X																								
-bow																																									
-shield		X															X																								
-dagger				X									/																												
-spearthr		X											/																												
-spear								X					X				X																								
-club		X						X				/					/							X					X		X			X							
WEAPON																					/																				
-float,si																/													/												
-net																																									
-spear																																									
-fishhook		X																/					/								X						X				
FISHING																																									
hunting													/																												
-model	X																																								
-ornament																																									
-paddle	X																X										X														
NAVIGATIO																																									
-barkclot	X																																								
-weaving																																									
-needle,a																																									
-chisel																																									
-rasp																																									
-grinding																																									
-pounding																																									
-adze			/										X											X																/	
TOOL								/																							X										
fire,ligh																																									
smoking pi													X																												
pottery								X																																	
utensil																																									
lime spat													X																												
dish,vesse		/																																							
lime cont.													/																												

Name	Wellcome Collection Science Museum	LONDON (WELLCOME
Address	Exhibition Road South Kensington London SW7 2DD	Sources & Dates of Information
		R. Hutchings 1966
		Visit
Telephone	01-589 3456	MEG 1978
Contact	Keeper, Wellcome Museum of the History of Medicine	Letter 1979

Notes

Several thousand objects, including Oceanic. In store pending inspection and transfer to Science Museum in the next three years. Thus inaccessible.

Dates of Collection/Acquisition	Donors/Collectors/Former Owners
	Wellcome

Documentation

Will be recorded on cards; at present no reliable list of material.

Comment

Presumably the residue of Wellcome Collection dispersed after 1951.

MACCLESFIELD

Name: West Park Museum & Art Gallery

Address: Prestbury Road
Macclesfield
Cheshire

Telephone: 0625-24067

Contact: Assistant Director (Museums), Cheshire Museum Service, Weaver Hall Museum, 162 London Rd., Northwich CW9 8AB (tel. 0606-41331)

Sources & Dates of Information	
R. Hutchings	1966
Visit	
MEG	1978
Letter	1979

Notes

Dates of Collection/Acquisition	Donors/Collectors/Former Owners
collected late 19th Century-early 20th	Brocklehurst family

Documentation

Catalogued on MDA system.

Comment

West Park Museum & Art Gallery MACCLESFIELD

Artifact → / Provenance →	OCEANIA UN.	AUSTRALIA	MELA.UNPROV.	Admiralty	Banks	Bismarck	D'Entrecast.	Fiji	Louisiade	Loyalty	N. Britain	N. Caledonia	N. Guinea	N. Hebrides	N. Ireland	Santa Cruz	Solomon	Trobriand	MICRO.UNPROV.	Caroline	Gilbert	Mariana	Marshall	POLY.UNPROV.	Austral	Chatham	Cook	Easter	Hawaii	Marquesas	New Zealand	Niue	Pitcairn	Samoa	Society	Tokelau	Tonga	Tuamotu	Tuvalu
box																																							
bag																																							
basket																																							
mat																																							
headrest																																							
transport																																							
currency																																							
-rattle																																							
-flute,pipe																																							
-drum,gong																																							
MUSICAL INS.																																							
charm																																							
magic,med.																																							
fig.,image																																							
carving																																							
-bullroarer																																							
-paddle																																							
-adze																																							
-board																																							
-mask																																							
CERE. OBJ.																																							
staff,stick																																							
toilet app.																																							
fan																																							
comb																																							
-neck,breast																																							
-arm																																							
-ear,nose																																							
-head																																							
PERS. ORN.																																							
-cloak																																							
-belt																																							
-skirt																																							
CLOTHING																																							
barkcloth																																							
OTHER																																							
TOTAL	X																																						

West Park Museum & Art Gallery

MACCLESFIELD

Artefact → / Provenance →	OCEANIA UN.	AUSTRALIA	MELA.UNPROV.	Admiralty	Banks	Bismarck	D'Entrecast.	Fiji	Louisiade	Loyalty	N. Britain	N. Caledonia	N. Guinea	N. Hebrides	N. Ireland	Santa Cruz	Solomon	Trobriand	MICRO.UNPROV.	Caroline	Gilbert	Mariana	Marshall	POLY.UNPROV.	Austral	Chatham	Cook	Easter	Hawaii	Marquesas	New Zealand	Niue	Pitcairn	Samoa	Society	Tokelau	Tonga	Tuamotu	Tuvalu	
cord																																								
raw mate																																								
-sling,s.																																								
-arrow																																								
-bow																																								
-shield																																								
-dagger																																								
-spearthr																																								
-spear																																								
-club																																								
WEAPON																																								
-float,s.																																								
-net																																								
-spear																																								
-fishhoo																																								
FISHING																																								
hunting																																								
-model																																								
-ornamen																																								
-paddle																																								
NAVIGATIO																																								
-barkclo																																								
-weaving																																								
-needle,e																																								
-chisel																																								
-rasp																																								
-grinding																																								
-pounding																																								
-adze																																								
TOOL																																								
fire,lig																																								
smokng p																																								
pottery																																								
utensil																																								
lime spa																																								
dish,vess																																								
lime cont																																								

Name	Henry Reitlinger Bequest
Address	Oldfield Guard's Club Road Maidenhead SL6 8DN
Telephone	0628-21818
Contact	Resident trustee curator

MAIDENHEAD

Sources & Dates of Information

R. Hutchings 1966

Visit

MEG 1978

Letter 1979

Notes

Oceania: fishing spears 2
spears 3 (in carved wooden case)
wood dart carrier 1

Closed October to April.

Private till 1950.

Dates of Collection/Acquisition	Donors/Collectors/Former Owners
1910-40	Henry Reitlinger

Documentation

Comment

Name	Maidstone Museum and Art Gallery
Address	St. Faith's Street Maidstone ME14 1LH
Telephone	0622-54497
Contact	Keeper of Archaeology

MAIDSTONE

Sources & Dates of Information

R. Hutchings 1966

Visit 1974 GSP

MEG 1978

Letter

personal communication, M. Hoad, 1979

Notes

Total Oceanic: several thousand objects.

Disposals: Material on loan to Museum of Mankind.

*Chatham-- club: patu onewa
*New Zealand-- clubs: includes taiaha 5, tewhatewha 1, paehaka 1

Dates of Collection/Acquisition	Donors/Collectors/Former Owners
Acquired mainly 1873	Brenchley, 1865, Solomons Charles Collection, 1856, Oceania

Documentation

Reference: J. Brenchley and other collections in Museum of Mankind from Solomon Islands discussed by D. Waite, 1979, Capt. Cook and the South Pacific, British Museum Yearbook 3.

Comment

Important collection from Brenchley, HMS Curaçoa.

Museum and Art Gallery

MAIDSTONE

Artefact → / Provenance ↓	OCEANIA UN.	AUSTRALIA	MELA.UNPROV.	Admiralty	Banks	Bismarck	D'Entrecast.	Fiji	Louisiade	Loyalty	N. Britain	N. Caledonia	N. Guinea	N. Hebrides	N. Ireland	Santa Cruz	Solomon	Trobriand	MICRO.UNPROV.	Caroline	Gilbert	Mariana	Marshall	POLY.UNPROV.	Austral	Chatham	Cook	Easter	Hawaii	Marquesas	New Zealand	Niue	Pitcairn	Samoa	Society	Tokelau	Tonga	Tuamotu	Tuvalu
box																																							
bag																															X								
basket																																							
mat																																							
headrest																																							
transport																																							
currency																																							
-rattle																																							
-flute,pipe																																							
-drum,gong																																							
MUSICAL INS																																							
charm																																							
magic,med.																																							
fig.,image																																							
carving																																							
-bullroarer																																							
-paddle																																							
-adze																																							
-board																																							
-mask																																							
CERE. OBJ.																																							
staff,stick																																							
toilet app.																															X								
fan																																							
comb																																							
-neck,breast																															1								
-arm																																							
-ear,nose																																							
-head																																							
PERS. ORN.																																							
-cloak																															2								
-belt																																							
-skirt																															2								
CLOTHING																																							
barkcloth																																							
OTHER																																							
TOTAL	X							X					X	X			X									X			X		X								

Museum and Art Gallery MAIDSTONE

Artefact → / Provenance ↓	OCEANIA UN.	AUSTRALIA	MELA.UNPROV.	Admiralty	Banks	Bismarck	D'Entrecast.	Fiji	Louisiade	Loyalty	N. Britain	N. Caledonia	N. Guinea	N. Hebrides	N. Ireland	Santa Cruz	Solomon	Trobriand	MICRO.UNPROV	Caroline	Gilbert	Mariana	Marshall	POLY.UNPROV.	Austral	Chatham	Cook	Easter	Hawaii	Marquesas	New Zealand	Niue	Pitcairn	Samoa	Society	Tokelau	Tonga	Tuamotu	Tuvalu
cord																																							
raw mater																																							
-sling,sto																																							
-arrow																																							
-bow																																							
-shield																																							
-dagger																																							
-spearthro																																							
-spear																																							
-club																																							
WEAPON																									1*					11*									
-float,si																																							
-net																														1									
-spear																																							
-fishhook																																							
FISHING																														1									
hunting																																							
-model																														1									
-ornament																														1									
-paddle																																							
NAVIGATIO																														3									
-barkclot																																							
-weaving																																							
-needle,aw																																							
-chisel																																							
-rasp																									1														
-grinding																																							
-pounding																																							
-adze																																							
TOOL																									8					12									
fire,ligh																																							
smoking pi																																							
pottery																																							
utensil																																							
lime spat																																							
dish,vesse																																							
lime cont.																																							

MALDON

Name Maldon Museum Society

Address Maldon
Essex

Telephone

Contact Secretary

Sources & Dates of Information

R. Hutchings 1966

Visit PG 1974

MEG 1978

Letter

Notes

Dates of Collection/Acquisition

Donors/Collectors/Former Owners

Dr. Salter

Documentation

Comment

All Salter Collection. Salter was a local doctor with wide collection interests, c. 1900. Oldman acquired some of his material, and other collections (natural history) are in Colchester Museum. (Other Salter material was once in Chelmsford Museum.)

Museum Society

MALDON

Artcfact → / Provenance ↓	TOTAL	OTHER	barkcloth	CLOTHING	-skirt	-belt	-cloak	PERS. ORN.	-head	-ear,nose	-arm	-neck,breast	comb	fan	toilet app.	staff,stick	CERE. OBJ.	-mask	-board	-adze	-paddle	-bullroarer	carving	fig.,image	magic,med.	charm	MUSICAL INS.	-drum,gong	-flute,pipe	-rattle	currency	transport	headrest	mat	basket	bag	box
OCEANIA UN.																																					
AUSTRALIA	8																																				
MELA.UNPROV.																																					
Admiralty																																					
Banks																																					
Bismarck																																					
D'Entrecast.																																					
Fiji																																					
Louisiade																																					
Loyalty																																					
N. Britain																																					
N. Caledonia																																					
N. Guinea																																					
N. Hebrides																																					
N. Ireland																																					
Santa Cruz																																					
Solomon	7																																				
Trobriand																																					
MICRO.UNPROV.																																					
Caroline																																					
Gilbert																																					
Mariana																																					
Marshall																																					
POLY.UNPROV.																																					
Austral																																					
Chatham																																					
Cook																																					
Easter																																					
Hawaii																																					
Marquesas																																					
New Zealand																																					
Niue																																					
Pitcairn																																					
Samoa	1																																				
Society																																					
Tokelau																																					
Tonga	2																																				
Tuamotu																																					
Tuvalu																																					

Museum Society

MALDON

Artefact →

Provenance →

Artefact (rows): cord; raw mater; -sling,st; -arrow; -bow; -shield; -dagger; -spearthr; -spear; -club; WEAPON; -float,si; -net; -spear; -fishhook; FISHING; hunting; -model; -ornament; -paddle; NAVIGATIO; -barkclot; -weaving; -needle,aw; -chisel; -rasp; -grinding; -pounding; -adze; TOOL; fire,ligh; smokng pi; pottery; utensil; lime spat; dish,vesse; lime cont.

Provenance (columns): OCEANIA UN.; AUSTRALIA; MELA.UNPROV.; Admiralty; Banks; Bismarck; D'Entrecast.; Fiji; Louisiade; Loyalty; N. Britain; N. Caledonia; N. Guinea; N. Hebrides; N. Ireland; Santa Cruz; Solomon; Trobriand; MICRO.UNPROV; Caroline; Gilbert; Mariana; Marshall; POLY.UNPROV.; Austral; Chatham; Cook; Easter; Hawaii; Marquesas; New Zealand; Niue; Pitcairn; Samoa; Society; Tokelau; Tonga; Tuamotu; Tuvalu

1 7 1 2

Name	The Manchester Museum	MANCHESTER
Address	The University of Manchester Oxford Road Manchester M13 9PL	Sources & Dates of Information R. Hutchings 1966 Visit SP 1975
Telephone	061-2733333	MEG 1978
Contact	Keeper of Ethnology	Letter

Notes

For table explanatory notes, see Manchester (C).

Dates of Collection/Acquisition	Donors/Collectors/Former Owners
	Hadfield (missionary), Loyalty Islands, collected c. 1900 Salford Museum Bankfield Museum

Documentation

Complete card catalogue.

Reference: F. Willett, 1955, "A Maori Store-Chamber Slab in the Manchester Museum", Man, LV, p. 177 (no. 197).

Comment

Clearly important. Card index recently revised.

Artefact → / Provenance ↓	TOTAL	OTHER	barkcloth	CLOTHING	-skirt	-belt	-cloak	PERS. ORN.	-head	-ear,nose	-arm	-neck,breast	comb	fan	toilet app.	staff,stick	CERE. OBJ.	-mask	-board	-adze	-paddle	-bullroarer	carving	fig.,image	magic,med.	charm	MUSICAL INS.	-drum,gong	-flute,pipe	-rattle	currency	transport	headrest	mat	basket	bag	box
OCEANIA UN.	42	7						1					6																							1	
AUSTRALIA	745			106*				x									34																		1*		
MELA. UNPROV.	28	5		1				13																													
Admiralty	48							8																													
Banks																																					
Bismarck	11																																				
D'Entrecast.																																					
Fiji	385	15	41	13				11				14		9	2*	2	18*											1	2				8	8	9		
Louisiade																																					
Loyalty	107	6						22																												3	
N. Britain	78							23								7															8				3		
N. Caledonia	46+			1				5								1																				5	
N. Guinea	884	44		12		2		133					12			3		2						1		7		8	2					4			
N. Hebrides	243	5		9				34										2					1													2	
N. Ireland	14							3								1		1						1													
Santa Cruz	42	2						2									6																			1	
Solomon	578	28						37									10						3	1													
Trobriand																																					
MICRO. UNPROV.																																					
Caroline	4																																				
Gilbert	61							6						1																						1	
Mariana																																					
Marshall	2																																				
POLY. UNPROV.	45	8	27						1*																										7		
Austral	14																																				
Chatham																																					
Cook	24																			13																	
Easter	1																							1													
Hawaii	81	5	10								1	2		1																							
Marquesas	11							3						1									3*														
New Zealand	191	2			6	2	11	12				6				5	4		1				1	1											10		4*
Niue	64			3				5						3																				2		1	
Pitcairn																																				1	
Samoa	97	1	8									9	23	8	3*													1					1	7			
Society	21	1	2	1								2																									
Tokelau																																					
Tonga	41		1	1				5					7																				1				
Tuamotu																																					
Tuvalu	2							2																													
[illegible]	2																																				

The Manchester Museum

MANCHESTER

Artefact → / Provenance ↓	lime cont	dish,vess	lime spat	utensil	pottery	smokng pi	fire,ligh	TOOL	-adze	-pounding	-grinding	-rasp	-chisel	-needle,a	-weaving	-barkclot	NAVIGATIO	-paddle	-ornament	-model	hunting	FISHING	-fishhook	-spear	-net	-float,si	WEAPON	-club	-spear	-spearthro	-dagger	-shield	-bow	-arrow	-sling,st	raw mater	cord
OCEANIA UN.									2														12		2		11										
AUSTRALIA								154																			45										
MELA.UNPROV.		2																							2		5										
Admiralty																												8	24		6					2	
Banks																																					
Bismarck																													11*								
D'Entrecast.																																					
Fiji		42		12	5				8	1				1		2		1									2	146	12								
Louisiade																																					
Loyalty		2							23																			10	18					12	11		
N. Britain																												14	23								
N. Caledonia								2	5							2												15	1					8	X		
N. Guinea			34			13		25	43									14		1	4		2		5		6	85	27		8	24	6	357			
N. Hebrides								3	14																			31	12		6		2	115		7	
N. Ireland																		2										4	2								
Santa Cruz		2																													1			28			
Solomon																	1*	13					22				100*		X			5		358			
Trobriand																																					
MICRO.UNPROV.																																					
Caroline									1									1											2								
Gilbert																							4				49*										
Mariana																																					
Marshall																							2														
POLY.UNPROV.									2																												
Austral									1									13																			
Chatham																																					
Cook		1							4	2								1		1								2									
Easter																																					
Hawaii								25	26	2						8								1													
Marquesas																												4									
New Zealand		1						X	36	3					1		2	9	1	2			12					59*									
Niue								6										4		3			5					15	17								
Pitcairn									2																												
Samoa		1		2					1														2					28	1		1						
Society									5							1							7				2										
Tokelau																																					
Tonga																							2					23	1								
Tuamotu																																					
Tuvalu																																					
Rotuma																												2									
N.G. - Asmat		1							1									1											2		2	2					

MANCHESTER

The Manchester Museum (C)

*Australia-- clothing: '106' includes ornaments
basket: from Tasmania

*Melanesia unprovenanced-- other: misc. 5

*Bismarck-- spears: 11, from New Hanover

*Fiji-- toilet apparatus: tattooing
ceremonial objects: tambua 18
other: hook 1, flywhisks 3, misc. 11

*Loyalty-- other: misc. 6

*New Guinea-- includes from Matty/Wuvulu Is.: weapons 6, paddles 3, axes 2, ornament 1
other: containers(unspecified) 40, skulls 4

*New Hebrides-- other: containers 5

*Santa Cruz-- other: misc. 2

*Solomons-- weapons: most are spears
other: containers 14, misc. 14

*Gilberts-- weapons: 12 pieces armour

*Polynesia unprovenanced-- headdress: possibly Society
other: misc. 8

*Hawaii-- other: games 5

*Marquesas-- carvings: stilt steps

*New Zealand-- clubs: patu paraoa 9, patu onewa 10, merė (wood) 9, taiaha 25, tewhatewha 5, pouwhenna 1
other: heads 2

*Samoa-- toilet apparatus: tattooing
other: misc. 1

*Society-- other: flywhisk

*New Guinea Asmat-- other: head

MANSFIELD

Name Mansfield Museum and Art Gallery

Address Leeming Street
Mansfield, Notts.

Telephone 0623-22561

Contact Curator

Sources & Dates of Information

R. Hutchings 1966

Visit

MEG 1978

Letter 1979

Notes

*Australia-- other: boomerang

Dates of Collection/Acquisition	Donors/Collectors/Former Owners
	W.J. Thompson, acquired 1950

Documentation

Comment

Cf. other material from Thompson Collection at Nottingham.

Museum and Art Gallery

MANSFIELD

Artefact → / Provenance ↓	OCEANIA UN.	AUSTRALIA	MELA.UNPROV.	Admiralty	Banks	Bismarck	D'Entrecast.	Fiji	Louisiade	Loyalty	N. Britain	N. Caledonia	N. Guinea	N. Hebrides	N. Ireland	Santa Cruz	Solomon	Trobriand	MICRO.UNPROV.	Caroline	Gilbert	Mariana	Marshall	POLY.UNPROV.	Austral	Chatham	Cook	Easter	Hawaii	Marquesas	New Zealand	Niue	Pitcairn	Samoa	Society	Tokelau	Tonga	Tuamotu	Tuvalu
box																																							
bag																																							
basket																																							
mat																																							
headrest																																							
transport																																							
currency																																							
-rattle																							X																
-flute, pipe																																							
-drum, gong																																							
MUSICAL INS.																																							
charm													X																										
magic, med.																																							
fig., image																																							
carving																																							
-bullroarer																																							
-paddle																																							
-adze																																							
-board																																							
-mask																																							
CERE. OBJ.																																							
staff, stick																																							
toilet app.		2																																					
fan																																							
comb																																							
-neck, breast																																							
-arm																																							
-ear, nose																																							
-head																																							
PERS. ORN.																																							
-cloak																																							
-belt																																							
-skirt																																							
CLOTHING																																							
barkcloth																																							
OTHER		1																																					
TOTAL		12						3					7+	2			1				1		X														2		

Museum and Art Gallery

MANSFIELD

Artefact → / Provenance ↓	OCEANIA UN.	AUSTRALIA	MELA.UNPROV.	Admiralty	Banks	Bismarck	D'Entrecast.	Fiji	Louisiade	Loyalty	N. Britain	N. Caledonia	N. Guinea	N. Hebrides	N. Ireland	Santa Cruz	Solomon	Trobriand	MICRO.UNPROV	Caroline	Gilbert	Mariana	Marshall	POLY.UNPROV.	Austral	Chatham	Cook	Easter	Hawaii	Marquesas	New Zealand	Niue	Pitcairn	Samoa	Society	Tokelau	Tonga	Tuamotu	Tuvalu
cord																																							
raw mater																																							
-sling,sto																																							
-arrow																																							
-bow																																							
-shield																																							
-dagger																																							
-spearthro		3																																					
-spear		5		2																																			
-club								1						2			1																				1		
WEAPON																					1																		
-float,sin																																							
-net																																							
-spear		1						2					6																										
-fishhook																																							
FISHING																																							
hunting																																							
-model																																					1		
-ornament																																							
-paddle																																							
NAVIGATION																																							
-barkclot																																							
-weaving																																							
-needle,aw																																							
-chisel																																							
-rasp																																							
-grinding																																							
-pounding																																							
-adze																																							
TOOL																																							
fire,ligh																																							
smoking pi																																							
pottery																																							
utensil																																							
lime spat																																							
dish,vesse																																							
lime cont.																																							

Name	Captain Cook Birthplace Museum
Address	Stewart's Park Middlesbrough
Telephone	0642-311211
Contact	Leisure Officer, Museums and Art Galleries, c/o Middlesbrough Recreation & Amenities Dept. P.O. Box, Zetland ~~House, Zetland Rd., Middlesbrough (tel. 0642-245432)~~

MIDDLESBROUGH

Sources & Dates of Information

R. Hutchings	1966
Visit	-
MEG	1978
Letter	1979

Notes

The Oceanic section of the collections is being developed.

*Oceania-- toilet apparatus: backscratcher
*Australia-- other: boomerangs 2, post-European 1
*Fiji-- other: flywhisk

Dates of Collection/Acquisition	Donors/Collectors/Former Owners
Acquired mainly 1900-20	G.L. Dorman 1904 Dr. Weatherell 1904 Mrs. Mallabar 1937

Documentation

Libary, iconographic.

Comment

Note some material is on loan from the Hancock Museum, Newcastle. May therefore have fair age.

Captain Cook Birthplace Museum

MIDDLESBROUGH

Provenance ↓ / Artefact →	TOTAL	OTHER	barkcloth	CLOTHING	-skirt	-belt	-cloak	PERS. ORN.	-head	-ear,nose	-arm	-neck,breast	comb	fan	toilet app.	staff,stick	CERE. OBJ.	-mask	-board	-adze	-paddle	-bullroarer	carving	fig.,image	magic,med.	charm	MUSICAL INS.	-drum,gong	-flute,pipe	-rattle	currency	transport	headrest	mat	basket	bag	box
OCEANIA UN.	62														1*	1																			1	1	
AUSTRALIA	45+	3		1								1																									
MELA.UNPROV.																																					
Admiralty																																					
Banks																																					
Bismarck																																					
D'Entrecast.																																					
Fiji		1																																			
Louisiade																																					
Loyalty																																					
N. Britain																																					
N. Caledonia	1																																				
N. Guinea	4																											1									
N. Hebrides	5												4																								
N. Ireland																																					
Santa Cruz																																					
Solomon	23																																				
Trobriand																																					
MICRO.UNPROV.																																					
Caroline																																					
Gilbert	2																																				
Mariana																																					
Marshall																																					
POLY.UNPROV.																																					
Austral																																					
Chatham																																					
Cook																																					
Easter																																					
Hawaii																																					
Marquesas																																					
New Zealand	9			1																			1	1													2
Niue	3			1																																2	
Pitcairn																																					
Samoa																																					
Society																																					
Tokelau																																					
Tonga																																					
Tuamotu																																					
Tuvalu																																					

Captain Cook Birthplace Museum

MIDDLESBROUG

Provenance	lime cont	dish,vess	lime spat	utensil	pottery	smokng pi	fire,ligh	TOOL	-adze	-pounding	-grinding	-rasp	-chisel	-needle,a	-weaving	-barkclot	NAVIGATIO	-paddle
OCEANIA UN.		2						1										
AUSTRALIA							2		6									
MELA.UNPROV.																		
Admiralty																		
Banks																		
Bismarck																		
D'Entrecast.																		
Fiji		1																
Louisiade																		
Loyalty																		
N. Britain																		
N. Caledonia																		
N. Guinea		1		2														
N. Hebrides																		
N. Ireland																		
Santa Cruz																		
Solomon									1									
Trobriand																		
MICRO.UNPROV.																		
Caroline																		
Gilbert																		
Mariana																		
Marshall																		
POLY.UNPROV.																		
Austral																		
Chatham																		
Cook																		
Easter																		
Hawaii																		
Marquesas																		
New Zealand														1				
Niue																		
Pitcairn																		
Samoa																		
Society																		
Tokelau																		
Tonga																		
Tuamotu																		
Tuvalu																		

Provenance	-ornament	-model	hunting	FISHING	-fishhook	-spear	-net	-float,si	WEAPON	-club	-spear	-spearthr	-dagger	-shield	-bow	-arrow	-sling,s	raw mate	cord
OCEANIA UN.									1	2	3				3	46			
AUSTRALIA				1		2			2	1	15			4				7+	
MELA.UNPROV.																			
Admiralty																			
Banks																			
Bismarck																			
D'Entrecast.																			
Fiji						2				5									
Louisiade																			
Loyalty																			
N. Britain																			
N. Caledonia										1									
N. Guinea																			
N. Hebrides										1									
N. Ireland																			
Santa Cruz																			
Solomon										1					1	20			
Trobriand																			
MICRO.UNPROV.																			
Caroline																			
Gilbert													2						
Mariana																			
Marshall																			
POLY.UNPROV.																			
Austral																			
Chatham																			
Cook																			
Easter																			
Hawaii																			
Marquesas																			
New Zealand										1	2								
Niue																			
Pitcairn																			
Samoa																			
Society																			
Tokelau																			
Tonga																			
Tuamotu																			
Tuvalu																			

MONTROSE

Name	Montrose Museum
Address	Panmure Place Montrose Angus Scotland
Telephone	0674-3232
Contact	District Curator

Sources & Dates of Information

R. Hutchings 1966

Visit

MEG 1978

Letter 1979

Notes

*Micronesia unprovenanced-- daggers: all sharkstooth
*Pitcairn-- barkcloth: made by Adams family, survivors of Bounty
weaving: cloth samples made by Adams family

Dates of Collection/Acquisition	Donors/Collectors/Former Owners
Collected mainly 1840-80	Capt. Young, 1837, Australs George Smart, 1842 & 1873, New Zealand ?Capt. Simpson, 1843, Oceania Capt. G. Burnett, 1843, Oceania C. Wood, 1846, New Zealand A. Bower, 1879, New Zealand A. Cruickshank, 1842, Fiji W. Low, 1915, Australia & "Gama" Is. Rev. Tait-Scott, 1882 & 1887, New Guinea M.A. Lyall, 1889, New Ireland

Documentation

Comment

Note early material. Not seen but appears interesting and important, especially Smart, Cruickshank and Wood collections.

Montrose Museum

MONTROSE

Artefact → / Provenance ↓	TOTAL	OTHER	barkcloth	CLOTHING	-skirt	-belt	-cloak	PERS. ORN.	-head	-ear,nose	-arm	-neck,breast	comb	fan	toilet app.	staff,stick	CERE. OBJ.	-mask	-board	-adze	-paddle	-bullroarer	carving	fig.,image	magic,med.	charm	MUSICAL INS.	-drum,gong	-flute,pipe	-rattle	currency	transport	headrest	mat	basket	bag	box
OCEANIA UN.	9															3																					
AUSTRALIA	35											3																									
MELA. UNPROV.																																					
Admiralty																																					
Banks																																					
Bismarck																																					
D'Entrecast.	1																																				
Fiji	8																																				
Louisiade																																					
Loyalty																																					
N. Britain																																					
N. Caledonia																																					
N. Guinea	6																																			2	
N. Hebrides																																					
N. Ireland	2																																				
Santa Cruz																																					
Solomon																																					
Trobriand																																					
MICRO. UNPROV.	4																																				
Caroline																																					
Gilbert	4																																				
Mariana																																					
Marshall																																					
POLY. UNPROV.																																					
Austral	1																																				
Chatham																																					
Cook	2											2																									
Easter																																					
Hawaii																																					
Marquesas																																					
New Zealand	10					1																															
Niue																																					
Pitcairn	24		1*																																		
Samoa																																					
Society																																					
Tokelau																																					
Tonga																																					
Tuamotu																																					
Tuvalu	3																																				
"[illegible]" (1)	5										4	1																									

Montrose Museum

MONTROSE

Provenance ↓ / Artefact →	lime cont.	dish,vesse	lime spat.	utensil	pottery	smoking pip	fire,light	TOOL	-adze	-pounding	-grinding	-rasp	-chisel	-needle,aw	-weaving	-barkcloth	NAVIGATION	-paddle	-ornament	-model	hunting	FISHING	-fishhook	-spear	-net	-float,sin	WEAPON	-club	-spear	-spearthro	-dagger	-shield	-bow	-arrow	-sling,sto	raw mater.	cord
OCEANIA.UN.																												1	5								
AUSTRALIA									1					9													1		18	1						1	1
MELA.UNPROV.																																					
Admiralty																																					
Banks																																					
Bismarck																																					
D'Entrecast.									1																												
Fiji																													8								
Louisiade																																					
Loyalty																																					
N. Britain																																					
N. Caledonia																																					
N. Guinea		2																1				1															
N. Hebrides																																					
N. Ireland																													2								
Santa Cruz																																					
Solomon																																					
Trobriand																																					
MICRO.UNPROV.																															4*						
Caroline																																					
Gilbert																											2		2								
Mariana																																					
Marshall																																					
POLY.UNPROV.																																					
Austral																		1																			
Chatham																																					
Cook																																					
Easter																																					
Hawaii																																					
Marquesas																																					
New Zealand									7									2																			
Niue																																					
Pitcairn															1*																						
Samoa																																					
Society																																					
Tokelau																																					
Tonga																																					
Tuamotu																																					
Tuvalu																											2		1								
"Gama" (?)																																					

NEWCASTLE (BROWN

Name George Brown Ethnographical Collection

Address Department of Social Studies
University of Newcastle upon Tyne
Newcastle upon Tyne

Telephone Head of Department

Contact

Sources & Dates of Information

R. Hutchings 1966

Visit

MEG 1978

Letter

Catalogue 1971

Notes

For table explanatory notes, see Newcastle (Brown) C.

Collection moved from Bowes Museum, Barnard Castle to King's College, Durham University, finally settling at Newcastle University in 1953.

Dates of Collection/Acquisition

Collected 1860+

Donors/Collectors/Former Owners

George Brown

Documentation

Completely catalogued.
Photographic.

Comment

Collection written up by Caroline Upton for Master's thesis, 1971. George Brown (1835-1917) was a well-known missionary and writer, active in the South Pacific 1860-1917. Upton was unable to tie down provenances for all objects from his writings, as he was not sufficiently precise. A copy of her report* in Anthropology Museum at Cambridge. (Other Brown collections in Australian Museum, Sydney; Hobart Museum, Tasmania. Papers, photographs, etc., in Mitchell Library, Sydney and in private hands.)

* to Social Science Research Council

George Brown Collection

NEWCASTLE (BROW[N]

Artefact → / Provenance ↓	TOTAL	OTHER	barkcloth	CLOTHING	-skirt	-belt	-cloak	PERS. ORN.	-head	-ear,nose	-arm	-neck,breast	comb	fan	toilet app.	staff,stick	CERE. OBJ.	-mask	-board	-adze	-paddle	-bullroarer	carving	fig.,image	magic,med.	charm	MUSICAL INS.	-drum,gong	-flute,pipe	-rattle	currency	transport	headrest	mat	basket	bag	box
OCEANIA UN.	111	2	83	2		3						4																									
AUSTRALIA																																					
MELA.UNPROV.	131	5		4				2			8	15	3														5	1							2	2	
Admiralty	see Bismarck																																				
Banks																																					
Bismarck *	598	6		11		1		29	14	8	77	9	1				1	20					21			2	6*	6	6		13				22	16	
D'Entrecast.	see New Guinea																																				
Fiji	118	10	2	2								4	4	2		2	8										1						3	1	5		
Louisiade *	6									3																											
Loyalty																																					
N. Britain	see Bismarck																																				
N. Caledonia																																					
N. Guinea	632	13		39		19		15	2	8	89	31	108			21							2			2		5				2	1		76	3	
N. Hebrides	32			3												1																		3			
N. Ireland	see Bismarck																																				
Santa Cruz	61	2				4		1			1												2								2			11	14		
Solomon	636	36		4		3		25		12	44	22	4	1	1*	2	4	1					16				7*		3		7			10	44	12	
Trobriand	380	6		2						1		15											23					6							5		
MICRO.UNPROV.	2																													1							
Caroline																																					
Gilbert																																					
Mariana																																					
Marshall	5			4																															1		
POLY.UNPROV.	30			1										1																				22		2	
Austral	1																																				
Chatham																																					
Cook																																					
Easter																																					
Hawaii																																					
Marquesas																																					
New Zealand																																					
Niue																																					
Pitcairn																																					
Samoa	210	16	4	15*				15	3			3	25	42														1					1	9	15		
Society																																					
Tokelau																																					
Tonga	38	2	2	14									9																				1	3	4		
Tuamotu																																					
Tuvalu	4			2																																	
Rotuma	2																																		1		

George Brown Collection

NEWCASTLE (BROWN

Artefact → / Provenance ↓	lime con	dish,ves	lime spa	utensil	pottery	smokng p	fire,lig	TOOL	-adze	-poundin	-grindin	-rasp	-chisel	-needle,	-weaving	-barkclo	NAVIGATI	-paddle	-ornamen	-model	hunting	FISHING	-fishhoo	-spear	-net	-float,s	WEAPON	-club	-spear	-spearth	-dagger	-shield	-bow	-arrow	-sling,s	raw mat	cord
OCEANIA UN.		1							4									1										1					3			7	
AUSTRALIA																																					
MELA.UNPROV.									34									2							17			1	5				11	13		1	
Admiralty																																					
Banks																																					
Bismarck		12		3				4	16								1	8			4		1		7		3	77	168		12	1			9	3	
D'Entrecast.																																					
Fiji		21		2	15				3	1						8						2						17	4							1	
Louisiade	1								1																			1									
Loyalty																																					
N. Britain																																					
N. Caledonia																																					
N. Guinea	4	21	27	15		25		7	54	2		1						2	11			2			1		6	10	1		1	5	3				1
N. Hebrides									1																			11	1					6		6	
N. Ireland																																					
Santa Cruz				1				1		3		1			17*																					1	
Solomon	15	19	1	3	2	2		8	7	2					8		2*	7	5	2		4	53		2	2	29	31				1	9	155		5	1
Trobriand	47	64	104	1				14	1	15								4	7	1	5		1		4			25	3			8			1	20	
MICRO.UNPROV.																											1										
Caroline																																					
Gilbert																																					
Mariana																																					
Marshall																																					
POLY.UNPROV.									1																			1								2	
Austral																		1																			
Chatham																																					
Cook																																					
Easter																																					
Hawaii																																					
Marquesas																																					
New Zealand																																					
Niue																																					
Pitcairn																																					
Samoa		17							1											7		6						12								2	
Society																																					
Tokelau																																					
Tonga																							3														
Tuamotu																																					
Tuvalu		2																																			
Rotuma									1																												

CONT NEXT PAGE (8)

George Brown Collection (B)

NEWCASTLE (BR

Artefact → / Provenance	Line	Norfolk
box		
bag		
basket		
mat		
headrest		
transport		
currency		
-rattle		
-flute,pipe		
-drum,gong		
MUSICAL INS.		
charm		
magic,med.		
fig.,image		
carving		
-bullroarer		
-paddle		
-adze		
-board		
-mask		
CERE. OBJ.		
staff,stick		
toilet app.		
fan		
comb		
-neck,breast		
-arm		5
-ear,nose		
-head		
PERS. ORN.		
-cloak		
-belt		
-skirt		
CLOTHING		
barkcloth		
OTHER		
TOTAL	2	5

George Brown Collection (B)

NEWCASTLE (BROWN

- cord
- raw mat
- -sling,s
- -arrow
- -bow
- -shield
- -dagger
- -spearth
- -spear
- -club
- WEAPON
- -float,s — Z
- -net
- -spear
- -fishhoo
- FISHING
- hunting
- -model
- -ornamen
- -paddle
- NAVIGATI
- -barkclo
- -weaving
- -needle,
- -chisel
- -rasp
- -grindin
- -poundin
- -adze
- TOOL
- fire,lig
- smoking p
- pottery
- utensil
- lime spa
- dish,ves
- lime con

Artefact →

Provenance →

Line

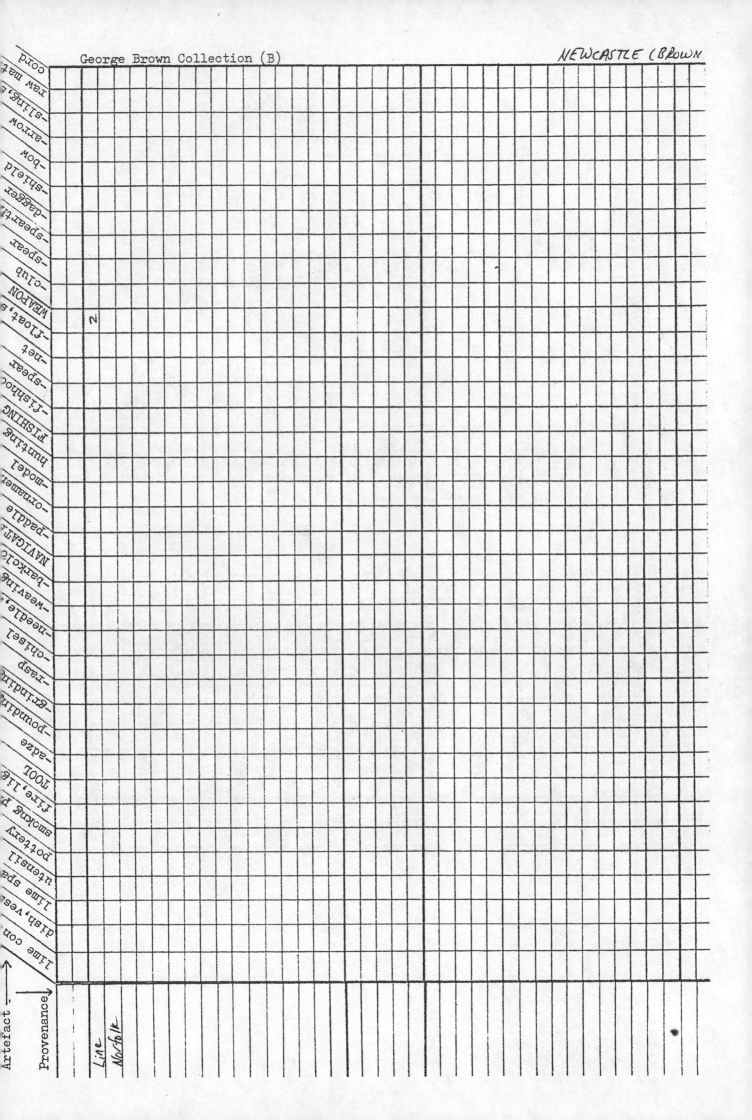

Norfolk

NEWCASTLE
(BROWN)

Newcastle (Brown) (C)

*Oceania unprovenanced-- other: misc. 2

*Melanesia unprovenanced-- other: cloth 3, misc. 2

*Bismarck (including Duke of York, New Hanover, Emirau, Wuvulu)--
musical instrument: jewsharps 6
other: cloth 3, misc. 2

*Fiji-- other: house model, flywhisks 3, misc. 6

*Louisiade-- includes only Rossel

*New Guinea (including D'Entrecasteaux, Fergusson, Laughlin, Woodlark)--
other: toys 7, cloth 1, misc. 5

*Santa Cruz-- weaving tools: looms 17
other: cloth 2

*Solomon (including Ontong Java, Shortlands, Nukumanu, Niguria)--
toilet apparatus: tattooing
musical instrument: jewsharps 5
other: cloth 11, toys 11, sunshades 5, misc. 9

*Trobriand-- other: house models 2, toy 1, misc. 3

*Samoa-- clothing: hats 15
other: flywhisks 14, toy 1, misc. 1

*Tonga--. other: flywhisks 2

NEWCASTLE (HANCOCK)

Name: Hancock Museum

Address: Barras Bridge
Newcastle upon Tyne NE2 4PT

Telephone: 0632-22359

Contact: Curator

Sources & Dates of Information

R. Hutchings 1966

Visit LDS 1972

MEG 1978

Letter

UNESCO I circular 1971

Notes

Table lists material on display only (by Cambridge student 1972).
H.D. Skinner also listed, in 1915, the following from New Zealand: preserved heads 3, pendant, flutes 4, weaving peg, decorated calabash, adzes 13, paddles 4, fishhooks 8, figure 1, navigation 2.

*Australia-- other: boomerang
*New Hebrides-- other: effigy
*Gilberts-- weapons: includes armour suit
*Hawaii-- other: house model
*New Zealand-- utensil: chief's feeding funnel

Dates of Collection/Acquisition

Acquired mainly 1910-50

Donors/Collectors/Former Owners

George Allen

Documentation

Being catalogued.

Photographic, iconographic.

Comment

Some early material. Important collection, with some Cook items (cf. Kaeppler, 1974, "Cook Voyage Provenance of the 'Artificial Curiousities' from Bullock's Museum", Man, 9:68-92).

Hancock Museum

NEWCASTLE (HANC

Provenance ↓ / Artefact →	TOTAL	OTHER	barkcloth	CLOTHING	-skirt	-belt	-cloak	PERS. ORN.	-head	-ear,nose	-arm	-neck,breast	comb	fan	toilet app.	staff,stick	CERE. OBJ.	-mask	-board	-adze	-paddle	-bullroarer	carving	fig.,image	magic,med.	charm	MUSICAL INS.	-drum,gong	-flute,pipe	-rattle	currency	transport	headrest	mat	basket	bag	box
OCEANIA UN.	95							1																													
AUSTRALIA		1										1																							X		
MELA.UNPROV.	3																																				
Admiralty	11																																				
Banks																																					
Bismarck																																					
D'Entrecast.																																					
Fiji	53				1							1					1												1				2		1		
Louisiade																																					
Loyalty	5								x																1												
N. Britain	2																																				
N. Caledonia	4																																				
N. Guinea	105							1	1	1																		1									
N. Hebrides	32	1																2						X													
N. Ireland	3																							1													
Santa Cruz	21																														1						
Solomon	52								1	1	1	X																									
Trobriand																																					
MICRO.UNPROV																																					
Caroline	2																																				
Gilbert	6																																				
Mariana																																					
Marshall																																					
POLY.UNPROV.	14		1																										1								
Austral	1																																				
Chatham																																					
Cook	1																																				
Easter	2																																				
Hawaii	9	1										1																									
Marquesas	2																																				
New Zealand	92			1	1		4																1				X		x					X	X		
Niue	6					1																															
Pitcairn																																					
Samoa	10												X																								
Society	X																																				
Tokelau	15																																				
Tonga												1																					1				
Tuamotu																																					
Tuvalu																																					
Tahiti	3+										X	1																									

Hancock Museum

NEWCASTLE (HANCOCK

Artefact → / Provenance ↓	lime cont	dish,vess	lime spat	utensil	pottery	smokng pi	fire,ligh	TOOL	-adze	-pounding	-grinding	-rasp	-chisel	-needle,a	-weaving	-barkclot	NAVIGATIO	-paddle	-ornament	-model	hunting	FISHING	-fishhook	-spear	-net	-float,si	WEAPON	-club	-spear	-spearthr	-dagger	-shield	-bow	-arrow	-sling,st	raw mate	cord
OCEANIA UN.	1	2							1							1							2+					2	1								
AUSTRALIA								2																			1	1	x	2		1				1	
MELA.UNPROV.																																					
Admiralty																																					
Banks																																					
Bismarck																																					
D'Entrecast.																																					
Fiji		1		1	2					1																		2	1								
Louisiade																																					
Loyalty																														1							
N. Britain																																					
N. Caledonia		1																										1									
N. Guinea																												2									
N. Hebrides																												2									
N. Ireland																																					
Santa Cruz																																					
Solomon	1	2						1																									1				
Trobriand																																					
MICRO.UNPROV																																					
Caroline																																					
Gilbert																											2*		1								
Mariana																																					
Marshall																																					
POLY.UNPROV.		1																7										3								1	
Austral																																					
Chatham																																					
Cook																																					
Easter																																					
Hawaii																				1																	
Marquesas																																					
New Zealand				1*					x	2								1	2			1				1	4	17+								1	
Niue																				1																	
Pitcairn																																					
Samoa																												1									
Society																																					
Tokelau																																					
Tonga		1								1																		1									
Tuamotu																																					
Tuvalu																																					
Tahiti										1																											
Woodlark																												1									

Name	Northampton Museums and Art Gallery (including Abington Museum)
Address	Central Museum and Art Gallery Guildhall Road Northampton NN1 1DP
Telephone	0604-34881
Contact	Keeper of Archaeology

NORTHAMPTON (M+AG)

Sources & Dates of Information

R. Hutchings 1969

Visit GSP 1974

MEG 1978

Letter 1979

Notes

Important collection of musical instruments.

Dates of Collection/Acquisition	Donors/Collectors/Former Owners

Documentation

Comment

Museums and Art Gallery NORTHAMPTON

Artefact →

Provenance ↓

Provenance	box	bag	basket	mat	headrest	transport	currency	-rattle	-flute, pipe	-drum, gong	MUSICAL INS.	charm	magic, med.	fig., image	carving	-bullroarer	-paddle	-adze	-board	-mask	CERE. OBJ.	staff, stick	toilet app.	fan	comb	-neck, breast	-arm	-ear, nose	-head	PERS. ORN.	-cloak	-belt	-skirt	CLOTHING	barkcloth	OTHER	TOTAL
OCEANIA UN.												X																									
AUSTRALIA																																					
MELA. UNPROV.																																					
Admiralty																																					
Banks																																					
Bismarck																																					
D'Entrecast.																																					
Fiji																																					X
Louisiade																																					
Loyalty																																					
N. Britain																																					
N. Caledonia																																					
N. Guinea																																					X
N. Hebrides																																					
N. Ireland																																					
Santa Cruz																																					X
Solomon																																					X
Trobriand																																					
MICRO. UNPROV.																																					
Caroline																																					
Gilbert																																					
Mariana																																					
Marshall																																					
POLY. UNPROV.																																					
Austral																																					X
Chatham																																					
Cook																																					X
Easter																																					
Hawaii																																					
Marquesas																																					
New Zealand																																					4
Niue																																					
Pitcairn																																					
Samoa																																					
Society																																					
Tokelau																																					
Tonga																																					X
Tuamotu																																					
Tuv[illegible]																																					X

Museums and Art Gallery NORTHAMPTON (H+A

Artefact → / Provenance →	OCEANIA UN.	AUSTRALIA	MELA.UNPROV.	Admiralty	Banks	Bismarck	D'Entrecast.	Fiji	Louisiade	Loyalty	N. Britain	N. Caledonia	N. Guinea	N. Hebrides	N. Ireland	Santa Cruz	Solomon	Trobriand	MICRO.UNPROV	Caroline	Gilbert	Mariana	Marshall	POLY.UNPROV.	Austral	Chatham	Cook	Easter	Hawaii	Marquesas	New Zealand	Niue	Pitcairn	Samoa	Society	Tokelau	Tonga	Tuamotu	Tuvalu	Tahiti
cord																																								
raw mater																																								
-sling,sto																																								
-arrow																																								
-bow																																								
-shield																																								
-dagger																																								
-spearthro																																								
-spear	/							X																																
-club	/							X								X	X																							
WEAPON																																								
-float,si																																								
-net																																								
-spear																																								
-fishhook																																								
FISHING																																								
hunting																																								
-model																																								
-ornament																																								
-paddle																										X										X			
NAVIGATIO																																								
-barkclot																																								
-weaving																																								
-needle,aw																																								
-chisel																																								
-rasp																																								
-grinding																																								
-pounding																																								
-adze																														/									
TOOL																																								
fire,ligh																																								
smokng pi																																								
pottery																																								
utensil								/																																
lime spat																																								
dish,vesse																																								
lime cont.																																								

Name	Museum of the Northamptonshire Regiment	NORTHAMPTON (REG)
Address	Abington Park Northampton	Sources & Dates of Information R. Hutchings 1966 Visit ESP 1974
Telephone	0604-31454	MEG 1978
Contact	Curator, c/o Regimental Headquarters, Royal Anglian Regiment, Gibralter Barracks, Barracks Road, Northampton NN1 ~~3RE (tel. 0604-35412)~~	Letter

Notes

Dates of Collection/Acquisition	Donors/Collectors/Former Owners

Documentation

Comment

Maori objects probably from 2nd Maori Wars, (Regiment, as 58th (Rutlandshire) Regiment, was in N.Z. 1845-46, 1847-1858).

Regimental Museum NORTHAMPTON CRE

Artifact → / Provenance	OCEANIA UN.	AUSTRALIA	MELA.UNPROV.	Admiralty	Banks	Bismarck	D'Entrecast.	Fiji	Louisiade	Loyalty	N. Britain	N. Caledonia	N. Guinea	N. Hebrides	N. Ireland	Santa Cruz	Solomon	Trobriand	MICRO.UNPROV	Caroline	Gilbert	Mariana	Marshall	POLY.UNPROV.	Austral	Chatham	Cook	Easter	Hawaii	Marquesas	New Zealand	Niue	Pitcairn	Samoa	Society	Tokelau	Tonga	Tuamotu	Tuvalu
box																																							
bag																																							
basket																																							
mat																																							
headrest																																							
transport																																							
currency																																							
-rattle																																							
-flute,pipe																																							
-drum,gong																																							
MUSICAL IN																																							
charm																																							
magic,med.																																							
fig.,image																																							
carving																																							
-bullroarer																																							
-paddle																																							
-adze																																							
-board																																							
-mask																																							
CERE. OBJ.																																							
staff,stick																																							
toilet app.																																							
fan																																							
comb																																							
-neck,breast																																							
-arm																																							
-ear,nose																																							
-head																																							
PERS. ORN.																																							
-cloak																																							
-belt																																							
-skirt																																							
CLOTHING																																							
barkcloth																																							
OTHER																																							
TOTAL																																							

Regimental Museum

NORTHAMPTON (REG

Artefact → / Provenance	OCEANIA UN.	AUSTRALIA	MELA.UNPROV.	Admiralty	Banks	Bismarck	D'Entrecast.	Fiji	Louisiade	Loyalty	N. Britain	N. Caledonia	N. Guinea	N. Hebrides	N. Ireland	Santa Cruz	Solomon	Trobriand	MICRO.UNPROV.	Caroline	Gilbert	Mariana	Marshall	POLY.UNPROV.	Austral	Chatham	Cook	Easter	Hawaii	Marquesas	New Zealand	Niue	Pitcairn	Samoa	Society	Tokelau	Tonga	Tuamotu	Tuvalu
cord																																							
raw mate																																							
-sling,st																																							
-arrow																																							
-bow																																							
-shield																																							
-dagger																																							
-spearthr																																							
-spear																																							
-club																																							
WEAPON																																							
-float,si																																							
-net																																							
-spear																																							
-fishhook																																							
FISHING																																							
hunting																																							
-model																																							
-ornament																																							
-paddle																																							
NAVIGATIO																																							
-barkclot																																							
-weaving																																							
-needle,a																																							
-chisel																																							
-rasp																																							
-grinding																																							
-pounding																																							
-adze																																							
TOOL																																							
fire,ligh																																							
smokng pi																																							
pottery																																							
utensil																																							
lime spat																																							
dish,vess																																							
lime cont																																							

NORWICH (NMS)

Name: Norfolk Museums Service

Address: Castle Museum
Norwich NR1 3JU

Telephone: 0603-22233

Contact: Keeper of Archaeology

Sources & Dates of Information

R. Hutchings 1969

Visit PG 1974, D. Jones 1978

MEG 1978

Letter

Notes

Disposals: To Liverpool and to the British Museum.

Norfolk Museums Service includes items formerly at the Castle Museum, Norwich; Thetford Ancient House Museum; and some from Lynn Museum, King's Lynn. All now stored at Gressenhall, Norfolk.

*Australia-- other: boomerangs 12, toy 1
*Hawaii-- navigation: canoe

Dates of Collection/Acquisition	Donors/Collectors/Former Owners
	Mr. & Mrs. Armstrong, Hawaii, 1891

Documentation

Comment

Most of collections transferred to Merseyside County Museums, Liverpool, and to Canterbury Museum, Christchurch, New Zealand (cf. Duff, 1969, No Sort of Iron). Presume canoe too heavy to move.

NORWICH (

Provenance ↓ / Artefact →	TOTAL	OTHER	barkcloth	CLOTHING	-skirt	-belt	-cloak	PERS. ORN.	-head	-ear,nose	-arm	-neck,breast	comb	fan	toilet app.	staff,stick	CERE. OBJ.	-mask	-board	-adze	-paddle	-bullroarer	carving	fig.,image	magic,med.	charm	MUSICAL INS.	-drum,gong	-flute,pipe	-rattle	currency	transport	headrest	mat	basket	bag	box
OCEANIA UN.																																					
AUSTRALIA	29	13																				2														1	
MELA.UNPROV.																																					
Admiralty	1																																				
Banks																																					
Bismarck																																					
D'Entrecast.																																					
Fiji	4																																				
Louisiade																																					
Loyalty																																					
N. Britain	2																																				
N. Caledonia	1																																				
N. Guinea	4																																				
N. Hebrides	1																																				
N. Ireland																																					
Santa Cruz																																					
Solomon	2																																				
Trobriand	1																																				
MICRO.UNPROV.																																					
Caroline																																					
Gilbert	1																																				
Mariana																																					
Marshall																																					
POLY.UNPROV.																																					
Austral																																					
Chatham																																					
Cook																																					
Easter																																					
Hawaii	1																																				
Marquesas																																					
New Zealand	1																																				
Niue																																					
Pitcairn																																					
Samoa																																					
Society																																					
Tokelau																																					
Tonga																																					
Tuamotu																																					
Tuvalu																																					
[illegible]	1																																				

Norfolk Museum Service NORWICH(NHS

Provenance / Artefact	lime cont	dish, vess	lime spat	utensil	pottery	smoking pi	fire, ligh	TOOL	-adze	-pounding	-grinding	-rasp	-chisel	-needle, a	-weaving	-barkclot	NAVIGATIO	-paddle	-ornament	-model	hunting	FISHING	-fishhook	-spear	-net	-float, si	WEAPON	-club	-spear	-spearthr	-dagger	-shield	-bow	-arrow	-sling, st	raw mater	cord
OCEANIA UN.																																					
AUSTRALIA								2	1															1				4	1	3		1					
MELA. UNPROV.																																					
Admiralty																													1								
Banks																																					
Bismarck																																					
D'Entrecast.																																					
Fiji																												4									
Louisiade																																					
Loyalty																																					
N. Britain																												2									
N. Caledonia																												1									
N. Guinea		1						1	1					1																							
N. Hebrides																																		1			
N. Ireland																																					
Santa Cruz																																					
Solomon																																		2			
Trobriand		1																																			
MICRO. UNPROV																																					
Caroline																																					
Gilbert																															1						
Mariana																																					
Marshall																																					
POLY. UNPROV.																																					
Austral																																					
Chatham																																					
Cook																																					
Easter																																					
Hawaii																	1*																				
Marquesas																																					
New Zealand																												1									
Niue																																					
Pitcairn																																					
Samoa																																					
Society																																					
Tokelau																																					
Tonga																																					
Tuamotu																																					
Tuvalu																																					
Tahiti									1																												

Name	Sainsbury Centre for the Visual Arts	NORWICH (UEA)
Address	The University of East Anglia Norwich	**Sources & Dates of Information** R. Hutchings 1966 Visit MEG 1978 Letter catalogue 1978
Telephone		
Contact	Keeper	

Notes

Objects all collected because of their aesthetic significance; hence, difficult to classify them according to type.

*New Guinea-- breakdown provided since information available (see B).
*Middle Sepik-- other: suspension hook
*Papua-- other: crocodile skull

Dates of Collection/Acquisition	Donors/Collectors/Former Owners
Acquired in 1973. Collected c. 1930-75.	Sir Robert Sainsbury

Documentation

Museum publication: Opening exhibition catalogue, 1978, University of East Anglia.

Comment

Superb material, very well displayed and catalogued. Published exhibition catalogue will presumably be supplemented as further items are acquired.

Provenance \ Artefact	TOTAL	OTHER	barkcloth	CLOTHING	-skirt	-belt	-cloak	PERS. ORN.	-head	-ear,nose	-arm	-neck,breast	comb	fan	toilet app.	staff,stick	CERE. OBJ.	-mask	-board	-adze	-paddle	-bullroarer	carving	fig.,image	magic,med.	charm	MUSICAL INS.	-drum,gong	-flute,pipe	-rattle	currency	transport	headrest	mat	basket	bag	box
OCEANIA UN.																																					
AUSTRALIA																																					
MELA.UNPROV.																																					
Admiralty	3							1																													
Banks																																					
Bismarck																																					
D'Entrecast.																																					
Fiji																																					
Louisiade																																					
Loyalty																																					
N. Britain	1																	1																			
N. Caledonia																																					
N. Guinea	see		(B)																																		
N. Hebrides	2																						1														
N. Ireland																																					
Santa Cruz	1																							1													
Solomon	5							1									1							1							1						
Trobriand	2															1	1																				
MICRO.UNPROV																																					
Caroline																																					
Gilbert																																					
Mariana																																					
Marshall																																					
POLY.UNPROV.																																					
Austral																																					
Chatham																																					
Cook	3															1								1									1				
Easter																								1													
Hawaii											1													2													
Marquesas								1		1														1													
New Zealand								1								1							3	1					1								
Niue																																					
Pitcairn																																					
Samoa																																					
Society																																					
Tokelau																																					
Tonga																								1													
Tuamotu																																					
Tuvalu																																					
Torres Straits	2																	1																			

Sainsbury Centre NORWICH (UEA)

Provenance ↓ / Artefact →	cord	raw mater	sling,st	arrow	bow	shield	dagger	spearthr	spear	club	WEAPON	float,st	net	spear	fishhook	FISHING	hunting	model	ornamen	paddle	NAVIGATIO	barkclot	weaving	needle,a	chisel	rasp	grinding	pounding	adze	TOOL	fire,ligh	smoking pi	pottery	utensil	lime spat	dish,vess	lime cont
OCEANIA UN.																																					
AUSTRALIA																																					
MELA.UNPROV.																																					
Admiralty																																		1	1		
Banks																																					
Bismarck																																					
D'Entrecast.																																					
Fiji																																					
Louisiade																																					
Loyalty																																					
N. Britain																																					
N. Caledonia																																					
N. Guinea																																				see (B)	
N. Hebrides									1																												
N. Ireland																																					
Santa Cruz																																					
Solomon																			1																		
Trobriand																																					
MICRO.UNPROV																																					
Caroline																																					
Gilbert																																					
Mariana																																					
Marshall																																					
POLY.UNPROV.																																					
Austral																																					
Chatham																																					
Cook																																					
Easter																																					
Hawaii																																					
Marquesas										1																											
New Zealand										3																											
Niue																																					
Pitcairn																																					
Samoa																																					
Society																																					
Tokelau																																					
Tonga																																					
Tuamotu																																					
Tuvalu																																					
Torres Straits				1																																	
CONT. NEXT PAGE (B)																																					

Sainsbury Centre (B) NORWICH (UE

Artefact → / Provenance ↓	NEW GUINEA:	West Irian	lower Sepik	middle Sepik	Huon & Tami	Papua
box						
bag						
basket						
mat						
headrest						
transport						
currency						
-rattle						
-flute,pipe			2			
-drum,gong						
MUSICAL INS.						
charm						
magic,med.						
fig.,image		1		1		
carving						1
-bullroarer						
-paddle						
-adze						
-board						
-mask			1			
CERE. OBJ.						
staff,stick						
toilet app.						
fan						
comb						
-neck,breast						
-arm				2		
-ear,nose						
-head						
PERS. ORN.						
-cloak						
-belt						
-skirt						
CLOTHING						
barkcloth						
OTHER				1		1
TOTAL		1	3	8	1	4

Sainsbury Centre (B) NORWICH (UEA)

Artefact → / Provenance ↓	NEW GUINEA:	West Irian	lower Sepik	middle Sepik	Huon + Tami	Papua
cord						
raw mater						
-sling,st						
-arrow						
-bow						
-shield						
-dagger						
-spearthr				/		
-spear						
-club						
WEAPON						
-float,si						
-net						
-spear						
-fishhook						
FISHING						
hunting						
-model						
-ornament						
-paddle				/		
NAVIGATIO						
-barkclot						
-weaving						
-needle,a						
-chisel						
-rasp						
-grinding						
-pounding						
-adze						
TOOL						
fire,ligh						
smokng pi						
pottery						
utensil						/
lime spat						/
dish,vess				/	/	
lime cont				/		

Name	Nottingham Castle Museum	NOTTINGHAM
Address	The Castle Nottingham NG1 6EL	Sources & Dates of Information R. Hutchings 1966 Visit PG 1976
Telephone	0602-411881	MEG 1978
Contact	Senior Keeper, Human History	Letter 1979 Thompson Collection Catalogue

Notes

Table entries are almost entirely Thompson Collection. Two other Oceanic collections (1878 & 1882) being sorted.

*Australia-- stick: message
other: includes 3 boomerangs
*New Guinea-- head ornament: headdresses 2
musical instrument: shell trumpet
*Gilbert-- weapons: includes 1 armour cuirass
*Hawaii-- barkcloth: samples, Bloxam, 1825
*New Zealand-- clubs: taiaha 2, patu onewa 1, wahaika 2
*Samoa-- bows: some Tongan?
*Torres Straits-- head ornaments: headdresses 3

Small number of archaeological specimens.

Dates of Collection/Acquisition	Donors/Collectors/Former Owners
Acquired mainly 1878-1956	Bloxam, 1825 W.J. Thompson Brooke/Walker (Dunedin), New Zealand Fillingham-Parr, 1887

Documentation

Library, archival, photographic.

Being catalogued.

Comment

Almost all Thompson Collection, checked by B. Cranstone. Thompson was a local dealer who made good. Quite important. (Other Thompson material at Mansfield Museum, ultimately to be transferred to Nottingham.)

Castle Museum NOTTINGHAM

Provenance ↓ / Artefact →	TOTAL	OTHER	barkcloth	CLOTHING	-skirt	-belt	-cloak	PERS. ORN.	-head	-ear,nose	-arm	-neck,breast	comb	fan	toilet app.	staff,stick	CERE. OBJ.	-mask	-board	-adze	-paddle	-bullroarer	carving	fig.,image	magic,med.	charm	MUSICAL INS.	-drum,gong	-flute,pipe	-rattle	currency	transport	headrest	mat	basket	bag	box
OCEANIA UN.	X	3																																			
AUSTRALIA		16+											1			1*						1	1		1											1	
MELA.UNPROV.								7					1															1	1								
Admiralty											1																										
Banks																																					
Bismarck																																					
D'Entrecast.																																					
Fiji		X	5									3		2			2																1				
Louisiade																																					
Loyalty																																					
N. Britain																1																					
N. Caledonia																																					
N. Guinea						1		5	8	X										1			2				1*	1								2	
N. Hebrides																																					
N. Ireland																		6																			
Santa Cruz																																					
Solomon								1					5			3	1				9																
Trobriand	1																			1																	
MICRO.UNPROV.																																					
Caroline																																					
Gilbert																																					
Mariana																																					
Marshall																																					
POLY.UNPROV.																																					
Austral																					3																
Chatham																																					
Cook																				6																	
Easter																								1													
Hawaii			12*																																		
Marquesas																																					
New Zealand		X			1	1	2					1											1														1
Niue																																					
Pitcairn																																					
Samoa																																					
~~Society~~ Tahiti																																	1				
Tokelau																																					
Tonga																																					
Tuamotu																																					
Tuvalu																																					
Torres Straits									3*																												

Castle Museum

NOTTINGHAM

Provenance ↓ / Artefact →	lime cont.	dish,vesse	lime spat.	utensil	pottery	smokng pip	fire,ligh	TOOL	-adze	-pounding	-grinding	-rasp	-chisel	-needle,aw	-weaving	-barkcloth	NAVIGATIO	-paddle	-ornament	-model	hunting	FISHING	-fishhook	-spear	-net	-float,sin	WEAPON	-club	-spear	-spearthro	-dagger	-shield	-bow	-arrow	-sling,sto	raw mater	cord
OCEANIA UN.									1																				2								
AUSTRALIA		1					3	X	1																		X	29	17	20		6		1			
MELA.UNPROV.																								3	1			5									
Admiralty				1																									11								
Banks																																					
Bismarck																																					
D'Entrecast.																																					
Fiji		3			1											5		X									1	X	X				X	X			
Louisiade																																					
Loyalty																																					
N. Britain																												6	3								
N. Caledonia		1						1	1																			5							X		
N. Guinea	2					2			9													2		7	1		1	17	8		2		6	116	1		
N. Hebrides																								7				10	4					49			
N. Ireland																												2	1								
Santa Cruz																												4									
Solomon	1								1									3	1				2					6	38+			1	X	135+			
Trobriand																																					
MICRO.UNPROV									1																												
Caroline																																					
Gilbert																											13*				1						
Mariana																																					
Marshall																							1														
POLY.UNPROV.																																					
Austral																																					
Chatham																																					
Cook																		1																			
Easter																												1									
Hawaii										1																											
Marquesas																																					
New Zealand									1									1	1				2					5									
Niue																												1									
Pitcairn																																					
Samoa																							1					6					3*				
~~Society~~ Tahiti																							1														
Tokelau																																					
Tonga																												5					*				
Tuamotu																																					
Tuvalu																							1														
Torres Straits																																		29			
Woodlark									1																												

NUNEATON

Name Museum and Art Gallery

Address Riversley Park
Nuneaton CV11 5TU

Telephone 0682-382683

Contact Curator

Sources & Dates of Information

R. Hutchings 1966

Visit GSP 1974

MEG 1978

Letter 1979

Notes

Some unidentified material.

*Australia-- stick: message
tool: digging stick
other: boomerangs 14
*Fiji-- tool: "rake"
*New Guinea-- head ornament: headdress
*Solomon-- currency: 19 also breast ornaments
*Gilbert-- weapon: 18th Century sword
*New Zealand-- other: preserved head

Dates of Collection/Acquisition

1966+

Donors/Collectors/Former Owners

Documentation

Collection catalogued.

Comment

This seems to be an unknown collection. Some derived from Coventry Museum. Perhaps also from Rugby School, 1939.

Museum and Art Gallery

NUNEATON

Artefact →
Provenance ↓

Provenance	TOTAL	OTHER	barkcloth	CLOTHING	-skirt	-belt	-cloak	PERS. ORN.	-head	-ear,nose	-arm	-neck,breast	comb	fan	toilet app.	staff,stick	CERE. OBJ.	-mask	-board	-adze	-paddle	-bullroarer	carving	fig.,image	magic,med.	charm	MUSICAL INS.	-drum,gong	-flute,pipe	-rattle	currency	transport	headrest	mat	basket	bag	box
OCEANIA UN.	42							1			5		1																								
AUSTRALIA	75	14		1				1								1*						1			2				1							2	
MELA.UNPROV.	1																																				
Admiralty	1																																				
Banks																																					
Bismarck																																					
D'Entrecast.																																					
Fiji	23		1																																	2	1
Louisiade																																					
Loyalty																																					
N. Britain						1					4																										
N. Caledonia																																					
N. Guinea	14								1*									2		2								1									
N. Hebrides	2																																				
N. Ireland																																					
Santa Cruz																																					
Solomon	61										5	4	1															1			19*						
Trobriand																																					
MICRO.UNPROV.																																					
Caroline																																					
Gilbert																																					
Mariana																																					
Marshall																																					
POLY.UNPROV.																																					
Austral																																					
Chatham																																					
Cook																																					
Easter																																					
Hawaii																																					
Marquesas	1																																				
New Zealand	25	1			2	4																	1													2	
Niue																																					
Pitcairn																																					
Samoa	1																																				
Society																																					
Tokelau																																					
Tonga																																					
Tuamotu																																					
Tuvalu																																					

Museum and Art Gallery NUNEATON

Artefact → / Provenance ↓

Artefact	OCEANIA UN.	AUSTRALIA	MELA.UNPROV.	Admiralty	Banks	Bismarck	D'Entrecast.	Fiji	Louisiade	Loyalty	N. Britain	N. Caledonia	N. Guinea	N. Hebrides	N. Ireland	Santa Cruz	Solomon	Trobriand
cord																		
raw mater		1																
-sling,st																		
-arrow	X												1					
-bow														1			1	
-shield		6																
-dagger				1														
-spearthr		6																
-spear	X	25															2	
-club	2	8						7					5		2		8	
WEAPON	31												1					
-float,si																		
-net																		
-spear		4												1			1	
-fishhook																		
FISHING																		
hunting																		
-model																		
-ornament																		
-paddle	2																4	
NAVIGATIO																		
-barkclot								4										
-weaving																		
-needle,aw																		
-chisel								1										
-rasp																		
-grinding																		
-pounding																		
-adze			1					3										
TOOL		1*						1*										
fire,ligh																		
smoking pi																		
pottery		1																
utensil								2									12	
lime spat													1					
dish,vess								1									3	
lime cont.																		

Artefact	MICRO.UNPROV	Caroline	Gilbert	Mariana	Marshall	POLY.UNPROV.	Austral	Chatham	Cook	Easter	Hawaii	Marquesas	New Zealand	Niue	Pitcairn	Samoa	Society	Tokelau	Tonga	Tuamotu	Tuvalu
cord																					
raw mater													2								
-sling,st																					
-arrow																					
-bow																					
-shield																					
-dagger																					
-spearthr																					
-spear													1								
-club												1	4			1					
WEAPON			1*																		
-float,si																					
-net																					
-spear																					
-fishhook													1								
FISHING																					
hunting																					
-model																					
-ornament																					
-paddle																					
NAVIGATIO																					
-barkclot																					
-weaving																					
-needle,aw																					
-chisel													1								
-rasp																					
-grinding																					
-pounding																					
-adze													4								
TOOL																					
fire,ligh																					
smoking pi																					
pottery																					
utensil													2								
lime spat																					
dish,vess																					
lime cont.																					

ORPINGTON

Name: Bromley Museum

Address: The Priory
Church Hill
Orpington
Kent BR6 OHH

Telephone

Contact: Curator

Sources & Dates of Information

R. Hutchings 1966

Visit

MEG 1978

Letter

Notes

Dates of Collection/Acquisition	Donors/Collectors/Former Owners
Acquired 1960's	Sir John Lubbock, first Lord Avebury Mrs. H. Stock

Documentation

Archival, photographic, iconographic.

Catalogue information available. Hold Lubbock catalogue.

Comment

Lubbock Collection may contain some comparative Oceanic material illustrated in his Prehistoric Times (1st edition, 1865).

Bromley Museum

ORPINGTON

Provenance \ Artefact	TOTAL	OTHER	barkcloth	CLOTHING	skirt	belt	cloak	PERS. ORN.	head	ear,nose	arm	neck,breast	comb	fan	toilet app.	staff,stick	CERE. OBJ.	mask	board	adze	paddle	bullroarer	carving	fig.,image	magic,med.	charm	MUSICAL INS.	drum,gong	flute,pipe	rattle	currency	transport	headrest	mat	basket	bag	box
OCEANIA UN.	300																																				
AUSTRALIA																																					
MELA. UNPROV.																																					
Admiralty																																					
Banks																																					
Bismarck																																					
D'Entrecast.																																					
Fiji																																					
Louisiade																																					
Loyalty																																					
N. Britain																																					
N. Caledonia																																					
N. Guinea																																					
N. Hebrides																																					
N. Ireland																																					
Santa Cruz																																					
Solomon																																					
Trobriand																																					
MICRO. UNPROV.																																					
Caroline																																					
Gilbert																																					
Mariana																																					
Marshall																																					
POLY. UNPROV.																																					
Austral																																					
Chatham																																					
Cook																																					
Easter																																					
Hawaii																																					
Marquesas																																					
New Zealand																																					
Niue																																					
Pitcairn																																					
Samoa																																					
Society																																					
Tokelau																																					
Tonga																																					
Tuamotu																																					
Tuvalu																																					

Bromley Museum

ORPINGTON

Artefact → / Provenance →	OCEANIA UN.	AUSTRALIA	MELA.UNPROV.	Admiralty	Banks	Bismarck	D'Entrecast.	Fiji	Louisiade	Loyalty	N. Britain	N. Caledonia	N. Guinea	N. Hebrides	N. Ireland	Santa Cruz	Solomon	Trobriand	MICRO.UNPROV	Caroline	Gilbert	Mariana	Marshall	POLY.UNPROV.	Austral	Chatham	Cook	Easter	Hawaii	Marquesas	New Zealand	Niue	Pitcairn	Samoa	Society	Tokelau	Tonga	Tuamotu	Tuvalu
cord																																							
raw mater																																							
-sling,st																																							
-arrow																																							
-bow																																							
-shield																																							
-dagger																																							
-spearthr																																							
-spear																																							
-club																																							
WEAPON																																							
-float,si																																							
-net																																							
-spear																																							
-fishhook																																							
FISHING																																							
hunting																																							
-model																																							
-ornament																																							
-paddle																																							
NAVIGATIO																																							
barkclot																																							
-weaving																																							
-needle,a																																							
-chisel																																							
-rasp																																							
-grinding																																							
-pounding																																							
-adze																																							
TOOL																																							
fire,ligh																																							
smokng pi																																							
pottery																																							
utensil																																							
lime spat																																							
dish,vess																																							
lime cont																																							

Name Ashmolean Museum of Art and Archaeology	OXFORD (ASH)
Address Beaumont Street Oxford OX1 3PP	Sources & Dates of Information R. Hutchings 1966 Visit MEG 1978 Letter
Telephone 0865-57522 Contact Keeper of Antiquities	

Notes

Disposals : All ethnographic material transferred to the Pitt Rivers Museum, beginning in 1886 and ending in 1969, to Oxfordshire County Museum in 1969 and to the Tower Armouries in 1969, excepting that displayed in Tradescant Room (non-Oceanic).

Dates of Collection/Acquisition	Donors/Collectors/Former Owners
Acquired 1683-1886	Tradescant Ashmole

Documentation

Archival (catalogue from 1656+).

Comment

Name	Pitt Rivers Museum	OXFORD (PRM)
Address	The University Department of Ethnology and Prehistory Parks Road Oxford OX1 3PP	Sources & Dates of Information R. Hutchings 1969 Visits AC 1979 MEG 1978 Letter
Telephone	0865-54979	
Contact	Curator	

Notes

Major museum re-organisation continuing, hence material may be inaccessible or accessible with difficulty.

For table explanatory notes, see Pitt Rivers (E)ff.

Dates of Collection/Acquisition	Donors/Collectors/Former Owners
1883+	See separate page (D).

Documentation

Excellent double entry card index (geographical & typological). Donors' index.

Library, archival, photographic, iconographic, film, sound recordings.

Museum publications: Blackwood, The Kukukuku of the Upper Watut
Blackwood, The Technology of a Modern Stone Age People in New Guinea (1950)
Blackwood, The Origin and Development of the Pitt Rivers Museum (1970)
Gathercole "From the Islands of the South Seas 1773-4" (Exhibition catalogue, Forster Collection. 1970

Comment

A highly important and wide ranging collection; not the largest, but the most balanced in the U.K., with good coverage from large and small islands. This range, and good catalogues, make the collection a rich research tool simply waiting for extensive use. (Spoken from the heart.)

Pitt Rivers Museum

OXFORD (P

Provenance ↓ / Artefact →	TOTAL	OTHER	barkcloth	CLOTHING	-skirt	-belt	-cloak	PERS. ORN.	-head	-ear,nose	-arm	-neck,breast	comb	fan	toilet app.	staff,stick	CERE. OBJ.	-mask	-board	-adze	-paddle	-bullroarer	carving	fig.,image	magic,med.	charm	MUSICAL INS.	-drum,gong	-flute,pipe	-rattle	currency	transport	headrest	mat	basket	bag	box
OCEANIA UN.	136	13	14	4				4			5	4	2	1		5*				1*							2*		1	1				8		3	
AUSTRALIA	see attached																																				
MELA.UNPROV.	45			4				3			9	13	1																					3			
Admiralty	218	2	1	5				15			5		3			1										3	1*		1								
Banks	158			7				15				1	2	1		1	1								2				5		16				16	4	
Bismarck	220	2	2	10				16			60		3				2										1	3		1	2	1	3		7	5	
D'Entrecast.	544	7		15				51			70	7	13		2	1	3						3	1	4		5*	5	3			7		3*	13	6	
Fiji	746	18	88	14				35	4		3	19	6	4		3	3						3	1			9*	6	11				19	3	7	1	2
Louisiade	68	4		1				11			1	11					1																				
Loyalty	24			1				2			3	1																	1		1					1	
N. Britain	383+	20	16	1*	6			4	7	2	5	4			X*		8	2				2		1		2	7*	1	15	1	18*				4	10	
N. Caledonia	223	4		1				10			2	6	8			1	3									7					1				1	12	2
N. Guinea	see attached																																				
N. Hebrides	743	14	4	43				37			52	12	26			4	43						5	11			2*		13		1			2	1	12	
N. Ireland	86		1					9									22						9	4			1		3	1	4						
Santa Cruz	384	2	3	13				38			25	10		1			14												1	2	5	3	2	9	1	7	
Solomon	see attached																																				
Trobriand	123	1		3				1			4					3	3											4				1	2		4		
MICRO.UNPROV.	11							9																													
Caroline	181	3	2	23				9			17	20	4				2*														4			1		2	3
Gilbert	160+			9				7				23	2	1																	3			2			1
Mariana																																					
Marshall	41			1								5		2																			3	8			
POLY.UNPROV.	45	3	4	2				2			1	4																									
Austral	83	4						1								4	7*				24			1				1									
Chatham	73																							1													
Cook	97	1	2	4		3*		3				8		1		4	3*	1*		15	6						2*							1	1		
Easter	216	X						7				1				2	4						11*	16													
Hawaii	171	9	51				3	7	1*		2	8		5	1*									4			3*	1		3			2				
Marquesas	79	1	1				1	17	2		2	5		6		3					1		11*	2*			3*	1						1			
New Zealand	1054	29		17	X		48	65*				19*	8		11*	9	2					1	21	4					17*			3		18	12	38	16
Niue	92	6	10	4								2	3	6														1	2				1		1		
Pitcairn	99	2	5*																																		
Samoa	233	17	25	10				4				3	31	25	1*																			8	3	1	
Society	41	3	14	1								2		1		2											1*						2				
Tokelau	1																																				
Tonga	199	4	7	5				1	1*		2	11	11	2			1				3						1*		7		10*		4	2	9	1	
Tuamotu	17	1						4				2																							1		
Tuvalu	161	9		11			13				4	1		7	1													1			1	4*	5		5		2
Tahiti	87	2	17	1				3			3				5*	1	2*							5				1	5		1		1				

Pitt Rivers Museum

OXFORD (PRM

Provenance ↓ / Artefact →	lime cont	dish,vesse	lime spat	utensil	pottery	smokng pi	fire,ligh	TOOL	-adze	-pounding	-grinding	-rasp	-chisel	-needle,a	-weaving	-barkclot	NAVIGATIO	-paddle	-ornament	-model	hunting	FISHING	-fishhook	-spear	-net	-float,si	WEAPON	-club	-spear	-spearthro	-dagger	-shield	-bow	-arrow	-sling,st	raw mater	cord
OCEANIA UN.		12						2	12			1	1				1	1		1			1					2	1				2	15		13	3
AUSTRALIA																																					
MELA.UNPROV.						1			3													2	3				1	2									
Admiralty		7		1				2	6									1		1							72	1	90								
Banks		12		15			1	6	7												1	2						5					5	33			
Bismarck		9		6				9	10	8							2			1	1	11					1	3	41								
D'Entrecast.	10	44	28	41	3	11		22	43	8							1	3	9	2		37	12				9	22	9							2	9
Fiji		64		16	15			18	42	1						18	3			4		6	1*					234*	46				2*			7	10
Louisiade		3		5	1			4	8	1								9		1		3						1								1	2
Loyalty					5			1	1														4							2							1
N. Britain	1			8			1	2	64	3						9		2	1		1	6		2			22	25*	61			2	1		5	29	1
N. Caledonia		1			1				27								1						1				64	36*	27	2				5			
N. Guinea																																					
N. Hebrides		8		11	5			5	23												9	11					5	121	45				38	176		2	2
N. Ireland								5	1									1				1	1					22	1								
Santa Cruz		5		8				6	3	3					21*			2			1	19					1	2					16	158		3	
Solomon																																					
Trobriand	9	12	16	4		1		2	4	7								4	9	1		3	1					18				6					
MICRO.UNPROV.																							2														
Caroline		11		10				11	26	5							1	1		1		4	16				3		2								
Gilbert		1						6										1		1	2	2	9				55+*		10		25						
Mariana																																					
Marshall																	1*					4*	16*														1
POLY.UNPROV.		1					1		3														20	2*									1				1
Austral		2		1				1	18	6			2			8								2		1											
Chatham									63	1													5				1	2*									
Cook		1					1						1	2		3		4		3			15*						12								
Easter		1						70+*	21	8													4			1		2	35							29	3
Hawaii		11					5	7	17	4	1					11				3*		1				4			1					3	3		
Marquesas		5								1								6					2					7									1
New Zealand		7		6*			5	59	157	5							10	20	15	5	3	11*	226				7	88*	4							85+*	3
Niue		1					1	2*	4	1							1			6*		5	3	6	1		1	10	12								2
Pitcairn								8	74	3			4																					2		1	
Samoa		1					1	4	32							3				5*			6		1			36	10							4	2
Society				1					9							2						3															
Tokelau																							1														
Tonga		4		3			1	1	2							3				1		9	8		1			55*	15				10			3	1
Tuamotu																							9														
Tuvalu		4		8				7	4	3		1		4			1	1		3	5		38		6		1									6	5*
Tahiti				3					6	7			1	2								2	11				1		4					2		2	

CONT. NEXT PAGE

Pitt Rivers Museum (B)

OXFORD (PRM

Provenance	TOTAL	OTHER	barkcloth	CLOTHING	-skirt	-belt	-cloak	PERS. ORN.	-head	-ear,nose	-arm	-neck,breast	comb	fan	toilet app.	staff,stick	CERE. OBJ.	-mask	-board	-adze	-paddle	-bullroarer	carving	fig.,image	magic,med.	charm	MUSICAL INS.	-drum,gong	-flute,pipe	-rattle	currency	transport	headrest	mat	basket	bag	box
Gambier	37	1																																			
Mangareva	42	4																																	2		
Link	4																																				1
Futuna (E.)	2		2																																		
Uvea (E)	3		1	1																															1		
Kotuma	27			1										4																				1			
Tikopia	4							2				1																									
Ontong Java	8							5																													
Bellona	16												1																							2	
Rennell	1																																				
Sikiana	6	3																																2			
W. Uvea	3	1																											2								
W. Futuna	1							1																													
Mae	14	3						9																													
Mele	4											1	2																								
Norfolk	4							3																													
Woodlark	30	2						1					1																								
Marshall Bennett	42	2						1																													
Ninigo	270	8		6							12	1	3			5	13														1					3	6
Torres Strait	211	5		5				35			8	9	1	1		15						1		1	5	7	2*	3		2		1			5		
New Guinea un.	427	9		17				36			27	23	13		6*	4	2					3	1			3	8*	6		3	1	2	1		2	4	
West Irian	163	5		2				18			3	5	3			1							3	6			2*	6					2				
MT unprov.	96			1				4			14	4												1					1*		3		1			1	
Highlands	144	11		14				9			5	8					1						1				1*		2		13					8	
Sepik	79	4						2									12							10			2*	3	3		4		6			2	
Ramu	420	17		18		24*		48			6	14	4	1			13					1	9*	10	1	3	2*	3	3		2	1	2		1	5	
other Madang	22		3	1													1											1			1				3		
Huon + Tami	53	1	1	2				1			5	1	1											1			1*	1			2		1		1	1	
other Morobe	500	17	9	11				59			58	29													5		16*	1	7	4	4	1				6	
Papua unprov.	753	12	11	18				54			127	24	5	1		3	1						1	1	1	8	8*	4	4	4	13	1	5		4	11	
Fly	301	4		18				9			20	6	2			2	5					1	3	1		2	3*	7	6	2		1			1	5	
Gulf	547		8	31				93			11	26	12		1*		31					41	2	1		18	1*	7	3	1		1		1		15	
Massim *	725	16	29	34				86			31	42	11		4*	2	25						2	3		9	5*	2	3	4	1	1	2			7	1
other Papuan	487		25	26			14	52			25	76	6				2					2			1	2	3*	6	6	1	5					16	

Pitt Rivers Museum (B)

OXFORD (PRM

Provenance ↓ / Artefact →	lime cont.	dish, vesse	lime spat.	utensil	pottery	smokng pi	fire, ligh.	TOOL	-adze	-pounding	-grinding	-rasp	-chisel	-needle, aw	-weaving	-barkclot	NAVIGATIO	-paddle	-ornament	-model	hunting	FISHING	-fishhook	-spear	-net	-float, si	WEAPON	-club	-spear	-spearthro	-dagger	-shield	-bow	-arrow	-sling, sto	raw mater	cord
Gambier				1				1	15	3			3	5				2				4	1			1											
Mangareva		1						4	12	9				3				2		2*		1	1			1											
Line																							2					1									
Futuna (E)																																					
Uvea (E)																																					
Rotuma									11	5												1						3	1								
Tikopia																												1									
Ontong Java																							2														1
Bellona																												4	3					6			
Rennell																												1									
Sikiana								1																													
W. Uvea																																					
W. Futuna																																					
Mac																												2									
Mele									1																												
Norfolk																							1														
Woodlark		5		1				3	17																												
Marshall Bennett		4		6				1	8	7									8			4	1														
Ninigo		9		24			1	7	8								1*	6		3		4	74				13	2	52							2	6
Torres Strait		1			1	7		5											1	1	1	3	5				2		6	2			4	62		2	2
New Guinea un.		6		17	1	3	6	8	25								7	4	3	1	1	6					21	25	7			1	12	101			1
West Irian		3		1		5	3	3	16								1	6	6			1					5		12			4	6	35			
MT unprov.		2		2				1	3										1			1		3			1		4	4		1	7	36			
Highlands				4		11		7	11																				12			5		18			3
Sepik		5			2			4	1																		1		1			2	1	14			
Ramu		15		21	10			37	79	2									5		4	3	3				10		16	6		3		7		11	
other Madang		2			1			2													3	1										1		1			
Huon + Tami		4		3	1			4												1		10	7											2		3	
other Morobe		5		8	2	4	4	36	114												8	2						35				2	4	43		5	1
Papua unprov.		21		58	3	7	4	22	62	5								18	3	4		5	3				32	19	10			4	8	142			2
Fly		4		3		3	5	8	4									2		1	2	12					11	2					9	133		3	1
Gulf		13		43		2	8	20	32	1												12					15	21				4	2	67		1	2
Massim *		25		101	7		5	84	24	7							2	7	2		6	38	21				8	30	10			3	2	19		4	
other Papuan	2	11		58	3	19	7	27	35									2				1					1	43				1		1			2

Pitt Rivers Museum (C)

OXFORD (PR

Artefact →
Provenance ↓

Provenance	TOTAL	OTHER	barkcloth	CLOTHING	-skirt	-belt	-cloak	PERS. ORN.	-head	-ear,nose	-arm	-neck,breast	comb	fan	toilet app.	staff,stick	CERE. OBJ.
Australia un.	236	79						1				3				5*	2
Central	102	13		5				9				4			5*		3
N. Territories	389	9		25				34			35	12				2*	8
Arnhemland*	54	5		1				9			4						3
Queensland	277	93	1	3				7				5				4*	1
Cape York*	141	18						2	1	1		4				1	2
New S. Wales	108+	25+															4
Victoria	120+	11+						1				1					
Western	202	25		4			1	13				9				4*	13
Northwestern*	162	13						16				8				4*	3
South Australia	71	5										1				3*	
Tasmania	2130*																
Solomons un.	984	4		10				69			64	30	22				
Buka & Bougainville	522	8		9				37			16	2	59	4		6	14
Central	1065	31	11	13				85			67	49	36			9	34

Provenance	-mask	-board	-adze	-paddle	-bullroarer	carving	fig.,image	magic,med.	charm	MUSICAL INS.	-drum,gong	-flute,pipe	-rattle	currency	transport	headrest	mat	basket	bag	box
Australia un.					1					1								1		
Central					19			6							2					
N. Territories						1		3	5						2			5	17	
Arnhemland*					1					2		3	1				1	6	1	
Queensland					4			2	1									13	3	
Cape York*					3								1					5	1	
New S. Wales					3	2													6	
Victoria					10			6												
Western					18*	1		3					1						2	
Northwestern*					3	2		10												
South Australia					7			5	1									3	2	
Tasmania																				
Solomons un.						4	7			5*		4	1	12				2	4	8
Buka & Bougainville								18		9*	2	10	2	9			1	7	1	
Central						10	10	1	4	14*		14	3	31				11	13	24

OKFORD (PRM

PITT RIVERS MUSEUM (D)

Table Explanatory Notes

Note: Not all of the types of object on the form were in use when this collection was classified. The following were added afterwards and therefore are only sporadically recorded for the Pitt Rivers Collection:

skirt	rasp
belt	chisel
head ornament	needle & awl
ear & nose ornament	weaving tool
ceremonial board	barkcloth-making tool
" adze & axe	fish spear
" paddle	fish net
lime container	float & sinker
lime spatula	dagger
grinding tool	sling & stone

*Torres Straits includes Mawata, on the Papuan coast.

*Massim- mainland only. Coastal peoples from Kukipi to Cape Nelson.

*Arnhemland- area north of the Roper River and east of the Mary River.

*Cape York- area north of the Gulf Highway and west of Cairns.

*Northwest Australia- area north of the Fitzroy, Mary & Elvira Rivers.

for Hermit Is., see Admiralty.
for Wuvulu, see Ninigo Group.
for Aua, see Ninigo Group.

Oceania unprovenanced-- ceremonial axe: fake?
stick: includes 4 walking sticks, of which 2 are probably European
musical instrument: shell trumpet, "seaweed trumpet"
other: flywhisk 2, misc. 11

Admiralty-- musical instrument: shell trumpet
other: map (G. Pitt Rivers), physical anthropology 1

Banks-- includes 76 specimens from Torres Islands

Bismarck-- other: toy, hook

d'Entrecasteaux- musical instrument: jewsharps 5
mat: weather protection "cloaks"
other: toy 7

Fiji-- musical instrument: jewsharp, shell trumpets 8
fishhook: 1Tongan
club: includes ula 49, cylindrical 11, duck-head 6, flat blade 9, lotus 4, paddle 8, pineapple 14, roothead 19, spurred head 38, two-hand 3; some possibly of Tongan origin.
bow: 1 European made
other: hooks 2, house models 2, flywhisk 1, toys 10, punishment 1, misc. 2

Louisade-- other: misc. 4

New Britain-- clothing: dance costume
toilet apparatus: razors
musical instrument: includes musical bow 1, jewsharp 1
currency: 1 from Admiralty
club: 1 from Solomons, 1 from Admiralty
other: preserved heads 3, stone tools, physical anthropology 14, misc.3

Pitt Rivers Museum (C) OXFORD (PR

Artefact → / Provenance →

Artefact	Australian un.	Central	N. Territories	Arnhemland	Queensland	Cape York	New S. Wales	Victoria	Western	Northwestern	South Australia	Tasmania	Solomons un.	Buka-Bougainville	Central
lime cont.															
dish,vessel	3		3	2				1	1	2	3		39	26	49
lime spat.															
utensil													9	5	31
pottery														2	
smoking pipe			1			1							2	8	1
fire,light			1		10	8	2	8		7			2	1	13
TOOL	2	7	16	1	6	4	5	4	9*	13	5		13	12	25
-adze	29	4	6		29		27	17	7*	3	4		16	39	68
-pounding			2		3		6	5	1		2		2	2	12
-grinding															
-rasp															
-chisel		1	2		1			1							
-needle,awl	1		2					1							
-weaving			1											1*	
-barkcloth															
NAVIGATION				1*											3
-paddle	1												15	22	27
-ornament													17		37
-model						1				1*			2	2	1
hunting	1		4						3				15		3
FISHING	1	1	4		1		2			2			6	11	80
-fishhook			2		5								38	24	56
-spear	21				1	15					1				
-net					1				2		3				
-float,sinker															
WEAPON					2			4					1	1	3
-club	65	2	12	1	32		7	14	9		8		61		35
-spear		7	122	9	1	52	3	7	16	63			45	39	37
-spearthrower	6	4	29	3	21	6	9	16	34*		13				
-dagger															
-shield	7	5	19		22	2	6	12	11	5	4		6		17
-bow						1							37	1	14
-arrow						12							405	70	68
-sling,stone															
raw mater.	5	4	2		4		1	1	5	5			1	38	14
cord	1	1	3		1					2	1		6	4	1

Pitt Rivers Museum (D) cont. ii

New Caledonia-- clubs: includes 18 mushroom, 1 bird-headed
other: physical anthropology 2, misc. 2

New Hebrides-- musical instrument: musical bows 2
other: physical anthropology 11, misc. 3

Santa Cruz-- weaving: includes 5 looms
other: toy 1, sunshade 1

Trobriand-- other: toy 1

Caroline-- ceremonial object: burial goods
other: weaving samples 3

Gilbert-- weapons: include 6 suits armour; jackets, belts & helmets
other: physical anthropology 1

Marshall-- navigation: chart 1
fishooks: 2 possibly Cape York

Polynesia unprovenanced-- fishspears: 2 possibly Torres Straits
other: physical anthropology 2, stone implement 1

Austral-- ceremonial objects: include 3 ladles, 2 bowls
other: 3 boards (with handles), flywhisk 1

Chatham-- clubs: 1 mere shape

Cook-- belts: 3 Danger Is. wrestling
ceremonial objects: includes ceremonial spear, ladles 2
mask: includes dance dress
musical instrument: shell trumpets 2
fishooks: includes 5 Danger Is.
other: flywhisk

Easter-- carvings: 1 a cast
other: numerous stone & obsidian implements and fragments

Hawaii-- head ornament: feather helmet
toilet apparatus: mirror
musical instruments: musical bows 2, ukelele 1
models: outrigger 2, dugout 1
other: toys 5, time-measuring device 1, physical anthropology 1, misc. 2

Marquesas-- carvings: all stilt
figures: include a cast
musical instrument: 3 trumpets, 2 shell, 1 wood
other: toy stilts

New Zealand-- personal ornaments: 3 European style
neck ornaments: 18 tikis, of which 1 a cast, 2 forgeries
toilet apparatus: 11 tatooing designs
flutes: 3 forgeries
utensils: include 2 feeding funnels
fishing: 11 lines
clubs: taiaha/hani 19, pouwhenna 5, tewhatewha 9, patu onewa 8, patu paraoa 10 (including 1 forgery), patu kotiate 5, wahaika 12, wood mere 1, metal mere 2 (1 Banks, 1 European cast), patuki 2, hoeroa 1, unspecified 3
raw material: includes plant, animal, flax, nephrite, pigments
other: European 7, toy 1, physical anthropology 6, numerous archaeological incl. 10 chisels, misc. 14

OXFORD(P

Pitt Rivers Museum (D) cont. iii

Niue-- tool: pump drill 1
models: outrigger 5, dugout 1
other: toys 4, house model 1, model machine 1

Pitcairn-- barkcloth: 1 made by European

Samoa-- toilet apparatus: tattooing
models: include dugout 2, outrigger 2
other: toys 4, flywhisks 9, misc. 4

Society-- musical instrument: shell trumpet
other: flywhisks 3

Tonga--head ornament: plaited war helmet 1
musical instrument: jewsharp
currency: foreign coins 2, discs 3 (game?), notes 5
clubs: 12 possibly ceremonial (based on shape)
other: physical anthropology 2, shell totem, food hook

Tuamotu-- other: physical anthropology 1

Tuvalu-- transport: includes 1 climbing aid
cord: barkcloth 1, sennit 4
other: flywhisk, toys 5, eyeshades 4

Tahiti-- toilet apparatus: tattooing
ceremonial objects: mourning dress, club
other: flywhisk, physical anthropology 1

Gambier-- other: misc. 1

Mangareva-- models: raft 1, outrigger 1
other: misc. 4

Sikiana-- other: weaving samples 3

W. Uvea-- other: flywhisk

Mae-- other: misc. 3

Woodlark-- other: misc. 2

Marshall Bennett-- other: misc. 2

Ninigo-- navigation: canoe 1
other: hook 3, maps (G. Pitt Rivers) 2, toy 1, misc. 2

Torres Straits-- musical instruments: jewsharp, musical whip
other: smoking apparatus, toy, misc. 3

New Guinea unprovenanced-- musical instruments: jewsharps 6, bell 1, shell trumpet
other: archaeological 2, physical anthropology 1, skull
misc. 4

West Irian-- musical instruments: bamboo trumpets
other: toy, misc. 5

MT unprovenanced-- flute: from Schouten Is.

Highlands-- musical instrument: jewsharp
other: bamboo tubes (some with holes) 9, toy, archaeological 1

Sepik-- musical instruments: musical bow, jewsharp
other: toys 4

Ramu-- belts: of barkcloth
carvings: include house ornaments 5
musical instruments: include 1 jewsharp
other: toys 15, flywhisk 2
mainly Bosmun tribe

OXFORD (PRM)

Pitt Rivers Museum (D) iv

Huon & Tami-- musical instrument: jewsharp
other: hook

other Morobe-- 3 films
musical instruments: monochord 2, jewsharp, bells 13
other: toys 16, misc. 1
(mainly Kukukuku)

Papus unprovenanced-- musical instruments: jewsharps 7, monochord 1
other: bamboo tubes 4, physical anthropology 1, misc. 7

Fly-- musical instruments: monochord, jewsharps 2
other: toy, misc. 3

Gulf-- toilet apparatus: depilatory
musical instrument: shell trumpet

other Papuan-- musical instruments: jewsharps 2, shell trumpet
other: toys 2, misc. 1

Massim-- toilet apparatus: razors
musical instruments: jewsharps 4, oboe
other: hook, house models 2, toys 3, misc. 10

Australia unprovenanced-- sticks: message 3
other: boomerangs 56, physical anthropology 5, toys 2, stone tools, European 15

Central-- toilet apparatus: surgical 5
other: boomerangs 8, toy, misc. 2, 2 hold-alls containing ornaments, tools, string, awls, fishhooks, etc.

N. Territories-- sticks: message
other: boomerangs 5, toy, stone implements 2, misc. 1, physical anthropology 2

Arnhemland-- navigation: canoe (or model) from Melville Is.
other: bark paintings 2, physical anthropology 3

Queensland-- sticks: include 3 message
other: boomerangs 88, stone implements, physical anthropology 2, murder 2

Cape York-- other: boomerangs 5, toys 13

New South Wales-- other: boomerangs 21, many stone implements, misc. 3

Victoria-- other: boomerangs 7, many stone implements, misc. 3

Western-- sticks: message 3
bullroarers: 1 also a musical rasp
tools: digging stick 1
adzes: 4 are axe-hammers
spearthrowers: 3 are also musical rasps; 1 is musical rasp & chisel
other: boomerangs 16, stone implements 3, 'passports' 5, toy

Northwestern-- sticks: include 2 message
model: raft
other: boomerangs 8, stone implement, toy 1, passport 1, misc. 2

South-- sticks: message 3
other: boomerangs 3, many stone implements, murder 1

Tasmania-- large collection of stone implements

Solomon unprovenanced-- musical instruments: jewsharps 3, shell trumpets 2
other: toy, eyeshade, misc. 2

Pitt Rivers Museum (D) v

Buka & Bougainville-- musical instruments: musical bow, bells 3, jewsharp, shell trumpets 2, misc. 2
other: toys 4, misc. 4
weaving: loom

Central Solomon-- musical instruments: zither, musical bows 4, shell trumpet, jewsharps 8
other: toys 5, hook, 'native drawings' 5, eyeshades 6, misc. 8

Photographs

Fiji (von Hügel Collection)
New Caledonia
New Hebrides
New Guinea
- Sepik
- Papua
- Massim

Solomon Is.
Micronesia (Wood Collection)
Easter
New Zealand (Smith Collection)
Samoa
Tonga
Tuvalu
- Nukufetau

E. Futuna
W. Futuna
Rotuma

OXFORD (PRM

PITT RIVERS MUSEUM (E)

Donors/Collectors/Former Owners

Ashmolean Museum	Melanesia, Polynesia, Micronesia	1886+
Rev. J.D. Badger	Papua	1941
G. Balfour	Micronesia	1896
H. Balfour	New Guinea, Australia, Polynesia, Solomon Is.	1888+
H.G. Beasley	New Guinea, Solomon Is., Oceania	1951-55
Capt. Beechey	Polynesia	1896
Capt. Belcher	Polynesia	1896
G. Bennet	Polynesia	1896
B. Blackwood	New Guinea, Papua, Bismarck Archipelago, Solomon Is.	1931
Bloxam	Polynesia	1896
Chignell	Melanesia	
L.C.G. Clarke	Tasmania	1919+
Rev. R.H. Codrington	Polynesia, New Hebrides, Santa Cruz, Solomon Is.	1920
Capt. Cook (see Forster)	Polynesia, New Hebrides, New Caledonia	
W.A. Cooke-Daniels	Papua	
B.A.L. Cranstone	New Guinea	1969
Rev. F.H. Drew	Solomon Is., Santa Cruz	1911
R. & G. Forster	Polynesia, New Hebrides, New Caledonia	1775-76
Capt. G.C. Frederick.	New Hebrides	1896
N.H. Hardy	Australia (Stockdale Collection), Melanesia	1900
A.C. Haddon	Torres Strait	1888+
A.M. Hocart	Polynesia, Fiji	1914+
A.W. Horn	Australia	1897
A.S. Kenyon	Australia	1915-17
Makareti (M. Papakura)	New Zealand	1910
Admiral Monro	Polynesia, Solomon Islands	1926
H.N. Moseley	Admiralty Is., New Guinea, Caroline Is.	1915+
Lord Moyne	New Guinea	1936-38
G. Pitt Rivers	Papua, Ninigo Is., Anchorite Is.	1924-25
Ramsden	Polynesia	
W.S. Routledge	Polynesia	1899
C.G. Seligmann	Papua	1899+
C. Smith	New Zealand (19th Century Collection)	1923
Cdr. B.T. Somerville	New Hebrides, Solomon Is., New Guinea	1893+
W.B. Spencer	Australia	1897
H. Tufnell	Polynesia, Melanesia, Micronesia	1899-1900
E. Westlake	Tasmania	1934+
C.F. Wood	Fiji, New Hebrides	1921
C.W. Wood	Rotuma, Solomon Is., Marshall Is., Caroline Is.	1873

Name	Museum and Art Gallery
Address	High Street Paisley PA1 2BA
Telephone	041-889 3151
Contact	Senior Depute Curator

PAISLEY

Sources & Dates of Information

R. Hutchings 1966
Visit
MEG 1978
Letter 1977

Notes

*Oceania unprovenanced-- navigation: dugout canoe
*Australia-- other: boomerangs 9

Dates of Collection/Acquisition	Donors/Collectors/Former Owners

Documentation

Comment

Information is from general ethnographic list; needs to be checked. Hitherto totally unknown collection.

Museum PAISLEY

Provenance ↓ / Artefact →	TOTAL	OTHER	barkcloth	CLOTHING	-skirt	-belt	-cloak	PERS. ORN.	-head	-ear,nose	-arm	-neck,breast	comb	fan	toilet app.	staff,stick	CERE. OBJ.	-mask	-board	-adze	-paddle	-bullroarer	carving	fig.,image	magic,med.	charm	MUSICAL INS.	-drum,gong	-flute,pipe	-rattle	currency	transport	headrest	mat	basket	bag	box
OCEANIA UN.	140+		1	1																				1										1			
AUSTRALIA	38+	9		1						1																						1		1		4+	
MELA.UNPROV.																																					
Admiralty																																					
Banks																																					
Bismarck																																					
D'Entrecast.																																					
Fiji	5				1																													1			
Louisiade																																					
Loyalty																																					
N. Britain																																					
N. Caledonia																																					
N. Guinea	8												1			1					2														1		
N. Hebrides																																					
N. Ireland																																					
Santa Cruz																																					
Solomon	1																																				
Trobriand																																					
MICRO.UNPROV.																																					
Caroline																																					
Gilbert	2																																	1			
Mariana																																					
Marshall																																					
POLY.UNPROV.																																					
Austral																																					
Chatham																																					
Cook																																					
Easter																																					
Hawaii																																					
Marquesas																																					
New Zealand	15		5	2			3							1		1																					
Niue																																					
Pitcairn																																					
Samoa																																					
Society																																					
Tokelau																																					
Tonga																																					
Tuamotu																																					
Tuvalu																																					

Museum PAISLEY

Provenance ↓ / Artefact →	lime cont	dish,vess	lime spat	utensil	pottery	smokng pi	fire,ligh	TOOL	-adze	-pounding	-grinding	-rasp	-chisel	-needle,a	-weaving	-barkclot	NAVIGATIO	-paddle	-ornament	-model	hunting	FISHING	-fishhook	-spear	-net	-float,si	WEAPON	-club	-spear	-spearthr	-dagger	-shield	-bow	-arrow	-sling,st	raw mater	cord
OCEANIA UN.		1															1*	1			4+	1		91				19	16			1	4				
AUSTRALIA				1					1												X							7	X	5		4	X				
MELA.UNPROV.																																					
Admiralty																																					
Banks																																					
Bismarck																																					
D'Entrecast.																																					
Fiji																												3									
Louisiade																																					
Loyalty																																					
N. Britain																																					
N. Caledonia																																					
N. Guinea																												3									
N. Hebrides																																					
N. Ireland																																					
Santa Cruz																																					
Solomon																												1									
Trobriand																																					
MICRO.UNPROV.																																					
Caroline																																					
Gilbert																											1										
Mariana																																					
Marshall																																					
POLY.UNPROV.																																					
Austral																																					
Chatham																																					
Cook																																					
Easter																																					
Hawaii																																					
Marquesas																																					
New Zealand																								1	1											1	
Niue																																					
Pitcairn																																					
Samoa																																					
Society																																					
Tokelau																																					
Tonga																																					
Tuamotu																																					
Tuvalu																																					

PERTH

Name: Perth Museum and Art Gallery

Address: George Street
Perth
Scotland

Telephone: 0738-32488

Contact: Assistant Keeper of Human History

Sources & Dates of Information

R. Hutchings 1963

Visit 6SP 1974, DRS 1978

MEG 1978

Letter from D. Idiens 197

Notes

*Fiji-- cloaks: flax 2, 1 dating from 1850
*New Zealand-- clubs: taiaha 7, collected 1842
other: heads 2, collected 1825
*Tahiti-- clothing: mourning dress, including headdress, breast pieces & tapa fragments

Dates of Collection/Acquisition	Donors/Collectors/Former Owners
1840-1940	Donors known. Dr. David Ramsay, Oceania & New Zealand, donated 1840's

Documentation

Partial catalogue; ethnographic collection being sorted and re-catalogued.
Catalogue to be published by D. Idiens of Royal Scottish Museum.
Library, archival.

Comment

Important. Note especially early (Ramsay) collection, particularly Maori preserved heads, weapons, clothing. Two flax cloaks from Fiji are a bit of a puzzle.

Museum and Art Gallery

PERTH

Artefact → / Provenance ↓	TOTAL	OTHER	barkcloth	CLOTHING	-skirt	-belt	-cloak	PERS. ORN.	-head	-ear,nose	-arm	-neck,breast	comb	fan	toilet app.	staff,stick	CERE. OBJ.	-mask	-board	-adze	-paddle	-bullroarer	carving	fig.,image	magic,med.	charm	MUSICAL INS.	-drum,gong	-flute,pipe	-rattle	currency	transport	headrest	mat	basket	bag	box
OCEANIA UN.	19																											X									
AUSTRALIA	68																																				
MELA. UNPROV.																																					
Admiralty	3																																				
Banks																																					
Bismarck																																					
D'Entrecast.																																					
Fiji	49						#																														
Louisiade																																					
Loyalty																																					
N. Britain																																					
N. Caledonia																																					
N. Guinea	27																																				
N. Hebrides	42																																				
N. Ireland	1																																				
Santa Cruz	6																																				
Solomon	43																																				
Trobriand																																					
MICRO. UNPROV.	5																																				
Caroline																																					
Gilbert																																					
Mariana																																					
Marshall																																					
POLY. UNPROV.																																					
Austral	12																																				
Chatham																																					
Cook	4																																				
Easter																																					
Hawaii	14																																				
Marquesas	19																																				
New Zealand	69	2			1		6	5		2		2	1			1	1				2		4						1			1				2	5
Niue																																					
Pitcairn																																					
Samoa																																					
Society																																					
Tokelau																																					
Tonga	7																																				
Tuamotu																																					
Tuvalu																																					
Tahiti	23			*																																	

Museum and Art Gallery PERTH

Artefact → / Provenance →	OCEANIA UN.	AUSTRALIA	MELA.UNPROV.	Admiralty	Banks	Bismarck	D'Entrecast.	Fiji	Louisiade	Loyalty	N. Britain	N. Caledonia	N. Guinea	N. Hebrides	N. Ireland	Santa Cruz	Solomon	Trobriand	MICRO.UNPROV	Caroline	Gilbert	Mariana	Marshall	POLY.UNPROV.	Austral	Chatham	Cook	Easter	Hawaii	Marquesas	New Zealand	Niue	Pitcairn	Samoa	Society	Tokelau	Tonga	Tuamotu	Tuvalu
cord																																							
raw mater																																							
-sling,st																																							
-arrow																																							
-bow																																							
-shield																																							
-dagger																																							
-spearthr																																							
-spear																																							
-club																														𝍸								
WEAPON,sl																																							
-float,si																																							
-net																																							
-spear																																							
-fishhook																														5								
FISHING																																							
hunting																																							
-model																														1								
-ornament																																							
-paddle																														1								
NAVIGATIO																																							
-barkclot																																							
-weaving																														1								
-needle,a																														1								
-chisel																																							
-rasp																																							
-grinding																																							
-pounding																														1								
-adze																														5								
TOOL																														3								
fire,ligh																																							
smokng p																																							
pottery																																							
utensil																																							
lime spa																																							
dish,vess																																							
lime cont																																							

Name City Museum and Art Gallery **Address** Priestgate Peterborough PE1 1LF **Telephone** 0733-43329 **Contact** Curator	**PETERBOROUGH** Sources & Dates of Information R. Hutchings 1966 Visit MEG 1978 Letter personal communication H.D. Skinner list 1915

Notes

Disposal: Material went to either Cambridge or Horniman Museum, London.
Included a tewhatewha (seen by Skinner 1915).

Dates of Collection/Acquisition	Donors/Collectors/Former Owners

Documentation

Comment

PETERHEAD

Name: North-East of Scotland Museums Service

Address: Arbuthnot Museum
St. Peter Street
Peterhead
Aberdeenshire

Telephone: 0779-2554

Contact: Museums Organiser

Sources & Dates of Information

R. Hutchings 1966

Visit

MEG 1978

Letter 1979

Notes

This entry includes items from Arbuthnot Museum, Peterhead; Carnegie Museum, Inverurie; and Huntly Brander Museum, Huntly.

Disposals: There have been some; details still unknown.

*Australia-- other: boomerangs

Dates of Collection/Acquisition

Acquired mainly 1900-20

Donors/Collectors/Former Owners

Documentation

Archival, photographic. Catalogue being prepared.

Comment

Being sorted and catalogued. Other specimens may still be found.

North-East of Scotland Museums Service

PETERHEAD

Provenance ↓ / Artefact →	TOTAL	OTHER	barkcloth	CLOTHING	-skirt	-belt	-cloak	PERS. ORN.	-head	-ear,nose	-arm	-neck,breast	comb	fan	toilet app.	staff,stick	CERE. OBJ.	-mask	-board	-adze	-paddle	-bullroarer	carving	fig.,image	magic,med.	charm	MUSICAL INS.	-drum,gong	-flute,pipe	-rattle	currency	transport	headrest	mat	basket	bag	box
OCEANIA UN.	X																																		X*		
AUSTRALIA	3	3																																			
MELA.UNPROV.																																					
Admiralty																																					
Banks																																					
Bismarck																																					
D'Entrecast.																																					
Fiji																																					
Louisiade																																					
Loyalty																																					
N. Britain																																					
N. Caledonia																																					
N. Guinea																																					
N. Hebrides																																					
N. Ireland																																					
Santa Cruz																																					
Solomon																																					
Trobriand																																					
MICRO.UNPROV.																																					
Caroline																																					
Gilbert																																					
Mariana																																					
Marshall																																					
POLY.UNPROV.																																					
Austral																																					
Chatham																																					
Cook																																					
Easter																																					
Hawaii																																					
Marquesas																																					
New Zealand	2			2																																	
Niue																																					
Pitcairn																																					
Samoa																																					
Society																																					
Tokelau																																					
Tonga																																					
Tuamotu																																					
Tuvalu																																					

North-East of Scotland Museums Service

PETERHEAD

Artefact → / Provenance →	OCEANIA UN.	AUSTRALIA	MELA.UNPROV.	Admiralty	Banks	Bismarck	D'Entrecast.	Fiji	Louisiade	Loyalty	N. Britain	N. Caledonia	N. Guinea	N. Hebrides	N. Ireland	Santa Cruz	Solomon	Trobriand	MICRO.UNPROV.	Caroline	Gilbert	Mariana	Marshall	POLY.UNPROV.	Austral	Chatham	Cook	Easter	Hawaii	Marquesas	New Zealand	Niue	Pitcairn	Samoa	Society	Tokelau	Tonga	Tuamotu	Tuvalu
cord																																							
raw mater																																							
-sling,sto																																							
-arrow																																							
-bow																																							
-shield																																							
-dagger																																							
-spearthro																																							
-spear																																							
-club																																							
WEAPON																																							
-float,si																																							
-net																																							
-spear																																							
-fishhook																																							
FISHING																																							
hunting																																							
-model																																							
-ornament																																							
-paddle																																							
NAVIGATIO																																							
-barkclot																																							
-weaving																																							
-needle,aw																																							
-chisel																																							
-rasp																																							
-grinding																																							
-pounding																																							
-adze																																							
TOOL																																							
fire,ligh																																							
smokng pi																																							
pottery																																							
utensil																																							
lime spat																																							
dish,vess																																							
lime cont																																							

PLYMOUTH

Name: City Museum and Art Gallery

Address: Drake Circus
Plymouth PL4 8AJ

Telephone: 0752-68000

Contact: Keeper of Archaeology

Sources & Dates of Information

R. Hutchings 1966

Visit PG / ALR } 1973, 6SP 197?

MEG 1978

Letter

Notes

Disposals: Some on long-term (since 1950's) loan to Exeter.

Dates of Collection/Acquisition	Donors/Collectors/Former Owners
Acquired mainly 1899-1934	H.M. Dauncey, late 19th Century, New Guinea Gertrude Benham

Documentation

Library, archival, photographic.

Comment

Not accessible- had to work from card catalogue.

City Museum

PLYMOUTH

Provenance ↓ / Artefact →	TOTAL	OTHER	barkcloth	CLOTHING	-skirt	-belt	-cloak	PERS. ORN.	-head	-ear,nose	-arm	-neck,breast	comb	fan	toilet app.	staff,stick	CERE. OBJ.	-mask	-board	-adze	-paddle	-bullroarer	carving	fig.,image	magic,med.	charm	MUSICAL INS.	-drum,gong	-flute,pipe	-rattle	currency	transport	headrest	mat	basket	bag	box
OCEANIA UN.																																					
AUSTRALIA	24																																				
MELA.UNPROV.																																					
Admiralty																																					
Banks																																					
Bismarck																																					
D'Entrecast.																																					
Fiji	40+																																				
Louisiade																																					
Loyalty																																					
N. Britain	2																																				
N. Caledonia	5																																				
N. Guinea	178																																				
N. Hebrides	2																																				
N. Ireland																																					
Santa Cruz																																					
Solomon	30+																																				
Trobriand																																					
MICRO.UNPROV																																					
Caroline																																					
Gilbert	27+																																				
Mariana																																					
Marshall																																					
POLY.UNPROV.																																					
Austral																																					
Chatham	2																																				
Cook	23+																																				
Easter	2																																				
Hawaii																																					
Marquesas																																					
New Zealand	16+																																				
Niue																																					
Pitcairn	1																																				
Samoa	6+																																				
Society																																					
Tokelau																																					
Tonga	5																																				
Tuamotu																																					
Tuvalu	27+																																				

City Museum PLYMOUTH

Artefact → / Provenance →	OCEANIA UN.	AUSTRALIA	MELA.UNPROV.	Admiralty	Banks	Bismarck	D'Entrecast.	Fiji	Louisiade	Loyalty	N. Britain	N. Caledonia	N. Guinea	N. Hebrides	N. Ireland	Santa Cruz	Solomon	Trobriand	MICRO.UNPROV	Caroline	Gilbert	Mariana	Marshall	POLY.UNPROV.	Austral	Chatham	Cook	Easter	Hawaii	Marquesas	New Zealand	Niue	Pitcairn	Samoa	Society	Tokelau	Tonga	Tuamotu	Tuvalu	
cord																																								
raw mater																																								
-sling,st																																								
-arrow																																								
-bow																																								
-shield																																								
-dagger																																								
-spearthr																																								
-spear																																								
-club																																								
WEAPON																																								
-float,si																																								
-net																																								
-spear																																								
-fishhook																																								
FISHING																																								
hunting																																								
-model																																								
-ornament																																								
-paddle																																								
NAVIGATIO																																								
-barkclot																																								
-weaving																																								
-needle,a																																								
-chisel																																								
-rasp																																								
-grinding																																								
-pounding																																								
-adze																																								
TOOL																																								
fire,ligh																																								
smoking pi																																								
pottery																																								
utensil																																								
lime spat																																								
dish,vess																																								
lime cont																																								

Name Burnby Hall Museum Trust
The Stewart Collection

Address Burnby Hall Gardens
Pocklington
near Bridlington
Humberside

Telephone

Contact Administrator

POCKLINGTON

Sources & Dates of Information

R. Hutchings 1966

Visit SP 1975

MEG 1978

Letter

Notes

Total collection about 30 objects, with additional unidentified pieces.

Dates of Collection/Acquisition	Donors/Collectors/Former Owners
	Major Stewart, collected 1904-30

Documentation

Comment

Stewart Collection worth following up.

Burnby Hall Museum Trust

POCKLINGTON

Provenance ↓ / Artefact →	box	bag	basket	mat	headrest	transport	currency	-rattle	-flute,pipe	-drum,gong	MUSICAL INS.	charm	magic,med.	fig.,image	carving	-bullroarer	-paddle	-adze	-board	-mask	CERE. OBJ.	staff,stick	toilet app.	fan	comb	-neck,breast	-arm	-ear,nose	-head	PERS. ORN.	-cloak	-belt	-skirt	CLOTHING	barkcloth	OTHER	TOTAL
OCEANIA UN.																																					X
AUSTRALIA																																					
MELA.UNPROV.																																					
Admiralty														1																							1
Banks																																					
Bismarck																																					
D'Entrecast.																																					
Fiji																																			1		3
Louisiade																																					
Loyalty																																					
N. Britain																																					
N. Caledonia																																					
N. Guinea										1						1																					3
N. Hebrides																																					
N. Ireland																				1																	1
Santa Cruz																																					
Solomon														1																							1
Trobriand																						1															1
MICRO.UNPROV.																																					
Caroline																																					
Gilbert																																					2
Mariana																																					
Marshall																																					
POLY.UNPROV.																																					
Austral																																					
Chatham																																					
Cook																																					
Easter																																					
Hawaii																																					
Marquesas																																					
New Zealand														1												1					1						3
Niue																																					
Pitcairn																																					
Samoa																																					
Society																																					
Tokelau																																					
Tonga																																					
Tuamotu																																					
Tuvalu																																					

Burnby Hall Museum Trust POCKLINGTON

Artefact → / Provenance →	OCEANIA UN.	AUSTRALIA	MELA.UNPROV.	Admiralty	Banks	Bismarck	D'Entrecast.	Fiji	Louisiade	Loyalty	N. Britain	N. Caledonia	N. Guinea	N. Hebrides	N. Ireland	Santa Cruz	Solomon	Trobriand	MICRO.UNPROV	Caroline	Gilbert	Mariana	Marshall	POLY.UNPROV.	Austral	Chatham	Cook	Easter	Hawaii	Marquesas	New Zealand	Niue	Pitcairn	Samoa	Society	Tokelau	Tonga	Tuamotu	Tuvalu
cord																																							
raw mater																																							
-sling,sto																																							
-arrow																																							
-bow																																							
-shield																																							
-dagger																																							
-spearthro																																							
-spear																																							
-club																																							
WEAPON																					2																		
-float,si																																							
-net																																							
-spear																																							
-fishhook																																							
FISHING																																							
hunting																																							
-model																																							
-ornament																																							
-paddle																																							
NAVIGATIO																																							
-barkcloth																																							
-weaving																																							
-needle,aw																																							
-chisel																																							
-rasp																																							
-grinding																																							
-pounding																																							
-adze																																							
TOOL																																							
fire,ligh																																							
smoking pi												1																											
pottery																																							
utensil																																							
lime spat																																							
dish,vesse								2																															
lime cont.																																							

Name	Museums and Art Gallery	PORTSMOUTH
Address	Museum Road Old Portsmouth P01 2LJ	Sources & Dates of Information R. Hutchings 1966 Visit GSP 1979 MEG 1978 Letter 1979
Telephone	0705-811527	
Contact	Keeper of Local History	

Notes

Pitcairn: 3 stone artefacts including an axehead, used by survivors of Bounty.

Dates of Collection/Acquisition	Donors/Collectors/Former Owners
	Collected by Capt. Beechey of Blossom 1825; transferred fro Royal United Service Museum in 1963.

Documentation

Comment

PORT SUNLIGHT

Name Lady Lever Art Gallery

Address Port Sunlight
Wirral
Merseyside L62 5EQ

Telephone 051-645 3623

Contact Director, Walker Art Gallery, William Brown Street, Liverpool L3 8EL (tel. 051-2275234)

Sources & Dates of Information

R. Hutchings 1966

Visit

MEG 1978

Letter

Notes

This museum has recently come under the jurisdiction of the Walker Art Gallery. A check of the collections has begun. Neither the provenances nor numbers given in the table, therefore, can be considered definite. Much of the material is still on loan to other institutions.

*Oceania-- clothing: hemp dress
barkcloth tools: 'fan-shaped' beaters
arrows: probably many Solomons

Dates of Collection/Acquisition	Donors/Collectors/Former Owners

Documentation

Comment

Lady Lever Art Gallery

PORT SUNLIGHT

Artifact → / Provenance ↓	OCEANIA UN.	AUSTRALIA	MELA.UNPROV.	Admiralty	Banks	Bismarck	D'Entrecast.	Fiji	Louisiade	Loyalty	N. Britain	N. Caledonia	N. Guinea	N. Hebrides	N. Ireland	Santa Cruz	Solomon	Trobriand	MICRO.UNPROV.	Caroline	Gilbert	Mariana	Marshall	POLY.UNPROV.	Austral	Chatham	Cook	Easter	Hawaii	Marquesas	New Zealand	Niue	Pitcairn	Samoa	Society	Tokelau	Tonga	Tuamotu	Tuvalu
box																																							
bag																1																							
basket	1															2																							
mat	10															4																							
headrest																																							
transport																																							
currency																																							
-rattle																																							
-flute,pipe																																							
-drum,gong																																							
MUSICAL IN																																							
charm																																							
magic,med.																																							
fig.,image																																							
carving																																							
-bullroarer																																							
-paddle																																							
-adze																																							
-board																																							
-mask																																							
CERE. OBJ.																1																							
starf,stick	2																1																						
toilet app.																																							
fan																																							
comb	2																																						
-neck,breast	24																																						
-arm	1																																						
-ear,nose																																							
-head																																							
PERS. ORN.																																							
-cloak																																							
-belt	1																																						
-skirt																																							
CLOTHING	1*																																						
barkcloth	5																																						
OTHER	X	2																																					
TOTAL	194	2						1								8	20																				1		

Lady Lever Art Gallery

PORT SUNLIGHT

Artefact → / Provenance ↓	OCEANIA UN.	AUSTRALIA	MELA.UNPROV.	Admiralty	Banks	Bismarck	D'Entrecast.	Fiji	Louisiade	Loyalty	N. Britain	N. Caledonia	N. Guinea	N. Hebrides	N. Ireland	Santa Cruz	Solomon	Trobriand	MICRO.UNPROV	Caroline	Gilbert	Mariana	Marshall	POLY.UNPROV.	Austral	Chatham	Cook	Easter	Hawaii	Marquesas	New Zealand	Niue	Pitcairn	Samoa	Society	Tokelau	Tonga	Tuamotu	Tuvalu
cord																																							
raw mater																																							
-sling,st																																							
-arrow	129*																																						
-bow	1																7																						
-shield																	1																						
-dagger																																							
-spearthr																																							
-spear	10+																8																						
-club	1							1																													1		
WEAPON																																							
-float,sl																																							
-net																																							
-spear																																							
-fishhook																																							
FISHING																																							
hunting																																							
-model																	1																						
-ornament																	1																						
-paddle																	1																						
NAVIGATIO																																							
-barkclot	2*																																						
-weaving																																							
-needle,a																																							
-chisel																																							
-rasp	1																																						
-grinding																																							
-pounding																																							
-adze																																							
TOOL																																							
fire,ligh																																							
smoking pi																																							
pottery																																							
utensil																																							
lime spat																																							
dish,vess	3																																						
lime cont.																																							

Name Eastgate House

Address High Street
Rochester, Kent ME1 1EW

Telephone 0634-44176

Contact Curator

ROCHESTER

Sources & Dates of Information

R. Hutchings 1966

Visit

MEG 1978

Letter 1979

M.I. Hoad, personal communication

Notes

Eastgate House Museum is in the process of being moved to the Guildhall, Rochester. The effective date of this change will be 1 September 1979.

*Australia-- arrows: Cape York??

Dates of Collection/Acquisition

Mainly acquired 1900-35.

Donors/Collectors/Former Owners

Documentation

Comment

Eastgate House

ROCHESTER

Provenance ↓ / Artefact →	TOTAL	OTHER	barkcloth	CLOTHING	-skirt	-belt	-cloak	PERS. ORN.	-head	-ear,nose	-arm	-neck,breast	comb	fan	toilet app.	staff,stick	CERE. OBJ.	-mask	-board	-adze	-paddle	-bullroarer	carving	fig.,image	magic,med.	charm	MUSICAL INS.	-drum,gong	-flute,pipe	-rattle	currency	transport	headrest	mat	basket	bag	box
OCEANIA UN.	X		X					X																							X						
AUSTRALIA	X																																				
MELA.UNPROV.																																					
Admiralty	X																																				
Banks																																					
Bismarck																																					
D'Entrecast.																																					
Fiji	X		X																																		
Louisiade																																					
Loyalty																																					
N. Britain																																					
N. Caledonia																																					
N. Guinea	X																																				
N. Hebrides	X																																				
N. Ireland																																					
Santa Cruz	X																																				
Solomon																																					
Trobriand	X																																				
MICRO.UNPROV.																																					
Caroline																																					
Gilbert																																					
Mariana																																					
Marshall																																					
POLY.UNPROV.																																					
Austral																																					
Chatham																																					
Cook																																					
Easter																																					
Hawaii																																					
Marquesas																																					
New Zealand																																					
Niue																																					
Pitcairn																																					
Samoa	X		X																																		
Society																																					
Tokelau																																					
Tonga																																					
Tuamotu																																					
Tuvalu																																					

Eastgate House ROCHESTER

Artefact → / Provenance →	OCEANIA UN.	AUSTRALIA	MELA.UNPROV.	Admiralty	Banks	Bismarck	D'Entrecast.	Fiji	Louisiade	Loyalty	N. Britain	N. Caledonia	N. Guinea	N. Hebrides	N. Ireland	Santa Cruz	Solomon	Trobriand	MICRO.UNPROV	Caroline	Gilbert	Mariana	Marshall	POLY.UNPROV.	Austral	Chatham	Cook	Easter	Hawaii	Marquesas	New Zealand	Niue	Pitcairn	Samoa	Society	Tokelau	Tonga	Tuamotu	Tuvalu
cord																																						
raw mater.																																						
-sling,stone																																						
-arrow	X	[illegible]*											47																									
-bow																																						
-shield																																						
-dagger				1																																		
-spearthrow		2																																				
-spear	X			3				1										2																				
-club		1						2								1																		1					
WEAPON		X		X				X					X	X		X																						
-float,sinker																																						
-net																																						
-spear																																						
-fishhook																																						
FISHING																																						
hunting																																						
-model																																						
-ornament																																						
-paddle													2																									
NAVIGATION																																						
-barkcloth								1																										2					
-weaving																																						
-needle,awl								1																														
-chisel																																						
-rasp																																						
-grinding																																						
-pounding																																						
-adze																																		1					
TOOL																																						
fire,light																																						
smoking pipe																																						
pottery																																						
utensil																																						
lime spat.																		1																				
dish,vessel																																		2					
lime cont.																																						

Name	Rossendale Museum	ROSSENDALE
Address	Whitaker Park Rawtenstall Rossendale BB4 6RE	**Sources & Dates of Information** R. Hutchings 1966 Visit SP1975 MEG 1978 Letter 1979
Telephone	07062-7777/26509	
Contact	Curator	

Notes

Total Oceanic around 82; table incomplete.

Many items on loan are being returned to Lady Lever Art Gallery (Port Sunlight).

*Australia-- other: boomerang
*New Zealand-- other: model meeting house

Dates of Collection/Acquisition	Donors/Collectors/Former Owners
Acquired mainly 1900-30	

Documentation

Comment

Some things on loan from Lady Lever Art Gallery, Port Sunlight, including good W.D. Webster object. (Webster was a dealer operating from Bicester, Oxfordshire, and London about 1890-1910, who published important series of sales catalogues; a near complete set in Cambridge.)

Rossendale Museum

ROSSENDALE

Provenance ↓ / Artefact →	box	bag	basket	mat	headrest	transport	currency	-rattle	-flute,pipe	-drum,gong	MUSICAL INS.	charm	magic,med.	fig.,image	carving	-bullroarer	-paddle	-adze	-board	-mask	CERE. OBJ.	staff,stick	toilet app.	fan	comb	-neck,breast	-arm	-ear,nose	-head	PERS. ORN.	-cloak	-belt	-skirt	CLOTHING	barkcloth	OTHER	TOTAL
OCEANIA UN.																																					3
AUSTRALIA																																				1	5
MELA.UNPROV.																																					
Admiralty																																					1
Banks																																					
Bismarck																																					
D'Entrecast.																																					
Fiji																																					9
Louisiade																																					
Loyalty																																					
N. Britain																																					3
N. Caledonia																																					
N. Guinea																																					14
N. Hebrides																																					2
N. Ireland																																					
Santa Cruz		1																																			1
Solomon								1																													3
Trobriand																																					4
MICRO.UNPROV.																																					
Caroline																																					1
Gilbert																																					
Mariana																																					
Marshall																																					
POLY.UNPROV.																																					
Austral																		2					2														4
Chatham																																					
Cook																																					
Easter																																					
Hawaii																																					
Marquesas																																					
New Zealand																																				1	5
Niue																																					1
Pitcairn																																					
Samoa																																					1
Society																																					
Tokelau																																					
Tonga																																					2
Tuamotu																																					
Tuvalu																																					

Rossendale Museum

ROSSENDALE

Provenance ↓ / Artefact →	lime cont	dish,vess	lime spa	utensil	pottery	smokng p	fire,lig	TOOL	-adze	-pounding	-grinding	-rasp	-chisel	-needle,s	-weaving	-barkclo	NAVIGATI	-paddle	-ornamen	-model	hunting	FISHING	-fishhoo	-spear	-net	-float,s	WEAPON	-club	-spear	-spearth	-dagger	-shield	-bow	-arrow	-sling,s	raw mate	cord
OCEANIA UN.									2			1																									
AUSTRALIA																												1	3								
MELA.UNPROV.																																					
Admiralty																													1								
Banks																																					
Bismarck																																					
D'Entrecast.																																					
Fiji																												9									
Louisiade																																					
Loyalty																																					
N. Britain																												3									
N. Caledonia																																					
N. Guinea									2									1										2					1	8			
N. Hebrides																												1	1								
N. Ireland																																					
Santa Cruz																																					
Solomon																												2									
Trobriand									2									1										1									
MICRO.UNPROV																																					
Caroline									1																												
Gilbert																																					
Mariana																																					
Marshall																																					
POLY.UNPROV.																																					
Austral																																					
Chatham																																					
Cook																																					
Easter																																					
Hawaii																																					
Marquesas																																					
New Zealand																												4									
Niue																												1									
Pitcairn																																					
Samoa																												1									
Society																																					
Tokelau																																					
Tonga																												2									
Tuamotu																																					
Tuvalu																																					

ROTHERHAM

Name	Rotherham Museum
Address	Clifton Park Rotherham S65 2AA
Telephone	0709-2121
Contact	Keeper of Antiquities

Sources & Dates of Information

R. Hutchings 1966
Visit

MEG 1978
Letter

personal communication C. Millar, 1979

Notes

Oceania: 6 objects

Dates of Collection/Acquisition

Acquired mainly 1893-1950

Donors/Collectors/Former Owners

Documentation

Documentation fragmentary.

Photographic.

Comment

To be examined in near future by ethnographer at Leeds.

RUGBY

Name Rugby School

Address Rugby
Warwickshire

Telephone

Contact

Sources & Dates of Information

R. Hutchings 1966

Visit PG ALK 1970

MEG 1978

Letter

Notes

Disposals : The Art Museum, which undoubtedly included Oceanic artefacts, was disbanded and many items went on permanent loan to other museums. A New South Wales axe was recorded in 1915. Dispersal in 1939 because of war.

Dates of Collection/Acquisition	Donors/Collectors/Former Owners

Documentation

Comment Bloxam family resident in Rugby in 19 century; so Link via Andrew and Richard with HMS Blonde and Hawaii (1825).

SAFFRON WALDEN

Name Saffron Walden Museum

Address Museum Street
Saffron Walden, Essex CB10 1JL

Telephone 0799-22494

Contact Curator

Sources & Dates of Information

R. Hutchings 1966

Visit PG 1975

MEG 1978

Letter

Notes

A few sales in 1940's (Hawaiian feather cloak in 1948).

*Gilberts-- weapon: armour suit
*Hawaii-- other: toy
*Marquesas-- carving: stilt step
*New Zealand-- mus. instrument: shell trumpet
other: heads
*Tahiti-- mus. instrument: shell trumpet
neck ornament: mourning dress pectoral

Dates of Collection/Acquisition

Donors/Collectors/Former Owners

Bennet; Chelmsford Museum? St Albans City Museum

Documentation

1845 catalogue; several others published since 1933. Careful accessions records since 1880.

Museum publication: Saffron Walden Museum Guide (n.d.?)

Comment

Good material, some early. Includes George Bennet material from Tahiti (some went to Sheffield, then transferred to Cambridge 1891).

Saffron Walden Museum

Provenance ↓ / Artefact →	TOTAL	OTHER	barkcloth	CLOTHING	-skirt	-belt	-cloak	PERS. ORN.	-head	-ear,nose	-arm	-neck,breast	comb	fan	toilet app.	staff,stick	CERE. OBJ.	-mask	-board	-adze	-paddle	-bullroarer	carving	fig.,image	magic,med.	charm	MUSICAL INS.	-drum,gong	-flute,pipe	-rattle	currency	transport	headrest	mat	basket	bag	box
OCEANIA UN.																																					
AUSTRALIA																																					
MELA.UNPROV.																																					
Admiralty																																					
Banks	X																																				
Bismarck																																					
D'Entrecast.																																					
Fiji	7		1									1	1																								
Louisiade																																					
Loyalty																																					
N. Britain																																					
N. Caledonia	3																																				
N. Guinea	17+				1	1		X			2+		1					1		1				1													
N. Hebrides	3																												1					1			
N. Ireland																																					
Santa Cruz								1																													
Solomon	16+							3+			X	1	1																								
Trobriand																																					
MICRO.UNPROV.																																					
Caroline																																					
Gilbert	5																																				
Mariana																																					
Marshall																																					
POLY.UNPROV.	7+							1			X		X																								
Austral	6																																				
Chatham	1																																				
Cook	2																			1								1									
Easter																																					
Hawaii	8	1	4																																		
Marquesas	3											1											1*														
New Zealand	28	2			1		2			1			1														1*		2							1	
Niue																																					
Pitcairn																																					
Samoa	2													1																							
Society																																					
Tokelau																																					
Tonga	3											1																									
Tuamotu																																					
Tuvalu																																					
Tahiti	13		1									1*												1			1*		1				1				

Saffron Walden Museum SAFFRON WALDE

Artefact → / Provenance ↓	OCEANIA UN.	AUSTRALIA	MELA.UNPROV.	Admiralty	Banks	Bismarck	D'Entrecast.	Fiji	Louisiade	Loyalty	N. Britain	N. Caledonia	N. Guinea	N. Hebrides	N. Ireland	Santa Cruz	Solomon	Trobriand
cord																		
raw mater																		
-sling,sto												1						
-arrow																		
-bow																		
-shield																		
-dagger																		
-spearthro																		
-spear																		
-club								3				1						
WEAPON																		
-float,sin																	1	
-net														1				
-spear																		
-fishhook																	2	
FISHING																		
hunting																		
-model																		
-ornament													1				1	
-paddle																		
NAVIGATION																		
-barkcloth																		
-weaving																		
-needle,aw																		
-chisel																		
-rasp																		
-grinding																		
-pounding													1					
-adze													4					
TOOL																		
fire,light																		
smoking pip													1					
pottery								1										
utensil					X													
lime spat.																		
dish,vesse												2					1	
lime cont.																	5	

Artefact → / Provenance ↓	MICRO.UNPROV	Caroline	Gilbert	Mariana	Marshall	POLY.UNPROV.	Austral	Chatham	Cook	Easter	Hawaii
cord											
raw mater											
-sling,sto											
-arrow											
-bow											
-shield											
-dagger			1								
-spearthro											
-spear			3								
-club											
WEAPON			1*								
-float,sin											
-net											
-spear											
-fishhook						1					1
FISHING											
hunting											
-model											
-ornament											
-paddle							5				
NAVIGATION											
-barkcloth						1					
-weaving											
-needle,aw											
-chisel											
-rasp											
-grinding											
-pounding											
-adze							1				
TOOL											
fire,light											
smoking pip											
pottery											
utensil											
lime spat.											
dish,vesse						2	1				2
lime cont.											

Artefact → / Provenance ↓	Marquesas	New Zealand	Niue	Pitcairn	Samoa	Society	Tokelau	Tonga	Tuamotu	Tuvalu	Tahiti	Gambier
cord												
raw mater												
-sling,sto												
-arrow												
-bow												
-shield												
-dagger												
-spearthro												
-spear												
-club	1	6			1			2				
WEAPON												
-float,sin												
-net												
-spear												
-fishhook		1									2	
FISHING											1	
hunting												
-model		1									1	
-ornament												
-paddle												
NAVIGATION												
-barkcloth												
-weaving												
-needle,aw												
-chisel												
-rasp											1	
-grinding												
-pounding												
-adze		9									2	
TOOL												
fire,light												
smoking pip												
pottery												
utensil												
lime spat.												
dish,vesse												
lime cont.												

Name City Museum

ST. ALBANS

Address Hatfield Road
St. Albans AL1 3RR

Telephone 0727-56679

Contact Keeper, Social History & Folk Life

Sources & Dates of Information

R. Hutchings 1966

Visit

MEG 1978

Letter 1979

personal communication L. Pole 1979

Notes

Disposal: Maori adze and Australian boomerangs transferred to Saffron Walden Museum.
Remainder being transferred to Ipswich Museum.

Dates of Collection/Acquisition

Acquired mainly 1898-1969

Donors/Collectors/Former Owners

Documentation

Undocumented.

Comment

Soon to be disposed of.

City Museum ST. ALBANS

Provenance ↓ / Artefact →	TOTAL	OTHER	barkcloth	CLOTHING	-skirt	-belt	-cloak	PERS. ORN.	-head	-ear,nose	-arm	-neck,breast	comb	fan	toilet app.	staff,stick	CERE. OBJ.	-mask	-board	-adze	-paddle	-bullroarer	carving	fig.,image	magic,med.	charm	MUSICAL INS.	-drum,gong	-flute,pipe	-rattle	currency	transport	headrest	mat	basket	bag	box
OCEANIA UN.																																					
AUSTRALIA	X	X																																			
MELA.UNPROV.																																					
Admiralty																																					
Banks																																					
Bismarck																																					
D'Entrecast.																																					
Fiji																																					
Louisiade																																					
Loyalty																																					
N. Britain																																					
N. Caledonia																																					
N. Guinea	X																																				
N. Hebrides																																					
N. Ireland																																					
Santa Cruz																																					
Solomon	2↑																																				
Trobriand																																					
MICRO.UNPROV.																																					
Caroline																																					
Gilbert																																					
Mariana																																					
Marshall																																					
POLY.UNPROV.																																					
Austral																																					
Chatham																																					
Cook																																					
Easter																																					
Hawaii	2																																				
Marquesas																																					
New Zealand	1																																				
Niue																																					
Pitcairn																																					
Samoa																																					
Society																																					
Tokelau																																					
Tonga																																					
Tuamotu																																					
Tuvalu																																					

City Museum ST. ALBANS

Artefact → / Provenance →	OCEANIA UN.	AUSTRALIA	MELA.UNPROV.	Admiralty	Banks	Bismarck	D'Entrecast.	Fiji	Louisiade	Loyalty	N. Britain	N. Caledonia	N. Guinea	N. Hebrides	N. Ireland	Santa Cruz	Solomon	Trobriand	MICRO.UNPROV	Caroline	Gilbert	Mariana	Marshall	POLY.UNPROV.	Austral	Chatham	Cook	Easter	Hawaii	Marquesas	New Zealand	Niue	Pitcairn	Samoa	Society	Tokelau	Tonga	Tuamotu	Tuvalu
cord																																							
raw mater.																																							
-sling,ston																																							
-arrow													X																										
-bow																																							
-shield																																							
-dagger																																							
-spearthrow																																							
-spear																	X												/										
-club																	/																						
WEAPON																																							
-float,sink																																							
-net																																							
-spear																																							
-fishhook																																							
FISHING																																							
hunting																																							
-model																													/										
-ornament																																							
-paddle																																							
NAVIGATION																																							
-barkcloth																																							
-weaving																																							
-needle,awl																																							
-chisel																																							
-rasp																																							
-grinding																																							
-pounding																																							
-adze																															/								
TOOL																																							
fire,light																																							
smoking pipe																																							
pottery																																							
utensil																																							
lime spat.																																							
dish,vessel																																							
lime cont.																																							

ST. HELENS

Name: St. Helens Museum and Art Gallery

Address: Gamble Institute
Victoria Square
St. Helens
Merseyside WA10 1DY

Telephone: 0744-24061

Contact: Curator

Sources & Dates of Information

R. Hutchings 1966

Visit

MEG 1978

Letter 1979

Notes

Australia: shields 3
boomerangs 2
New Guinea: knife 1

A few unidentified artefacts.

Dates of Collection/Acquisition

Acquired 1896-1954

Donors/Collectors/Former Owners

E.E. Hurt, 1954, Australia
F.J. Horniman, 1899, New Guinea

Documentation

Comment

Name	The Longsands Museum	ST. NEOTS
Address	Longsands Road St. Neots Cambridgeshire PE19 1LQ	Sources & Dates of Information R. Hutchings 1966 Visit PG 1979
Telephone	0480-72740	MEG 1978
Contact	Curator	Letter

Notes

*Fiji-- adze: Fijian haft, Society blade

Dates of Collection/Acquisition	Donors/Collectors/Former Owners
	Material on long-term loan from Norris Museum, St. Ives, & University Museum of Archaeology & Anthropology, Cambridge (Lucas Barrett Collection)

Documentation

Comment

Longsands Museum

ST. NEOT

Provenance	TOTAL	OTHER	barkcloth	CLOTHING	-skirt	-belt	-cloak	PERS. ORN	-head	-ear,nose	-arm	-neck,breast	comb	fan	toilet app.	staff,stick	CERE. OBJ.	-mask	-board	-adze	-paddle	-bullroarer	carving	fig.,image	magic,med.	charm	MUSICAL INS	-drum,gong	-flute,pipe	-rattle	currency	transport	headrest	mat	basket	bag	box
OCEANIA UN.	9																																				
AUSTRALIA	7																																				
MELA.UNPROV.																																					
Admiralty																																					
Banks																																					
Bismarck																																					
D'Entrecast.																																					
Fiji	6																																				
Louisiade																																					
Loyalty																																					
N. Britain																																					
N. Caledonia																																					
N. Guinea	5																																				
N. Hebrides																																					
N. Ireland																																					
Santa Cruz																																					
Solomon																																					
Trobriand																																					
MICRO.UNPROV.																																					
Caroline																																					
Gilbert																																					
Mariana																																					
Marshall																																					
POLY.UNPROV.	1																																				
Austral																																					
Chatham																																					
Cook																																					
Easter																																					
Hawaii																																					
Marquesas																																					
New Zealand	3																																				
Niue																																					
Pitcairn																																					
Samoa																																					
Society	1																																				
Tokelau																																					
Tonga																																					
Tuamotu																																					
Tuvalu																																					

Artifact →
Provenance →

Longsands Museum

ST. NEOTS

Artefact → / Provenance ↓	OCEANIA UN.	AUSTRALIA	MELA.UNPROV.	Admiralty	Banks	Bismarck	D'Entrecast.	Fiji	Louisiade	Loyalty	N. Britain	N. Caledonia	N. Guinea	N. Hebrides	N. Ireland	Santa Cruz	Solomon	Trobriand	MICRO.UNPROV.	Caroline	Gilbert	Mariana	Marshall	POLY.UNPROV.	Austral	Chatham	Cook	Easter	Hawaii	Marquesas	New Zealand	Niue	Pitcairn	Samoa	Society	Tokelau	Tonga	Tuamotu	Tuvalu
cord																																						
raw mater																																						
-sling,sto																																						
-arrow																																						
-bow																																						
-shield																																						
-dagger		1																																				
-spearthro																																						
-spear		2																																				
-club		2																																				
WEAPON		1						5					1																									
-float,si																																						
-net																																						
-spear																																						
-fishhook																																						
FISHING																																						
hunting																																						
-model																																						
-ornament																																						
-paddle																																						
NAVIGATIO																																						
-barkclot																																						
-weaving																																						
-needle,aw																																						
-chisel																																						
-rasp																																						
-grinding																																						
-pounding																																						
-adze																																						
TOOL	9	1						1*					4											1							3				1				
fire,ligh																																						
smoking pi																																						
pottery																																						
utensil																																						
lime spat																																						
dish,vess																																						
lime cont																																						

Name Salford Museum and Art Gallery

SALFORD

Address Peel Park
Salford M5 4WU

Telephone 061-736 2649/737 7692

Contact Curator

Sources & Dates of Information	
R. Hutchings	1969
Visit	
MEG	1978
Letter SP	1975

Notes

Disposals : Substantial ethnographical collection, including a number of items from Pacific and New Guinea, exchanged with Manchester Museum around 1969.

Dates of Collection/Acquisition

Donors/Collectors/Former Owners

Documentation

Comment

Name	Salisbury and South Wiltshire Museum	SALISBURY
Address	42 St. Ann Street Salisbury SP1 2DT	**Sources & Dates of Information** R. Hutchings 1966 Visit MEG 1978 Letter 1979
Telephone	0722-4465	
Contact	Curator	

Notes

Disposals: former Blackmore Museum Collection (19th Century) given or sold to other museums, from 1930's, especially Squire & Davies, British Museum.

Stored in 2 places; accessible with advance notice.

*New Guinea-- tools: includes a digging stick weight
*Carolines-- tool: digging stick

Dates of Collection/Acquisition	Donors/Collectors/Former Owners
Acquired 1974-75	Pitt Rivers (Farnham) Collection

Documentation

A list of articles exists, but documentation is scanty.

Extensive photos by George Pitt Rivers, taken in 1920-21 in New Guinea & Bismarck Archipelago (G. Pitt Rivers maps, etc., also in Pitt Rivers Museum, Oxford).

Comment

Note that Pitt Rivers Collection here is from P.R. Museum, Farnham, and therefore acquired by General Pitt Rivers after his donation to Oxford (i.e. after about 1887).

Salisbury Museum

SALISBURY

Provenance / Artifact	box	bag	basket	mat	headrest	transport	currency	rattle	flute,pipe	drum,gong	MUSICAL INS.	charm	magic,med.	fig.,image	carving	bullroarer	paddle	adze	board	mask	CERE. OBJ.	staff,stick	toilet app.	fan	comb	neck,breast	arm	ear,nose	head	PERS. ORN.	cloak	belt	skirt	CLOTHING	barkcloth	OTHER	TOTAL
OCEANIA UN.																																				
AUSTRALIA																																				
MELA. UNPROV.																																				
Admiralty																																				4
Banks																																				
Bismarck																																				
D'Entrecast.																																				
Fiji																																				3
Louisiade																																				
Loyalty																																				
N. Britain																																				
N. Caledonia																																				2
N. Guinea																																				14
N. Hebrides																																				
N. Ireland																																				
Santa Cruz																																				
Solomon																																				
Trobriand																																				
MICRO. UNPROV.																																				
Caroline																																				1
Gilbert																																				
Mariana																																				
Marshall																																				
POLY. UNPROV.																																				
Austral																																				
Chatham																																				
Cook																																				
Easter																																				2
Hawaii																																				
Marquesas																																				
New Zealand																																				
Niue																																				
Pitcairn																																				
Samoa																																				2
Society Tahiti																																				1
Tokelau																																				
Tonga																																				
Tuamotu																																				
Tuvalu																																				
[illegible]																																				2

Salisbury Museum

SALISBURY

Provenance ↓ / Artefact →	lime cont.	dish,vesse	lime spat	utensil	pottery	smoking pi	fire,ligh	TOOL	-adze	-pounding	-grinding	-rasp	-chisel	-needle,aw	-weaving	-barkclot	NAVIGATIO	-paddle	-ornament	-model	hunting	FISHING	-fishhook	-spear	-net	-float,si	WEAPON	-club	-spear	-spearthr	-dagger	-shield	-bow	-arrow	-sling,st	raw mater	cord
OCEANIA UN.																																					
AUSTRALIA																																					
MELA.UNPROV.																																					
Admiralty																													4								
Banks																																					
Bismarck																																					
D'Entrecast.																																					
Fiji									2															1													
Louisiade																																					
Loyalty																																					
N. Britain																																					
N. Caledonia									2																												
N. Guinea								3*	5																		2	2			2						
N. Hebrides																																					
N. Ireland																																					
Santa Cruz																																					
Solomon																																					
Trobriand																																					
MICRO.UNPROV																																					
Caroline								1*																													
Gilbert																																					
Mariana																																					
Marshall																																					
POLY.UNPROV.																																					
Austral																																					
Chatham																																					
Cook																																					
Easter								2																													
Hawaii																																					
Marquesas																																					
New Zealand																																					
Niue																																					
Pitcairn																																					
Samoa									2																												
~~Society~~ Tahiti										1																											
Tokelau																																					
Tonga																																					
Tuamotu																																					
Tuvalu																																					
Aua (Ninigo)									2																												
Woodlark									1																												

Name	Department of Tourism and Amenities	SCARBOROUGH
Address	Normanton Rise Holbeck Hill Scarborough YO11 2XD	**Sources & Dates of Information** R. Hutchings 1966 Visit MEG 1978 Letter 1979
Telephone	0723-69151	
Contact	Arts and Museums Officer	

Notes

Oceania: fishnet 1
club 1
Australia: axe 1
spearpoints 7

A number of unidentified objects; may include Oceanic.

Disposals: see Doncaster.

Dates of Collection/Acquisition	Donors/Collectors/Former Owners
Mainly latter 19th Century	

Documentation

Comment

SHEFFIELD (CH)

Name: Sheffield City Museum

Address: Weston Park
Sheffield S10 2TP

Telephone: 0742-27226

Contact: Keeper of Antiquities

Sources & Dates of Information

R. Hutchings 1966

Visit SP 1975

MEG 1978

Letter

Notes

*Australia-- other: boomerangs 13
*New Zealand-- other: head

Dates of Collection/Acquisition	Donors/Collectors/Former Owners
Acquired mainly 1875-1936	George Bennet, 1820's Fordham, 1864, Fiji Sheffield Literary and Philosophical Society

Documentation

Photographic.

Sheffield Literary and Philosophical Society register.

Comment

Good material, some early. Includes a few George Bennet pieces; other Bennet transferred to Cambridge in 1891.

City Museum

SHEFFIELD (CH)

Provenance ↓ / Artefact →	TOTAL	OTHER	barkcloth	CLOTHING	-skirt	-belt	-cloak	PERS. ORN.	-head	-ear,nose	-arm	-neck,breast	comb	fan	toilet app.	staff,stick	CERE. OBJ.	-mask	-board	-adze	-paddle	-bullroarer	carving	fig.,image	magic,med.	charm	MUSICAL INS.	-drum,gong	-flute,pipe	-rattle	currency	transport	headrest	mat	basket	bag	box
OCEANIA UN.																																					
AUSTRALIA	57	13						4																													
MELA.UNPROV.	13																																				
Admiralty	13																																				
Banks																																					
Bismarck																																					
D'Entrecast.																																					
Fiji	34		3					1																													
Louisiade																																					
Loyalty																																					
N. Britain	5																																				
N. Caledonia	2																																				
N. Guinea	83				2	3							1						2				1	1								1					
N. Hebrides	17																																				
N. Ireland	5																	1																			
Santa Cruz	5															1																					
Solomon	70										1		1																								
Trobriand	1																																				
MICRO.UNPROV.																																					
Caroline																																					
Gilbert	3																																				
Mariana																																					
Marshall																																					
POLY.UNPROV.	6		1																																		
Austral	6																																				
Chatham																																					
Cook	7																			2																	
Easter																																					
Hawaii																																					
Marquesas																																					
New Zealand	27	1				1		1				1																								2	
Niue	2																																				
Pitcairn																																					
Samoa	4		1																															2			
Society																																					
Tokelau	1																																				1
Tonga	2																																				
Tuamotu																																					
Tuvalu																																					
Tahiti	8		1																																		

City Museum SHEFFIELD (CM)

Artefact / Provenance	OCEANIA UN.	AUSTRALIA	MELA.UNPROV.	Admiralty	Banks	Bismarck	D'Entrecast.	Fiji	Louisiade	Loyalty	N. Britain	N. Caledonia	N. Guinea	N. Hebrides	N. Ireland	Santa Cruz	Solomon	Trobriand	MICRO.UNPROV.	Caroline	Gilbert	Mariana	Marshall	POLY.UNPROV.	Austral	Chatham	Cook	Easter	Hawaii	Marquesas	New Zealand	Niue	Pitcairn	Samoa	Society	Tokelau	Tonga	Tuamotu	Tuvalu	Tahiti
cord								1																																
raw mater																								2							1									
-sling,st																																								
-arrow													29	2		2	25																							
-bow			3										2			2	2																							
-shield		5																1																						
-dagger				13									4								2																			
-spearthr		5																																						
-spear		9	9								2			1			16																							
-club		12						23			3	1	12	7	4		10														10			1			2			
WEAPON																																								
-float,sl.																																								
-net																																								
-spear																																								
-fishhook																					1										3									1
FISHING																																								
hunting													1																											
-model								1																							1	2								
-ornament																	1																							
-paddle																	12								6															
NAVIGATIO																																								
-barkclot																																								2
-weaving																																								
-needle,a																																								
-chisel																																								
-rasp																								3																
-grinding		1																																						
-pounding														2																										
-adze		1						2				1	12														5				6									2
TOOL		6																																						1
fire,ligh		1																																						
smoking pl																																								
pottery																																								
utensil								1					2																											
lime spat					4								7																											
dish,vess			1					2					3	5																										1
lime cont																	2																							

SHEFFIELD (REG)

Name: York and Lancaster Regimental Museum

Address: Regimental Headquarters
Endcliffe Hall
Endcliffe Vale Road
Sheffield S10 3EU

Telephone: 0742-662734

Contact: Curator

Sources & Dates of Information

R. Hutchings 1966

Visit

MEG 1978

Letter

Notes

Total number of objects: less than 10 Oceanic.

Dates of Collection/Acquisition

Donors/Collectors/Former Owners

Documentation

Comment

Regimental Museum SHEFFIELD (R

Artefact → / Provenance ↓	OCEANIA UN.	AUSTRALIA	MELA.UNPROV.	Admiralty	Banks	Bismarck	D'Entrecast.	Fiji	Louisiade	Loyalty	N. Britain	N. Caledonia	N. Guinea	N. Hebrides	N. Ireland	Santa Cruz	Solomon	Trobriand	MICRO.UNPROV.	Caroline	Gilbert	Mariana	Marshall	POLY.UNPROV.	Austral	Chatham	Cook	Easter	Hawaii	Marquesas	New Zealand	Niue	Pitcairn	Samoa	Society	Tokelau	Tonga	Tuamotu	Tuvalu
TOTAL	10																																						
OTHER																																							
barkcloth																																							
CLOTHING																																							
-skirt																																							
-belt																																							
-cloak																																							
PERS. ORN.																																							
-head																																							
-ear,nose																																							
-arm																																							
-neck,breast																																							
comb																																							
fan																																							
toilet app.																																							
staff,stick																																							
CERE. OBJ.																																							
-mask																																							
-board																																							
-adze																																							
-paddle																																							
-bullroarer																																							
carving																																							
fig.,image																																							
magic,med.																																							
charm																																							
MUSICAL INS.																																							
-drum,gong																																							
-flute,pipe																																							
-rattle																																							
currency																																							
transport																																							
headrest																																							
mat																																							
basket																																							
bag																																							
box																																							

Regimental Museum SHEFFIELD (REG

Artefact → / Provenance →	OCEANIA UN.	AUSTRALIA	MELA.UNPROV.	Admiralty	Banks	Bismarck	D'Entrecast.	Fiji	Louisiade	Loyalty	N. Britain	N. Caledonia	N. Guinea	N. Hebrides	N. Ireland	Santa Cruz	Solomon	Trobriand	MICRO.UNPROV	Caroline	Gilbert	Mariana	Marshall	POLY.UNPROV.	Austral	Chatham	Cook	Easter	Hawaii	Marquesas	New Zealand	Niue	Pitcairn	Samoa	Society	Tokelau	Tonga	Tuamotu	Tuvalu
lime cont.																																						
dish,vesse																																						
lime spat.																																						
utensil																																						
pottery																																						
smokng pip																																						
fire,light																																						
TOOL																																						
-adze																																						
-pounding																																						
-grinding																																						
-rasp																																						
-chisel																																						
-needle,aw.																																						
-weaving																																						
-barkcloth																																						
NAVIGATION																																						
-paddle																																						
-ornament																																						
-model																																						
hunting																																						
FISHING																																						
-fishhook																																						
-spear																																						
-net																																						
-float,sin																																						
WEAPON																																						
-club																																						
-spear																																						
-spearthro.																																						
-dagger																																						
-shield																																						
-bow																																						
-arrow																																						
-sling,sto.																																						
raw mater.																																						
cord																																						

Name Bargate Guildhall Museum

SOUTHAMPTON

Address The Bargate
High Street
Southampton

Telephone 0703-22544

Contact Senior Keeper, Museums, c/o Tudor House Museum, Bugle St., Southampton (tel. 0703-24216)

Sources & Dates of Information

R. Hutchings 1966

Visit GSP 1974

MEG 1978

Letter

Notes

Dates of Collection/Acquisition

Donors/Collectors/Former Owners

Documentation

Comment

No trace of the Northesk Collection seen by H.D. Skinner during first World War.

Bargate Guildhall Museum

SOUTHAMPTON

Artefact → / Provenance	box	bag	basket	mat	headrest	transport	currency	-rattle	-flute,pipe	-drum,gong	MUSICAL INS	charm	magic,med.	fig.,image	carving	-bullroarer	-paddle	-adze	-board	-mask	CERE. OBJ.	staff,stick	toilet app.	fan	comb	-neck,breast	-arm	-ear,nose	-head	PERS. ORN.	-cloak	-belt	-skirt	CLOTHING	barkcloth	OTHER	TOTAL
OCEANIA UN.																																				
AUSTRALIA																																				
MELA.UNPROV.																																				
Admiralty																																				
Banks																																				
Bismarck																																				
D'Entrecast.																																				
Fiji																																				
Louisiade																																				
Loyalty																																				
N. Britain																																				
N. Caledonia																																				
N. Guinea																																				3
N. Hebrides																																				3
N. Ireland																																				
Santa Cruz																																				
Solomon																																				6
Trobriand																																				
MICRO.UNPROV.																																				
Caroline																																				
Gilbert																																				
Mariana																																				
Marshall																																				
POLY.UNPROV.																																				
Austral																																				
Chatham																																				
Cook																																				
Easter																																				
Hawaii																																				
Marquesas																																				
New Zealand																																				2
Niue																																				
Pitcairn																																				
Samoa																																				
Society																																				
Tokelau																																				
Tonga																																				
Tuamotu																																				
Tuvalu																																				

Bargate Guildhall Museum SOUTHAMPTON

Artefact → / Provenance →	OCEANIA UN.	AUSTRALIA	MELA.UNPROV.	Admiralty	Banks	Bismarck	D'Entrecast.	Fiji	Louisiade	Loyalty	N. Britain	N. Caledonia	N. Guinea	N. Hebrides	N. Ireland	Santa Cruz	Solomon	Trobriand	MICRO.UNPROV	Caroline	Gilbert	Mariana	Marshall	POLY.UNPROV.	Austral	Chatham	Cook	Easter	Hawaii	Marquesas	New Zealand	Niue	Pitcairn	Samoa	Society	Tokelau	Tonga	Tuamotu	Tuvalu
cord																																							
raw mate																																							
-sling,s																																							
-arrow																																							
-bow																																							
-shield																																							
-dagger																																							
-spearth																																							
-spear																																							
-club																																							
WEAPON																																							
-float,s																																							
-net																																							
-spear																																							
-fishhoo																																							
FISHING																																							
hunting																																							
-model																																							
-ornamen																																							
-paddle																																							
NAVIGATI																																							
-barkclo																																							
-weaving																																							
-needle,e																																							
-chisel																																							
-rasp																																							
-grindin																																							
-poundin																																							
-adze																																							
TOOL													2				6																						
fire,lig																																							
smoking p																																							
pottery																																							
utensil																																							
lime spa																																							
dish,vess																																							
lime con																																							

Name	Botanic Gardens Museum
Address	Churchtown Southport Merseyside PR9 7NB
Telephone	0704-27547
Contact	Keeper of Museums

SOUTHPORT

Sources & Dates of Information

R. Hutchings 1966

Visit

MEG 1978

Letter 1979

Notes

Some unidentified material.

Disposals: Waterloo Museum (Sefton) destroyed in war; no inventory of its contents.

*Australia-- other: boomerang
*Fiji & Samoa-- clubs said to have been captured from Maoris during wars of 1860-70.

Dates of Collection/Acquisition	Donors/Collectors/Former Owners
Acquired mainly 1938-51	Bootle and Crosby Libraries Collections R.W.B. Sparkes, S. Australia

Documentation

Comment

Possible trade/gift from Samoa and Fiji to Maoris before 1860? -Interesting.

Botanic Gardens Museum SOUTHPORT

Artefact → / Provenance ↓	OCEANIA UN.	AUSTRALIA	MELA.UNPROV.	Admiralty	Banks	Bismarck	D'Entrecast.	Fiji	Louisiade	Loyalty	N. Britain	N. Caledonia	N. Guinea	N. Hebrides	N. Ireland	Santa Cruz	Solomon	Trobriand	MICRO.UNPROV	Caroline	Gilbert	Mariana	Marshall	POLY.UNPROV.	Austral	Chatham	Cook	Easter	Hawaii	Marquesas	New Zealand	Niue	Pitcairn	Samoa	Society	Tokelau	Tonga	Tuamotu	Tuvalu
box																																							
bag																																							
basket																																							
mat																																							
headrest																																							
transport																																							
currency																																							
-rattle																																							
-flute,pipe																																							
-drum,gong																																							
MUSICAL INS.																																							
charm																																							
magic,med.																																							
fig.,image																																							
carving																																							
-bullroarer																																							
-paddle																																							
-adze																																							
-board																																							
-mask																																							
CERE. OBJ.																																							
staff,stick																																							
toilet app.																																							
fan																																							
comb																																							
-neck,breast																																							
-arm																																							
-ear,nose																																							
-head																																							
PERS. ORN.																																							
-cloak																																							
-belt																																							
-skirt																																							
CLOTHING																																							
barkcloth																																							
OTHER		1																																					
TOTAL		1						3																										2					

Botanic Gardens Museum SOUTHPORT

Artefact → / Provenance →	OCEANIA UN.	AUSTRALIA	MELA.UNPROV.	Admiralty	Banks	Bismarck	D'Entrecast.	Fiji	Louisiade	Loyalty	N. Britain	N. Caledonia	N. Guinea	N. Hebrides	N. Ireland	Santa Cruz	Solomon	Trobriand	MICRO.UNPROV.	Caroline	Gilbert	Mariana	Marshall	POLY.UNPROV.	Austral	Chatham	Cook	Easter	Hawaii	Marquesas	New Zealand	Niue	Pitcairn	Samoa	Society	Tokelau	Tonga	Tuamotu	Tuvalu
cord																																							
raw mater.																																							
-sling,sto																																							
-arrow																																							
-bow																																							
-shield																																							
-dagger																																							
-spearthro																																							
-spear																																							
-club																																							
WEAPON								3*																										2*					
-float,si																																							
-net																																							
-spear																																							
-fishhook																																							
FISHING																																							
hunting																																							
-model																																							
-ornament																																							
-paddle																																							
NAVIGATIO																																							
barkcloth																																							
-weaving																																							
-needle,aw																																							
-chisel																																							
-rasp																																							
-grinding																																							
-pounding																																							
-adze																																							
TOOL																																							
fire,ligh																																							
smoking pi																																							
pottery																																							
utensil																																							
lime spat																																							
dish,vesse																																							
lime cont.																																							

Name	South Shields Museum and Art Gallery	SOUTH SHIELDS
Address	Ocean Road South Shields Tyne and Wear	Sources & Dates of Information R. Hutchings 1966 Visit MEG 1978 Letters 1975
Telephone	08943-68740	
Contact	Keeper	

Notes

*New Zealand-- neck ornament: wood "tiki"
navigation: steering paddle
clubs: taiaha 2, patu pounamu 2

Dates of Collection/Acquisition	Donors/Collectors/Former Owners

Documentation

Comment

By correspondence. Not seen.

Museum and Art Gallery

SOUTH SHIEL

Artefact / Provenance	OCEANIA UN.	AUSTRALIA	MELA.UNPROV.	Admiralty	Banks	Bismarck	D'Entrecast.	Fiji	Louisiade	Loyalty	N. Britain	N. Caledonia	N. Guinea	N. Hebrides	N. Ireland	Santa Cruz	Solomon	Trobriand	MICRO.UNPROV	Caroline	Gilbert	Mariana	Marshall	POLY.UNPROV.	Austral	Chatham	Cook	Easter	Hawaii	Marquesas	New Zealand	Niue	Pitcairn	Samoa	Society	Tokelau	Tonga	Tuamotu	Tuvalu
box																																							
bag																															3								
basket																																							
mat																																							
headrest																																							
transport																																							
currency																																							
-rattle,pipe																																							
-flute																																							
-drum,gong																																							
MUSICAL INS.																																							
charm																																							
magic,med.																																							
fig.,image																																							
carving																																							
-bullroarer																																							
-paddle																																							
-adze																																							
-board																																							
-mask																																							
CERE. OBJ.																																							
staff,stick																																							
toilet app.																																							
fan																																							
comb																																							
-neck,breast																															1*								
-arm																																							
-ear,nose																																							
-head																																							
PERS. ORN.																																							
-cloak																																							
-belt																																							
-skirt																																							
CLOTHING																																							
barkcloth																																							
OTHER																															3								
TOTAL																															14								

Museum and Art Gallery

SOUTH SHIELDS

Artefact → / Provenance ↓	OCEANIA UN.	AUSTRALIA	MELA.UNPROV.	Admiralty	Banks	Bismarck	D'Entrecast.	Fiji	Louisiade	Loyalty	N. Britain	N. Caledonia	N. Guinea	N. Hebrides	N. Ireland	Santa Cruz	Solomon	Trobriand	MICRO.UNPROV.	Caroline	Gilbert	Mariana	Marshall	POLY.UNPROV.	Austral	Chatham	Cook	Easter	Hawaii	Marquesas	New Zealand	Niue	Pitcairn	Samoa	Society	Tokelau	Tonga	Tuamotu	Tuvalu
cord																																							
raw mate																																							
-sling,st																																							
-arrow																																							
-bow																																							
-shield																																							
-dagger																																							
-spearthr																																							
-spear																																							
-club																															4*								
WEAPON																																							
-float,si																																							
-net																																							
-spear																																							
-fishhook																																							
FISHING																																							
hunting																																							
-model																																							
-ornament																																							
-paddle																																							
NAVIGATIO																																							
-barkclot																															1*								
-weaving																																							
-needle,a																																							
-chisel																																							
-rasp																																							
-grinding																																							
-pounding																																							
-adze																															1								
TOOL																																							
fire,ligh																																							
smoking pi																																							
pottery																																							
utensil																															1								
lime spat																																							
dish,vess																																							
lime cont																																							

Name	Stamford Museum
Address	High Street Stamford PE9 2BB
Telephone	0780-55611
Contact	Curator

STAMFORD

Sources & Dates of Information

R. Hutchings 1966

Visit

MEG 1978

Letters 1979

Notes

*Australia-- other: boomerang

Dates of Collection/Acquisition	Donors/Collectors/Former Owners
Acquired mainly 1960-70	Some known

Documentation

Documentation fragmentary.

Comment

STAMFORD

Artefact → / Provenance ↓	TOTAL	OTHER	barkcloth	CLOTHING	-skirt	-belt	-cloak	PERS. ORN.	-head	-ear,nose	-arm	-neck,breast	comb	fan	toilet app.	staff,stick	CERE. OBJ.	-mask	-board	-adze	-paddle	-bullroarer	carving	fig.,image	magic,med.	charm	MUSICAL INS.	-drum,gong	-flute,pipe	-rattle	currency	transport	headrest	mat	basket	bag	box
OCEANIA UN.																																					
AUSTRALIA	2	1																																			
MELA.UNPROV.																																					
Admiralty																																					
Banks																																					
Bismarck																																					
D'Entrecast.																																					
Fiji																																					
Louisiade																																					
Loyalty																																					
N. Britain																																					
N. Caledonia																																					
N. Guinea																																					
N. Hebrides																																					
N. Ireland																																					
Santa Cruz																																					
Solomon	4																																				
Trobriand																																					
MICRO.UNPROV.																																					
Caroline																																					
Gilbert	1																																				
Mariana																																					
Marshall																																					
POLY.UNPROV.																																					
Austral																																					
Chatham																																					
Cook																																					
Easter																																					
Hawaii																																					
Marquesas																																					
New Zealand																																					
Niue																																					
Pitcairn																																					
Samoa																																					
Society																																					
Tokelau																																					
Tonga																																					
Tuamotu																																					
Tuvalu																																					

STAMFORD

Artefact → / Provenance ↓	lime cont.	dish,vesse	lime spat.	utensil	pottery	smokng pip	fire,light	TOOL	-adze	-pounding	-grinding	-rasp	-chisel	-needle,aw.	-weaving	-barkcloth	NAVIGATION	-paddle	-ornament	-model	hunting	FISHING	-fishhook	-spear	-net	-float,sin	WEAPON	-club	-spear	-spearthro	-dagger	-shield	-bow	-arrow	-sling,sto	raw mater.	cord
OCEANIA UN.																																					
AUSTRALIA																															/						
MELA.UNPROV.																																					
Admiralty																																					
Banks																																					
Bismarck																																					
D'Entrecast.																																					
Fiji																																					
Louisiade																																					
Loyalty																																					
N. Britain																																					
N. Caledonia																																					
N. Guinea																																					
N. Hebrides																																					
N. Ireland																																					
Santa Cruz																																					
Solomon																																					
Trobriand																																					
MICRO.UNPROV																																					
Caroline																																					
Gilbert																														/							
Mariana																																					
Marshall																																					
POLY.UNPROV.																																					
Austral																																					
Chatham																																					
Cook																																					
Easter																																					
Hawaii																																					
Marquesas																																					
New Zealand																																					
Niue																																					
Pitcairn																																					
Samoa																																					
Society																																					
Tokelau																																					
Tonga																																					
Tuamotu																																					
Tuvalu																																					

Name Stirling Smith Art Gallery and Museum

STIRLING

Address Albert Place
Stirling FK8 2RQ

Telephone 0786-2849

Contact Curator, c/o Old High School, Academy Road, Stirling FK8 1DZ (tel. 0786-2849)

Sources & Dates of Information

R. Hutchings 1966

Visit GSP 1974, DRS 197[illegible]

MEG 1978

Letters 1979

Notes

*Australia-- other: stone implements 14

*New Guinea-- other: container
*New Hebrides-- clubs: 1 possibly Samoan
other: container
*Gilbert-- boat model & mat: "Gilbert & Ellice"- not distinguished
*Cook-- clubs: possibly Tongan
*New Zealand-- personal ornament: 18th Century pendant
fan: 1 possibly Tongan
box: 18th Century papa hou
*Tonga-- fans: 1 possibly Samoan, 1 possibly New Zealand
other: flywhisk

Dates of Collection/Acquisition	Donors/Collectors/Former Owners
Acquired mainly 1880-1910	

Documentation

Comment

A collection with a few early items (those from New Zealand identified by D.R. Simmons, 1978). Some well-attributed later material. Needs to be examined in detail.

Art Gallery and Museum

STIRLING

Provenance	TOTAL	OTHER	barkcloth	CLOTHING	-skirt	-belt	-cloak	PERS. ORN.	-head	-ear,nose	-arm	-neck,breast	comb	fan	toilet app.	staff,stick	CERE. OBJ.	-mask	-board	-adze	-paddle	-bullroarer	carving	fig.,image	magic,med.	charm	MUSICAL INS.	-drum,gong	-flute,pipe	-rattle	currency	transport	headrest	mat	basket	bag	box
OCEANIA UN.	1																																				
AUSTRALIA	37	14																				1															
MELA. UNPROV.	7											2									1																
Admiralty																																					
Banks																																					
Bismarck	2																																				
D'Entrecast.																																					
Fiji	8																																				
Louisiade																																					
Loyalty																																					
N. Britain																																					
N. Caledonia																																					
N. Guinea	41	1				2				1		2	1														1										
N. Hebrides	78	1									4	3	2														1										
N. Ireland																																					
Santa Cruz																																					
Solomon	35								1																												
Trobriand																																					
MICRO. UNPROV.																																					
Caroline																																					
Gilbert	6																																	1*			
Mariana																																					
Marshall																																					
POLY. UNPROV.																																					
Austral																																					
Chatham																																					
Cook	2																																				
Easter																																					
Hawaii																																					
Marquesas																																					
New Zealand	13							2*						2*																				1	3	2	2*
Niue																																					
Pitcairn	1											1																									
Samoa	2																																				
Society																																					
Tokelau																																					
Tonga	10	1			1	1								4*																							
Tuamotu																																					
Tuvalu	1													1																							

Art Gallery and Museum

STIRLING

Provenance ↓ / Artefact →	lime con	dish,vess	lime spa	utensil	pottery	smokng p.	fire,lig	TOOL	-adze	-pounding	-grinding	-rasp	-chisel	-needle,a	-weaving	-barkclo.	NAVIGATION	-paddle	-ornamen	-model	hunting	FISHING	-fishhook	-spear	-net	-float,s	WEAPON	-club	-spear	-spearthr	-dagger	-shield	-bow	-arrow	-sling,s	raw mate	cord
OCEANIA UN.																											1										
AUSTRALIA								3	1																			15				1			1	1	
MELA.UNPROV.																																		4			
Admiralty																																					
Banks																																					
Bismarck																												2									
D'Entrecast.																																					
Fiji									2																			6									
Louisiade																																					
Loyalty																																					
N. Britain																																					
N. Caledonia																																					
N. Guinea		1	1	1					1																			1	1			1	2	2			
N. Hebrides																												9*	13		1		4	40			
N. Ireland																																					
Santa Cruz																																					
Solomon																							23					2	1				1	7			
Trobriand																																					
MICRO.UNPROV.																																					
Caroline																																					
Gilbert																				1*							1	1	2								
Mariana																																					
Marshall																																					
POLY.UNPROV.																																					
Austral																																					
Chatham																																					
Cook																												2*									
Easter																																					
Hawaii																																					
Marquesas																																					
New Zealand																												1									
Niue																																					
Pitcairn																																					
Samoa																												2									
Society																																					
Tokelau																																					
Tonga																												3									
Tuamotu																																					
Tuvalu																																					

Name	City Museum and Art Gallery
Address	Broad Street Hanley Stoke-on-Trent ST1 4HY
Telephone	0782-29611
Contact	Keeper of Archaeology

STOKE-ON-TRENT

Sources & Dates of Information

R. Hutchings	1966
Visit GSP	1974
MEG	1978
Letter	1979

Notes

Disposal : Ethnographic collection was transferred to Birmingham Museum in 1978 (including Maori figure).

Dates of Collection/Acquisition

Donors/Collectors/Former Owners

Documentation

Comment

City Museum STOKE-ON-TRE

Artefact → / Provenance	OCEANIA UN.	AUSTRALIA	MELA.UNPROV.	Admiralty	Banks	Bismarck	D'Entrecast.	Fiji	Louisiade	Loyalty	N. Britain	N. Caledonia	N. Guinea	N. Hebrides	N. Ireland	Santa Cruz	Solomon	Trobriand	MICRO.UNPROV.	Caroline	Gilbert	Mariana	Marshall	POLY.UNPROV.	Austral	Chatham	Cook	Easter	Hawaii	Marquesas	New Zealand	Niue	Pitcairn	Samoa	Society	Tokelau	Tonga	Tuamotu	Tuvalu
cord																																							
raw mater.																																							
-sling,stone																																							
-arrow																																							
-bow																																							
-shield																																							
-dagger																																							
-spearthrow																																							
-spear																																							
-club																																							
WEAPON																																							
-float,sinkr																																							
-net																																							
-spear																																							
-fishhook																																							
FISHING																																							
hunting																																							
-model																																							
-ornament																																							
-paddle																																							
NAVIGATION																																							
-barkcloth																																							
-weaving																																							
-needle,awl																																							
-chisel																																							
-rasp																																							
-grinding																																							
-pounding																																							
-adze																																							
TOOL																																							
fire,light																																							
smoking pipe																																							
pottery																																							
utensil																																							
lime spat.																																							
dish,vessel																																							
lime cont.																																							

TORQUAY

Name: Torquay Natural History Society
The Museum

Address: 529 Babbacombe Road
Torquay TQ1 1HG

Telephone: 0803-23975

Contact: Curator

Sources & Dates of Information

R. Hutchings 1966

Visit PG ALK } 1973

MEG 1978

Letters 1979

Notes

More artefacts will doubtless be recorded; sorting continues, and there is some unidentified material.

*Australia-- other: boomerangs 16
*Fiji-- clubs: plain 4, root 6, gunstock 7, pineapple 4, ula 4, paddle 3
*Gilberts-- toilet apparatus: scarifying

+ archaeological axes & chisels: Australia 1, New Zealand 15, Fiji 8, Solomons 1

Dates of Collection/Acquisition

Acquired mainly 1874-1940

Donors/Collectors/Former Owners

Dr. C. Paget-Blake, collected 1840+ ; on permanent loan from 1928
Correy, Everett, Brewster, Pike: Australia

Documentation

Identification and cataloguing continuing.

Comment

Some very good pieces from Paget-Blake collection on display. Future of collection in doubt - may go to Exeter.

The Museum

TORQUAY

Provenance ↓ / Artefact →	TOTAL	OTHER	barkcloth	CLOTHING	-skirt	-belt	-cloak	PERS. ORN.	-head	-ear,nose	-arm	-neck,breast	comb	fan	toilet app.	staff,stick	CERE. OBJ.	-mask	-board	-adze	-paddle	-bullroarer	carving	fig.,image	magic,med.	charm	MUSICAL INS.	-drum,gong	-flute,pipe	-rattle	currency	transport	headrest	mat	basket	bag	box
OCEANIA UN.	96																																				
AUSTRALIA	44	16																				4															
MELA.UNPROV.																																					
Admiralty	1																																				
Banks																																					
Bismarck																																					
D'Entrecast.																																					
Fiji	44		1									3																									
Louisiade																																					
Loyalty																																					
N. Britain																																					
N. Caledonia																																					
N. Guinea	161											1																									
N. Hebrides	1																																				
N. Ireland																																					
Santa Cruz	1																1																				
Solomon	24																							1													
Trobriand																																					
MICRO.UNPROV.																																					
Caroline	3																																				
Gilbert	20												3	2	2*																						
Mariana																																					
Marshall	2																																				
POLY.UNPROV.																																					
Austral																																					
Chatham																																					
Cook	8																			1																	
Easter																																					
Hawaii	1																						1														
Marquesas	1																																				
New Zealand	12															2																					
Niue																																					
Pitcairn																																					
Samoa	3																																				
Society																																					
Tokelau																																					
Tonga	9																																				
Tuamotu																																					
Tuvalu																																					
Tahiti	2																																				

The Museum

TORQUAY

Artefact → / Provenance ↓	lime cont.	dish,vesse	lime spat	utensil	pottery	smoking pi	fire,ligh	TOOL	-adze	-pounding	-grinding	-rasp	-chisel	-needle,aw	-weaving	-barkclot	NAVIGATIO	-paddle	-ornament	-model	hunting	FISHING	-fishhook	-spear	-net	-float,si	WEAPON	-club	-spear	-spearthro	-dagger	-shield	-bow	-arrow	-sling,sto	raw mater	cord
OCEANIA UN.																		8											35					53			
AUSTRALIA									2													2						10		5		5					
MELA.UNPROV.																																					
Admiralty																						1															
Banks																																					
Bismarck																																					
D'Entrecast.																																					
Fiji	4				3				2							3												28*									
Louisiade																																					
Loyalty																																					
N. Britain																																					
N. Caledonia																																					
N. Guinea	1	4							2	2								2										2			1			146			
N. Hebrides																													1								
N. Ireland																																					
Santa Cruz																																					
Solomon																		5					8					10									
Trobriand																																					
MICRO.UNPROV.																																					
Caroline	1																						2														
Gilbert	1																					2	2	2			6										
Mariana																																					
Marshall																							2														
POLY.UNPROV.																																					
Austral																																					
Chatham																																					
Cook																		7																			
Easter																																					
Hawaii																																					
Marquesas																												1									
New Zealand																		3					1					6									
Niue																																					
Pitcairn																																					
Samoa																												3									
Society																																					
Tokelau																																					
Tonga																												9									
Tuamotu																																					
Tuvalu																																					
Tahiti																							2														
Woodlark									2																												

Name	Royal Institution of Cornwall
Address	County Museum 25 River Street Truro Cornwall
Telephone	0872-2205
Contact	Curator

TRURO

Sources & Dates of Information

R. Hutchings	1966
Visit	PG, ALK 1973
MEG	1978
Letter	

Notes

Total Oceanic collection around 100 objects.

Dates of Collection/Acquisition	Donors/Collectors/Former Owners
	Cumming; Molesworth family

Documentation

Comment

3 ex-Cumming Collection. Note Molesworth tiki (1840-1).

Royal Institution of Cornwall TRURO

Artefact → / Provenance →	OCEANIA UN.	AUSTRALIA	MELA.UNPROV.	Admiralty	Banks	Bismarck	D'Entrecast.	Fiji	Louisiade	Loyalty	N. Britain	N. Caledonia	N. Guinea	N. Hebrides	N. Ireland	Santa Cruz	Solomon	Trobriand	MICRO.UNPROV.	Caroline	Gilbert	Mariana	Marshall	POLY.UNPROV.	Austral	Chatham	Cook	Easter	Hawaii	Marquesas	New Zealand	Niue	Pitcairn	Samoa	Society	Tokelau	Tonga	Tuamotu	Tuvalu
box																																							
bag																																							
basket																																							
mat																																							
headrest																																							
transport																																							
currency																																							
-rattle																																							
-flute,pipe																																							
-drum,gong																																							
MUSICAL INS.																																							
charm																																							
magic,med.																																							
fig.,image																																							
carving																																							
-bullroerer																																							
-paddle																																							
-adze																																							
-board																																							
-mask																																							
CERE. OBJ.																																							
staff,stick																																							
toilet app.																																							
fan																																							
comb																																							
-neck,breast																																							
-arm																															1								
-ear,nose																																							
-head																																							
PERS. ORN.																																							
-cloak																																							
-belt																																							
-skirt																																							
CLOTHING																																							
barkcloth																																							
OTHER																																							
TOTAL								X					X				X												X		5								

Royal Institution of Cornwall TRURO

Artefact → / Provenance ↓	OCEANIA UN.	AUSTRALIA	MELA.UNPROV.	Admiralty	Banks	Bismarck	D'Entrecast.	Fiji	Louisiade	Loyalty	N. Britain	N. Caledonia	N. Guinea	N. Hebrides	N. Ireland	Santa Cruz	Solomon	Trobriand	MICRO.UNPROV	Caroline	Gilbert	Mariana	Marshall	POLY.UNPROV.	Austral	Chatham	Cook	Easter	Hawaii	Marquesas	New Zealand	Niue	Pitcairn	Samoa	Society	Tokelau	Tonga	Tuamotu	Tuvalu
cord																																							
raw mate-																																							
-sling,st																																							
-arrow																																							
-bow																																							
-shield																																							
-dagger																																							
-spearthr																																							
-spear																																							
-club																																							
WEAPON																																							
-float,si																																							
-net																																							
-spear																																							
-fishhook																																							
FISHING																																							
hunting																																							
-model																																							
-ornament																																							
-paddle																																							
NAVIGATIO																																							
-barkclot																																							
-weaving																																							
-needle,a																																							
-chisel																																							
-rasp																																							
-grinding																																							
-pounding																																							
-adze																																							
TOOL																																							
fire,ligh																																							
smoking pi																																							
pottery																																							
utensil																																							
lime spat																																							
dish,vess																																							
lime cont																																							

Name	Municipal Museum
Address	Civic Centre Mount Pleasant Tunbridge Wells TN1 1RS
Telephone	0892-26121
Contact	Assistant Curator

TUNBRIDGE WELLS

Sources & Dates of Information

R. Hutchings 1966

Visit

MEG 1978

Letter 1979

Notes

Australia: club
New Zealand: utensil

Possibly others in stone tool collection.

Disposals: Foreign ethnography sold to the Wellcome Museum in 1933.

Dates of Collection/Acquisition	Donors/Collectors/Former Owners

Documentation

Photographic.

Comment

WAKEFIELD (H)

Name	Wakefield Museum
Address	Wood Street Wakefield West Yorkshire
Telephone	0924-61767
Contact	Keeper, Social History

Sources & Dates of Information

R. Hutchings 1966

Visit

MEG 1978

Letter

Notes

Dates of Collection/Acquisition

Acquired between 1930's & 1950's

Donors/Collectors/Former Owners

Documentation

Index needs to be updated.

Comment

Wakefield Museum

WAKEFIELD (

Artefact ⟶

Provenance ⟶

Artefact \ Provenance	OCEANIA UN.	AUSTRALIA	MELA.UNPROV.	Admiralty	Banks	Bismarck	D'Entrecast.	Fiji	Louisiade	Loyalty	N. Britain	N. Caledonia	N. Guinea	N. Hebrides	N. Ireland	Santa Cruz	Solomon	Trobriand	MICRO.UNPROV.	Caroline	Gilbert	Mariana	Marshall	POLY.UNPROV.	Austral	Chatham	Cook	Easter	Hawaii	Marquesas	New Zealand	Niue	Pitcairn	Samoa	Society	Tokelau	Tonga	Tuamotu	Tuvalu
TOTAL	6																																						
OTHER																																							
barkcloth																																							
CLOTHING																																							
-skirt																																							
-belt																																							
-cloak																																							
PERS. ORN.																																							
-head																																							
-ear,nose																																							
-arm																																							
-neck,breast																																							
comb																																							
fan																																							
toilet app.																																							
staff,stick																																							
CERE. OBJ.																																							
-mask																																							
-board																																							
-adze																																							
-paddle																																							
-bullroarer																																							
carving																																							
fig.,image																																							
magic,med.																																							
charm																																							
MUSICAL INS.																																							
-drum,gong																																							
-flute,pipe																																							
-rattle																																							
currency																																							
transport																																							
headrest																																							
mat																																							
basket																																							
bag																																							
box																																							

Wakefield Museum

WAKEFIELD (M)

Artefact → / Provenance →	OCEANIA UN.	AUSTRALIA	MELA.UNPROV.	Admiralty	Banks	Bismarck	D'Entrecast.	Fiji	Louisiade	Loyalty	N. Britain	N. Caledonia	N. Guinea	N. Hebrides	N. Ireland	Santa Cruz	Solomon	Trobriand	MICRO.UNPROV.	Caroline	Gilbert	Mariana	Marshall	POLY.UNPROV.	Austral	Chatham	Cook	Easter	Hawaii	Marquesas	New Zealand	Niue	Pitcairn	Samoa	Society	Tokelau	Tonga	Tuamotu.	Tuvalu
cord																																							
raw mate																																							
-sling,st																																							
-arrow																																							
-bow																																							
-shield																																							
-dagger																																							
-spearthr																																							
-spear																																							
-club																																							
WEAPON																																							
-float,si																																							
-net																																							
-spear																																							
-fishhook																																							
FISHING																																							
hunting																																							
-model																																							
-ornament																																							
-paddle																																							
NAVIGATIO																																							
-barkclot																																							
-weaving																																							
-needle,a																																							
-chisel																																							
-rasp																																							
-grinding																																							
-pounding																																							
-adze																																							
TOOL																																							
fire,ligh																																							
smoking pi																																							
pottery																																							
utensil																																							
lime spat																																							
dish,vess																																							
lime cont																																							

Name	School Museum & Resource Service Yorkshire Consortium for Education Joint Services	WAKEFIELD (SMRS)
Address	71C Northgate Wakefield WF1 3BT	Sources & Dates of Information R. Hutchings 1966 Visit
Telephone	0942-70211	MEG 1978
Contact	Senior Advisor	Letter 1979 Catalogue 1979

Notes

Accessibility improbable, since a school service.

*Australia-- other: bark paintings 2, boomerangs 3+

Dates of Collection/Acquisition	Donors/Collectors/Former Owners
1956+	

Documentation

Photographic, sound recordings, films.

Publication: Museum Materials, updated in 1977.

Comment

School Museum & Resource Service

WAKEFIELD (SMR

Provenance / Artefact	TOTAL	OTHER	barkcloth	CLOTHING	-skirt	-belt	-cloak	PERS. ORN.	-head	-ear,nose	-arm	-neck,breast	comb	fan	toilet app.	staff,stick	CERE. OBJ.	-mask	-board	-adze	-paddle	-bullroarer	carving	fig.,image	magic,med.	charm	MUSICAL INS.	-drum,gong	-flute,pipe	-rattle	currency	transport	headrest	mat	basket	bag	box
OCEANIA UN.																																					
AUSTRALIA	12t	5t																					2	1		1											
MELA.UNPROV.																																					
Admiralty																																					
Banks																																					
Bismarck																																					
D'Entrecast.																																					
Fiji																																					
Louisiade																																					
Loyalty																																					
N. Britain																																					
N. Caledonia																																					
N. Guinea																																					
N. Hebrides																																					
N. Ireland																																					
Santa Cruz																																					
Solomon																																					
Trobriand																																					
MICRO.UNPROV																																					
Caroline																																					
Gilbert																																					
Mariana																																					
Marshall																																					
POLY.UNPROV.																																					
Austral																																					
Chatham																																					
Cook																																					
Easter																																					
Hawaii																																					
Marquesas																																					
New Zealand																																					
Niue																																					
Pitcairn																																					
Samoa																																					
Society																																					
Tokelau																																					
Tonga																																					
Tuamotu																																					
Tuvalu																																					

School Museum & Resource Service WAKEFIELD (SMRS

Artefact → / Provenance →	OCEANIA UN.	AUSTRALIA	MELA.UNPROV.	Admiralty	Banks	Bismarck	D'Entrecast.	Fiji	Louisiade	Loyalty	N. Britain	N. Caledonia	N. Guinea	N. Hebrides	N. Ireland	Santa Cruz	Solomon	Trobriand	MICRO.UNPROV.	Caroline	Gilbert	Mariana	Marshall	POLY.UNPROV.	Austral	Chatham	Cook	Easter	Hawaii	Marquesas	New Zealand	Niue	Pitcairn	Samoa	Society	Tokelau	Tonga	Tuamotu	Tuvalu
cord																																							
raw mater.																																							
-sling,sto																																							
-arrow																																							
-bow																																							
-shield		/																																					
-dagger																																							
-spearthro		/																																					
-spear																																							
-club		X																																					
WEAPON																																							
-float,sin																																							
-net																																							
-spear																																							
-fishhook																																							
FISHING																																							
hunting																																							
-model																																							
-ornament																																							
-paddle																																							
NAVIGATION																																							
barkcloth																																							
-weaving																																							
-needle,aw																																							
-chisel																																							
-rasp																																							
-grinding																																							
-pounding																																							
-adze																																							
TOOL																																							
fire,ligh																																							
smoking pi																																							
pottery																																							
utensil																																							
lime spat																																							
dish,vesse																																							
lime cont.																																							

Name Warrington Museum and Art Gallery

WARRINGTON

Address Bold Street
Warrington WA1 1JG

Sources & Dates of Information

R. Hutchings 1966

Visits 6SP/974, SP 1975

MEG 1978

Letter

Telephone 0925-30550

Contact Curator of Museums & Art Galleries

Notes

*New Zealand-- clubs: patu paraoa 2, patu onewa 2, wood 2
other: head (donated 1843)
*Santa Cruz-- other: cloth
*Oceania unprovenanced-- musical instrument: shell trumpet
*Australia-- stick: message
*Fiji-- toilet apparatus: tattooing
ceremonial object: tambua
other: hook, flywhisk
*New Guinea-- musical instrument: jewsharp
headrest: Tami Island

Dates of Collection/Acquisition	Donors/Collectors/Former Owners
Acquired mainly in 1920's	Miss Birkbeck, 1921, Australia & New Guinea

Documentation

Comment

Note some early material (e.g. Maori preserved head, 1843). Could any of this material come from the Warrington Dissenters Academy- a notable school in the 18th Century?

WARRINGTON

Museum and Art Gallery

Provenance ↓ / Artefact →	TOTAL	OTHER	barkcloth	CLOTHING	-skirt	-belt	-cloak	PERS. ORN.	-head	-ear,nose	-arm	-neck,breast	comb	fan	toilet app.	staff,stick	CERE. OBJ.	-mask	-board	-adze	-paddle	-bullroarer	carving	fig.,image	magic,med.	charm	MUSICAL INS.	-drum,gong	-flute,pipe	-rattle	currency	transport	headrest	mat	basket	bag	box
OCEANIA UN.	10										4			2													1*							1			
AUSTRALIA	85							26								1*						7	1	2												5	
MELA.UNPROV.	12																																				
Admiralty	1																																				
Banks	1									1																											
Bismarck																																					
D'Entrecast.																																					
Fiji	30	2	3									1			1		1																2			1	
Louisiade																																					
Loyalty																																					
N. Britain	2										1																										
N. Caledonia																																					
N. Guinea	27+			2		1				2		X	2					1+				1					1*						1*			X	
N. Hebrides	5										3													1													
N. Ireland																																					
Santa Cruz	7	1							1																											1	
Solomon	12									2	1		3																								
Trobriand	1																																				
MICRO.UNPROV.											—																										
Caroline																																					
Gilbert	3											1																									
Mariana																																					
Marshall	1																																				
POLY.UNPROV.																																					
Austral	1																																				
Chatham																																					
Cook	X																																				
Easter																																					
Hawaii	2																																				
Marquesas	1								1																												
New Zealand	27	1			1		2					3																								1	1
Niue																																					
Pitcairn																																					
Samoa	3		1																																		
Society																																					
Tokelau			3																																		
Tonga	5												1																								
Tuamotu																																					
Tuvalu	1																																				
Tahiti	2		1																																		

Museum and Art Gallery

WARRINGTON

Artefact → / Provenance ↓	lime cont.	dish,vesse	lime spat	utensil	pottery	smokng pi	fire,ligh	TOOL	-adze	-pounding	-grinding	-rasp	-chisel	-needle,a	-weaving	-barkclot	NAVIGATIO	-paddle	-ornament	-model	hunting	FISHING	-fishhook	-spear	-net	-float,si	WEAPON	-club	-spear	-spearthr	-dagger	-shield	-bow	-arrow	-sling,st	raw mate	cord
OCEANIA UN.		1										1																									
AUSTRALIA		1						9																			25		1	2		5					
MELA.UNPROV.																																		12			
Admiralty																															1						
Banks																																					
Bismarck																																					
D'Entrecast.																																					
Fiji		5		2												3												9									
Louisiade																																					
Loyalty																																					
N. Britain																												1									
N. Caledonia																																					
N. Guinea			3	1		1																		X	1			2					1	7			
N. Hebrides																					1																
N. Ireland																																					
Santa Cruz																																		4			
Solomon		3																					3														
Trobriand									1																												
MICRO.UNPROV																																					
Caroline																																					
Gilbert								1															1														
Mariana																																					
Marshall																							1														
POLY.UNPROV.																																					
Austral																		1																			
Chatham																																					
Cook																																					
Easter																																					
Hawaii																2																					
Marquesas																																					
New Zealand									7	1													4					6*									
Niue																																					
Pitcairn																																					
Samoa																1							1														
Society																																					
Tokelau																																					
Tonga																							1														
Tuamotu																																					
Tuvalu																											1										
Tahiti																							1														

WARWICK (WMS)

Name Warwickshire Museum Service

Address Market Place
Warwick CV34 4SA

Telephone 0926-43431

Contact Keeper of Archaeology

Sources & Dates of Information

R. Hutchings 1966

Visit SP 1975

MEG 1978

Letter 1979

Notes

*Australia-- other: boomerangs
*Melanesia unprovenanced-- other: pyro-engraved hollow bamboo

Dates of Collection/Acquisition

Mostly 19th Century

Donors/Collectors/Former Owners

Warwickshire Natural History & Archaeological Society

Documentation

Comment

Some material may have come from Rugby School Museum, when much of its collection was dispersed in 1939.

Museum Service

WARWICK (W

Provenance ↓ / Artefact →	TOTAL	OTHER	barkcloth	CLOTHING	-skirt	-belt	-cloak	PERS. ORN.	-head	-ear,nose	-arm	-neck,breast	comb	fan	toilet app.	staff,stick	CERE. OBJ.	-mask	-board	-adze	-paddle	-bullroarer	carving	fig.,image	magic,med.	charm	MUSICAL INS.	-drum,gong	-flute,pipe	-rattle	currency	transport	headrest	mat	basket	bag	box
OCEANIA UN.	8																																				
AUSTRALIA	33	7																																			
MELA.UNPROV.	10+	1	1	1																																	
Admiralty																																					
Banks																																					
Bismarck																																					
D'Entrecast.																																					
Fiji	7																																				
Louisiade																																					
Loyalty																																					
N. Britain																																					
N. Caledonia																																					
N. Guinea	9																																				
N. Hebrides																																					
N. Ireland																																					
Santa Cruz	6																																				
Solomon	2												1																								
Trobriand																																					
MICRO.UNPROV	1				1																																
Caroline																																					
Gilbert																																					
Mariana																																					
Marshall																																					
POLY.UNPROV.	3		3																																		
Austral	2																																				
Chatham																																					
Cook	2																																				
Easter	1																							1													
Hawaii	15		14																																		
Marquesas	1																																				
New Zealand	7						4																														1
Niue	1																																				
Pitcairn	1																																				
Samoa	2																																				1
Society																																					
Tokelau																																					
Tonga																																					
Tuamotu																																					
Tuvalu																																					
Tahiti	4		2																																		

Museum Service

WARWICK(W...

Artefact → / Provenance ↓	lime cont.	dish,vesse	lime spat.	utensil	pottery	smokng pi	fire,ligh.	TOOL	-adze	-pounding	-grinding	-rasp	-chisel	-needle,aw	-weaving	-barkcloth	NAVIGATION	-paddle	-ornament	-model	hunting	FISHING	-fishhook	-spear	-net	-float,sin	WEAPON	-club	-spear	-spearthro	-dagger	-shield	-bow	-arrow	-sling,sto	raw mater.	cord
OCEANIA UN.									1														1						2				1	2			
AUSTRALIA																												5	9	8		2					
MELA.UNPROV.																													1					6			
Admiralty																																					
Banks																																					
Bismarck																																					
D'Entrecast.																																					
Fiji																		1										5					1				
Louisiade																																					
Loyalty																																					
N. Britain																																					
N. Caledonia																																					
N. Guinea																																	1	8			
N. Hebrides																																					
N. Ireland																																					
Santa Cruz																																	1	5			
Solomon																																		1			
Trobriand																																					
MICRO.UNPROV																																					
Caroline																																					
Gilbert																																					
Mariana																																					
Marshall																																					
POLY.UNPROV.																																					
Austral																		2																			
Chatham																																					
Cook									2																												
Easter																																					
Hawaii																													1								
Marquesas		1																																			
New Zealand																							1					1									
Niue																													1								
Pitcairn																																					
Samoa												1											1					1									
Society																																					
Tokelau																																					
Tonga																																					
Tuamotu																																					
Tuvalu																																					
Tahiti										1												1															

Name	Powysland Museum
Address	Salop Road Welshpool, Powys Wales
Telephone	0938-3001
Contact	Curator

WELSHPOOL

Sources & Dates of Information

R. Hutchings 1966
Visit

MEG 1978
Letter

Notes

Total Oceanic c. 40 items.

Disposals: to other museums, by 1960's.

Dates of Collection/Acquisition	Donors/Collectors/Former Owners
Acquired 1870's	

Documentation

1878 Catalogue includes list of the original collection.

Comment

Collection awaiting sorting, identification and cataloguing.

Powysland Museum

WELSHPOOL

Provenance ↓ / Artefact →	box	bag	basket	mat	headrest	transport	currency	-rattle	-flute,pipe	-drum,gong	MUSICAL INS	charm	magic,med.	fig.,image	carving	-bullroarer	-paddle	-adze	-board	-mask	CERE. OBJ.	staff,stick	toilet app.	fan	comb	-neck,breast	-arm	-ear,nose	-head	PERS. ORN.	-cloak	-belt	-skirt	CLOTHING	barkcloth	OTHER	TOTAL
OCEANIA UN.																																					X
AUSTRALIA																																					X
MELA.UNPROV.																																					
Admiralty																																					
Banks																																					
Bismarck																																					
D'Entrecast.																																					
Fiji																																					
Louisiade																																					
Loyalty																																					
N. Britain																																					
N. Caledonia																																					
N. Guinea																																					
N. Hebrides																																					
N. Ireland																																					
Santa Cruz																																					
Solomon																																					
Trobriand																																					
MICRO.UNPROV																																					
Caroline																																					
Gilbert																																					
Mariana																																					
Marshall																																					
POLY.UNPROV.																																					
Austral																																					
Chatham																																					
Cook																																					
Easter																																					
Hawaii																																					
Marquesas																																					
New Zealand																																					
Niue																																					
Pitcairn																																					
Samoa																																					
Society																																					
Tokelau																																					
Tonga																																					
Tuamotu																																					
Tuvalu																																					

Powysland Museum

WELSHPOOL

Artefact → / Provenance ↓	OCEANIA UN.	AUSTRALIA	MELA.UNPROV.	Admiralty	Banks	Bismarck	D'Entrecast.	Fiji	Louisiade	Loyalty	N. Britain	N. Caledonia	N. Guinea	N. Hebrides	N. Ireland	Santa Cruz	Solomon	Trobriand	MICRO.UNPROV.	Caroline	Gilbert	Mariana	Marshall	POLY.UNPROV.	Austral	Chatham	Cook	Easter	Hawaii	Marquesas	New Zealand	Niue	Pitcairn	Samoa	Society	Tokelau	Tonga	Tuamotu	Tuvalu
cord																																							
raw mater																																							
-sling,st																																							
-arrow																																							
-bow																																							
-shield																																							
-dagger																																							
-spearthr																																							
-spear																																							
-club																																							
WEAPON																																							
-float,si																																							
-net																																							
-spear																																							
-fishhook																																							
FISHING																																							
hunting																																							
-model																																							
-ornament																																							
-paddle																																							
NAVIGATIO																																							
-barkclot																																							
-weaving																																							
-needle,aw																																							
-chisel																																							
-rasp																																							
-grinding																																							
-pounding																																							
-adze																																							
TOOL																																							
fire,ligh																																							
smokng pi																																							
pottery																																							
utensil																																							
lime spat																																							
dish,vess																																							
lime cont.																																							

Name Whitby Museum

Address Pannett Park
Whitby YO21 1RE

Telephone 0947-2908

Contact Honorary Keeper

WHITBY

Sources & Dates of Information

R. Hutchings 1966

Visit SP 1975

MEG 1978

Letter

Notes

*Australia-- other: boomerangs 6
*New Zealand-- other: beads 2, kauri gum head 1, taniko band

Dates of Collection/Acquisition	Donors/Collectors/Former Owners
Mainly 1823+	Cook Scoresby

Documentation

Photographic (New Zealand, Samoa).
Archival.

Museum publication: Catalogue of Whitby Museum, Whitby Literary and Philosophical Society, esp. pp. 87-8.

Comment

Interesting collection from local sources requiring detailed assesment.

Provenance ↓ / Artefact →	TOTAL	OTHER	barkcloth	CLOTHING	-skirt	-belt	-cloak	PERS. ORN.	-head	-ear,nose	-arm	-neck,breast.	comb	fan	toilet app.	staff,stick	CERE. OBJ.	-mask	-board	-adze	-paddle	-bullroarer	carving	fig.,image	magic,med.	charm	MUSICAL INS.	-drum,gong	-flute,pipe	-rattle	currency	transport	headrest	mat	basket	bag	box
OCEANIA UN.																												1									
AUSTRALIA	15	6																				1													1		
MELA.UNPROV.	3										2																				X						
Admiralty																																					
Banks																																					
Bismarck																																					
D'Entrecast.																																					
Fiji	8																																		1		
Louisiade																																					
Loyalty																																					
N. Britain																																					
N. Caledonia	1																																				
N. Guinea	10					1						1				1	1		2																		
N. Hebrides	2			1																																	
N. Ireland	2																						1	1													
Santa Cruz																																					
Solomon																																					
Trobriand	9																						2														
MICRO.UNPROV	13							4																									2				
Caroline																																					
Gilbert	1																																				
Mariana																																					
Marshall																																					
POLY.UNPROV.	4							1				2				1																					
Austral	5											2																									
Chatham																																					
Cook	3																			3																	
Easter																																					
Hawaii	9	6					1	1																													
Marquesas																																					
New Zealand	48	4					5					1					1						2	1												1	1
Niue	1				1																																
Pitcairn																																					
Samoa	3																																				
Society																																					
Tokelau																																					
Tonga	1																																				
Tuamotu	X																																				
Tuvalu																																					
Tahiti	9		2									1																									

Whitby Museum

WHITBY

Provenance ↓ / Artefact →	lime cont.	dish,vesse	lime spat.	utensil	pottery	smokng pi	fire,ligh	TOOL	-adze	-pounding	-grinding	-rasp	-chisel	-needle,aw	-weaving	-barkcloth	NAVIGATION	-paddle	-ornament	-model	hunting	FISHING	-fishhook	-spear	-net	-float,sin	WEAPON	-club	-spear	-spearthro	-dagger	-shield	-bow	-arrow	-sling,sto	raw mater.	cord
OCEANIA UN.																																					
AUSTRALIA		1							2																			1		2		1					
MELA.UNPROV.																																					
Admiralty																																					
Banks																																					
Bismarck																																					
D'Entrecast.																																					
Fiji																												7									
Louisiade																																					
Loyalty																																					
N. Britain																																					
N. Caledonia																																				1	
N. Guinea									1																			3									
N. Hebrides																												1									
N. Ireland																																					
Santa Cruz																																					
Solomon																																					
Trobriand			4																									3									
MICRO.UNPROV																											6				1						
Caroline																																					
Gilbert																																					
Mariana																							1														
Marshall																																					
POLY.UNPROV.																																					
Austral																		3																			
Chatham																																					
Cook																																					
Easter																																					
Hawaii																																					
Marquesas																																			1		
New Zealand									8	2									1	2			9					5								5	
Niue																																					
Pitcairn																																					
Samoa									1														2														
Society																																					
Tokelau																																					
Tonga																						1															
Tuamotu																							X														
Tuvalu																																					
Tahiti		1							1	1		1										1	1														
Matty (Wuvulu)				1					1																												

WINCHESTER

Name: Winchester City Museum

Address: The Square
Winchester
Hampshire

Telephone: 0962-68166

Contact: Keeper of Archaeology

Sources & Dates of Information

R. Hutchings 1966

Visit GSP 1974

MEG 1978

Letters 1979

Notes

Dates of Collection/Acquisition

19th Century-1940

Donors/Collectors/Former Owners

Documentation

Documentation fragmentary.

Comment

City Museum

WINCHESTER

Artefact → / Provenance ↓	OCEANIA UN.	AUSTRALIA	MELA.UNPROV.	Admiralty	Banks	Bismarck	D'Entrecast.	Fiji	Louisiade	Loyalty	N. Britain	N. Caledonia	N. Guinea	N. Hebrides	N. Ireland	Santa Cruz	Solomon	Trobriand	MICRO.UNPROV	Caroline	Gilbert	Mariana	Marshall	POLY.UNPROV.	Austral	Chatham	Cook	Easter	Hawaii	Marquesas	New Zealand	Niue	Pitcairn	Samoa	Society	Tokelau	Tonga	Tuamotu	Tuvalu	Tahiti
box																																								
bag																																								
basket																																								
mat																																								
headrest																																					3			
transport																																								
currency																																								
-rattle																																								
-flute,pipe								1																																
-drum,gong																																								
MUSICAL INS.																																								
charm																																								
magic,med.																																								
fig.,image																																								
carving																																								
-bullroarer																																								
-paddle																																								
-adze																																								
-board																																								
-mask																																								
CERE. OBJ.																																								
staff,stick																																								
toilet app.																																								
fan																																								
comb																																					4			
-neck,breast																																								
-arm																																								
-ear,nose																																								
-head																																								
PERS. ORN.																																								
-cloak																																								
-belt																																								
-skirt																																								
CLOTHING																																								
barkcloth																																								
OTHER		1																																						
TOTAL		1	X					3					13				3														1	2					7		1	

City Museum WINCHESTER

Artefact → / Provenance ↓	OCEANIA UN.	AUSTRALIA	MELA.UNPROV.	Admiralty	Banks	Bismarck	D'Entrecast.	Fiji	Louisiade	Loyalty	N. Britain	N. Caledonia	N. Guinea	N. Hebrides	N. Ireland	Santa Cruz	Solomon	Trobriand	MICRO.UNPROV.	Caroline	Gilbert	Mariana	Marshall	POLY.UNPROV.	Austral	Chatham	Cook	Easter	Hawaii	Marquesas	New Zealand	Niue	Pitcairn	Samoa	Society	Tokelau	Tonga	Tuamotu	Tuvalu	Tahiti
cord																																								
raw mater																																								
-sling,st																																								
-arrow			X										2				2																							
-bow													3																											
-shield																																								
-dagger																																								
-spearthr																																								
-spear			X										X																											
-club																															1									
WEAPON																																								
-float,si																																								
-net																																								
-spear													1																											
-fishhook																																								
FISHING																																								
hunting																																								
-model																																2								
-ornament																																								
-paddle																	1																							
NAVIGATIO																																								
-barkclot																																								
-weaving																																								
-needle,aw																																								
-chisel																																								
-rasp																																								
-grinding																																								
-pounding																																								
-adze													6																											
TOOL																																								
fire,ligh																																								
smokng pi																																								
pottery																																								
utensil																																								
lime spat																																								
dish,vesse								2					1																											1
lime cont.																																								

Name	Wisbech and Fenland Museum	WISBECH
Address	Museum Square Wisbech PE13 1ES Cambridgeshire	**Sources & Dates of Information** R. Hutchings 1966 Visit 16 1974 MEG 1978 Letter 1979
Telephone	0945-3817	
Contact	Curator	

Notes

More material may be found. 25 items acquired between 1836 & 1860.

Dates of Collection/Acquisition	Donors/Collectors/Former Owners
	Lt. W.G. England, RN,1848-1850's, Polynesia & Fiji Rev. W. Ellis, 1840's, Polynesia & Fiji Capt. Swaine, 1836, Tahiti King's Lynn Museum, 1932, Australia

Documentation

Comment

Swaine (of Vancouver's Voyage 1790's) was from Leverington, near Wisbech, but most of his collection appears to have been transferred to Cambridge or Christchurch, N.Z. Polynesian material was given to Canterbury Museum 1949-50. Cambridge Museum has correspondence relating to this.

Wisbech & Fenland Museum

WISBECH

Provenance ↓ / Artefact →	TOTAL	OTHER	barkcloth	CLOTHING	-skirt	-belt	-cloak	PERS. ORN.	-head	-ear,nose	-arm	-neck,breast	comb	fan	toilet app.	staff,stick	CERE. OBJ.	-mask	-board	-adze	-paddle	-bullroarer	carving	fig., image	magic,med.	charm	MUSICAL INS.	-drum,gong	-flute,pipe	-rattle	currency	transport	headrest	mat	basket	bag	box
OCEANIA UN.	1																																				
AUSTRALIA	9																																				
MELA.UNPROV.																																					
Admiralty																																					
Banks																																					
Bismarck																																					
D'Entrecast.																																					
Fiji	6																																				
Louisiade																																					
Loyalty																																					
N. Britain																																					
N. Caledonia																																					
N. Guinea	6																																				
N. Hebrides	1																																				
N. Ireland																																					
Santa Cruz																																					
Solomon	7																																				
Trobriand																																					
MICRO.UNPROV.	X									X																											
Caroline																																					
Gilbert																																					
Mariana																																					
Marshall																																					
POLY.UNPROV.																																					
Austral	3	3																																			
Chatham																																					
Cook	1																																				
Easter																																		1			
Hawaii	8	1	4																																		
Marquesas																																					
New Zealand	6					1				1					1																					1	
Niue																																					
Pitcairn																																					
Samoa																																					
Society																																					
Tokelau																																					
Tonga	2																																				
Tuamotu																																					
Tuvalu																																					
Tahiti	3	1	2																																		

Wisbech & Fenland Museum

WISBECH

Artefact → / Provenance →	OCEANIA UN.	AUSTRALIA	MELA.UNPROV.	Admiralty	Banks	Bismarck	D'Entrecast.	Fiji	Louisiade	Loyalty	N. Britain	N. Caledonia	N. Guinea	N. Hebrides	N. Ireland	Santa Cruz	Solomon	Trobriand	MICRO.UNPROV	Caroline	Gilbert	Mariana	Marshall	POLY.UNPROV.	Austral	Chatham	Cook	Easter	Hawaii	Marquesas	New Zealand	Niue	Pitcairn	Samoa	Society	Tokelau	Tonga	Tuamotu	Tuvalu	Tahiti
cord																																								
raw mater.																																								
-sling,sto																																								
-arrow														1			6																							
-bow																																								
-shield																	1																							
-dagger																																								
-spearthro.																																								
-spear		5																																						
-club	1	4						6																							1						2			
WEAPON,sin																																								
-float,sin																																								
-net																																								
-spear													6																											
-fishhook																													3											
FISHING																																								
hunting																																								
-model																																								
-ornament																																								
-paddle																																								
NAVIGATION																																								
-barkcloth																																								
-weaving																																								
-needle,aw.																																								
-chisel																																								
-rasp																																								
-grinding																																								
-pounding																																								
-adze																															1									
TOOL																																								
fire,ligh																																								
smoking pip																																								
pottery																																								
utensil																																								
lime spat.																																								
dish,vesse																																								
lime cont.																																								

Name	Central Art Gallery
Address	Lichfield Street Wolverhampton WV1 1DU
Telephone	0902-24549
Contact	Curator

WOLVERHAMPTON

Sources & Dates of Information

R. Hutchings 1966
Visit

MEG 1978
Letter

Notes

Oceania: 2-3 objects

Dates of Collection/Acquisition

Acquired mainly 1912-50's

Donors/Collectors/Former Owners

Documentation

Comment

Name	Maritime Museum for East Anglia	YARMOUTH
Address	Marine Parade Great Yarmouth NR30	Sources & Dates of Information R. Hutchings 1966 Visit 16/1973 ALKS MEG 1978 Letter
Telephone	0493-2267	
Contact	Curator, Great Yarmouth Museums	

Notes

*New Zealand-- utensil: chief's feeding funnel

Dates of Collection/Acquisition	Donors/Collectors/Former Owners
Acquired 1964	

Documentation

Comment Museum was Seamen's Home for 100 years. Funnel probably came from there.

Maritime Museum YARMOUTH

Provenance / Artifact →	TOTAL	OTHER	barkcloth	CLOTHING	-skirt	-belt	-cloak	PERS. ORN.	-head	-ear,nose	-arm	-neck,breast	comb	fan	toilet app.	staff,stick	CERE. OBJ.	-mask	-board	-adze	-paddle	-bullroarer	carving	fig.,image	magic,med.	charm	MUSICAL INS.	-drum,gong	-flute,pipe	-rattle	currency	transport	headrest	mat	basket	bag	box
OCEANIA UN.	X																																			
AUSTRALIA																																				
MELA.UNPROV.																																				
Admiralty																																				
Banks																																				
Bismarck																																				
D'Entrecast.																																				
Fiji																																				
Louisiade																																				
Loyalty																																				
N. Britain																																				
N. Caledonia																																				
N. Guinea																																				
N. Hebrides																																				
N. Ireland																																				
Santa Cruz																																				
Solomon																																				
Trobriand																																				
MICRO.UNPROV.																																				
Caroline																																				
Gilbert																																				
Mariana																																				
Marshall																																				
POLY.UNPROV.																																				
Austral																																				
Chatham																																				
Cook																																				
Easter																																				
Hawaii																																				
Marquesas																																				
New Zealand	X																																			
Niue																																				
Pitcairn																																				
Samoa																																				
Society																																				
Tokelau																																				
Tonga																																				
Tuamotu																																				
Tuvalu																																				

Maritime Museum

YARMOUTH

Artefact → / Provenance →	OCEANIA UN.	AUSTRALIA	MELA.UNPROV.	Admiralty	Banks	Bismarck	D'Entrecast.	Fiji	Louisiade	Loyalty	N. Britain	N. Caledonia	N. Guinea	N. Hebrides	N. Ireland	Santa Cruz	Solomon	Trobriand	MICRO.UNPROV	Caroline	Gilbert	Mariana	Marshall	POLY.UNPROV.	Austral	Chatham	Cook	Easter	Hawaii	Marquesas	New Zealand	Niue	Pitcairn	Samoa	Society	Tokelau	Tonga	Tuamotu	Tuvalu
cord																																							
raw mate																																							
-sling,st																																							
-arrow																																							
-bow																																							
-shield																																							
-dagger																																							
-spearthr																																							
-spear																																							
-club																																							
WEAPON																																							
-float,st																																							
-net																																							
-spear																																							
-fishhook																																							
FISHING																																							
hunting																																							
-model																																							
-ornament																																							
-paddle																																							
NAVIGATIO																																							
-barkclot																																							
-weaving																																							
-needle,a																																							
-chisel																																							
-rasp																																							
-grinding																																							
-pounding																																							
-adze																																							
TOOL																																							
fire,ligh																																							
smoking pi																																							
pottery																																							
utensil																															/*								
lime spat																																							
dish,vess																																							
lime cont																																							

Name The Castle Museum

Address York YO1 1RY

Telephone 0904-53611

Contact Deputy Curator

YORK (CASTLE)

Sources & Dates of Information

R. Hutchings 1966

Visit SP 1975

MEG 1978

Letter

Notes

New Zealand : 3 taiaha

Dates of Collection/Acquisition	Donors/Collectors/Former Owners

Documentation

Comment

Skinner's 1917 manuscript, of which there is a copy in Cambridge, reports much more material. Now no trace.

Name	Yorkshire Museum	YORK (YM)
Address	Museum Gardens York YO1 2DR	Sources & Dates of Information
		R. Hutchings 1966 Visit
Telephone	0904-29745	MEG 1978
Contact	Curator	Letter

Notes

Disposals : Material sold, transferred to other museums, etc. between 1920's & 1970's.
Some went to Leeds in 1972.

Dates of Collection/Acquisition	Donors/Collectors/Former Owners

Documentation

Comment

Museum of Mankind
Notes

Oceania unprovenanced- navigation: steering paddle 1

Admiralty- other: carved steps for men's house
musical instrument: shell trumpet
drum/gong: slit gong 2
flute/pipe: pipe 2
dish/vessel: large vessel 8
navigation: bailer
spear: hafted 22

Banks- toilet apparatus: head scratcher
staff/stick: or club 3
flute/pipe: whistle
fishing: kite
("pudding" knives listed under utensil)

Bismarck- figure/image: chalk (New Hanover) 1; malanggan (Tabar) 1
flute/pipe: pipe
tool: cutting 2

D'Entrecasteaux- other: misc. 1
musical instrument: jewsharp
fishing: kite

Fiji- other: sunshade; suspension hook 12; house or temple model 3; game 10; misc. 10
barkcloth: map 4; Lau Group 10
head ornament: headdress 1
fan: flywhisk 10
ceremonial object: tambua 41
" paddle: Tongan style 4
musical instrument: shell trumpet 4
drum/gong: slit gong
flute/pipe: pipe 2
transport: potstand 2
utensil: "cannibal" fork 23
smoking pipe: cigar 4
tool: cutting 1
needle/awl: sail or fishing 39
barkcloth tool: beater 8; matrix 14; roller 9; pattern board 5; stencil 4
model: part 11
fishing: trap 2
club: throwing 44; cylindrical 41; pineapple 22; lotus 48; gunstock 11; paddle 36; root 33; mini 8; figure-headed 1; other 5

pottery: excavated pot & sherds from Vitu Levu

Louisiade- other: bamboo tube
ceremonial object: preserved head
flute/pipe: pipe 2
tool: cutting 4
model: prow 3

Loyalty- other: misc. 1

New Britain- mask: large 1
flute/pipe: pipe 1

New Caledonia- other: model house; misc. 1
head ornament: headdress 3
ceremonial object: club 1

New Hebrides- other: misc. 3
toilet apparatus: head scratcher 6
ceremonial object: preserved head 9; composition head 1; pig killing club 2
mask: composition 5
carving: fern root 3
figure/image: composition 7 (large 3)
musical instrument: shell trumpet 2
drum/gong: slit gong 2 (large 1)
flute/pipe: pipe 6
navigation: bailer
arrow: quiver 7

New Ireland- ceremonial object: modelled skull 1
mask: malanggan 24
carving: malanggan 21
figure/image: malanggan 21; chalk 9
musical instrument: jewsharp 1
drum/gong: slit gong 3
tool: cutting 2
club: or paddle 2
spear: or New Hanover 44
ceremonial board: malanggan 1

Santa Cruz- other: clothing hook; fornication tally 2; misc. 1
ceremonial object: club 17; commemorative post; skull; food bowl
figure/image: duka 13
dish/vessel: large 2
weaving: loom 10
navigation: bailer 5
fishing: trap 1

Trobriand- other: game 9; bamboo tube; misc. 1
head ornament: headdress 1
fan: flywhisk 1
flute/pipe: pipe 7
transport: potstand 4
tool: netting 8; drill 4
navigation: bailer 4
model: prow 16
(includes 689 items collected by B. Malinowski)

Micronesia unprovenanced- other: misc. 4

Caroline- other: model house 2; pattern block 8; wood bench; archaeologica
archaeological (ornaments?) 6
ceremonial object: sword (Palau Group)
drum/gong: slit gong 1
dish/vessel: turtleshell 27; large 2
utensil: turtleshell 5
tool: drill; archaeological shell (Ponape) 72
weaving: loom 3
navigation: canoe (Palau Group)

Gilbert- other: well dipper 2; misc. 1
head ornament: headdress:1
fan: flywhisk 3
toilet apparatus: scratcher 1
tool: drill 1
fishing: trap 2
weapon: sharkstooth 71; helmet 4; fibre armour, part or whole, 27

Mariana- other: archaeological (Guam) 1
head ornament: headdress

Marshall- other: misc. 1
head ornament: headdress
weaving: loom
navigation: sailing chart 3

Polynesia unprovenanced- other: misc. 9
barkcloth: sample size 23+
head ornament: headdress 2
tool: netting 1

Austral- other: stool 3; wood tablet; misc. 2
head ornament: headdress 6
fan: flywhisk 13
ceremonial object: ladle 9

Chatham- other: bark picture 4
tool: cutting 3,

Cook- other: stool (Atiu) 4
barkcloth: garment 2
clothing: mourning poncho; grass poncho; dancer's cap 2; war cap
head ornament: headdress 2
ceremonial object: ladle 4
figure/image: large 1
magic/medicine: soul trap
drum/gong: or Austral drum 1; slit gong 1
dish/vessel: large 1
model: large*(Manihiki) 2
(staff gods, feather gods, godsticks listed under figure/ima

Easter- other: archaeological; incised tablet 5 (cast 3); misc. 2
head ornament: headdress 6
figure/image: monumental 2
tool: netting 3

Hawaii- other: game 13; misc. 2
barkcloth: includes many of sample size
clothing: feather garment (?) 2; feather helmet 10
toilet apparatus: scarifying 2; mirror 2
ceremonial object: feather temple 1
figure/image: feather gods 5; figure (Necker) 1; figure figure (Hawaii) 1
drum/gong: drumstick 1
flute/pipe: whistle 5; pipe 1
transport: calabash holder 3
headrest: pillow
dish/vessel: vessel (Maui)1; vessel (Nihoa) 1
tool: netting 2
navigation: canoe 1
spear: spear rest 3

Marquesas- head ornament: headdress 1
carving: stilt footrest 15
figure/image: large 3
musical instrument: shell trumpet
transport: pair stilts 2
dish/vessel: large 1
model: large 1
club: paddle 4

*i.e. requires more than one person to move

New Zealand- other:model house 3; reed screen; kauri gum head 5, carving 4, cast 1; game 3; archaeological animal and bird bones; taaniko weaving sample 3; misc. 10
cloak: flax 40; flax a&d taaniko 17; feather 21; feather a&d flax 13; other 13
personal ornament: cloak pin 16; toggle 5
head ornament: headdress 2
neck ornament: tiki 45 (reproduction 9)
ceremonial object: poi ball 7; preserved head 7
" adze: tourist 2
carving: pumice 4; carved wood pieces, use unknown, 3
musical instrument: shell trumpet 6
flute/pipe: koauau 14; nguru 6; puturino 26
utensil: funnel 7
tool: digging stick 4, tread 6; cutting (netting- see needle/awl)
weaving: peg 6+
navigation: bailer 11; sail 1
model: large (Auckland) 3
hunting: parrot ring 4; bird snare 6; post European 5
weapon: kotaha 9
club: pouwhenua 7; hoeroa 6; patu paraoa 15 (reproduction 2 patu onewa 24 (reproduction 1); tewhatewha 21 (reproduction 2); taiaha/hani 62 (tourist 2);
patu p patu pounamu 20 (reproduction 5); kakauroa 2; patuki patu kotiate (wood) 8 (reproduction 1); patu kotiate (bone) 6; wahaika (wood) 14 (tourist 2); wahaika (bone) 7; granite patu 3; metal patu 3 (Banks cast 1)

Niue- other: pole; game 2
barkcloth: garment; mat 2
drum/gong: slit gong
headrest: pillow

Samoa- other: house model; game 10; misc. 4
barkcloth: mosquito net 1
head ornament: headdress 2
fan: flywhisk 8
drum/gong: slit gong 1
tool: drill 2
barkcloth tool: matrix 3
navigation: canoe 1

Society- other: eyeshade 2; stool 3
head ornament: headdress 1
neck ornament: feather gorget 2
fan: flywhisk 8; handle only 10
figure/image: (Moorea) 1
musical instrument: shell clappers (mourning) 3
transport: travelling case
headrest: pillow 2
tool: netting 3
hunting: fowl tether
arrow: quiver 4
(godsticks, feather gods, staff gods and stone representations listed under figure/image)

Tonga- other: game 17
barkcloth: mourning garment 1
fan: flywhisk 5
figure/image: ivory 5
flute/pipe: pipe 7

Tuamotu- head ornament: headdress 1
navigation: canoe 1

Tahiti- other: eyeshade; woven fibre (?); misc. 1
clothing: mourning dress 1
head ornament: headdress 4
neck ornament: feather gorget 8
staff/stick: possibly Austral 3
figure/image: god house 1; feather god 2
transport: travelling case 5
tool: netting 1
arrow: quiver 2

Torres Strait- other: game 9; misc. 1
head ornament: headdress 22
arm ornament: also head carrier 3
ceremonial object: modelled skull 2; dance ornament 2
musical instrument: jewsharp 2
transport: head carrier 4
tool: netting 2
bow: wristguard 4; string 1

Ninigo- dagger: sheath 4

Rotuma- head ornament: headdress

Massim unprovenanced-	other: suspension hook; bamboo tube; misc. 2 head ornament: headdress 8 ceremonial object: skull 1 musical instrument: jewsharp 1 flute/pipe: pipe 7 tool: netting 5; drill 2 navigation: bailer 1
Engineer-	musical instrument: jewsharp 1 flute/pipe: pipe 1 tool: netting 5; cutting 3 model: prow 5 fishing: trap
Marshall Bennett-	tool: netting 3 navigation: bailer 4 model: prow 28
Nukuoro-	musical instrument: shell trumpet
Ontong Java-	other: cloth 1 weaving: loom
Rennell-	ceremonial object: club; spear musical instrument: shell trumpet tool: netting 5 fishing: trap 1
Sikiana-	other: cloth 3; game 1 weaving: loom
Tikopia-	mat: or Anuta 1 weaving: loom
Uvea-	other: game
Mangareva-	other: misc. 1
Wallis-	other: game 2 fan: flywhisk 1 musical instrument: shell trumpet; bamboo trumpet tool: netting 4 navigation: bailer

Solomon unprovenanced- other: design sample 3; game; sunshade 4; bamboo tube; suspension hook; misc. 3+
ceremonial object: club 4
" board: shield
carving: architectural 3; house board 1
musical instrument: shell trumpet 6; jewsharp 1
flute/pipe: pipe 3
transport: potstand 1
dish/vessel: large 1
tool: drill 1
adze/axe: with European blade 5
navigation: canoe 5; bailer 1
fishing; trap 5; kite 3
bow: wristguard 1

Buka & Bougainville- other: game 2; sunshade 2; suspension hook
head ornament: headdress 1
ceremonial object: club 8; grave ornament 1
" board: shield 1
musical instrument: jewsharp
flute/pipe: pipe 3
transport: potstand
tool: netting 3
fishing: kite 1
bow: wristguard 1

Central- other: design sample; sunshade 2
ceremonial object: club; grave ornament 2; shrine
" board: shield 2
carving: tridacna shell 10
musical instrument: jewsharp
flute/pipe: pipe 3
dish/vessel: large 1
tool: drill 2
model: large 1
fishing: trap 1; kite 1

South East- other: cloth; design sample; game; sunshade; misc. 1
head ornament: headdress 4
ceremonial object: club 20
ceremonial board: shield 5
carving: houseboard
musical instrument: jewsharp 2
flute/pipe: pipe 2
dish/vessel: large 3
tool: drill 3
model: large 2

(Solomon maces listed under staff/stick)

New Guinea unprovenanced- other: eyeshade; woven sample 2; model house; game 3; misc. 14
head ornament: headdress 1
fan: flywhisk 2
ceremonial object: preserved head 2
musical instrument: shell trumpet 1; jewsharp 3
flute/pipe: pipe 2
tool: drill 3; cutting 3; netting 10
fishing: trap 3

West Irian unprovenanced- musical instrument: jewsharp

South unprovenanced- barkcloth: skirt 2
head ornament: headdress 7
weapon: cuirass
bow: wristguard 2

Geelvinck- musical instrument: shell trumpet 2
(includes from Schouten Islands (West);
personal ornament 2
figure/image 2
dish/vessel 1
canoe ornament 1)

Humboldt & Sentani- other: suspension hook
figure/image: large 1

Highlands- weapon: cuirass 3

Tapiro- head ornament: headdress
toilet apparatus: head scratcher 5
musical instrument: jewsharp
tool: cutting 4

Kampong & Eilanden- ceremonial object: grave goods
navigation: bailer

Asmat- other: misc. 1
head ornament: headdress
mask: large 1
carving: bis pole 2
musical instrument: trumpet 10
bow: wristguard 3

Marind-Anim & Merauke- ceremonial object: preserved head
fishing: trap
bow: wristguard 1

Trust Territory unprovenanced- other: stepladder; suspension hook
barkcloth: apron 2
head ornament: headdress 2
musical instrument: shell trumpet
tool: drill
navigation: bailer
fishing: trap 2
spear: or arrow 17

(includes from Schouten Islands (East): breast ornament
shell trumpet
bag
adze
bailer
fishhook 5

Sepik- other: suspension hook 3; stool 4
breast ornament: (Tamara Is.) 1
ceremonial object: preserved head 16
carving: houseboard 7
drum/gong: slit gong 2
flute/pipe: flute ornament 2
transport: potstand 2
lime spatula: (Tamara Is.) 1
pottery: roof finial 1

Ramu- toilet apparatus: scratcher

Sepik/Ramu- other: part of structure; stool 3; suspension hook 2; misc. 1
head ornament: headdress 8
musical instrument: wood trumpet 3
flute/pipe: flute ornament 2; whistle (Manam Is.) 1
bag: sago strainer 1
canoe ornament: (Manam Is.) 1
weapon: cuirass

Madang- pottery: pot (Bilibili Is.) 1

Highlands- other: part of structure 3; garden spike 3; suspension hook 2
game 18
head ornament: headdress 1
toilet apparatus: massage 6
ceremonial object: pig killing club 2; spear 1
musical instrument: musical bow 1; jewsharp 4
flute/pipe: pipe 2; whistle 1
transport: climbing ring & belt 2
headrest: pillow board
smoking pipe: cigar holder 20
tool: cutting 6
weapon: cuirass

Huon & Tami- tool: cutting
navigation: bailer
(the only items from Tami Is. are 1 vessel & 1 stool)

Morobe- smoking: cigar holder
tool: netting 1; cutting 1

Papua unprovenanced- other: whip 2; misc. 2
fan: flywhisk 6
ceremonial object: preserved head 1
mask: large 1
tool: drill 1; cutting 1; netting 1
fishing: trap 2

Western- other: misc. 5
head ornament: headdress 26
ceremonial object: dancing club 1; preserved head 9
carving: post 1
musical instrument: jewsharp 2
transport: head carrier 7
tool: cutting 9
hunting: man catcher 4
club: also digging stick 1
bow: wristguard 1

Gulf- other: stool; bark painting; misc. 1
barkcloth: animal 9
belt/girdle: bark 32
head ornament: headdress 1
ceremonial object: preserved head 9
mask: barkcloth 50
charm: or sago pomander 3
musical instrument: jewsharp
rattle/jingle: pig rattle 1
bag: sago strainer 6
tool: drill 3; netting 2
fishing: trap 1
bow: wristguard 2
arrow: quiver 1; toy 65+

Central- other: eyeshade; hammock 2; game 10
barkcloth: skirt 1
head ornament: headdress 36
toilet apparatus: foot cleaner 2
ceremonial object: clan badge 5; grave goods 1
musical instrument: jewsharp 4
transport: pair stilts
tool: cutting 2; netting 2; drill 7
fishing: trap 2

Mainland Massim- other: suspension hook
barkcloth: cap 2
musical instrument: shell trumpet
flute/pipe: pipe 2
pottery: excavated pot & sherds from Collingwood Bay
tool: drill 1; netting 6
navigation: bailer
model: part
fishing: trap

North East- tool: drill 1; netting 2
fishing: trap

Australia unprovenanced- other: 34 rock rubbings of rock engravings from New South Wales, South Australia, Western Australia, & Northern Territory; misc. 3
fan: flywhisk
bullroarer: churinga 5
tool: digging stick 1; stone tools
weapon: boomerang

Queensland- other: blanket 2; drawing 3; game 4; decorated objects (Clack 5; misc. 5
staff/stick: message 24
tool: paintbrush 6; cutting 16; digging stick 3
fishing: trap 2
weapon: boomerang 50

Cape York- head ornament: headdress 1
weapon: bboomerang

head ornament: headdress 1
fan: flywhisk 1

Northern Territory-	other: misc. 1 staff/stick: message 15 ceremonial object: skull bullroarer: churinga 12 tool: cutting 4; digging stick 1 weaving: spindle weapon: boomerang 18
Arnhemland-	other: house board; bark painting 9; misc. 3 fan: flywhisk staff/stick: message 2 ceremonial object: spear 1; grave post 4 headrest: bark pillow tool: cutting 3 weapon: boomerang 2
Western-	other: painting; bark cradle staff/stick: message 17 bullroarer: churinga 14 tool: netting 2; cutting 21; digging stick 3 weaving: spindle 2; loom (Sunday Is.) 1 weapon: boomerang 45
Northwestern-	other: wood painting; engraved baobab nut 2 staff/stick: message 1 bullroarer: churinga 7 weaving: spindle navigation: raft 1 weapon: boomerang
Central-	other: game headornament: headdress 1 bullroarer: churinga 21 tool: cutting 10 weapon: boomerang 17
South-	bullroarer: churinga 1 tool: digging stick 2 weapon: boomerang 6
New South Wales-	other: misc. 1 ceremonial object: widow's cap 1; gravemarker 9 tool: digging stick 1 weapon: boomerang 25

Victoria-	other: bark drawing; misc. 1 ceremonial object: skull navigation: canoe 1 weapon: boomerang 10
South East-	weapon: boomerang 34
Tasmania-	other: stone tools

OCEANIA

Early collections of importance

AUSTRALIA		Neil Talbot (1832, 1839) Spencer and Gillen (1903)
MELANESIA		Brenchley (1870)
	Solomon Islands	Lords of the Admiralty and Surgeon Guppy of HMS Lark (1884) Woodford (1902)
	New Hebrides	Capt. Cross (1889)
	New Guinea (including Bismarck Archipelago and Torres Strait)	Capt. Stanley of HMS Rattlesnake (1851) Sir Wyville Thomson of HMS Challenger (1872-80) Duke of Bedford (1884; Romilly collection) H.J. Veitch (1889) Sexton (Holmes collection of 1890's) Cooke-Daniels Expedition (1906; Seligman coll.) British Ornithologists' Union Expedition (1910-13) (Wollaston) Williamson (1913) Malinowski (1922) Lord Moyne (1934 and 1936) Haddon (1889)
POLYNESIA		Cook material London Missionary Society collection (1890)
	New Zealand	Sir George Grey (1854) Meinertzhagen (1895)
	Samoa	King Malietoa (1887)
	Fiji	Sir Arthur Gordon (1878)
MICRONESIA		
	Palau	Capt. Wilson of the Antelope (collection of 1783)
	Gilbert Islands	Arthur Grimble (1921)